THE SMALL BUSINESS HANDBOOK

A COMPREHENSIVE GUIDE TO STARTING AND RUNNING YOUR OWN BUSINESS

REVISED EDITION

IRVING BURSTINER

PRENTICE HALL PRESS

NEW YORK   LONDON   TORONTO   SYDNEY   TOKYO

With love to Razel;
Our children, Harry, Alan, and
Roseann;
Our grandchildren, Joseph, Brian,
and David;
and
In loving memory of Ronald and Stuart

Prentice Hall Press
Gulf+Western Building
One Gulf+Western Plaza
New York, New York 10023

Library of Congress Cataloging-in-Publication Data

Burstiner, Irving.
    The small business handbook: a comprehensive guide to starting and running your own
business / by Irving Burstiner.—Rev. ed.
        p.   cm.
    Includes index.
    ISBN 0-13-814344-7 (pbk.) : $16.95
    1. Small business—Management—Handbooks, manuals, etc.   2. Small business—Hand-
books, manuals, etc.   I. Title.
HD62.7.B84 1988
658′.022—dc19   88-4585
                                                                                                                            CIP

Designed by Robert Bull Design
Manufactured in the United States of America

10 9 8 7 6 5 4 3 2 1

Revised Edition

Contents

Preface

Relinquishing the security of a job to launch one's own business venture is both an American tradition and part of the great American dream. Every year, several hundred thousand new enterprises are started up. Unfortunately, a nearly equal number annually close up shop.

The most often quoted reason for business failure is managerial ineptitude. Obviously, education and experience are fundamental. People who start businesses do need help. Few are expert in even a single major area, such as production, finance, or sales. Fewer still understand the details of legal requirements, tax regulations, financial and risk management, and other specialized facets of business administration.

Still, interest in owning a business grows each year. Attendance at small business shows and conventions is way up; colleges and universities show their increasing awareness of public interest by offering courses in entrepreneurship; and the federal government frequently sponsors small business institutes.

Small business *is* American business. Nearly nine out of every ten manufacturing firms, wholesale establishments, retail stores, and service operations are small enterprises—small in annual sales volume, in number of employees, and in scope of operations. Yet, despite its size, the small business sector is where most new jobs are being created.

The Small Business Handbook has been designed to be an informative, comprehensive, and balanced guide to profitable small business management. Written in clear, nontechnical language, it is packed with facts and techniques needed to: (1) make the initial decision to start your own business; (2) plan, organize, arrange financing for, locate, staff, and finally launch the new enterprise; (3) ensure its viability; and (4) sustain both profitability and growth over the long term.

The Handbook is an invaluable reference for the dissatisfied job-holder who occasionally toys with the notion of managing a business of his or her own. Although it has been targeted primarily at the general public, colleges may find it suitable for the basic course in Entrepreneurship or as recommended reading for several of the offerings in their management curricula. It should also be of interest to continuing education departments as well as small business institutes.

This revised edition contains twenty-six chapters, two more than the earlier edition. It is organized into nine sections.

Part I aims at helping you to make two important decisions: (1) whether or not to go into a business of your own; and (2) what type of business to go into, if you do decide to proceed. First you learn about the benefits and the drawbacks of either choice (business or job); the kinds of risks new entrepreneurs can expect to face; and what you need to make a success of your enterprise. Useful facts are then presented about four major sectors of our economy: manufacturing, wholesaling, retailing, and the service sector.

Part II deals with the major "start-up" questions most often asked by aspiring entrepreneurs. It begins by stressing the importance of knowing—and targeting—your customer and offers basic insights into buyer psychology. Next, the various routes by which you can enter the business community are discussed, along with the advantages and disadvantages of operating your business as a sole proprietorship, partnership, or corporation. You are shown how to estimate your financial needs; introduced to sources of capital, balance sheets, and profit-and-loss statements; and learn how to prepare your business plan. Finally, you are given valuable insights into the areas of location choice and layout planning.

Part III is actually a three-chapter "minicourse" in organization management. The four major management functions—planning, organizing, directing, and controlling—are explained, and the importance of good communications within the organization is emphasized. A detailed overview of the "human resources" area then follows, along with worthwhile information about personnel management, leadership dynamics, employee motivation, and the decision-making process.

Part IV explores the manufacturing function. Production processes and methods are reviewed, and you are introduced to the different kinds of departments found in the typical plant. Thorough descriptions are provided of such significant activity areas as production planning, operations management, inventory control, and materials management.

Part V offers a thorough grounding in the fundamentals of marketing. Each of the five chapters is devoted to a single major marketing area. In the product/services area, you learn about the product life cycle concept and its marketing implications, the new product development process (and creative thinking techniques), packaging, branding, and the marketing of services. Following this, you are introduced to the approaches that companies use to set prices and to a variety of pricing policies and promotional pricing techniques. Next, you delve into the exciting promotion areas: personal selling (and sales force management), advertising, sales promotion, and public relations. You are then made aware of the roles that agents and wholesalers play in the marketing channels and learn about transportation and warehousing. A useful introduction to marketing research methods concludes Part V.

Important aspects of financial management for the small business manager are outlined in Part VI. Following a brief review of the basic accounting statements, the usefulness and methods of ratio analysis are explained. You then learn how to avoid cash flow problems, keep records, prepare budgets, manage expenses, and handle credit sales. Finally, an entire chapter is devoted to risk reduction; this includes a thorough discussion of your business's insurance needs and suggestions as to the measures you can take to help reduce both internal and external theft.

Part VII begins with a review of those aspects of the legal environment with which an entrepreneur should be familiar. A detailed discussion of the entire taxation area is then provided, along with valuable, up-to-date information and sample federal tax return forms.

Part VIII makes a unique contribution not found in other small business books. It consists of four chapters, each of which offers helpful suggestions for improving results in a different type of business, once that enterprise has been successfully launched. Manufacturing, wholesaling, retailing, and service businesses are covered.

The final section of the book, Part IX, focuses on the future of your new business. Outlined here are approaches to growth and continuity, mergers and acquisitions, and management succession.

Before concluding, I wish to express my gratitude to those who helped and encouraged me throughout this endeavor: first and foremost, my lovely wife and companion, Razel; my family; my congenial friends and colleagues at Baruch College: Professors Mel Unger, Bernard Belasco, Tom Killoran, and Conrad Berenson; my invaluable graduate assistant, Jacob Ho; Dean John Haynie and Professor Michael Tuttle of Northwood Institute, West Palm Beach, Fla.; Alan M. Goldberg, of Parliament Brokerage, Massapequa, N.Y.; Jerri Goldberg, of American Assurance Underwriters Group, Deerfield Beach, Fla.; Alan B. Burstiner, CLU, ChFC of Financial Underwriters, North Haven, Conn.; and Harry Burstiner, videographer par excellence, of Long Beach, N.Y.

Finally, my sincere thanks to the editorial staff at Prentice Hall Press for their guidance throughout the preparation of both the original work and this revised edition.

—IRVING BURSTINER

I
MAKING THE DECISION

1

What It Takes to Succeed in Your Own Business

Ever think about going into business for yourself?

Even if you haven't yet explored the thought, you probably will at some point in your life. Most people do.

Each year well over half a million Americans try their hand at businesses of their own. Increase that figure tenfold, and you'll probably still be far short of the number of people who *think* about going into business but who put it off to the indeterminate future. To some it represents the kind of freedom and challenge they cannot hope to find working for others—and much more money than they could ever earn in a job. Others are completely turned off by the thought, preferring the security of a steady position.

In this first chapter you'll be led into exploring the advantages and disadvantages of working for other people and for yourself. You'll learn a few of the reasons why some people go into business—and the kinds of risks they face. And—most important of all if you follow the instructions carefully—you'll find out if *you* have what it takes to make a go of it.

SHOULD YOU GO INTO BUSINESS?

The decision to try your hand at business should never be approached lightly. This is a major decision. Once you've committed yourself, you can be certain that the road ahead will be long, winding, tumultuous on occasion, and blocked by obstacles. If the business fails—and it *could*—it may not only wreak havoc with your personal savings (and perhaps other assets as well), it may also deal a blow to your ego. Indeed, business owners who are compelled to declare bankruptcy often show severe signs of psychological strain. The question that floors many people after declaring bankruptcy is, "Where do I go from here?"

3

No, I am not planning to discourage you from trying your own business. Rather, I am attempting to paint a realistic picture and foster caution on your part, because as many as one-half of all enterprises started up each year are nowhere to be found five or six years later.

If your notion of a satisfying career involves being situated in an agreeable environment, working five days a week at your assigned tasks while accepting little responsibility, leaving your job promptly after eight hours, and then forgetting all about your firm until the next working day, then don't think about venturing into a business of your own. On the other hand, if you are lucky enough to possess a higher-than-average level of self-confidence, if you can think positively about (and are not turned off by) the prospect of hard work, long hours, and onerous responsibility, if each new problem challenges you to tackle it with everything at your command, then owning your own business might be the proper route to chart.

The balance of this chapter may help you make up your mind one way or the other.

What's Good about Working for Others?

Holding a job is not the worst thing in the world. Working for someone else offers lots of advantages; some of the more significant ones for you to think about follow:

- Most likely, as an employee, you work regular hours and no more than eight each day. Your evenings and weekends remain free to enjoy family, friends, hobbies, and other leisure activities.
- You have occasional holidays off with pay, paid vacations after a while, and maybe some medical benefits, too.
- You have security, in the form of a regular income that you can count on: for your rent, utility bills, groceries, clothing, transportation, and all the other expenses that characterize modern living.
- Your personal savings remain relatively untouched—at least, they won't be risked on an enterprise of your own.
- You can expect to receive occasional pay increases as the years roll by.
- You may be blessed with special bonuses or profit-sharing.
- The chances are fairly good that your efforts will be recognized, leading to one or more promotions.
- Even though you may be saddled with more and more responsibilities as the years pass, the business will always remain someone else's. You'll be able to spend evenings and weekends with a relatively clear head.
- You may find that your job provides adequately for the personal needs most people want filled, such as status and a sense of belonging, pride in your work, and the like.

But There Are Drawbacks, Too!

Only a few disadvantages of working for others need to be mentioned. For one, you're subject to the vagaries of the economy. Should conditions deteriorate, your company may decide to lay off some employees (including you, perhaps), close down, or make a major move to another part of the country. Also, since you're working for others, you're subject to their whims and pleasures. For example, you may discover that your supervisor is totally illogical, unfair, and highly emotional; he or she could make working conditions rather unpleasant. Or, you may find yourself unexpectedly replaced by a brother, friend, or cousin of the owner, despite the fact that you have put in quite a few years on your job.

There's really no such thing as job security, no matter what you may believe. (Even civil service positions with tenure are no longer totally secure.) As you must know, your only security is *you*. Even though you may move up over the years into the higher echelons of management, you may ultimately be replaced if your firm is acquired by another company. Should you be replaced (and many hundreds of thousands of people have been), you might find it difficult to secure another comparable position.

Finally, while you may rise to a position where you enjoy a fine salary, your job, like most, will have a "cap" or ceiling on it. Your earnings are therefore limited.

WHY SOME PEOPLE BECOME ENTREPRENEURS

Consider this partial list of reasons, presented in no particular order, as to why people go into business:

- A strong desire to be my own master, independent, not taking orders from others and relying on my own talents
- The chance to work at something I enjoy, instead of settling for second- or third-best because of a desire for security in the form of a steady income
- The feeling that I would like to operate at my own pace
- A yearning for recognition and prestige
- A powerful drive to accumulate wealth—and the opportunity to earn far more than I ever could working for others
- The discovery of an opportunity that others have overlooked or ignored
- The challenge of pitting my resources and skills against the environment

Of the many more reasons for going into business, some are thoroughly logical, others emotional, and most probably a combination of the two.

WEIGH THE DRAWBACKS, TOO

While there are indeed many benefits to starting one's own business, disadvantages such as the following need to be borne in mind:

- You can forget about the eight-hour day, as well as carefree evenings and weekends—at least for the first few months (or perhaps years) of business operation. You'll put in long, irregular hours and take your business home with you religiously.

- You may lose your capital investment and, perhaps, other people's money as well.
- You probably won't be able to count on a regular income—or any income, for that matter—at the beginning. Indeed, it may take years before you attain the same salary level you enjoyed on the job.
- You'll carry a tremendous weight of responsibility on your shoulders. You'll have to make all the decisions (unless you share them with a partner—who presents another problem completely). You'll be embroiled in all phases of your business.
- Along these lines, you may find yourself having to perform chores that you dislike or actually abhor.
- By no means can you escape "boss-free." Your customers—and your suppliers—will, in effect, become your new bosses (in the sense that you'll have to accede to their wishes and commands).
- Like it or not, your business will tend to consume just about all your time and all your energies. You'll have little time to spare for family, friends, or fun (except for the fun of running your own business!).

THE KINDS OF RISKS YOU FACE

Each new business venture represents a considerable gamble involving time, effort, and money on the part of the gambler. Moreover, the odds of surviving for the first few years may be no greater than fifty-fifty.

To quote from Dun & Bradstreet's *Business Failure Record:*

> Every year thousands of firms are started, many either fail or discontinue, and others transfer ownership or control. Each business day, over 35,000 changes are made to the Dun & Bradstreet database of over nine million businesses at our National Business Information Center. New names are added and closed businesses are deleted, name styles altered, and financial information revised. This is all evidence of the dynamic change and turnover constantly taking place in the business population.*

In table 1–1, more than 61,000 businesses that failed in 1987 are analyzed by both the type of business and the age of the firm. The results are cross-tabulated. As Dun & Bradstreet wisely cautions with regard to this analysis:

> Business failures do not represent total business closings, which consist of both business failures and business discontinuances. As defined in Dun & Bradstreet's statistics, business failures consist of businesses involved in court proceedings or voluntary actions involving losses to creditors. In contrast, businesses that discontinue operations for reasons such as loss of capital, inadequate profits, ill health, retirement, etc., are not recorded as failures by

---

*The Dun & Bradstreet Corporation, *Business Failure Record: 1986 Final/1987 Preliminary* (New York: The Dun & Bradstreet Corporation, 1988), inside front cover. Used with permission.

TABLE 1–1. AGES OF 61,209 BUSINESSES THAT FAILED IN 1987*

Age of Business	All Types Combined**	Manufacturing	Wholesale Trade	Retail Trade	Services
1 year or less	10.0%	7.8%	7.7%	12.0%	14.9%
2 years	12.4	13.0	12.5	15.9	12.7
3 years	11.4	11.3	11.3	13.7	11.2
4 years	9.4	9.9	9.5	10.1	8.9
5 years	7.5	7.0	8.4	7.6	7.8
Total 5 years or less	50.7%	49.0%	49.4%	59.3%	55.5%
6 to 10 years	24.6	23.3	25.5	22.0	24.6
Over 10 years	24.7	27.7	25.1	18.7	19.9
Total	100.0%	100.0%	100.0%	100.0%	100.0%

Source: The Dun & Bradstreet Corporation, *Business Failure Record: 1986 Final/1987 Preliminary* (New York: The Dun & Bradstreet Corporation, 1988), 17. Used with permission.

*These are preliminary statistics for 1987.

**Other categories included in total, although not shown, are: agriculture, forestry, and fishing; mining; construction; transportation and public utilities; and finance, insurance, and real estate.

Dun & Bradstreet if creditors are paid in full. Although they represent only a percentage of total closings, failures have the most severe impact upon the economy.*

Note that across the various businesses covered in the analysis, some 50.7 percent of the failures were companies that had been in operation for five or fewer years.

Business Mortality

Regardless of your mode of entry into the business arena—through purchasing an existing company, signing up for a franchise, or launching a brand-new enterprise—the gambling aspect is not your only concern. Any new business represents a contest—a struggle over the long term, replete with an unending series of challenges to your knowledge and skills. Some might look at these challenges as a steady stream of small, gambling situations that must be resolved—the outcomes of which, when totaled up, will result in a business success or demise.

Yes, businesses fail. Indeed, many knowledgeable advisors ascribe such failures, in the main, to initial errors in judgment. Among these are selecting the wrong business location; offering the wrong product or product line; deciding to proceed with insufficient capital; ignoring the need for doing one's homework (projections and the like); or even choosing the wrong type of business to go into in the first place.

As we probe behind these initial errors, we find several other major factors, such as a lack of experience in the particular field of endeavor or sheer incompetence in business management. Indeed, Dun & Bradstreet's study of the prelimi-

*Ibid.

nary 1987 data concerning business failures underscores the seriousness of various experience causes by ranking them second only to economic factors causes (insufficient profits, high interest rates, loss of market, and so on) in their deleterious effects upon the enterprises concerned. (See exhibit 1–1.)

WHAT YOU NEED TO MAKE IT

Before rushing into a business of your own, you owe it to yourself to increase your chances for success by:

1. Preparing for the challenge by obtaining a good education, preferably one that includes some business courses

EXHIBIT 1-1. More significant causes of business failures, 1987

Note: These are preliminary statistics for 1987. Due to the fact that some failures are attributed to a combination of causes, the total of the major categories exceeds 100.00 percent. The individual major category total was used to achieve the percents in the minor categories.

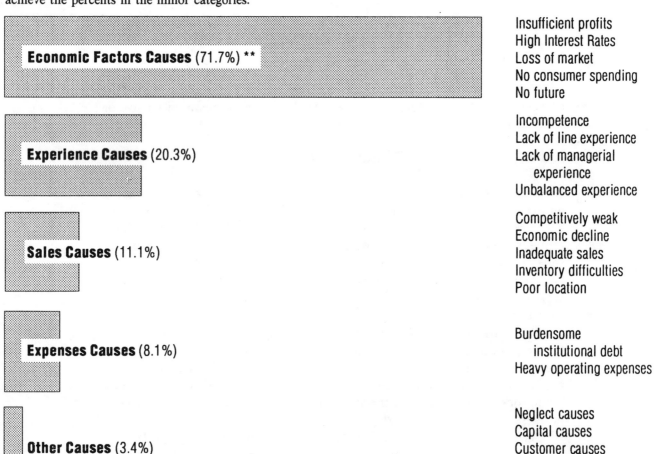

Economic Factors Causes (71.7%) **
- Insufficient profits
- High Interest Rates
- Loss of market
- No consumer spending
- No future

Experience Causes (20.3%)
- Incompetence
- Lack of line experience
- Lack of managerial experience
- Unbalanced experience

Sales Causes (11.1%)
- Competitively weak
- Economic decline
- Inadequate sales
- Inventory difficulties
- Poor location

Expenses Causes (8.1%)
- Burdensome institutional debt
- Heavy operating expenses

Other Causes (3.4%)
- Neglect causes
- Capital causes
- Customer causes
- Fraud causes
- Assets causes

Adapted from The Dun & Bradstreet Corporation, *Business Failure Record: 1986 Final/1987 Preliminary* (New York: The Dun & Bradstreet Corporation, 1988), 19. Used with permission.

2. Accumulating months, or even a year or more, of experience in the field you seek to enter
3. Securing a managerial post in that field in order to gain as much exposure as possible to the many facets of business administration: sales, purchasing, production, inventory control, financial management, and so forth
4. Keeping up with change and innovation in the industry by reading business and trade publications, and through personal contacts

Only four ingredients are truly essential to a new business success:

- A qualified entrepreneur
- A potential business opportunity
- A solid and detailed plan
- Sufficient capital

Upon further reflection, we should add a fifth element to that list: *luck.*

Of course, the biggest single factor in this recipe for success is the entrepreneur. This man or woman needs business experience plus knowledge and skills. In addition to such obvious traits as drive, willingness to take chances, and persistence, the following personal qualities appear to characterize most individuals who make a go of their own businesses:

energy	imagination
good health	self-control
inquisitiveness	good sense of
confidence	timing
boldness	independence
empathy	self-discipline
innovativeness	consideration
sense of ethics	of others
tact	good judgment
adaptability	sociability

Moreover, the successful entrepreneur:

- Is willing to work hard
- Gets along well with others
- Has good communication skills
- Knows how to organize
- Takes pride in what he or she does
- Maintains good interpersonal relations
- Is a self-starter
- Welcomes responsibility
- Is willing and able to make decisions

You have checked over these characteristics and decided that they describe you very well. Moreover, you're ready, willing, and eager to go into business. Now you need to discover a bona fide business opportunity and then develop a comprehensive business plan.

The balance of Part I of this book, along with the four chapters that comprise Part II, will help you do just that. In addition, you can order helpful booklets from the U.S. Small Business Administration, such as *Checklist for Going into Business* and *Business Plan for Small Manufacturers.* *

What about money?

Yes, launching a business takes money. The days of starting out on a shoestring are long gone, although thousands of people still attempt this feat every year.

You'll need two kinds of capital: *initial capital* to set up the business properly; and *working capital* to keep it going until the business begins to pay off. Of course, the amount of money you'll need depends on the kind of business you select. There will be rent to pay, a deposit plus one or more month's rent in advance, utility deposits and monthly bills to meet, and equipment to buy. You'll also need funds for incidentals (legal fees, permits, and insurance premiums) and, of course, initial inventory to begin operations.

You'll learn more about capital—and about where to find it—in chapter 5 ("How to Estimate Your Financial Needs").

THINK BEFORE YOU LEAP—TRY SELF-ANALYSIS

Before committing yourself to the extraordinary investment of time, energy, and money that starting a business requires, wouldn't it make sense to engage in some personal soul-searching? You ought to pause and think about the following questions:

- What am I looking for? What do I want out of life?
- Are my aspirations realistic? Attainable?
- Am I prepared to struggle and make sacrifices?
- Am I a self-starter?
- Am I in good health?
- Am I blessed with plain, old-fashioned common sense?
- Can I usually control my emotions?
- Do I have self-discipline?
- Do I have good managerial skills?
- Do I have enough experience in this field?
- Am I more of a doer than a dreamer?

The entrepreneur *is* the business—its originator, its motivating force, its energy. Do you have what it takes to make a success of your own business? Review your pluses and your minuses, your strengths and your weaknesses. In toto, are you a suitable match for this challenge? A few hours of introspection—with a pencil for recording your own self-portrait—should be enough to make this decision.

---

*See "Pamphlets Available from the Small Business Administration" in the bibliography at the end of this chapter.

As a cautionary note, bear in mind that some individuals have difficulty seeing themselves in a realistic light. Many have overly inflated egos and believe they can do anything, even things that are definitely beyond their reach and capabilities. Such confidence is admirable when deserved; it becomes a powerful weapon in the struggle for success. On the other hand, when unreasonably egotistical people fail, they quickly blame others (competitors, luck or fate, or even their spouses or relatives).

The majority of people, however, can see themselves pretty much as they really are if they: (a) make the effort, and (b) proceed on an intellectual and unemotional basis. To help you along, we offer two aids designed to facilitate your self-analysis. These are exhibit 1–2 ("Do You Have What It Takes?") and exhibit 1–3 ("The Creativity/Leadership Self-Rating Chart").

EXHIBIT 1–2. Do you have what it takes?

Note: The small booklet *Checklist for Going into Business* (MA 2.016) is one of the many publications distributed by the U.S. Small Business Administration. It is worthwhile reading for everyone thinking about starting a new enterprise. Along with other useful information, it contains the short quiz shown below. Though tongue-in-cheek, this quiz will help you decide whether you "have what it takes" to start a business of your own. For the next few minutes, enjoy answering the questions! After you have finished, follow the scoring instructions and then read the last paragraph.

UNDER EACH QUESTION, CHECK THE ANSWER THAT SAYS WHAT YOU FEEL OR COMES CLOSEST TO IT. BE HONEST WITH YOURSELF.

Are you a self-starter?

_____ I do things on my own. Nobody has to tell me to get going.

_____ If someone gets me started, I keep going all right.

_____ Easy does it, man. I don't put myself out until I have to.

How do you feel about other people?

_____ I like people. I can get along with just about anybody.

_____ I have plenty of friends—I don't need anyone else.

_____ Most people bug me.

Can you lead others?

_____ I can get most people to go along when I start something.

_____ I can give the orders if someone tells me what we should do.

_____ I let someone else get things moving. Then I go along if I feel like it.

Can you take responsibility?

_____ I like to take charge of things and see them through.

_____ I'll take over if I have to, but I'd rather let someone else be responsible.

_____ There's always some eager beaver around wanting to show how smart he is. I say let him.

How good an organizer are you?

_____ I like to have a plan before I start. I'm usually the one to get things lined up when the gang wants to do something.

EXHIBIT 1-2. (*Continued*)

_____ I do all right unless things get too goofed up. Then I cop out.

_____ You get all set and then something comes along and blows the whole bag. So I just take things as they come.

How good a worker are you?

_____ I can keep going as long as I need to. I don't mind working hard for something I want.

_____ I'll work hard for a while, but when I've had enough, that's it, man!

_____ I can't see that hard work gets you anywhere.

Can you make decisions?

_____ I can make up my mind in a hurry if I have to. It usually turns out O.K., too.

_____ I can if I have plenty of time. If I have to make up my mind fast, I think later I should have decided the other way.

_____ I don't like to be the one who has to decide things. I'd probably blow it.

Can people trust what you say?

_____ You bet they can. I don't say things I don't mean.

_____ I try to be on the level most of the time, but sometimes I just say what's easiest.

_____ What's the sweat if the other fellow doesn't know the difference?

Can you stick with it?

_____ If I make up my mind to do something, I don't let *anything* stop me.

_____ I usually finish what I start—if it doesn't get fouled up.

_____ If it doesn't go right away, I turn off. Why beat your brains out?

How good is your health?

_____ Man, I *never* run down!

_____ I have enough energy for most things I want to do.

_____ I run out of juice sooner than most of my friends seem to.

Now count the checks you made.

How many checks are there beside the *first* answer to each question? _____

How many checks are there beside the *second* answer to each question? _____

How many checks are there beside the *third* answer to each question? _____

If most of your checks are beside the first answers, you probably have what it takes to run a business. If not, you're likely to have more trouble than you can handle by yourself. Better find a partner who is strong on the points you're weak on. If many checks are beside the third answer, not even a good partner will be able to shore you up.

Source: Small Marketers Aid No. 71 (Washington, D.C.: U.S. Small Business Administration, 1975), 4–5.

EXHIBIT 1-3. The Creativity/Leadership Self-Rating Chart

Note: I developed and copyrighted this chart some years ago and have used it in a few studies of supervisory and managerial personnel.

Essentially, the chart consists of two lists of characteristics—twenty-five "Creativity Traits" and twenty-five "Leadership Traits"—culled from literature and research in these two areas.

More likely than not, entrepreneurs who hope to succeed will register an above-average score on the total list of "leadership" characteristics. Although the need for a high score on "creativity" traits may not be as apparent, I believe that creativity is essential for success over the long term. Among other things, it enables the business owner to cope with both new and recurring challenges, the efforts of competitors, and an ever-changing business environment.

Top company executives appear to earn comparatively high scores in both dimensions of the Self-Rating Chart.

EXHIBIT 1–3. (*Continued*)

People who see themselves as "average" in all traits (a rating of "4" multiplied by 25 traits) would earn scores of 100 on each of the two parts. The majority of successful executives tested with this chart score in the "110 and above" range on the Creativity Traits—and even higher on the Leadership Traits. Total test scores above 240 are quite common among them.

How well do you know yourself?

Below is a list of nouns and short phrases. You are to consider each item carefully—and then place an *X* in one of the boxes alongside the trait you are rating. There are seven choices available to you (Columns *1* through *7*). Placing an *X* in Column *1* would indicate that you rate yourself "Extremely Low" in the particular trait; an *X* in Column *4* would signify an "Average" rating; and *X* in Column *7* would mean "Extremely High."

Forget your natural modesty, yet *do* be honest with your self-evaluation.

The Chart As a Diagnostic Instrument

If you are entirely honest with yourself—and perceive yourself clearly—an analysis of your responses on the chart will pinpoint your strengths and expose your weaknesses. Low ratings on any qualities (*X*s in "Extremely Low" to "Average" columns) show that you do realize your deficiencies. You can improve these through study and effort.

Finally, many leadership qualities develop on the job, as you work hard making your own business a success.

PART I: CREATIVITY TRAITS

Item	Extremely Low 1	Quite Low 2	Somewhat Low 3	Average 4	Somewhat High 5	Quite High 6	Extremely High 7
Ability to express oneself							
Adaptability							
Awareness							
Curiosity							
Drive							
Enthusiasm							
Facility with numbers							
Flexibility of thinking							
Independence of outlook							
Lack of compulsion to conform							
Open-mindedness							

EXHIBIT 1–3 (*Continued*)

Item	Extremely Low 1	Quite Low 2	Somewhat Low 3	Average 4	Somewhat High 5	Quite High 6	Extremely High 7
Originality							
Positive attitude							
Powers of concentration							
Productivity							
Resourcefulness							
Self-confidence							
Self-sufficiency							
Sense of humor							
Sensitivity to problems							
"Stick-to-itiveness"							
Verbal fluency							
Wide and varied interests							
Willingness to take chances							
Zest for solving puzzles							
Creativity Traits Totals:							

PART II: LEADERSHIP TRAITS

Item	Extremely Low 1	Quite Low 2	Somewhat Low 3	Average 4	Somewhat High 5	Quite High 6	Extremely High 7
Ability to clarify ideas for others							
Ability to enlist the cooperation of others							
Ability to judge people							
Ability to see the whole picture							
Ability to set priorities							
Communication skills							

EXHIBIT 1–3 (*Continued*)

Item	Extremely Low 1	Quite Low 2	Somewhat Low 3	Average 4	Somewhat High 5	Quite High 6	Extremely High 7
Decision-making capability							
Evaluation skills							
Giving credit when due							
Good judgment							
Interest in people (in contrast to things)							
Knack for interpersonal relations							
Planning ability							
Powers of persuasion							
Receptivity to change							
Self-control							
Sensitivity to others							
Skill at motivating others							
Skill in scheduling							
Supportive of subordinates							
Taking the initiative							
Talent for analyzing situations							
Technical knowledge of my job							
Warmth of personal relations							
Willingness to listen to subordinates							
Leadership Traits Totals:							

SCORING INSTRUCTIONS

To score the chart after rating yourself, follow these steps:

1. Part I of the Chart lists twenty-five "Creativity Traits"; Part II lists twenty-five "Leadership Traits." Mark each half of the Chart separately.
2. Put the total number of *X*s in Column 1 ("Extremely Low") at the bottom of the first column.

EXHIBIT 1–3. (*Continued*)

3. Continue totaling Columns 2, 3, 4, and so on, until you have totaled all seven columns.
4. (First, your various totals should add up to 25—the number of traits you have rated.) Now, multiply each column total by the number at the top of the column. For example, your self-report shows the following numbers of *X*s: 1, 2, 4, 8, 3, 5, and 2. Here's how you work out a sample score on Part I of the chart:
5. Write your Total Creativity Traits Score in the box on the Scoring Chart.
6. Repeat the entire procedure with Part II, "Leadership Traits." Write your total score in the "Leadership" box on the Scoring Chart.
7. Add up the totals in the Scoring Chart box. Write in "Total Test" score.

Column Number		Number of *X*s		Total Value
1	$\times$	1	=	1
2	$\times$	2	=	4
3	$\times$	4	=	12
4	$\times$	8	=	32
5	$\times$	3	=	15
6	$\times$	5	=	30
7	$\times$	2	=	14

TOTAL CREATIVITY TRAITS SCORE   =   108

Scoring Chart _____
Creativity Traits
_____
Leadership Traits
_____
Total Test:
_____

©Copyright Irving Burstiner 1972.
*Revised, 1974.

A FRIEND IN NEED:
THE SMALL BUSINESS ADMINISTRATION

The U.S. Small Business Administration (SBA) is a federal agency that renders valuable services to small enterprises—and to those interested in small business—in nearly ninety branch offices in major cities around the country. (See Exhibit 1–4.) The SBA provides an array of services: financial assistance, management aid, technical advice, help in securing government business, procurement advisement, and so forth. In the management assistance area, for example, the SBA arranges for:

- Conferences dealing with topics of interest to small business
- Business management courses cosponsored with educational institutions

EXHIBIT 1–4. FIELD OFFICES OF THE U.S. SMALL BUSINESS ADMINISTRATION

Agana, Guam	Denver, Colo.	Las Cruces, N. Mex.	Portland, Oreg.
Albany, N.Y.	Des Moines, Iowa	Las Vegas, Nev.	Providence, R.I.
Albuquerque, N. Mex.	Detroit, Mich.	Little Rock, Ark.	Rapid City, S. Dak.
Anchorage, Alaska	Eau Claire, Wis.	Los Angeles, Calif.	Richmond, Va.
Atlanta, Ga.	Elmira, N.Y.	Louisville, Ky.	Rochester, N.Y.
Augusta, Maine	El Paso, Tex.	Lubbock, Tex.	St. Louis, Mo.
Baltimore, Md.	Fairbanks, Alaska	Madison, Wis.	Salt Lake City, Utah
Birmingham, Ala.	Fargo, N. Dak.	Marquette, Mich.	San Antonio, Tex.
Boise, Idaho	Fresno, Calif.	Marshall, Tex.	San Diego, Calif.
Boston, Mass.	Gulfport, Miss.	Memphis, Tenn.	San Francisco, Calif.
Buffalo, N.Y.	Harlingen, Tex.	Miami, Fla.	Seattle, Wash.
Casper, Wyo.	Harrisburg, Pa.	Milwaukee, Wis.	Sioux Falls, S. Dak.
Charleston, W. Va.	Hartford, Conn.	Minneapolis, Minn.	Spokane, Wash.
Charlotte, N.C.	Hato Rey, P.R.	Montpelier, Vt.	Springfield, Ill.
Chicago, Ill.	Helena, Mont.	Nashville, Tenn.	Syracuse, N.Y.
Cincinnati, Ohio	Holyoke, Mass.	Newark, N.J.	Tampa, Fla.
Clarksburg, W. Va.	Honolulu, Hawaii	New Orleans, La.	Washington, D.C.
Cleveland, Ohio	Houston, Tex.	New York, N.Y.	Wichita, Kans.
Columbia, S.C.	Indianapolis, Ind.	Oklahoma City, Okla.	Wilkes-Barre, Pa.
Columbus, Ohio	Jackson, Miss.	Omaha, Nebr.	Wilmington, Del.
Concord, N.H.	Jacksonville, Fla.	Philadelphia, Pa.	
Corpus Christi, Tex.	Kansas City, Mo.	Phoenix, Ariz.	
Dallas, Tex.	Knoxville, Tenn.	Pittsburgh, Pa.	

For addresses and telephone numbers of the field offices, look under "United States Government" in the appropriate telephone directories.

Source: C. R. Stigelman, "Franchise Index/Profile: A Franchise Evaluation Process," *Small Business Management Series No. 35* (Washington, D.C.: U.S. Small Business Administration, 1986), 55.

- Information and counseling
- Small business clinics
- Many printed aids, leaflets, and pamphlets

Moreover, the SBA works closely with both the Active Corps of Executives (ACE) and the Service Corps of Retired Executives (SCORE). These organizations provide consulting services to small businesses free of charge.

Financial assistance may be made available in the form of loans, mostly in cooperation with banks. These include various types of special-purpose loans, such as those for disadvantaged individuals (Economic Opportunity Loans), for handicapped persons, and for businesses hit by disaster.

Small Business Investment Corporations (SBICs), licensed by the SBA, also make funds available and offer management assistance to small enterprises. These came into being following the enactment, in 1958, of the Small Business Investment Act. Minority Small Business Investment Corporations (MESBICs) provide the same services to minority group members.

FOR FURTHER INFORMATION

Books

Broom, H. N., J. G. Longenecker, and Carlos Moore. *Small Business Management,* 6th ed. Cincinnati: South-Western, 1983.

Kline, John B., Donald P. Stegall, and Lawrence L. Steinmetz. *Managing the Small Business,* 3d ed. Homewood, Ill.: Irwin, 1982.

Kuriloff, Arthur H., and John M. Hemphill, Jr. *Starting and Managing the Small Business.* New York: McGraw-Hill, 1983.

Moreau, James F. *Effective Small Business Management.* Boston: Houghton Mifflin, 1980.

Siropolis, Nicholas C. *Small Business Management: A Guide to Entrepreneurship,* 3d ed. Boston: Houghton Mifflin, 1982.

Sondero, Stanley R. *Small Business Management Principles.* Plano, Tex.: Business Publications, 1985.

Steinhoff, Dan, and J. Burgess. *Small Business Management Fundamentals,* 4th ed. New York: McGraw-Hill, 1986.

Tate, Curtis E., Jr., et al. *Successful Small Business Management,* 4th ed. Plano, Tex.: Business Publications, 1985.

Walthall, Wylie A., and Michael J. Wirth. *Getting into Business: An Introduction to Business,* 3d ed. New York: Harper & Row, 1983.

Pamphlets Available from the Small Business Administration

Note: All currently available business development pamphlets and booklets are listed in Forms SBA 115-A and 115-B. You may obtain copies of these two order forms by (a) writing to the U. S. Small Business Administration, P. O. Box 15434, Forth Worth, TX 76119; (b) contacting the nearest field office of the SBA; or (c) calling the SBA. Answer Desk in Washington, D.C. The desk is staffed weekdays from 9 A.M. to 5 P.M.; the service is designed to help answer small business problems with government. Outside of Washington, the toll-free number is 1-800-368-5855. Within the District of Columbia, call 653-7561.

MANAGEMENT AIDS

MA 2.007—"Business Plan for Small Manufacturers"
MA 2.008—"Business Plan for Small Construction Firms"
MA 2.016—"Checklist for Going into Business"
MA 2.020—"Business Plan for Retailers"
MA 2.022—"Business Plan for Small Service Firms"
MA 2.025—"Thinking About Going into Business?"
MA 2.026—"Feasibility Checklist for Starting a Small Business of Your Own"
MA 7.003—"Market Overseas with U.S. Government Help"

SMALL BUSINESS BIBLIOGRAPHIES

SBB # 2—"Home Businesses"

Booklets Available from the Superintendent of Documents*

S/N 003-008-00194-7—*Franchise Opportunities Handbook, 1984*—$13.50.

S/N 045-000-00164-4—*Buying and Selling a Small Business*—$5.00.

S/N 045-000-00207-1—*Starting and Managing a Small Service Business*—$4.50.

S/N 045-000-00212-8—*Starting and Managing a Small Business of Your Own*—$4.75.

S/N 045-000-00232-2—*Starting and Managing a Small Business from Your Home*—$1.75.

S/N 045-000-00237-3—*Small Business Incubator Handbook: A Guide for Start-up and Management*—$8.50.

*To order publications from the Superintendent of Documents, send S/N (Stock Number) and title together with check or money order for the amount indicated to: Superintendent of Documents, U.S. Government Printing Office, Washington, D.C. 20402. (*Note:* Prices indicated for government publications are subject to change without prior notice.) These publications may also be purchased from U.S. Department of Commerce field offices.

2

How to Choose the Right Business for *You*

If you've read the introductory material in chapter 1 thoroughly and have concluded from your self-analysis that you have what it takes to succeed in your own business, the logical next step is to think about the type of business that suits your needs better than any other.

To help you make up your mind, you should know something about the business world in general, the various types of businesses available to the new entrepreneur, and the general characteristics shared by each.

Ultimately, your choice will be influenced by a variety of factors, a few of which are listed below:

- The size of your pocketbook (how much capital you can invest)
- The potential payoff *(return on investment)*
- The nature of the work activities involved
- Your past work experiences
- The objectives you set
- Your attitudes and opinions
- Your personality
- Your knowledge and skills

THE WORLD OF SMALL BUSINESS IN AMERICA

Ours is a vigorous economy. Living standards here are among the highest in the world. In recent decades there has been infringement into the private sector by all levels of government. However, private control of business and industry is assured by custom and by statute. Ours is a capitalist society where business is open to everyone who has what it takes—including courage.

Today there are approximately 13 million firms in operation in the United States. According to the U.S. Small Business Administration, more than nine out of every ten would most likely be considered small businesses—at least for business loan eligibility. Below are typical agency sales size or employment standards for definition as a "small business"; they depend, in each situation, on the particular industry in which the firm operates:

Manufacturers: from 500 to 1,500 employees
Wholesale establishments: up to 500 employees; annual sales of up to 25 million
Retail firms: yearly sales not exceeding $3 million to $13 million
Service companies: Annual revenues of not more than $3 million to $14.5 million

Most small enterprises reflect the following characteristics:

- Independently owned and operated
- Localized scope of operations
- Not dominant in its field
- Relatively small size in the particular industry
- Comparatively limited initial investment of capital

The vast majority of today's giant corporations (like Macy's and J. C. Penney, the Southland Corporation, Timex, the Ford Motor Company, Tandy Corporation, and so on) were once small businesses. In fact, the entire aviation industry began in a small garage run by two brothers who earned their livelihood repairing bicycles. You never know—today's tiny home business or part-time hobby might become tomorrow's successful large corporation!

The law favors small business. Monopolies, unfair methods of competition, and restraint of free trade are illegal in the United States. In 1953 the Small Business Administration was created to "encourage, assist and protect the interests of small businesses."

According to the federal government's Standard Industrial Classification System, the country's business structure is divided into a number of categories. Among these categories are:

agriculture	wholesale trade
mining	retail trade
construction	finance, insurance,
manufacturing	and real estate
transportation	services

EXPLORING THE MAJOR BUSINESS ARENAS

Chances are your new venture will fall into one of the following areas: (1) manufacturing, (2) wholesaling, (3) retailing, or (4) service. Of the four, retailing is the area most favored by new entrepreneurs (possibly because it's easy to enter the field and because it's the one kind of business most familiar to consumers). On the other hand, services has been the fastest growing area in recent years.

Manufacturing

Manufacturers are makers or producers—companies and individuals that produce goods by hand or by machine. Several different types of manufacturing processes are found in the economy: the conversion of raw materials into finished products, the assembling of parts into wholes, the fabrication of machinery and equipment, and so on.

More often than not, the new manufacturing enterprise calls for a heavy initial investment in a plant and machinery, needs a number of specialized employees, and requires large purchases of raw or semiprocessed materials and supplies. Depending on what you manufacture, your customers may be the public at large (or special segments of the consumer population), wholesalers,

EXHIBIT 2-1. MANUFACTURING IN AMERICA: MORE COMMON TYPES AND APPROXIMATE NUMBER OF ESTABLISHMENTS, 1982

Printing and Publishing	53,406
Machinery, except electrical	52,912
Fabricated metal products	35,560
Apparel, other textile products	24,391
Food and kindred products	22,130
Stone, clay, and glass products	16,545
Electric and electronic equipment	16,454
Chemicals and allied products	11,889
Furniture and fixtures	10,003

Source: U.S. Department of Commerce, Bureau of the Census, *Statistical Abstract of the United States, 1986,* 106th ed. (Washington, D.C.: U.S. Government Printing Office, 1985), 745–49.

retailers, industry itself, commerce, the agricultural sector, or government agencies at any level.

Among the manufacturing enterprises favored by small operators are printing establishments, sportswear and other apparel plants, machine shops, and bakeries. Exhibit 2–1 lists some of the more common types of manufacturing businesses in the United States, along with the approximate number of establishments in each category in 1982.

Of far more interest at this point, however, are the financial percentages furnished in table 2–1 for some selected manufacturing types. All figures are expressed as percentages of net sales. For example, the first entry (SIC Number 3993—Advertising displays and devices) indicates a 58.4 percent cost of sales. The term *gross profit* (or *gross margin*) refers to what is left over after the cost of sales is subtracted from the net sales figure. Hence, the gross profit in this case is 41.6 percent.

Note that gross profit percentages for these different types of manufacturing enterprises run from as low as 32.4 percent (miscellaneous plastic products) to as high as 43.3 percent (sporting and athletic goods). The range of operating profit before taxes for this group runs from 2.7 percent (bread and other bakery products) to 8.7 percent (sporting and athletic goods).

Wholesaling

Wholesalers act as intermediaries between manufacturers and retailers—if their business is consumer products—or between manufacturers and industry, commerce, professionals, and other buyers if they are marketing industrial goods.

There are fewer than 400,000 wholesale establishments in the United States. More than two-thirds of these firms are merchant wholesalers; the balance are

TABLE 2–1. FINANCIAL DATA FOR SELECTED MANUFACTURING BUSINESSES*

SIC Number	Type of Business	Cost of Sales	Gross Profit	Operating Expenses	Operating Profit
3993	Advertising displays and devices	58.4%	41.6%	36.6%	5.0%
2051	Bread and other bakery products	59.4	40.6	37.9	2.7
3471, 79	Coating, engraving, and allied services	61.7	38.3	33.0	5.3
2751	Commercial printing (letterpress and screen)	59.6	40.4	35.6	4.7
3671, 72–79	Electronic components and accessories	62.1	37.9	34.4	3.5
2861, 65, 69	Industrial chemicals	64.0	36.0	33.0	2.9
3911	Jewelry, precious metals	61.1	38.9	32.5	6.5
3599	Machine shops—jobbing and repair	63.6	36.4	31.6	4.8
3079	Miscellaneous plastic products	67.6	32.4	28.9	3.6
3949	Sporting and athletic goods	56.7	43.3	34.5	8.7
2335	Women's dresses	61.4	38.6	33.8	4.8

Source: Robert Morris Associates, *'87 Annual Statement Studies* (Philadelphia: Robert Morris Associates, 1987). Copyright 1987 by Robert Morris Associates. Used with permission. (See "Interpretation of Statement Studies Figures" at end of table 2–6 on page 30.)

*Based on statement studies of firms with fiscal year-ends June 30, 1986 through March 31, 1987. All statistics are expressed in terms of percentages of annual sales volume. (*Note:* Only data for firms with from $0 to $1 million in assets have been shown since this would be characteristic of the beginning business.)

of several types, including manufacturers' sales branches and offices, merchandise agents and brokers, and others. Most merchant wholesalers buy large quantities of goods, store them in their warehouses, then break them down into smaller amounts to sell to their customers. Consequently, the typical wholesale firm needs (1) a warehouse (2) a large investment in inventory, and (3) a sales staff. In addition, an efficient inventory control system is mandatory.

More information about wholesalers can be found in chapter 15. In the meantime, more common types and the approximate number of organizations in each classification are shown in exhibit 2-2.

Budding entrepreneurs who enter the wholesale trade seem to be attracted to such major lines of goods as office supplies, ceramics, hardware, chemical cleaning compounds and janitorial supplies, plants and flowers, beauty salon supplies, confectionery, stationery, and wall coverings.

Table 2-2 contains significant financial data for selected types of wholesale enterprises. The table reveals that pretax operating profit figures run from a low

EXHIBIT 2-2. WHOLESALING IN AMERICA: MORE COMMON TYPES AND APPROXIMATE NUMBER OF ESTABLISHMENTS, 1982

Machinery, equipment, supplies	99,200
Motor vehicles, automotive equipment	39,500
Groceries and related products	38,500
Electrical goods	29,200
Hardware, plumbing, heating equipment	20,800
Petroleum, petroleum products	18,700
Lumber, construction materials	17,000
Apparel, piece goods, notions	14,300
Paper, paper products	13,900

Source: U.S. Department of Commerce, Bureau of the Census, Statistical Abstract of the United States, 1986, 106th ed. (Washington, D.C.: U.S. Government Printing Office, 1985), 786.

TABLE 2–2. FINANCIAL DATA FOR SELECTED WHOLESALING BUSINESSES*

SIC Number	Type of Business	Cost of Sales	Gross Profit	Operating Expenses	Operating Profit
5013	Automotive equipment	66.4%	33.6%	30.8%	2.8%
5161	Chemicals and allied products	66.1	33.9	30.2	3.7
5145	Confectionery	73.3	26.7	25.4	1.3
5063	Electrical supplies and apparatus	67.3	32.7	30.4	2.4
5199	Flowers and florists' supplies	60.7	39.3	34.5	4.8
5148	Fresh fruits and vegetables	78.2	21.8	19.3	2.5
5021	Furniture	67.9	32.1	30.0	2.1
5141	General groceries	77.0	23.0	21.1	2.0
5199	General merchandise	64.1	35.9	31.6	4.3
5072, 5198	Hardware and paints	68.2	31.8	28.7	3.1
5087	Janitorial supplies	64.1	35.9	32.8	3.1
5094	Jewelry	70.1	29.9	26.1	3.8
5112	Stationery supplies	66.5	33.5	31.2	2.3
5041	Sporting goods and toys	68.5	31.5	29.2	2.3

Source: Robert Morris Associates, *'87 Annual Statement Studies* (Philadelphia: Robert Morris Associates, 1987). Copyright 1987 by Robert Morris Associates. Used with permission. (See "Interpretation of Statement Studies Figures" at end of table 2–6 on page 30.)

*Based on statement studies of firms with fiscal year-ends June 30, 1986 through March 31, 1987. All statistics are expressed in terms of percentages of annual sales volume. (*Note:* Only data for firms with from $0 to $1 million in assets have been shown since this would be characteristic of the beginning business.)

of 1.3 percent of sales (confectionery) to a high of 4.8 percent (flowers and florists' supplies).

Retailing

Like wholesalers, retailers are intermediaries in the marketing channels that forward goods from the nation's producers through to the final consumer. Retailers attempt to satisfy consumer needs and wants by selling them merchandise and/or services.

Retailing is a vital sector of the economy that employs more than 15 million people. By 1981 total annual sales in this sector began to surpass $1 trillion, up from $293 million in 1967.*

Of all categories of business, retailing is the type most familiar to the more than 235 million consumers in the country. There are approximately 1.9 million retail establishments across the land. For the most part, these are *store* retailers. Many of them are "mom and pop" stores, run by a married couple.

Store retailers are shopkeepers—merchants who buy merchandise from wholesalers or manufacturers for resale to the public. For the new small store operation, you need: a good location, suitable space, fixtures, displays, and an

*U.S. Department of Commerce, Bureau of the Census, *Statistical Abstract of the United States, 1984–1985,* 105th ed. (Washington, D.C.: U.S. Government Printing Office, 1984), 799.

initial stock of merchandise to sell. Depending on the size of the business, your initial investment can either be as low as several thousand dollars or considerably more than $100,000.

The most common types of retail establishments are indicated in table 2–3, along with estimates of their average per-unit yearly sales. Eating places (restaurants, fast-food drive-ins, and the like) lead the pack by far—with grocery stores and bars running close behind.

Table 2–4 contains financial information for some of the types of retailing that appeal to small-scale operators. For this group, the spread of operating profit percentages of sales runs from 1.8 percent (books and stationery) to 4.8 percent (jewelry).

Nonstore Retailers. There are other types of retailers who do not depend on store premises to transact business. Three major types of *nonstore retailers* are the direct selling company, mail order house, and vending machine operator. Many other kinds of operations exist; examples include flea marketers and street vendors.

TABLE 2–3. STORE RETAILING IN AMERICA: SELECTED TYPES, 1982

Kind of Business	Approximate Number of Establishments	Estimated Average Annual Sales/Unit*
Eating places	301,700	$ 315,000
Grocery stores	168,000	1,370,000
Drinking places (alcoholic beverages)	80,000	119,000
Women's clothing and specialty stores (and furriers)	58,800	379,000
Drug and proprietary stores	52,000	701,000
Auto- and home-supply stores	48,800	434,000
Women's ready-to-wear stores	47,900	426,000
Liquor stores	44,600	407,000
Home furnishing stores	44,300	213,000
Gift, novelty, and souvenir stores	41,400	122,000
Building materials and supply stores	40,100	876,000
Shoe stores	39,400	290,000
Jewelry stores	38,700	228,000
Radio, television, and music stores	35,200	392,000
Furniture stores	38,300	461,000
Sporting goods stores, bicycle shops	34,700	231,000
Florists	34,700	108,000
Hardware stores	25,400	344,000
Family clothing stores	23,700	576,000
Retail bakeries	22,200	169,000
Men's and boys' clothing, furnishings stores	18,600	420,000

Source: U.S. Department of Commerce, Bureau of the Census, *Statistical Abstract of the United States, 1986,* 106th ed. (Washington, D.C.: U.S. Government Printing Office, 1985) 779.

*These estimates were derived by dividing the total sales volume for each category by the number of establishments recorded. (*Note:* The sales of large chain store units are included as well as those of smaller independent retailers.)

TABLE 2–4. FINANCIAL DATA FOR SELECTED RETAIL BUSINESSES*

SIC Number	Type of Business	Cost of Sales	Gross Profit	Operating Expenses	Operating Profit
5942, 43	Books and stationery	61.5%	38.5%	36.7%	1.8%
5999	Computers and software	62.8	37.2	33.0	4.2
5992	Cut flowers and growing plants	47.6	52.4	49.8	2.6
5912	Drugs	67.7	32.3	28.3	4.0
5399	Dry goods and general merchandise	64.2	35.8	32.0	3.8
5651	Family clothing	60.6	39.4	34.8	4.6
5713	Floor coverings	67.2	32.8	29.4	3.4
5712	Furniture	59.8	40.2	36.9	3.3
5541	Gasoline service stations	77.7	22.3	19.6	2.7
5411	Groceries and meats	76.3	23.7	21.7	2.0
5251	Hardware	65.3	34.7	31.7	3.0
5945	Hobby, toy, and game shops	59.7	40.3	38.2	2.1
5722	Household appliances	66.8	33.2	30.6	2.6
5944	Jewelry	54.0	46.0	41.2	4.8
5921	Liquor	76.7	23.3	20.8	2.5
5947, 48	Luggage and gifts	55.3	44.7	40.8	3.9
5611	Men's and boys' clothing	58.0	42.0	39.5	2.5
5733	Musical instruments and supplies	58.9	41.1	36.9	4.2
5943, 99	Office supplies and equipment	60.0	40.0	36.3	3.7
5231	Paint, glass, and wallpaper	63.5	36.5	33.3	3.2
5812	Restaurants	43.6	56.4	53.1	3.3
5661	Shoes	60.5	39.5	36.7	2.8
5941	Sporting goods and bicycles	66.2	33.8	30.1	3.7
5621	Women's ready-to-wear	59.3	40.7	37.7	3.0

Source: Robert Morris Associates, *'87 Annual Statement Studies* (Philadelphia: Robert Morris Associates, 1987). Copyright 1987 by Robert Morris Associates. Used with permission. (See "Interpretation of Statement Studies Figures" at end of table 2–6 on page 30.)

*Based on statement studies of firms with fiscal year-ends June 30, 1986 through March 31, 1987. All statistics are expressed in terms of percentages of annual sales volume. (*Note:* Only data for firms with from $0 to $1 million in assets have been shown since this would be characteristic of the beginning business.)

Direct selling companies sell directly to consumers through sales representatives. Many of these firms, like Fuller Brush and Avon, depend on door-to-door *canvassing* for contacting prospective buyers. Others rely on *party-plan selling,* arranging at-home or in-office "parties" where sales presentations are made to small groups of neighbors and friends or co-workers.

Vending machine operators install coin-actuated machines in locations where considerable numbers of people may be expected to pass by: in bus stations, large stores, movie theaters, and so forth. In addition to candy, beverages, snack foods, and cigarettes, a wide variety of other merchandise is offered to the public.

Mail-order houses promote merchandise of every conceivable description through catalogs, brochures, and other types of direct mail pieces. They distribute these to lists of shoppers or in response to media advertising (including advertising on both regular and cable television). America's original mail-order establishments, Montgomery Ward's and Sears, Roebuck—both store retailers today—date back to the late nineteenth century. Nowadays, two of the better known mail-order houses are Spiegel's and Sunset House.

An unusual and most promising innovation, akin to other mail-order selling (or *direct marketing*) approaches, is the expanding field of *Videotex.* * This is a computer-based system that offers goods and services via two-way communication between retailers and at-home shoppers.

Service Businesses

Services are "activities, benefits, or satisfactions which are offered for sale or are provided in connection with the sale of goods."**

In recent years the service sector has reflected the sharpest growth of all segments of American private enterprise. In 1983 alone service industries contributed more than $426 billion to our economy. This represented more than a fourfold increase over the $104 billion in national income posted by such businesses in 1970, only thirteen years earlier.† Today more than 20 million people are employed in this sector.

Perhaps the most plausible reason for the popularity of service businesses is that there is no need either to carry substantial merchandise inventory for resale—as is the case in retailing or wholesaling—or to make a heavy investment in machinery and other capital goods, as in manufacturing. Often, little more is required than purchasing several relatively inexpensive pieces of equipment, printing business cards, and placing a few advertisements. Indeed, your own home, garage, or apartment can serve as the place of business until the enterprise grows too big.

Here are just a few of the types of service businesses that can be launched with little money and some talent/training/knowledge/skill:

lawn care	painting	seminars
home typing	apparel design	delivery service
sewing	translation bureau	newsletter publishing
bookkeeping	automotive repair	baby-sitting
consulting	tutoring	dance instruction
flower decorating	equipment rental	résumé preparation
appliance repair	upholstering	travel agency

*See: George P. Moschis, Jac L. Goldstucker, and Thomas J. Stanley, "At-Home Shopping: Will Consumers Let Their Computers Do the Walking?" *Business Horizons* 28 (March-April 1985), 22–29; "The Big Rush to Videotex—and Its Big Risks," *U.S. News & World Report* (13 February 1984), BC3–4; "Super VISA Package Increases Members for Comp-U-Card," *Direct Marketing* 46 (November 1983), 32*ff.*

**Committee on Definitions, *Marketing Definitions: A Glossary of Marketing Terms* (Chicago: American Marketing Association, 1960), 21.

†U.S. Department of Commerce, Bureau of the Census, *Statistical Abstract of the United States, 1984–1985,* 105th ed. (Washington, D.C.: U.S. Government Printing Office, 1984), 780.

TABLE 2–5. SELECTED SERVICE INDUSTRIES, BY CATEGORIES (1982)*

Business Classification	Approximate Number of Establishments	Representative Types
Personal services	512,000	Laundries, dry cleaners, photographic studios, beauty and barber shops, shoe repair shops
Business services	(N.A.)**	Advertising, data processing services, cleaning and maintenance services, management consulting, public relations services, equipment rental and leasing, commercial photography
Automotive repair, services, and garages	227,600	Automotive repair shops, automotive rental and leasing, parking lots
Amusement and recreation services	214,400	Motion picture production and distribution services, theaters, orchestras and entertainers, bowling alleys, other recreation and amusement services
Legal services	203,000	(Not broken down)
Miscellaneous repair services	159,300	Electrical and electronic repair shops, reupholstery and furniture repair shops
Hotels, motor hotels, and motels	69,100	Hotels, motor hotels, motels, trailer parks and camps

Source: U.S. Department of Commerce, Bureau of the Census, *Statistical Abstract of the United States, 1986,* 106th ed. (Washington, D.C.: U.S. Government Printing Office, 1985) 790.

*Firms subject to federal income tax.

**The total number of establishments in this category exceeded 500,000 in 1982.

Many of today's successful service companies had their beginnings in part-time avocations, hobbies, or home enterprises before growing large enough to require expanded premises. No doubt the same will be true for tomorrow's successes. Because of certain inherent characteristics of services that distinguish them from products (such as their intangibility), the marketing of services can be more intricate than product marketing.*

Table 2–5 lists the more popular kinds of service industries along with representative types in each category. Financial operating data for a number of different types of service businesses are presented in table 2–6.

Note that the format in table 2–6 differs somewhat from that seen in the earlier tables; for example, there are no columns that show the cost of sales or the gross margin. Among the types of service enterprises listed, pretax profit

*See, for example: Gregory Upah, "Mass Marketing in Service Retailing: A Review and Synthesis of Major Methods," *Journal of Retailing* 56 (Fall 1980), 59–76; A. J. Magrath, "When Marketing Services, 4 Ps Are Not Enough," *Business Horizons* 29 (May–June 1986), 44–50.

TABLE 2–6. Financial data for selected service businesses*

SIC Number	Type of Business	Operating Expenses	All Other Expenses	Profit Before Taxes
8931	Accounting, auditing, and bookkeeping	83.9%	2.6%	13.6%
7538	Auto repair—general	94.9	1.4	3.7
7531	Auto repair—top and body shops	94.9	0.9	4.2
7933	Bowling alleys	93.5	4.3	2.2
7542	Car washes	92.5	3.3	4.3
7372	Computer programming and other software services	94.5	1.3	4.1
7361	Employment agencies	95.7	0.5	3.8
7231, 41	Hair stylists	95.2	1.1	3.7
7211, 7166	Laundries and dry cleaners	96.0	0.7	3.4
7394	Leasing—equipment	85.1	5.7	9.2
7392	Management consulting and public relations services	91.6	1.7	6.7
7011	Motels, hotels, and tourist courts	90.3	6.2	3.5
7832	Motion picture theaters, except drive-ins	96.2	2.3	1.5
7221, 7333	Photographic studios, including commercial photography	93.2	1.9	4.9
6531	Real estate agents and brokers	87.4	4.1	8.5
4722	Travel agencies	97.9	0.1	2.0

Source: Robert Morris Associates, *'87 Annual Statement Studies* (Philadelphia: Robert Morris Associates, 1987). Copyright 1987 by Robert Morris Associates. Used with permission. (See "Note Regarding Interpretation of Statement Studies Figures" at end of this table.)

*Based on statement studies of firms with fiscal year-ends June 30, 1986 through March 31, 1987. All statistics are expressed in terms of percentages of annual sales volume. (*Note:* Only data for firms with from $0 to $1 million in assets have been shown since this would be characteristic of the beginning business.)

Note Regarding Interpretation of Statement Studies Figures

RMA cautions that the Studies be regarded only as a general guideline and not as an absolute industry norm. This is due to limited samples within categories, the categorization of companies by their primary Standard Industrial Classification (SIC) number only, and different methods of operations by companies within the same industry. For these reasons, RMA recommends that the figures be used only as general guidelines in addition to other methods of financial analysis.

runs from a low of 1.5 percent of sales (motion picture theaters, except drive-ins) to a high of 13.6 percent (accounting, auditing, and bookkeeping services).

OPPORTUNITIES IN FRANCHISING

Many people regard franchising as something comparatively new on the American scene, but it has been around since the turn of the century. Around that time the new automobile manufacturers began to license car dealers, and gas stations opened up across the country.

In the early 1950s most of today's better-known franchisors began rapidly expanding their outlets. There are now close to a half million franchised businesses in the United States. Nearly nine out of every ten are retail enterprises.

In 1984 alone retail franchise outlets were expected to generate around $400 billion—or approximately 30 percent of all retail sales.*

The franchise concept is simple to grasp: You (the *franchisee*) sign a contract with a successful franchising company (the *franchisor*) that spells out the terms and conditions under which you are permitted to operate your business— a unit of a large chain. The contract is a license to operate under the parent corporation's trade name, and in accordance with their policies and marketing procedures.

The more popular franchises are fried chicken, hamburger, pizza, and other fast-food outlets; motels and hotels; ice cream stores; coffee and doughnut shops; employment agencies; and convenience stores. Such names as Stuckeys, Kentucky Fried Chicken, Burger King, Bonanza, Dunkin' Donuts, International House of Pancakes, H & R Block, and Howard Johnson's come readily to mind.

The advantages and disadvantages of selecting the franchise mode are presented in chapter 4, along with a list of some well-known franchisors, their home offices, and number of franchisees.

FOR FURTHER INFORMATION

Books

Burstiner, Irving. *Basic Retailing.* Homewood, Ill.: Irwin, 1986.
————. *Run Your Own Store.* Englewood Cliffs, N.J.: Prentice-Hall, 1981.
Danenburg, William P., Russell L. Moncrief, and William E. Taylor. *Introduction to Wholesale Distribution.* Englewood Cliffs, N.J.: Prentice-Hall, 1978.
Fitzsimmons, James A., and Robert S. Sullivan. *Service Operations Management.* New York: McGraw-Hill, 1982.
Fogarty, Donald W., and Thomas R. Hoffman. *Production and Inventory Management.* Cincinnati: South-Western, 1983.
Hax, Arnold C., and Don Candea. *Production and Inventory Management.* Englewood Cliffs, N.J.: Prentice-Hall, 1984.
Kotler, Philip, and Paul N. Bloom. *Marketing Professional Services.* Englewood Cliffs, N.J.: Prentice-Hall, 1984.
Kuriloff, Arthur H., and John M. Hemphill, Jr. *Starting and Managing the Small Business.* New York: McGraw-Hill, 1983.
Laufer, A. C. *Production and Operations Management,* 3d ed. Cincinnati: South-Western, 1984.
Lowry, James. *Retail Management.* Cincinnati: South-Western, 1983.
Mayer, Raymond E. *Production and Operations Management,* 4th ed. New York: McGraw–Hill, 1982.

*Bureau of Industrial Economics, U.S. Department of Commerce, *Franchising in the Economy: 1982–1984* (Washington, D.C.: U.S. Government Printing Office, January 1984), 13.

Pamphlets Available from the Small Business Administration

MANAGEMENT AIDS

MA 2.007—"Business Plan for Small Manufacturers"
MA 2.008—"Business Plan for Small Construction Firms"
MA 2.016—"Checklist for Going into Business"
MA 2.020—"Business Plan for Retailers"
MA 2.022—"Business Plan for Small Service Firms"
MA 2.025—"Thinking About Going into Business?"
MA 2.026—"Feasibility Checklist for Starting a Small Business of Your Own"
MA 7.003—"Market Overseas with U.S. Government Help"

SMALL BUSINESS BIBLIOGRAPHIES

SBB # 2—"Home Businesses"

Booklets Available from the Superintendent of Documents

S/N 003-008-00194-7—*Franchise Opportunities Handbook, 1984*—$13.50.
S/N 045-000-00207-1—*Starting and Managing a Small Service Business*—$4.50.
S/N 045-000-00212-8—*Starting and Managing a Small Business of Your Own*—$4.75.

II
STARTING-UP
ISSUES

3

Customer Targeting: How to Optimize Your Chances for Success

Let's assume you have finally selected the kind of business that you want to go into. Maybe you'll be fortunate enough to find a top-notch location, clever enough to manufacture or purchase a terrific line of merchandise, shrewd enough to price your goods so they're profitable yet marketable, and smart enough to institute tight financial controls. Yet unless you build a steady and loyal clientele, you'll find yourself going out of business in a very short time!

Customers are the people who make or break a business.

WHAT CUSTOMERS ARE LIKE

Most of us readily link the term *customers* with the final consumers in this country, like you and me. There are, however, many thousands of firms that do not sell directly to the 240-plus million consumers that make up our total population. These companies sell just about everything—raw materials, semi-processed goods, and finished products—to industry, commerce, schools and universities, banks and hospitals, government agencies, and countless other types of establishments and institutions. They sell *industrial* goods and services: items and materials that are generally consumed by companies or organizations as they conduct their day-to-day business. These products differ from *consumer* goods and services, which are sold to the final consumer either directly or through marketing channels (agents, wholesalers, retailers).

Marketing practitioners distinguish between *consumer marketing* and *industrial marketing,* on the basis of the kind of customer (or prospective customer) being targeted. For the purpose of gaining more insight into these two vast and distinct market areas, we might more appropriately classify them as the *consumer* and the *organizational* markets.

Contrasting These Two Super Markets

Sharp differences characterize these two markets, including the following:

> While the American consumer market consists of more than 240 million individuals, the "customers" that comprise the organizational market number far fewer than one-tenth that amount. At most, they total no more than 14 to 15 million.

> Those who buy for the organizational market are generally trained purchasing agents for the organizations they represent. On the other hand, most consumers lack training in the finer, more technical aspects of buying for personal and family needs. Moreover, the consumer's buying motives are more confused, often tinged with emotional overtones, and less rational than the motives for purchasing industrial goods and services.

> While the consumer usually buys often and in small amounts, larger and less frequent purchases are characteristic of the organizational market.

> Targeting in on the general consumer market can be a complex, time-consuming, even frustrating task because of this market's sheer magnitude. By comparison, although selling to organizational users is by no means a simple task, help is available from various government reference works, trade associations, and other sources. Consequently, firms that sell industrial goods and services can get assistance in customer targeting in such areas as company size, product usage, and so forth.

Today's professional industrial marketers think in terms of specific submarkets, rather than the total marketplace. They face a twofold task: (1) to select groups of customers (organizations) with similar needs, wants, purchasing power, and the authority to buy what is for sale; and (2) to develop the appropriate mix of products, prices, promotion, and distribution to reach those customers and sell the product effectively. (See chapter 12.)

Much the same approach applies to the far broader consumer marketplace. Ways must be explored to select and target in on groups of those consumers who seem to be excellent prospects for one's products or services; then one needs to learn all one can about those individuals in order to prepare the proper "concoction" (products, prices, promotion, distribution) for wooing and winning them.

CUSTOMER TARGETING HELPS YOU SUCCEED

Aiming at the entire consumer population is a foolish move. It's not much different from firing a shotgun indiscriminately into a flock of geese in flight. Here and there, a single pellet might find its mark—but what a waste of good ammunition!

This kind of umbrella targeting is aptly termed the *shotgun* approach (as opposed to the *rifle* approach) and is completely out of the question for the smaller enterprise. Small business has neither the promotional budget, the production capacity, nor the staff to conduct business in this manner.

Of course, no one firm should expect to be able to fulfill the needs of all buyers. Nevertheless, some companies subscribe to a policy of *mass marketing*—a strategy whereby the same basic marketing "package" is offered to large numbers of customers of diverse types. Another recognized name for this approach is *undifferentiated marketing*—so designated because the marketing company makes no attempt to differentiate among specific groups of customers at which to aim its promotional efforts.

Among the many examples of products that have been successfully mass marketed to the American consumer are white bread, butter, and sugar; car radiator antifreeze; metropolitan daily newspapers; and room air fresheners.

Nowadays, many firms favor a different strategy. They first identify and then take careful aim at one or more viable market segments—groups of prospects who share similar needs, wants, preferences, and other characteristics. This approach, known as *market segmentation,* makes more sense than mass marketing. It enables marketers to tailor their presentations directly to one or more specific customer groups, thus "rifling in" on the target or targets. The information they gather about the various "submarkets" is of value in planning every facet of the marketing process—from product development and pricing to the creation of copy and artwork for advertisements and the strengthening of sales presentations.

SEGMENTING CONSUMER MARKETS

Modern marketers usually segment the consumer population in one or more of the following ways:

- Geographically
- Demographically
- Psychographically
- By benefits
- By usage

Geographic Segmentation

The oldest and most readily understood of all approaches to differentiating among consumer markets is *geographic segmentation*—targeting people to market to on the basis of where they live. For example, clothing worn in California, Florida, and Louisiana is more informal and lighter in weight than the apparel popular in colder climates—a fact of considerable importance to the clothing retailer.

Geography also plays an important role when it comes to marketing swimming pools, ski equipment, insect sprays, and many seasonal items. For a good many other products and services, consumption patterns often differ considerably from one section of the country to the next. Thus, knowledge of local needs and preferences may be essential to business success. As a case in point, a manufacturer-retailer of confectionery products was astonished to encounter massive consumer resistance to its line of dark-covered chocolates (eminently successful in the mid-Atlantic region where the brand name was well known) when the firm offered the candies for sale in newly opened stores in several southwestern states. It seems that consumers in the warmer climes preferred light- or milk-chocolate-coated products.

Demographic Segmentation

Demography is the most popular of all avenues to segmenting the vast consumer market. In *demographic segmentation,* a total group is analyzed by studying statistical variables such as age, sex, income level, occupation, nationality, educational level, race, and religion.

People who fall into one classification may have quite different purchasing patterns from those in another category. For example, young married couples without children are typically more likely to furnish their apartments or homes with appliances, furniture, and other durable goods than adults at any other stage of the family life cycle. Consequently, manufacturers and distributors of durable products may deliberately tailor their promotional efforts specifically to this lucrative market, rather than try to sell to other consumer groups. A cosmetics manufacturer will design one product or product line for the young woman and target another product or line at the older woman. A menswear retailer might seek to cater primarily to big men by carrying only the larger sizes in clothing and accessories.

Psychographic Segmentation

Marketers who employ the much more recent method known as *psychographic segmentation* group consumers according to their attitudes, interests, lifestyles, or other personality attributes. There is merit to this approach, especially when it is used in combination with the more established demographic techniques. For example, all women are logical targets for cosmetic products. Yet when women are categorized according to lifestyle, the manufacturer (or retailer) must offer products and advertising with very specific appeal in order to be successful.

Likewise, classifying consumers according to different stages of the family life cycle (a demographic technique) leads to more effective results if they are also cross-categorized according to their interests and attitudes.

Remember, too, that consumers often select products—and retail stores as well—with "personalities" that correspond to their own self-images.

Benefit Segmentation

Still another method of differentiating among sizable groups of consumers is *benefit segmentation:* sectioning off groups of people according to the kinds of benefits they seek from a product or service.

In a study conducted during the 1960s, this technique was successfully applied to the American toothpaste market.* The researchers were able to identify several distinct and large groups of toothpaste users, including people who buy the product primarily because they want a clean, fresh taste in their mouths in the morning; those who use the product mostly for appearance's sake (they want white teeth); and those who seek to prevent cavities.

As a result of this study, toothpaste manufacturers were thereafter able to tailor their products and brands, pricing approaches, and promotional efforts to specific segments of the consumer population. Subsequently, too, other types of manufacturers began to rely on information acquired from benefit segmentation studies.

Today's automobile manufacturers, for instance, know that many prospective buyers are primarily looking for economy of operation, while others are more interested in ample interior space and a feeling of luxury. Still other consumers are simply seeking a dependable vehicle that will take them where they want to go. Each of these segments, of course, calls for a distinct product/marketing approach.

Usage Segmentation

In *usage* (or *usage-rate*) *segmentation,* the total consumer marketplace is first divided according to users and nonusers of the product or service. Then the user population is broken down further into *heavy, medium,* and *light* users according to quantities consumed. Finally, the characteristics of these user subgroups are studied and compared in order to uncover significant differences among them. Such differences are then used to give direction to the development of specific marketing mixes designed to reach and sell to those subgroups.

Usage segmentation can be an exceptionally valuable tool. In some product categories, the heavy users account for as much as 30, 40, and even 50 percent or more of the total sales.

CONSUMER PSYCHOLOGY

Depending upon the market(s) you are trying to reach, your customers may be consumers or they may be organizations. In the first part of this section we

---

*Russell I. Haley, "Benefit Segmentation: A Decision-Oriented Research Tool," *Journal of Marketing* 32 (July 1968), 30–35.

touch briefly on the shopping and purchasing behavior of consumers. After that we consider some aspects of the industrial sphere—including how organizations buy and how to market to them.

Consumer Purchasing Behavior

There have been literally hundreds of articles in the marketing literature in recent years reporting on the results of research into the shopping behavior of the American consumer. This subject has been investigated from just about every conceivable angle. At least half a dozen popular college textbooks, all titled *Consumer Behavior,* are currently available. (Several are mentioned in the list at the end of this chapter.)

The social sciences (particularly psychology) have furnished the basics for marketing researchers to investigate why people select certain products and services as opposed to others, and why they prefer to shop at certain stores. These investigators have probed motives, perceptions, individual needs and wants (both innate and learned), attitudes, how people learn and remember or forget, and many other facets of the human personality and psyche. All of these factors appear to affect purchasing behavior.

Marketing theorists have also devised intricate models of the purchasing process itself to aid the businessperson's understanding of the complexities of consumer behavior. Moreover, they have borrowed from studies in sociology and social psychology to demonstrate how social class, culture, subcultures, family influences, and reference groups—indeed, the entire social environment—affect the consumer's shopping behavior.

These studies are certainly fascinating! They are also valuable. The information yielded by a single textbook can provide you with dozens of tips that you can readily use in your business. Unfortunately, there isn't room in this book for even the more salient details of buyer psychology. The works listed at the end of this chapter contain invaluable information for successful consumer targeting.

Certainly a cardinal requirement for success in business is to *know your customer.*

Positioning

In the marketing of consumer goods and services, one of the more interesting management strategies these days is that of *positioning.* To gain an edge over its competitors, a manufacturing company may study and "map" the perceptions of consumers with regard to its product(s) (or brand) *in relation to those of its major competitors.* It will strive to determine its unique niche in the total marketplace and then target for sales one or more specific consumer segments to which its offerings are likely to appeal. As one text has put it, "a product's market position denotes the location it occupies in the public's mind in relation to similar, competitive products."*

---

*Irving Burstiner, *Basic Retailing* (Homewood, Ill.: Irwin, 1986), 116.

Packaging, branding, advertising, sales promotion, and other aspects of the promotional mix are then used to reinforce this position vis-a-vis competitive products or brands.

Marketing practitioners sometimes refer to this approach as *product positioning,* even though it can be applied just as well to positioning a company itself. Indeed, K Mart, Mervyn's and other well-known retail chain store organizations have successfully positioned their companies in recent years, each selecting specific consumer groups to market to.

INDUSTRIAL MARKETING: SELLING ORGANIZATIONS

In actuality, the organizational market comprises several distinct, and relatively large, submarkets. The principal submarkets here are the producer, reseller, and government markets. The producer market encompasses not only manufacturers of every conceivable type of goods but also firms/organizations engaged in other "productive" industries, such as agriculture, cattle raising, mining, fishing, and so on. Also included are many types of service-producing organizations: utilities (electric, gas, water); commercial banks, savings and loan associations, brokerage houses, and other organizations that offer financial services; public and private hospitals and schools; hotels and other places of lodging; computer service firms and telephone companies; theaters, racetracks, baseball and football stadiums, bowling alleys, and other recreational facilities; employment agencies, typing services, and legal services; and so on.

As you already know, these organizations must arrange to purchase (or rent) the kinds of goods and services they require for running their businesses. They buy raw materials, semifinished products, and components (parts). These goods may run the gamut from a complete manufacturing facility or the installation of heavy machinery to an astounding variety of accessory items, equipment, and supplies. Typically, the organization must also provide for a number of services, such as insurance, transportation, and advertising.

The reseller market consists of organizations and individuals who buy goods and/or services regularly and then resell them at higher prices to others, thereby earning a profit. Because of the part they play in the economy's marketing channels, the reseller is also known by the more familiar term *distributor.*

Indeed, businesspeople often apply the label *distributive trades* to this segment of the organizational market. Included in the category are the 400,000 or so organizations and individuals engaged in wholesaling activities and some 1.9 million retailers. Although most of the latter are "store" retailers, others operate without the aid of store premises. Among the more important groups of "nonstore" retailers are direct selling organizations, vending machine operators, and mail-order houses.

Of course, reseller purchases are not entirely limited to the goods and services they acquire for resale. These organizations must also buy *industrially*—that is, they must purchase products for their own use. Wholesale and retail establishments alike have need of facilities in which to run their machines or to display and sell their merchandise. They require different kinds of equipment and various supplies, office furniture, small tools and replacement parts, trucks, cleaning and maintenance services, stationery, and so forth.

Last, but certainly not least, is the government market. In sheer volume, it represents the largest segment of the organizational market. This vast market includes all agencies, sections, divisions, departments, committees, and other governmental units at all three levels—federal, state, and local (county, town, village). As you no doubt realize, between its annual expenditures for both civilian aspects and the military, the federal government accounts for far more than one-half of all governmental consumption each year in the United States.

At the state and local level, the government market includes many types of groups: state troopers and local police departments, city councils and public hospitals, state universities and community colleges, public school districts, motor vehicle agencies, departments of health, housing, and welfare, and so on.

Collectively, the government market seeks to purchase goods and services of all kinds. In addition to the complex requirements of the military branches (as well as local police and fire protection)—aircraft, ships, tanks, guns, munitions, firefighting equipment, and the like—these customers also require work premises; office furniture, equipment, and supplies; motor vehicles; janitorial services; and many other types of goods and services.

Segmenting the Industrial Market

As is the case in the marketing of consumer goods and services, market segmentation techniques are also profitably employed in the industrial marketing sector.

Although such familiar approaches as geographical, benefit, and usage-rate segmentation are used, other techniques are seen much more often. These include segmentation by end user, by type of company (SIC code), and by size of customer organization (large, average, and small accounts). Combinations of two or three approaches are also quite popular.

WHAT CONSUMERISM MEANS TO YOU

The present consumerist climate in America is not a new phenomenon. The twentieth century witnessed two earlier consumer movements. The first began just before the turn of the century, culminating (in 1906) in two major proconsumer legislative acts: the Pure Food and Drug Act and the Meat Inspection Act. The second movement originated in the Great Depression. In 1938 the FDA (Food and Drug Administration) was substantially strengthened by the passage of the Food, Drug, and Cosmetic Act.

The current movement, spurred during the early 1960s, seems to have resulted from many influences: a more affluent consumer, a higher level of education, a more relaxed work ethic, emphasis on self-assertiveness and other changing values, the unethical practices of some business firms, misleading advertising and promotion, inferior products, poor service, and so forth.

Among the more important pieces of federal legislation evolving out of the present movement are the Fair Packaging and Labeling Act (1966), the Consumer Credit Protection Act (1968), the Child Protection and Toy Safety Act (1969), the Consumer Product Safety Act (1972), and the Fair Debt Collection Practices Act (1977).

In addition to various consumer associations and cooperatives and the Better Business Bureaus, the welfare of the American public is monitored by government consumer protection agencies that have been established in metropolitan areas and in county seats.

This consumer protection trend means that small business owners need to obtain detailed information regarding pertinent consumer legislation at all levels (federal, state, and local). They also need to understand how such laws affect their own particular type of business. Today's enlightened customer tolerates no mishandling, mislabeling, misrepresentation, or misunderstanding. As a business owner, you'll need to be fair and aboveboard in your dealings with the public if you want to retain your clientele.

ETHICAL AND SOCIAL RESPONSIBILITIES OF THE BUSINESS OWNER

Business today is more than profits and growth—it has a greater obligation to the public good than ever before. The callous disregard for the human element that characterized the first few decades of this century no longer exists. Instead there is an increasing struggle to maintain the quality of modern life as a counterpoint to humankind's harmful behavior. The new ethos pursues higher and nobler objectives, rather than merely aiming at earning profits at any cost.

The small business owner of today must be aware of the needs of the physical environment. Our lakes, streams, and rivers are contaminated with industrial waste. The atmosphere is polluted with harmful levels of sulphur and carbon compounds from our nation's factories and from the millions of vehicles operating daily on our highways. Year after year, our fields and groves are battered—sprayed with pesticides and dusted with chemicals. Poultry, cattle, and other livestock are raised on chemical fatteners. Our giant industrial machine has nearly exhausted many natural resources; shortages are becoming more common. Our ears are assaulted by the din of city traffic, roaring machinery, and thundering aircraft overhead.

In recent decades the federal government has enacted many laws to protect our population from these ravages. Among them are the Clean Air Act of 1963 (and subsequent amendments), the Solid Waste Disposal Act and the Water Quality Act (both enacted in 1965), the Noise Control Act (1972), the Pesticide Control Act (1972), and the Resource Conservation and Recovery Act (1976).

As a small business owner, you'll need to be concerned with the social environment, too. Today's corporation is responsible not only to its shareholders and customers but to other groups as well: employees, suppliers, residents of the community where the business is located, and even society at large. Inherent in the concept of a democratic society is the belief that those who are more affluent are responsible for the less able and less fortunate: hence, the Social Security system, antidiscrimination laws, programs for training the hardcore unemployed, the welfare system, and so forth. All such programs aim at aiding the less fortunate, such as the unemployed or poor. Clearly, the rate of unemployment in the United States is disturbingly high. Moreover, it is not expected to drop in the next few years. Approximately 25 million Americans are living today at or below the poverty level. Indeed, the changes in the federal tax structure signed into law in 1986 were designed, in part, to release hundreds of thousands of low-income consumers from the requirement of paying any income tax whatsoever.

Small wonder, then, that the public now expects private enterprise, which has taken liberally from the environment and its resources, to return some portion of its profits to the society that nurtured it. At the very least, modern business managers need to bear in mind at all times the social implications of the decisions they make.

FOR FURTHER INFORMATION

Books

Ames, B. Charles, and James D. Hlavacek. *Managerial Marketing for Industrial Firms.* New York: Random House, 1984.

Bonoma, Thomas V., and Benson P. Shapiro. *Segmenting the Industrial Market.* Lexington, Mass.: Lexington Books, 1983.

Carroll, Archie B. *Business & Society: Managing Corporate Social Performance.* Boston: Little, Brown, 1981.

Hawkins, Delbert I., and Roger J. Best. *Consumer Behavior: Implications for Marketing Strategy,* 2d ed. Plano, Tex.: Business Publications, 1983.

Hunt, Michael, and Thomas Speh. *Industrial Marketing Management,* 2d ed. New York: Dryden Press, 1985.

Loudon, David L., and Albert J. Della Bitta. *Consumer Behavior: Concepts and Applications,* 2d ed. New York: McGraw-Hill, 1984.

Peter, J. Paul, and Jerry C. Olson. *Consumer Behavior: Marketing Strategy Perspectives.* Homewood, Ill.: Irwin, 1985.

Reynolds, Fred D., and William D. Wells. *Consumer Behavior.* New York: McGraw-Hill, 1977.

Schiffman, Leon G., and Leslie Lazar Kanuk. *Consumer Behavior,* 2d ed. Englewood Cliffs, N.J.: Prentice-Hall, 1983.

Wilkie, William L. *Consumer Behavior.* New York: Wiley, 1986.

Zaltman, Gerald, and Melanie Wallendorf. *Consumer Behavior: Basic Findings and Management Implications,* 2d ed. New York: Wiley, 1983.

Pamphlets Available from the Small Business Administration

MANAGEMENT AIDS

MA 4.019—"Learning About Your Market"

4

How to Join the
Business Community

Once upon a time, the aspiring entrepreneur had only two alternatives: either to start up a brand-new business from scratch or to purchase a thriving operation from someone else. (Some lucky people, of course, have a successful enterprise deeded over to them by a parent or wealthy relative!) Both alternatives represented a gamble. Obviously, the new business risked more than one already tested—provided that the ongoing business was not already on its way out.

Today, people are luckier. A third way to enter the business community has become popular over the last thirty years. Now you can go the franchise route. Moreover, a responsible, well-established company behind you improves your chances of succeeding.

Read the statistics on new ventures. They're grim. Many enterprises fail within the first few years of operation. A good franchised outlet, however, has an excellent chance to succeed. According to some reports, nine out of ten franchises are successful.

This chapter is designed to help you avoid becoming another grim statistic. You'll find details on these alternate routes to business. Each has its attractive features and its drawbacks. The differences among them include the amount of investment capital required, the chances of survival, and the profits you can expect.

LAUNCHING THE NEW ENTERPRISE

Most people who try their hand at business select the riskiest approach—they start a brand-new business. For many, the motivating factor behind this decision is probably a lack of sufficient capital to purchase an already existing business or a franchise. Other people may want to test their capabilities and ingenuity to the fullest. Still others may desire the challenge of creating their own future, stone by stone. Some people choose to start a new business because they see a timely opportunity for a new product or service, with no competition.

Whatever the reason for the choice, one thing is certain: This route is by far the most perilous of the three in the long run.

The Positives

Nevertheless, if you choose this route, you'll find all options wide open. You'll have total and unrestricted freedom of choice in your decision making—the pleasure of choosing when, where, and how you set up shop. You won't be bound to a specific location or facility. You won't be limited to what products or services to manufacture or sell. Nor will you be tied to any particular suppliers, employees, or customers. All policies and procedures will be up to you—they'll be yours alone to establish.

The Negatives

But there is another side to the coin. Here are some troublesome aspects to think about. You might choose the wrong business to go into in the first place. You might err in your choice of product(s) to manufacture or sell. Or you might select a poor location for your new enterprise. Further, a new business takes time to get rolling. Weeks—maybe months—may pass before sales reach a high enough level to allow you to draw a small salary. (Compare this to the purchase of a business. Here you also purchase instant sales and instant wages the day you take it over.)

If you need additional funds, you'll probably find it more difficult to borrow money for a brand-new enterprise than for an existing business or a franchise unit.

A new business generally starts off with *zero* customers and *zero* suppliers. Unless you have had prior experience with sources of supply in the same field, you'll have to search out and cultivate a string of suppliers for your new business. This task occupies a lot of your time and energy in the beginning. Also, other than a few friends and relatives who may buy from you, you'll have to take the initiative to build up, over time, a satisfied and loyal clientele.

With little or nothing charted for you, you should expect to make a good many mistakes along the way. A new business is strictly a "learning-by-doing" experience. You'll have to live with, and hopefully learn from, your errors. This may prove costly—in time, money, and perhaps emotions. You should definitely seek the assistance of professionals whenever possible.

How Do You Get Started?

Certainly, it is foolhardy to contemplate setting up a new business without being thoroughly convinced that your business will be special and useful to the network of free enterprise. This means that you must direct your proposed business toward fulfilling unmet needs of specific customer groups.

You need a detailed analysis of possible markets for your particular product(s) and/or service(s). You need to assess the strengths and weaknesses of competitors and to study industry trends. You must pay attention to many other facets of business planning: the type and location of the facility, the amount of financial backing, machinery and equipment needed, and so forth.

TAKING ON A FRANCHISE

The franchising concept was introduced in chapter 2, in the section on "Opportunities in Franchising." Now, let's explore the advantages and disadvantages of this form of business operation.

Advantages of the Franchise Form

A franchise offers you the opportunity to jump aboard the bandwagon and become part of a tried-and-true success story. This is certainly the least risky of the three avenues to business ownership. Reputedly, nearly 95 percent of all high-quality franchises are profitable. You ride with the popularity of the brand name: It is known by hundreds of thousands—if not millions—of people.

When you sign with a reputable franchisor, you purchase a complete package designed to help you succeed. You receive professional assistance in most phases of the business: location hunting, construction of the facility, the proper equipment to use, inventory control system, bookkeeping methods, and promotion approaches.

Moreover, the franchising organization has a vital stake in keeping your new branch alive and growing. Consequently, they will continue to give you assistance in such important areas as merchandising, advertising, sales promotion, and even finance. They will literally teach you the business. Most franchisors insist on an initial period of intensive training and continue to render management help through supervision.

Table 4–1 offers information regarding a number of popular franchisors.

The Disadvantages

The financial aspects of a franchise unit merit careful consideration. Depending on the operation, start-up costs can range from as little as several thousand dollars to $100,000, $200,000, and much more. These figures include not only the initial franchise fee but also the entire cost of constructing and equipping the facility. Some of these expenses may be spread out over a period of years under a financing arrangement. In addition, you'll probably be required to pay the franchisor a set percentage of your sales for the duration of your franchise.

If you plan to take on a franchise, you'll need a fundamental change in perspective. You'll have to relinquish some of your independence. You might feel more like a worker or junior partner than a boss.

The products you sell—as well as the methods that you follow—will be selected for you by the franchisor. You'll have little say in these areas, and as a result your business may be adversely affected. As a retail franchisee, for example, you may be required to carry one or more items that do not move at

TABLE 4–1. Selected Franchising Companies

Franchisor (and Home Offices)	Number of Franchisees	Type of Business
Barbizon International, Inc. 3 East 54th Street New York, NY 10022	88	Modeling/personal development schools
Baskin-Robbins, Inc. 31 Baskin-Robbins Place Glendale, CA 91201	3,000+	Ice cream stores
Budget Rent A Car Corporation 200 No. Michigan Avenue Chicago, IL 60601	3,158[a]	Automobile and truck rentals
Canteen Corporation 1430 Merchandise Mart Chicago, IL 60654	78	Food vending and other related services
ComputerLand Corporation 30985 Santana Street Hayward, CA 94544	800	Computer stores
Curtis Mathes Corporation P.O. Box 223607 Dallas, TX 75225-0607	645	Home entertainment centers
Davis Paint Company 1311 Iron Street North Kansas City, MO 64116	60	Paint and wallpaper stores
Days Inns of America, Inc. 2751 Buford Highway, N.E. Atlanta, GA 30324	334	Motels and restaurants
Dunhill Personnel System, Inc. One Old Country Road Carle Place, NY 11514	282	International personnel services
Dunkin' Donuts of America, Inc. P. O. Box 317 Randolph, MA 02368	1,447	Coffee and doughnut shops
Godfather's Pizza 151 Kalmus Drive, Bldg. E Costa Mesa, CA 92626	65	Pizza restaurants
Hickory Farms of Ohio, Inc. 1505 Holland Road Maumee, OH 43537	260[b]	Specialty food stores
H & R Block, Inc. 4410 Main Street Kansas City, MO 64111	4,000+[c]	Tax returns preparation
Holiday Inns, Inc. 3796 Lamar Avenue Memphis, TN 38195	1,500+	Hotels and restaurants

TABLE 4–1. (*Continued*)

Franchisor (and Home Offices)	Number of Franchisees	Type of Business
Insty-Prints, Inc. 1215 Marshall Street, N.E. Minneapolis, MN 55403	330	Instant printing centers
Kampgrounds of America, Inc. P. O. Box 30558 Billings, MT 59114	650+	Campgrounds for recreational vehicles
Lawn Doctor Inc. P. O. Box 512142 Highway #34 Matawan, NJ 07747	300+	Professional automated lawn services
Mac Tools, Inc. P. O. Box 370 South Fayette Street Washington Court House, OH 43160	1,600+	Tool distributors
Manpower, Inc. 5301 No. Ironwood Road P. O. Box 2053 Milwaukee, WI 53201	300+	Temporary help services
Pearle Vision Centers 2534 Royal Lane Dallas, TX 75229	500	Full-service optical retail outlets
Supercuts 555 Northgate Drive San Rafael, CA 94903	150[d]	Quality haircut establishments
Taco Bell Corporation Headquarters 16808 Armstrong Avenue Irvine, CA 92714	255[e]	Fast-service Mexican food restaurants
Western Sizzlin Steak House 1537 Walton Way Augusta, GA 30904	570	Family steak houses
White Hen Pantry, Inc. 660 Industrial Drive Elmhurst, IL 60126	320	Convenience food stores
Wild Tops, National Development Group, Inc. 400 Cochituate Road Framingham, MA 01701	40	T-shirt and sportswear stores

Source: International Trade Administration and Minority Business Development Agency, U.S. Department of Commerce, *Franchise Opportunities Handbook* (Washington, D.C.: U.S. Government Printing Office, November 1986).

[a]Number of locations.

[b]Plus 255 company stores.

[c]More than 9,000 offices, of which some 4,000+ are franchised.

[d]Some 485 shops are open.

[e]More than 2,217 units operating, of which franchised restaurants total 1,019.

all in your particular neighborhood. You might have to sell your merchandise at prices that are either too high or too low for your area.

Furthermore, the franchise is a license granted to you by the franchising company, and if you want to close up shop someday, you cannot simply sell your business to a third party without involving the franchisor.

The contract is generally written from year to year and most often contains an "escape clause" that favors the franchisor. For instance, if your sales do not meet the expectations spelled out in the agreement, the franchisor may exercise the option not to renew the contract. In this case, you would be forced to remove all identification, signs, products, materials, and so forth that denote your connection with the parent company, and begin operating on your own if you choose. Usually, there is a "buy-back" clause as well. This gives the franchisor the right to repurchase your franchise at will; this clause could be a serious drawback if you are doing extremely well in the location.

Look Before You Leap into Franchising

Because the franchising field can be lucrative, it attracts not only hundreds of responsible, well-managed companies but also many less respectable firms. These fly-by-night companies are more concerned with making a quick buck than with sustaining growth over a long period. Therefore, you need to proceed with caution and thoroughly investigate any franchise offer that comes your way.

At the very least, you should resist any pressure exerted by sales representatives who try to sell you franchise units. The rosy pictures they paint for you should be taken with more than a few grains of salt. Even when representing a reliable firm, a salesperson tends to present an overly optimistic assessment of the sales and profit potential of the franchise.

Before you sign anything, consult your accountant, your banker, the local Chamber of Commerce, Dun and Bradstreet's, and the trade organization(s) in your field for unbiased information about the company. Make it your business to visit several of the outlets currently operating under contract to the franchisor, and ask their operators how satisfied they are with the situation. Find out whatever additional facts you can. Of course, shy away from those units selected for you by the sales representative.

BUYING AN ESTABLISHED BUSINESS

Advantages

You avoid much of the tedious planning and downright hard work required to set up a new business when you buy an ongoing enterprise. There is no need to search for a desirable location or to construct a facility and lay out the premises. (You can, of course, make changes later on.)

Since the previous owner(s) may have dealt with a number of suppliers before you entered the picture, chances are excellent that you'll spend little time initially developing your own sources of supply. With an ongoing business you also acquire experienced employees. They'll help you over the hurdles during the transition period. Likewise, you're rewarded with a bank of customers you can draw on immediately.

This kind of business is often purchased at a good price because the owner wants to sell quickly for some compelling reason (poor health, retirement, or the like). He or she may even be willing to assist you in the financing. In cases like this, an owner may be satisfied with a partial payment and take notes for the balance; these notes stretch out your obligation for years.

Finally, since the business has had a history, internal records are available to guide you.

Disadvantages

You may have serious problems with one or two aspects of the business, and you may have to make changes before you move in. You may have to relocate or enlarge the premises. You may have to do extensive repairs or redecoration. The layout may be in dire need of improvement.

Some of the inventory may be unusable, or you may have too many of some items and too few of others. Merchandise may be imperfect, damaged, or outdated. Machinery and equipment may need to be repaired or replaced. Consider your new employees, suppliers, and customers. In the past, relations between these people and the former owner(s) may not have been good. The "good will" you've bought may prove to be "bad will" that will detract from your immediate success. You might inherit several below-par employees whom you'll have to replace in time. If these employees are unionized, this will pose another problem.

What to Look Into Before Buying

No matter how attractive the deal seems to you or how eager you are to get started, make up your mind to approach buying a business unemotionally and with caution. Thoroughly check out the following:

- The firm's location and premises
- Its past history and estimated future potential
- Its assets and liabilities

Location and Premises. Visit the location and the surrounding neighborhood. Talk with the manager of the local bank and with other business owners in the area. Interview neighborhood residents and shoppers. Survey the businesses of competitors in the area. Try to ascertain whether the area is growing, maintaining its status quo, or deteriorating. (See chapter 6 for more help in evaluating a location.)

Bring in a consultant with experience in the particular kind of business to examine the premises thoroughly. Examine everything closely and make detailed notes. Be sure to check the interior and exterior; lighting, heating, and plumbing; elevators and staircases; stairwells and basements; shipping and receiving docks.

Make certain the facility has ample room not only to conduct the business activities that you find necessary but also to expand within—or adjacent to—the facility.

Past History and Future Potential. Ask your accountant and your lawyer for help in piecing together a picture of the firm's past. You'll discover problem areas you would be dealing with if you decided to buy as well as trends for projecting into the company's future. Bear this in mind: Most businesses for sale are not of "dream quality." There's almost always a need for improvement.

Examine company records. In addition to copies of past tax returns and other vital financial reports (annual balance sheets, operating statements, and the like), you'll find important information for future decision making in records of sales figures, production records, inventory counts, personnel files— even the shipping and receiving room logs. If you properly analyze sales, production, and financial data, you'll possess helpful ratios that can be compared over a succession of years. (See chapter 17.)

Survey the market potential for your firm's products and services as compared to those of your competitors. Analyze the demographic characteristics of present customers, along with their needs and wants. Also survey other market segments from which you could draw additional customers in the future. A worthwhile exercise here is to translate such details into projected dollars-and-cents sales figures, at least for the first two or three years after your takeover.

Assets and Liabilities. Assets include not only the cash and securities owned by the company you plan to acquire but also all property, including machinery and equipment, inventories, accounts receivable, contracts, and the like. By extension, it might also include personnel! Exercise caution with the firm's assets. This is the primary area to which any buyer of an existing business must address his or her attention. The major concern here is the *condition* of the assets. *Liabilities* include short- and long-term loans, unpaid taxes, mortgages, accounts payable (moneys owned to suppliers), and other business obligations. These terms are explained more fully in the next chapter.

How to Set the Price

Determining the proper price to pay for a business is a difficult problem. The seller usually tries to get more money for the business than it is worth—and the buyer tries to get it for as little as possible. Somewhere between the two extremes lies a price that is fair to both parties and that is (hopefully) finally agreed upon.

The two common approaches to solving this dilemma are (1) the *total-the-assets* technique and (2) the *return-through-profits* method.

The Total-the-Assets Technique. This method is the more frequently used, though not, in fact, the more advantageous of the two to the buyer. As the name indicates, it calls for a complete audit of the enterprise, usually best conducted by independent auditors. They should appraise the real and other property owned by the firm—including inventories, equipment, machinery, and the like—check into all liabilities, and subtract the liabilities from the assets owned. You'll then have an estimate of the company's *net worth.*

The Return-Through-Profits Method. The logic behind this approach is as follows: Buying an established business represents a considerable capital investment; you therefore have every right to expect a solid return on your investment. Considering the complexity of investing in an enterprise—including the need for your personal involvement and dedication for years to come (as well as the risk of failure)—your rate of return should certainly exceed by far those rates currently available to investors at banks, in corporate or government bonds, and the like.

There are desirable alternatives to buying a going business, which require nothing more than plunking down capital. Government bonds, about the safest of all investments, may bring you 6 or more percent on your money. The return from a long-term savings certificate (federally insured) may pay you even more. The total yield from high-quality corporate bonds may run several points higher. It would be illogical to invest in an existing business for a return comparable to these other kinds of investments. So, an ideal target to shoot for would be something in the neighborhood of 18 to 25 percent—taking a few percentage points less *only* if you have to!

As an illustration, assume that you've discovered an attractive business for sale, and the asking price is $60,000. If you placed that sum of money in a long-term certificate or similar investment, you'd receive interest totaling somewhere between $3,600 and $5,000 annually. These earnings do not require your working hard to protect your money—or leaving your current employment! Suppose, however, that an analysis of the business's operations reveals that its net profit each year would probably be in the $12,000 range. This return would indicate that you could pay back to yourself the cost of your investment within five years. Simply by dividing $12,000 by $60,000, you could calculate an effective *return on investment* (R.O.I.) of 20 percent.

When it comes to setting a fair price for a going business, then, you can use the following rough rule of thumb: Multiply the average yearly profit by four (for an R.O.I. of 25 percent) or by five (for a 20 percent R.O.I.).

There's one additional factor to consider in determining how much you ought to pay for the business. If you invest your capital in bonds or certificates, you will be able to keep your current job. Once you purchase a business, you must leave your job and give up the salary you've been earning. The price you eventually pay for a business should take this earnings factor into consideration. Make sure your proposed operations budget covers your current salary (even if you do not choose to draw a salary in the beginning) and the desired annual profit as well.

Continuing with our example, the present owner(s) may be willing to accept a down payment—perhaps $15,000—and take notes for the rest. This arrangement makes it easier for you to buy. Your investment is then only one-quarter of what you originally thought. Don't be tempted to think that an annual profit of only $3,000 is needed to make this a sound investment (because it *seems* as if you'd be earning 20 percent on your money). The fallacy here is that you need to generate enough additional profit each year to cover the notes as they mature.

Some Additional Thoughts Before You Buy

Never enter into any major transaction such as the purchase of a business without the full knowledge, cooperation, and assistance of both your attorney and your accountant. Your attorney must check on many details including ownership titles; occupancy leases, as well as leases on equipment, machinery, vehicles, and the like; contracts with contractors, services, and employees; zoning restrictions and local permits; compliance with the bulk sales act; and so on. Your accountant must delve into all financial aspects of operations, assist you in preparing pro forma statements, and point out deficiencies and weaknesses.

Do not neglect to obtain from the former owner an agreement to the effect that he or she will not seek to compete with you, for example, by opening a similar business in the area.

Be sure to call in an independent appraiser to determine the value of any property. Don't rely on book inventories; insist on a physical count by you or your representative side by side with the owner.

It's a good idea to investigate all personnel records to ascertain the caliber of the employees and the size of the current payroll. Check union contracts, employee contracts, benefits to be paid, and so forth. Assess the general state of employee morale.

Lastly, check into the owner's real reason for selling. A declaration that he or she is ready to retire, wants to move to Arizona for reasons of health, or wants to be near the children may be the truth. On the other hand, such reasons may serve as a "cover" for a poor profit picture, increasing competition, anticipated changes in the neighborhood, or legal problems that threaten the life of the enterprise.

WHICH LEGAL FORM TO CHOOSE?

Early in the game you need to decide on the *legal form of ownership* for your business: the sole proprietorship, the partnership, or the corporation. Each form has drawbacks as well as advantages. Consider carefully the pros and cons of each. The key is to select the one that will best meet your specific needs.

This is the customary procedure followed by many people who launch an enterprise:

- Start out as a sole proprietor if you have enough funds for the required investment and if you have enough self-confidence.

- Select the partnership form if you don't have the funds or the confidence, or if the expected workload will be too much for one person to handle.

- Form a corporation if you are planning to expand. (This need not be done at the outset; a corporation can be formed after the business has demonstrated its viability.)

THE SOLE PROPRIETORSHIP

The sole proprietorship is the simplest of the three legal forms of ownership and the form in which the majority of new businesses start off. You can't beat this form for its simplicity of organization and its absolute obedience to your every wish and command (right or wrong!).

What's Good about a Proprietorship

The sole proprietorship is the easiest and quickest form to initiate. At least three-quarters of the 13 million businesses in the United States are in this category. If you believe in the old "safety in numbers" approach and know that so many choose this particular route, how can you go wrong? Barring the need for special licenses or permits, all you have to do to get a business off the ground is to start working at it.

There are no set-up costs involved, as long as you plan on doing business under your own name. You might decide (as many people do) that you prefer to operate under a *trade name* instead. In that case you have to file the details with the local authorities at the offices of the town/city/county clerk. The form used for this purpose is available at business stationery stores. It's called a "Certificate of Doing Business Under an Assumed (or 'Fictitious') Name." The fee for filing is minimal—a few dollars at most. In some states you must first publish your intent to conduct business under a fictitious name in a local newspaper before filing your certificate.

You also save on legal fees with a proprietorship; no special contracts or agreements need to be drawn up, as is the case with a partnership or corporation.

A sole proprietorship offers you the greatest psychological rewards because you can run the business as you see fit. There are no bosses to issue orders to you, supervise your comings and goings, challenge your decisions, or take you to task for errors. This means that you must pit all your resources—mental, physical, and emotional, as well as financial—against the challenging business environment. It's somewhat like playing football without teammates: You not only get to carry the ball, but if you make it through the goalposts, you also get to keep all the profits—after taxes, of course!

If you run your operation honorably and in an aboveboard fashion (and keep accurate records), no one will interfere with how you conduct your business. Furthermore, you will avoid unnecessary pressure from the Better Business Bureau, consumer groups, the Internal Revenue Service, or any other government agency. Of the three legal forms, this is the one that gets the least attention from the federal bureaucracy. (The corporate form receives the most!)

Tax-wise, you and your sole proprietorship are treated as inseparable companions. This identity can be helpful to you. Typically, the new venture ends up its first six months (and often longer) in the red. This initial lack of success can be disheartening, especially if you have left a good-paying job to try your hand at business. If your enterprise incurs a loss for the year, you're entitled to deduct those lost dollars on your tax return against any other income you may have earned that year. Moreover, this holds true for succeeding years.

Finally, terminating your proprietorship is also simple. To close down the operation, all you need to do is liquidate your assets, pay off your debts, lock the door, and walk away from it all. (Of course, it's much better all around to simply sell it—providing that it's a successful business.)

Now for the Minuses . . .

Perhaps the most serious drawback to the sole proprietorship is the problem of unlimited personal liability. Legally, you and the business are one and the same. All the liabilities of the enterprise are therefore yours.

Of course, no one expects to fail when he or she first starts up a venture. Despite all your preparation and planning (let alone your financial commitment!), however, you must have a healthy outlook and plan for the possibility of failure. Indeed, some business advisors claim that it's more probable than possible! If your business fails and the business assets you are able to muster aren't sufficient to cover your obligations, your creditors can move in and take away your home, your automobile, your bank accounts, and any other personal assets you hold until the debts are fully satisfied. (The types of items that can be taken from you depend on different state bankruptcy rules and regulations and on different civil procedure laws.) Consequently, if your personal holdings are considerable, you might be better off opting for the corporate mode.

As a one-person operation, your business is limited by your own skills and capabilities. Under the right circumstances, you can hire additional talent—specialists who can provide the expertise you lack. However, it is generally wise to avoid hiring high-priced experts until your business has expanded enough to absorb this additional cost, and then only if the enterprise is certain to prosper.

The success of your business will be in jeopardy if you become seriously ill or disabled through accidental injury. You can and should anticipate this possibility and take steps early in the game to prevent it. You ought to train one or two of your key people to shoulder the responsibility at the helm, in the event that you're incapacitated for any substantial period of time.

Furthermore, because the business *is* the proprietor, you'll probably find it difficult to attract more capital into your enterprise for growth or expansion. Understandably, banks and other financial sources might be reluctant to advance funds to you. After all, the debt would have to be paid back over time by a single, fragile human being. What if something were to happen that rendered you incapable of managing the business?

This point leads us to the last consideration: If you die while owning the business, your sole proprietorship automatically terminates.

THE PARTNERSHIP

You may consider forming a partnership if you can't personally generate enough capital to make your new business a success, or if the workload is too heavy for you alone, or if you simply need moral support and are afraid of going it alone.

The partnership consists of two or more persons, or *principals,* who have contracted to set up a business. In many respects, this form of ownership does not differ much from the sole proprietorship, except that you can count on one or more associates to help you share the responsibilities, the work, the problem solving and the decision making. Of course, you must expect to share the profits as well.

This sharing aspect is based on the assumption that two or more *ordinary,* or *general,* partners are involved in the business. Another type of partner is the *limited* partner; this kind of arrangement, which is recognized in most states, permits a quasi-corporate entity to exist. In this situation, one or more individuals make an investment in the business and are given part ownership in return. However, they cannot participate in the operation of the business; the enterprise is run by the general partner(s). Limited partners earn their share of company profits but avoid the danger of being held personally liable for business debts.

Two clarion notes of caution should be trumpeted at this point. First, take care that your emotions don't interfere with sound logic and common sense, such as being too eager to go into business with family or friends, or with anyone who happens to come up with the money; a clear head at this early stage can save you lots of grief later. Second, avoid the all-too-common temptation to back up your partnership with nothing more than a verbal understanding and an amicable handshake. Not only for the sake of good business practice but also for your own peace of mind thereafter, you should draw up a partnership agreement with the help of your attorney. This legal instrument not only spells out the duties and responsibilities of the partners but also should include a "buy-sell" clause to forestall future headaches.

As a concluding comment, don't go into a partnership, if at all possible, unless you hold 51 percent of the ownership.

Advantages of the Partnership Form

Like the sole proprietorship, a partnership is relatively easy and inexpensive to establish. You'll probably want to operate under an assumed name, requiring you to file a "Certificate of Conducting Business as Partners." Having the partnership contract prepared is an additional cost.

Naturally, you can count on more initial capital than if you go it alone; the pooled investments of two or more individuals are involved. You also have more leverage when seeking trade credit, loans, or additional equity capital in the future simply because several people are involved.

Rarely does one person possess all the skills and experience required to make a new enterprise a success. If you aren't that rare individual, taking on a partner or two can provide the missing elements. A broader array of talent can be brought to bear on your business operations. (Of course, you must be astute enough to select partners whose skills complement yours—who make up for your shortcomings.)

Finally, the partnership form is relatively free of governmental red tape. Little is required in the way of paperwork (as is the case with a corporation). Each year, however, you must complete an information return, Form 1065 "U.S. Partnership Return of Income". (See chapter 21.)

Drawbacks to the Partnership

If you elect this form of ownership, be prepared to relinquish a good deal of your freedom. You have to work along with one or more co-bosses; you must share the authority and the responsibilities. The need to cooperate can provide a continuing assault on your entrepreneurial spirit. No longer can you enjoy the thrill and the challenge of running the entire show.

There can also be formidable adjustment problems. Disagreements with partners can develop not only over important business problems but also over such insignificant trivia as who will open up (or close) on Wednesdays or Saturdays, when to take vacations (and for how long), who will run the machines, do the buying, supervise the office staff, and so forth. It's difficult enough at times for spouses to get along with each other. Imagine the tensions inherent in a situation where two or more individuals, often unrelated, must act, work, plan, and operate in tandem for years and years! It's wise to make certain that your new partner(s) are as highly motivated and cooperative as you are and that your personalities do not clash. Be especially wary of close friends and relatives. Your affection, loyalty, or friendship can easily blind you to their deficiencies and lead you to make allowances for their mistakes.

In any event, you and the other(s) have to learn to work together if your business is to be successful. If you do become unhappy with the situation, only three courses are open to you: (1) sell out your share of the business to the other(s); (2) buy your partner(s) out; or (3) stay put and learn to live with it.

Be aware that any business decisions or actions taken by your partner(s) legally bind you as well under the general rules of agency, which spell out the duties and financial liability of partners, even in a case where you knew nothing about the move. This obligation is something to think about: It applies to any contracts that may be signed as well as to other acts.

Again, as with the sole proprietorship, you will run the considerable risk of incurring personal liability. As a general partner, your personal assets (as well as those of other general partners) are subject to seizure for the payment of business debts.

Finally, this form of ownership is also subject to the frailties of human nature. The death of any one partner, unless provided for in the partnership contract, automatically terminates the partnership.

THE CORPORATION

The third major legal form of business ownership is the corporation. To set up a corporation, one or more individuals apply for a charter within the state where they want to transact business and where the principal office of the business is located. (*Note:* The number of persons involved depends on state regulations. Most states require only one director in order to create a corporate entity.) Application is accomplished by preparing a "Certificate of Incorporation" in detail (names and addresses of both the proposed corporation and of the incorporators, purpose and type of business activities contemplated, amount of stock authorized, and so on), filing the certificate with the Secretary of State, and paying the required fee.

While it isn't absolutely necessary, I strongly recommend that your attorney handle all the details. Corporation law is complicated; a lawyer will save you needless headaches in the future. At the very least, the attorney may widen the horizons of your business by broadening the purposes of your activities listed in the application. State law limits the activities of your corporation to those spelled out in the charter. Moreover, your attorney can help you prepare a Preincorporation Agreement with the other principals.

Why Incorporate?

Of the three legal forms, this is the only one with a built-in capacity for permanence in that the death of one or more of its founders or stockholders does not affect the business's legal status. Corporations are recognized as legal entities in and of themselves. They exist apart from their stockholders, who can come and go.

Consequently, you avoid the problem of unlimited liability that characterizes the other two forms of ownership. Your liability is limited to the amount of your investment. Your personal holdings do not come up for grabs if the corporation becomes insolvent and its assets are insufficient to satisfy the creditors. This fact alone explains the attraction of the corporate form for many who start their own businesses.

Banks and other lenders are generally more willing to advance loans to a corporation that has been operating successfully for some time or to a new corporation with sufficient equity and promise than to an individual or partnership. (The lender sometimes insists on collateral or requires personal signatures from stockholders as a precautionary measure.) Individuals with money to invest might purchase some of the new corporation's stock.

You aren't locked into the corporation forever. If you someday decide you want to embark on an entirely different enterprise, relocate, or retire, all you have to do is sell your stock in the company. Ownership of stock is readily transferred.

As a final point, there can be certain advantages to the corporate form in the area of fringe benefits, such as pension and stock plans, insurance, and the like.

Disadvantages of Incorporation

A major limitation to the corporate form is the problem of *double taxation.* Corporate profits are taxed once per se since a corporation is a distinct taxable entity. Then they are taxed again as income, when distributed to the stockholders. Although you serve as corporation president and chairman of the board, you're legally an employee of the business. Hence, you are liable for income tax not only on your salary but also on your share of the distributed profits. The total tax bite can be substantial. Unfortunately, any losses sustained by a corporation are not available to stockholders as deductions from other earned income!

It takes time and effort as well as money to set up a corporation. Your costs can run from as little as several hundred dollars to well over a thousand dollars.

Corporations are closely regulated by the state in which they are franchised. In your home state, yours is known as a *domestic corporation. Foreign corporation* is the term applied to your firm when you operate in another state. In reality, you're not supposed to conduct business in a second or third state without making formal application to the respective secretaries of state for permission to conduct operations there. (Generally, this regulation comes up in matters of a corporation's right to sue for nonpayments, etc.) A company doing business in another state isn't stopped merely because of failure to file.

A corporation is also required to promulgate bylaws, hold stockholders' meetings, and keep records. (Most states use preprinted forms that alleviate much of the initial preparations.) Of all three forms of ownership, the corporation comes under the most scrutiny by the federal government.

The S Corporation

Given certain specific qualifications and requirements, a corporation may choose to adopt the *S corporation* form. An outstanding advantage of this legal form (formerly known as a *subchapter S corporation*) is that both income and losses are usually taxed to the individual shareholders, rather than to the corporation itself. This can be especially important in the first year of operation, when new companies frequently lose money. Any loss suffered can be applied against other personal income, such as that from an earlier job. This will reduce the amount of income tax levied. In this respect, the firm is taxed more like a proprietorship or partnership, yet the unlimited personal liability problem common to those two legal forms is avoided.

A corporation can elect to be an S corporation if:

- It "qualifies" (see below)
- All shareholders give their consent to the firm's choice of S corporation status
- It has a permitted tax year
- It files Form 2553 ("Election by a Small Business Corporation")

Some of the requirements needed to "qualify": The company must be a domestic corporation; there should be only one class of stock; and the shareholders should number no more than thirty-five. (For further details, see IRS Publication 589—"Tax Information on S Corporations.")

YOUR NEED FOR PROFESSIONAL ASSISTANCE

If you're like most other entrepreneurs, you're undoubtedly highly motivated and convinced that you'll be able to manage all aspects of your new business masterfully and by yourself. You also plan to run your affairs in a professional, open, and aboveboard manner. You want to treat both your customers and suppliers well, conform to all legal requirements and restrictions, maintain accurate records, pay your taxes on time, and so on.

Despite your high level of self-confidence, however, you must realize that the complexities of today's business environment call for reliance on the assistance of specialists. At the very least you will need an accountant, a banker, an insurance agent or broker, possibly one or two business consultants, and, of course, an attorney. The accountant can help you set up your books according to approved accounting procedures. This will enable you to make vital merchandising and other decisions in the future. Your accountant can also help you keep tabs on your business growth, point out minor problems before they become serious, and complete your tax returns.

Your banker can furnish you with information about the kind of business you are considering and about the community where it will be situated. Furthermore, he or she will be happy to recommend other professionals if you need them, assist your operation with loans and lines of credit, and advise you generally on economic trends.

Your insurance representative takes care of your special business needs for protection against fire and other perils.

Consultants are usually tapped for a variety of one-shot problems: designing a plant or store layout, appraising a going business in which you are interested, making a feasibility study for a new location or for electronic data processing (EDP) equipment under consideration, setting up an initial advertising campaign, and so on.

If at all feasible, it's worth your while to engage an attorney for your business on a retainer basis. Your lawyer's services are valuable at the very beginning, in assisting you with all the legal aspects of starting an enterprise: setting up the legal form of the business, negotiating leases and contracts, securing the necessary licenses and permits, preparing partnership or stockholder agreements, and so forth. Subsequently, your attorney will see to it that you become thoroughly familiar with the details of pertinent legislative acts and local ordinances. These run the gamut from the minimum wage and labor laws, through health and safety regulations, to tax responsibilities. You'll probably call on your attorney later on for assistance in a variety of situations too numerous to mention.

FOR FURTHER INFORMATION

Books

Goldstein, Arnold S. *The Complete Guide to Buying and Selling a Business.* New York: Wiley, 1983.

Hagendorf, Stanley. *Tax Guide for Buying and Selling a Business,* 6th ed. Englewood Cliffs, N.J.: Prentice-Hall, 1986.

Mangold, M. J. *How to Buy a Small Business,* rev. ed. New York: Pilot Books, 1986.

Siegel, William L. *Franchising.* New York: Wiley, 1983.

Small, Samuel, and Pilot Books Staff. *Directory of Franchising Organizations,* rev. ed. New York: Pilot Books, 1986.

Materials Available from the Small Business Administration

MANAGEMENT AIDS

MA 2.026—"Feasibility Checklist for Starting a Small Business of Your Own"

Booklets Available from the Superintendent of Documents

S/N 003-008-00194-7—*Franchise Opportunities Handbook, 1984*—$13.50.
S/N 045-000-00164-4—*Buying and Selling a Small Business*—$5.00.

5

How to Estimate Your Financial Needs

Each year a surprisingly high percentage of new ventures are launched with insufficient funding behind them. Initial undercapitalization is a major cause of early business failure. Even when an enterprise manages to last for three or four years before going under, its demise is often directly traceable to poor financial planning at the beginning.

Unfortunately, there are individuals who scrape together whatever money they can, perhaps in their eagerness to get started, and go in with an amazingly slim financial commitment. Somehow, they don't realize that they need more than just a month's rent in advance, a few fixtures, and a minimum inventory. At the very least, some reserves are required to cover personal needs and family responsibilities until the profits start to trickle in.

Of course, we've all heard anecdotes about this or that entrepreneur who in no time at all was able to pyramid an insignificant investment of $300 or $500 to a moderate-sized, going business. Though such stories may contain a few elements of truth, the odds are probably a thousand to one (if not higher) *against* your being so fortunate!

Lots of careful thinking and sound planning must characterize your own approach to business, if you want to succeed. Your capital requirements should be diligently formulated well in advance of taking the plunge.

HOW MUCH CAPITAL DO YOU NEED?

It appears to be fashionable in financial circles to separate the term *capital* into a number of classifications. Terms such as *initial, operating, working,* and *reserve* are often attached to the word *capital.* Of course, all of these are variations on the same theme: Enough money must be available to see the business (and yourself) off to a good start.

You need *initial capital* to cover all your start-up costs: legal fees, deposits with public utility companies, licenses and permits, machinery and fixtures, advances for the rental of premises, franchise fees (if required), and the like. Included here are funds set aside for your opening promotion; this money is sometimes referred to as *promotional capital.*

You need *operating* (or *working*) *capital* to purchase raw materials or merchandise for resale and supplies, to pay your employees, and to liquidate obligations—in short, to keep on operating until profits begin to show up.

Finally, you'll need *reserve capital* not only for unexpected contingencies but also to be able to eat three meals a day, buy clothing, pay your monthly rent bill or mortgage, cover medical expenses, and so on.

How to Determine Your Requirements

Now that you know you need three kinds of capital, you must pin down the approximate sales volume you expect your business to attain during its first year. This *sales target* guides you in calculating your overall capital requirements. It should be as accurate as you can make it: neither an optimistic nor a pessimistic estimate, but a fair appraisal of just how much you believe your sales will total.

Using this figure as a base—with the aid of obtainable trade information such as average markups in your kind of business, space productivity, and other ratios—you should be able to deduce other important details. These include the kinds (and values) of assets required to reach that level of sales, the size of the facility needed, and approximate overhead costs.

As an illustration of this general approach, assume you're planning to open a small gift shop. First you tap the services of your trade association and, perhaps, other sources such as Robert Morris Associates (Philadelphia) or Dun & Bradstreet (New York City).

Let's assume you discover that the average gift shop of the size you intend to open generally operates on a gross margin (sales, less cost of goods sold) of about 44 percent of sales. Overhead amounts to another 35 percent of sales. When you think about it, these two little facts alone provide substantial direction for your planning. Say you've set a first year's sales figure of $200,000. From these percentages, you can then calculate that your overhead (for rent, utilities, labor, insurance, advertising, and other expenses) should total around $70,000. You should also realize a gross margin of about $88,000 on some $112,000 worth of merchandise (at cost) to be sold. Subtracting the $70,000 figure from this gross, you'd expect to come out with about $18,000 in profit before taxes.

By the same token, you may learn from available tables that the customary rate of inventory turnover in gift shops is about 2.4 times annually. By dividing your cost-of-merchandise figure of $112,000 by 2.4 turns of stock, you can then conclude that you'll need to keep on hand an average inventory of approximately $46,667. The basic formula to use for this kind of calculation is given on the following page.

$$\text{Stockturn (at cost)} = \frac{\text{Sales at cost}}{\text{Average stock at cost}}$$

From trade sources you can also gain information as to the dollar sales per square foot of selling space typical of gift shops. This information will help you to decide how many square feet you need in your own store to do the kind of sales volume you project. By checking with other retailers, local representatives, and your bank, you'll also be able to ascertain how much is required for deposits against utility bills and about how much you can expect to be billed each month for utilities, insurance, and other operating expenses.

A Worksheet to Help You Estimate Cash Needs

One of the more popular little pamphlets put out by the Small Business Administration is the "Checklist for Going into Business." In addition to a series of thought-provoking questions for the would-be entrepreneur to answer before attempting to launch a business, the booklet contains a valuable aid—"Worksheet No. 2." The form is designed to help you estimate the amount of capital you'll need to start your business.

Take a few minutes now to look over the form in exhibit 5–1. As you can see, it's just about self-explanatory.

WHERE TO FIND THE MONEY YOU WILL NEED

After you've devoted many hours to planning your new enterprise, and after you've worked and reworked your figures and pared them to the bone, you finally decide you need a minimum of five, ten, or perhaps twenty thousand dollars to assure your business success. Your next hurdle is to locate the required capital.

Many sources of capital are available—and most have strings attached. Perhaps the best type for you to use, if only because it's the least expensive in the long run, is your own personal resources.

Use Your Own Funds, If Possible

Knowledgeable business consultants recommend that at least one-half, if not more, of your business investment should come from your own reserves. Consequently, it makes sense for you to work at a job for a year or two while you try to accumulate some savings.

Understandably, you'll be somewhat reluctant to gamble your own hard-earned capital. Few individuals escape a confrontation with this dilemma: Why not play with *other people's* money, instead of with your own?

Face it. Neither individuals nor firms are likely to advance moneys to anyone without expecting some sort of gain on the loans they make. They desire a return on their investment either in the form of "equity" (part ownership) in your business or the payment of an attractive rate of interest. Incidentally,

EXHIBIT 5-1. A WORKSHEET FOR ESTIMATING YOUR FINANCIAL NEEDS

WORKSHEET NO. 2			
ESTIMATED MONTHLY EXPENSES			
Item	Your estimate of monthly expenses based on sales of $ _____ per year	Your estimate of how much cash you need to start your business (See column 3.)	What to put in column 2 (These figures are typical for one kind of business. you will have to decide how many months to allow for in your business.)
	Column 1	Column 2	Column 3
Salary of owner-manager	$	$	2 times column 1
All other salaries and wages			3 times column 1
Rent			3 times column 1
Advertising			3 times column 1
Delivery expense			3 times column 1
Supplies			3 times column 1
Telephone and telegraph			3 times column 1
Other utilities			3 times column 1
Insurance			Payment required by insurance company
Taxes, including Social Security			4 times column 1
Interest			3 times column 1
Maintenance			3 times column 1
Legal and other professional fees			3 times column 1
Miscellaneous			3 times column 1
STARTING COSTS YOU ONLY HAVE TO PAY ONCE			Leave column 2 blank
Fixtures and equipment			Fill in worksheet 3 on page 12 and put the total here
Decorating and remodeling			Talk it over with a contractor
Installation of fixtures and equipment			Talk to suppliers from who you buy these
Starting inventory			Suppliers will probably help you estimate this
Deposits with public utilities			Find out from utilities companies
Legal and other professional fees			Lawyer, accountant, and so on
Licenses and permits			Find out from city offices what you have to have
Advertising and promotion for opening			Estimate what you'll use
Accounts receivable			What you need to buy more stock until credit customers pay
Cash			For unexpected expenses or losses, special purchases, etc.
Other			Make a separate list and enter total
TOTAL ESTIMATED CASH YOU NEED TO START WITH		$	Add up all the numbers in column 2

Source: "Checklist for Going into Business," *Management Aid No. 2.016* (Washington, D.C.: Small Business Administration, 1975), 6–7.

you'll also find that banks and other lenders are unwilling to lend you money unless you're prepared to risk your own funds as well.

You need not invest all your savings, nor do you have to relinquish any part of your business. There are ways to borrow additional funds on favorable terms. A loan on your savings bank passbook, for example, can bring you supplementary capital at low cost. While the bank may charge you 9 or 10 percent, the funds you maintain on deposit in your account continue to earn interest. This interest offsets much of your cost and results in your paying a differential interest rate of only 4 or 5 percent.

If you own your own home or other real property, there's also the possibility of taking out a mortgage or refinancing an existing mortgage. The mortgage rates available at the time of the loan or refinancing must be balanced against your rate of return.

Another possibility is a life insurance policy that has accumulated cash value over the years. Loans on such policies generally bear a relatively low rate of interest.

Tapping the Resources of Family and Friends

A popular source of additional investment capital is your family. Needless to say, in most families it seems to be relatively easy (no pun intended!) to locate family members who might be willing to lend a relatively small sum of money to the entrepreneur. Good friends might also be eager to help out. Even acquaintances can be sold on investing in a new corporation, if you can persuade them to have faith in you and your ideas.

You have to decide for yourself whether this avenue is for you. It could be sticky. There are some things you ought to think about: How will your relationships with these individuals be affected if your business does *not* succeed? How will you be able to pay them back?

If you decide to borrow from family or friends, you should work out in advance some method of paying them back over time, possibly in installments. Be prepared: They'll have difficulty restraining themselves from getting involved in the operation of your business. You need to be firm from the beginning, to avoid psychological wear and tear on yourself.

Bank Loans

Banks lend money to launch a new business only occasionally—and only when you've accompanied your application with an attractive and comprehensive business plan. More often than not, a commercial bank is more interested in offering funds for operating capital to a business with some history of successful operations behind it. The bank's primary usefulness is for short-term loans for the leasing of equipment, the purchasing of real estate, the buying of additional stocks of goods for resale, and the like.

Finally, many individuals are able to secure personal loans of five thousand dollars or more on their signatures alone if they have a preferred credit rating from repaying past loans on time. It helps if you can show personal assets on your loan application in the form of bank accounts, stocks, bonds, and so forth.

Finance Companies

Business executives can often borrow short-term funds from commercial finance companies by offering inventories, receivables, and similar holdings as collateral. Many personal finance companies are more than willing to extend loans to persons in whom they have confidence. However, the high interest rates these firms generally charge should rule out this source for the alert entrepreneur.

Venture Capitalists

You may be able to locate private individuals, small investment groups, and companies in the business of investing in small enterprise. These *venture capitalists* are eager to put their excess financial resources to work. They seldom become involved with a new undertaking, however, unless they're convinced by a well-developed proposal that the new business will indeed be a winner. Yet these people can be of value to you *after* your new firm has demonstrated viability and vigor for several years and is in need of additional moneys for further growth or expansion. Venture capitalists are usually not interested in granting loans outright. They prefer to put additional capital into a growing business in exchange for part of the ownership. In short, they look to make capital gains.

Small Business Investment Corporations (SBICs)

These private companies were authorized by act of Congress back in the 1950s. SBICS are licensed to provide financial services to small business in the form of equity/venture financing for modernization, expansion, and the like. Especially interested in purchasing stock in the promising small corporation, the SBIC usually seeks to become involved in actual business operations by providing management direction.

The federal government encourages private enterprise by members of minority groups. Minority Enterprise Small Business Investment Corporations (MESBICs) have been licensed to provide the identical kind of aid to small enterprises owned by minority-group members.

Issuing Stock

If you've organized your new firm into a corporation, your charter specifies the amount of shares the corporation is authorized to issue. You may be able to raise equity funds by selling some shares to others, making them shareholders and thereby endowing them with part ownership of your business.

Stocks may be either *preferred* or *common* shares. Preferred shares include certain privileges for the shareholder—for example, if the business fails, the shareholder is guaranteed a proportionate share of the remaining assets. Usually, though, only holders of common stock enjoy voting rights in the company.

Suppliers' Credit

Business makes abundant use of *trade,* or *supplier's, credit,* a practice of special significance to retailers and wholesalers. For example, if you own a store, your suppliers generally extend credit to you, albeit after some favorable experience. This means they ship goods and supplies to your business, bill you, and give you time to pay the invoice (usually thirty days). This is tantamount to financing of a short-term nature.

Along the same lines, where fixtures, machinery, and other equipment are concerned, suppliers are often more than happy to extend long-term credit. After making a down payment, you pay them back the balance of the debt on an installment basis. Some may even lease the equipment to you instead of insisting on an outright sale.

THE BALANCE SHEET

Every business must balance its books properly at the close of its business year, for tax purposes if for nothing else. The culmination of this activity is the issuance of a major accounting statement—the *balance sheet.*

This summarizes the status of the business at that point in time—its assets, liabilities, and net worth. The balance sheet is useful, too, for purposes of control, management direction, and decision making. By interpreting this statement, management is able to glean insights that are of value in planning. For example, the *current ratio* (one of the so-called *liquidity ratios*) is calculated by dividing the business's current assets by its current liabilities in order to assess the firm's ability to pay off its debts promptly. As a general rule, this ratio should be at least two to one. (An expanded treatment of the topic of ratio analysis will be found in chapter 17.)

The sample balance sheet in exhibit 5–2 shows that the current ratio for the small manufacturing company is well in excess of the acceptable figure. A brief explanation of the major items on the balance sheet follows:

- *Assets*—cash, property, and other items owned by the company
- *Current assets*—cash and property temporarily in your firm's possession that can be quickly liquidated
- *Cash*—in addition to currency and coin, this includes checks and money orders
- *Accounts receivable*—a collective term for moneys owed the firm on credit
- *Fixed assets*—tangible property of a long-term or permanent nature
- *Liabilities*—the debts your business must pay back
- *Current liabilities*—debts that must be met within the year, such as your *accounts payable* (moneys owed out to suppliers), short-term loans, and accrued taxes
- *Accounts payable*—money you owe to creditors
- *Accrued payroll taxes*—payroll taxes you have accumulated but not yet sent in to the government

EXHIBIT 5–2. A SAMPLE BALANCE SHEET

ADG-TENAFLY MANUFACTURING COMPANY
Balance Sheet
December 31, 1987

Assets			*Liabilities*		
CURRENT ASSETS			CURRENT LIABILITIES		
Cash on hand	$300		Accounts payable	$4,700	
Cash in bank	7,150		Notes payable within one year	1,400	
Accounts receivable, less allowance for bad debts	9,720		Accrued payroll taxes	1,960	
Merchandise inventory	11,880				
Total current assets		$29,050	Total current liabilities		$8,060
FIXED ASSETS			LONG-TERM LIABILITIES		
Land	$7,560		Note payable, due 1993	$3,000	
Building, less depreciation	33,330		Note payable, due 1996	7,000	
Equipment, less depreciation	12,060				
Furniture and fixtures, less depreciation	5,950				
Total fixed assets		58,900	Total long-term liabilities		10,000
Total Assets		$87,950			
			Capital (Net Worth)		
			Capital, December 31, 1987		69,890
			Total Liabilities and Capital		$87,950

Source: Compiled by the author.

- *Long-term liabilities*—debts of a long-term nature (over one year)
- *Capital*—also referred to as *owner's equity* or *net worth,* this is the excess of your assets over your liabilities. It is equivalent to what you originally invested in the business plus subsequent additions or subtractions

In the case of a corporation, the outstanding capital stock (at its original issue price) is listed here, as well as any accumulated profit.

THE PROFIT AND LOSS STATEMENT

Also called an *income statement* or *operating statement,* the profit and loss statement (or *P&L*) is another major accounting device. Prepared at least once a year, it depicts the results of business operation for the period covered. An abbreviated statement for a small retail shop is shown in exhibit 5–3.

EXHIBIT 5–3. A SAMPLE P&L.

THE TWO SISTERS' DRESS SHOPPE
Profit and Loss Statement
May 1987

GROSS SALES FOR MAY	$19,700		
Less returns and allowances		420	
Net sales			$19,380
COST OF GOODS			
Merchandise inventory, May 1		11,550	
Purchases during month		6,100	
Freight charges		115	
Total merchandise handled		17,765	
Less inventory, May 31		6,315	
Cost of goods sold			11,450
Gross profit (margin)			7,930
OPERATING EXPENSES			
Salaries		3,100	
Utilities		420	
Rent		1,000	
Stationery and printing		140	
Insurance		260	
Advertising and promotion		245	
Telephone		140	
Travel and entertainment		65	
Dues and subscriptions		40	
Bad debts		220	
Depreciation		820	
Total operating expenses			6,450
Operating profit			1,480
OTHER INCOME			
Dividends		90	
Interest on bank account		60	
Total other income			150
Total income before taxes			1,630
Less provision for income taxes			560
Net Income (or Loss)			$1,070

Source: Compiled by the author.

A major element of the profit-and-loss statement is the *bottom-line* fig-ure—the one that reveals how much net profit the company earned during the particular period or, perhaps, the magnitude of the loss it may have suffered.

The major parts of a P&L are readily seen in the following skeletal outline:

Gross sales
— Returns and allowances

Net sales
— Cost of goods

Gross profit (or Gross margin)
— Operating expenses

Operating profit
+ Other Income

Total income before taxes
— Provision for income taxes

Net income (or loss)

Management that allows a full year to go by without seeing a P&L shows signs of shortsightedness. Any attempts to correct an unfavorable picture are negated once months have rolled past. Smart business owners insist on having income statements prepared by their accountant or bookkeeping staff on at least a quarterly basis—or, even better, each month. That way, they can keep current with what is happening and take immediate steps to rectify any problems. Moreover, they can take advantage of opportunities that crop up unexpectedly.

PREPARE YOUR STATEMENTS IN ADVANCE

One of the healthiest steps you can take before starting up your business is to work out, well ahead of time, both an estimated balance sheet and an estimated profit and loss statement for at least your first year of operation. Indeed, smart planners will prepare these pro forma statements for the first two or three years following the start-up.

This suggestion is not made simply to offer you an exercise in thinking things through. It should provide you with foresight: You'll be able to determine what is likely to happen, be prepared for it, and rule out the unexpected.

Listed at the end of this chapter are several helpful pamphlets dealing with the preparation of business plans for different types of enterprises (manufacturing, construction, retailing, and service firms). These are available from the U.S. Small Business Administration; all are in the *Management Aids* series (MA 2.007, 2.008, 2.020, and 2.022).

Featured in MA 2.020 is the "Expenses Worksheet" reproduced in exhibit 5–4. Study the form; you'll readily understand its value. Although it was evidently devised for a retail business (specifically, for a hardware store), you can easily adapt it to any other kind of business. You'll find it useful for computing your expected profit (or loss) on a month-by-month basis for the entire year. Approximate percentage-of-sales figures for most entries (cost of goods sold, salaries, rents)—and for most types of businesses—can usually be obtained from one's trade association or service firms such as Dun & Bradstreet.

EXHIBIT 5-4. SBA EXPENSES WORKSHEET

	Sample Figures for hardware stores (Percent of sales)	% of Your Sales	Your Dollars Jan	Your Dollars Feb	Your Dollars Mar	Your Dollars Apr	Your Dollars May	Your Dollars Jun	Your Dollars Jul	Your Dollars Aug	Your Dollars Sep	Your Dollars Oct	Your Dollars Nov	Your Dollars Dec	Your Annual Sales Dollar
Net Sales	100.00														
Cost of Goods Sold	66.05														
Margin	33.95														
Salery Expense:															
Owners and managers	7.15														
Salespeople, office and other	9.60														
Total Saleries	16.75														
Other Expenses:															
Office supplies and postage	0.40														
Advertising	1.55														
Donations	0.05														
Telephone and telegraphy	0.30														
Losses on notes and accounts recievable	0.15														
Delivery Expense (exclusive of wages)	0.50														
Depreciationof delivery equipment	0.25														
Depreciation of furniture, fixtures, and tools	0.35														
Rent	2.70														
Repairs to building	0.10														
Heat, light, water, and power	0.80														
Insurance	0.80														
Taxes (not including Federal income tax	1.10														
Interest on borrowed money	0.05*														
Unclassified (including store supplies)	1.20														
Total Expense (not including interest on investment)	27.05														
Net Profit	6.90														

*The interest on funds used for start-up costs if yours is a new store.

Source: "Business Plan for Retailers," *Management Aid No. 2.020* (Washington, D.C.: Small Business Administration. Reprinted April 1981), 1.

MAKING YOUR BUSINESS PLAN

At this point, it may prove worthwhile to list once more those ingredients mentioned in chapter 1 as being essential to the success of a new business. As you may recall, they are

- A qualified entrepreneur
- A potential business opportunity
- A solid and detailed plan
- Sufficient capital
- Luck

That third item—a solid and detailed plan—is not always perceived by many people as being an absolute requirement. It is often pointed out that many of today's successful companies were initially started without much in the way of real, solid planning.

While this may be true in some instances, logic tells us that careful and thorough planning cannot hurt our chances. It can only make things better.

Indeed, the U.S. Small Business Administration suggests that a detailed business plan:

- Offers a path to follow (shows you how to achieve your goals)
- May help in securing loans
- Can provide useful information for suppliers, personnel, and others
- Can help you develop your management capabilities*

Exhibit 5–5 contains a useful outline for your business plan. Note that the outline is intended only as a planning aid. It's not designed for the sole purpose of attracting venture capital. (For more on the venture proposal, refer to *Management Aid No. 1.009*—listed in the bibliography at the end of this chapter.)

EXHIBIT 5–5. AN OUTLINE FOR YOUR BUSINESS PLAN

    A. *An Overview of the Business:*
        1. Name of firm
        2. Nature of the business
        3. Major business objectives
        4. Legal form of business
        5. Desired image
    B. *The Physical Plant:*
        1. Description of location (area, neighborhood, site)
        2. Transportation facilities
        3. Parking facilities
        4. The building (description, condition, façade, renovation/remodeling required, and so forth)

---

*Management Assistance Support Services Section, U.S. Small Business Administration, "Business Plan for Retailers," *Management Aid No. 2.020.* (Washington, D.C.: U.S. Small Business Administration, April 1981 reprint), 2.

EXHIBIT 5–5. (*Continued*)

     5. Licenses and permits required
     6. Terms of lease and other occupancy details
     7. Arrangements to be made with utilities
     8. Machinery required
     9. Equipment needed
    10. Fixturization
    11. Interior layout
    12. Interior design
    13. Supplies required

C. *The Financial Plan:*
     1. Initial investment required
     2. Additional financing to be sought, along with likely sources
     3. Projected sales figures
     4. Pro forma balance sheets (2 to 3 years)
     5. Pro forma income statements (2 to 3 years)
     6. Cash flow projections
     7. Needed insurance program
     8. Internal risk-reduction measures to be taken
     9. Bookkeeping method
    10. Expected taxation liabilities and responsibilities

D. *The Marketing Plan:*
     1. Targeted customer groups: their characteristics, size of market segments, and so forth
     2. Analysis of the competition
     3. Product mix
     4. Services mix
     5. Pricing policies (price ranges, price lines, promotional pricing approaches, and so on)
     6. Discount policies
     7. Markdown (and markup) policies
     8. Budget for promotion
     9. First year's promotion calendar
    10. Advertising plans: media selection, schedules, use of cooperative advertising, and so forth
    11. Personal selling efforts and sales training programs
    12. Sales promotion tools to be used
    13. Plans for window and interior displays (if a retail store)
    14. Distribution methods and channels
    15. Needed marketing research
    16. Credit extension and supervision of program

E. *Personnel Plan:*
     1. Organizational chart for the business
     2. Key personnel—names, job titles, educational background, experience, and skills
     3. Written job specifications for all positions
     4. Openings still to be filled
     5. Personnel sources to draw on
     6. Details of employee compensation, including fringe benefits
     7. Plans for employee training

F. *Inventory Plan:*
     1. Initial inventory required (amount, depth and width, quality level, and so forth)
     2. Methods for inventory management, planning, and control
     3. Expected rates of inventory turnover
     4. Buying: names and addresses of suppliers
     5. Buying: terms, delivery policies, and the like

Source: Compiled by the author.

FOR FURTHER INFORMATION

Books

Campsey, B. J., and Eugene F. Brigham. *Introduction to Financial Management.* New York: Dryden, 1985.

Carey, Omer L., and Dean F. Olson. *Financial Tools for Small Business.* Reston, Va.: Reston, 1983.

Dible, Donald. *How to Plan and Finance a Growing Business.* Reston, Va.: Reston, 1981.

Hartley, W. C., and Yale Meltzer. *Cash Management: Planning, Forecasting, and Control.* Englewood Cliffs, N.J.: Prentice-Hall, 1979.

Kozmetsky, George, Michael D. Gill, Jr., and Raymond W. Smilor. *Financing and Managing Fast-Growth Companies: The Venture Capital Process.* Lexington, Mass.: Lexington Books, 1985.

Mancuso, Joseph R. *How to Prepare and Present a Business Plan.* Englewood Cliffs, N.J.: Prentice-Hall, 1983.

O'Connor, D., and A. Bueso. *Managerial Finance: Theory and Techniques.* Englewood Cliffs, N.J.: Prentice-Hall, 1981.

Pratt, Stanley E. *How to Raise Venture Capital.* New York: Scribner's, 1982.

Silver, A. David. *Venture Capital: The Complete Guide for Investors.* New York: Wiley, 1982.

Pamphlets Available from the Small Business Administration

MANAGEMENT AIDS

MA 1.001—"The ABC's of Borrowing"

MA 1.003—"Basic Budgets for Profit Planning"

MA 1.009—"A Venture Capital Primer for Small Business"

MA 1.015—"Budgeting in a Small Business Firm"

MA 1.016—"Sound Cash Management and Borrowing"

MA 2.007—"Business Plan for Small Manufacturers"

MA 2.008—"Business Plan for Small Construction Firms"

MA 2.020—"Business Plan for Retailers"

MA 2.022—"Business Plan for Small Service Firms"

Booklets Available from the Superintendent of Documents

S/N 045-000-00142-3—*Financial Recordkeeping for Small Stores*—$5.50.

S/N 045-000-00174-1—*Evaluating Money Sources*—$5.00.

S/N 045-000-00193-8—*Capital Planning*—$4.50.

S/N 045-000-00194-6—*Understanding Money Sources*—$4.75.

S/N 045-000-00208-0—*Handbook of Small Business Finance*—$4.50.

6

Finding the Right Location

Selecting the place to set up your operation is one of the most important decisions you have to make. More often than not, the seeds of business success or demise are sown along with the choice of location.

It's sad but true that many location decisions are based on personal preferences or whim, instead of on an objective, orderly approach. Often, an entrepreneur chooses to set up shop close to home purely for the sake of convenience, or discovers a promising-looking empty store along a busy thoroughfare, or rides past a vacant building that strikes him or her as ideal for a new plant.

This person is relying more on intuition than on logic. Underlying this approach to decision making are emotional, or nonrational, factors. Strangely, too, the typical new business owner often neglects, among other things, to seek out pertinent helpful materials on location finding that are readily available from the Small Business Administration, the Government Printing Office, or the local branch of the public library.

If you plan to gamble your life's savings in launching a new enterprise, as so many do, you would do well to seize the reins and proceed in a coldly logical, businesslike fashion.

HOW TO ANALYZE YOUR REQUIREMENTS

Obviously, the right choice of location for a retail store can easily mean the difference between success and failure. Many types of retail shops depend almost entirely on passersby for their sales. Your selection of a side street location or a deteriorating neighborhood could indeed prove to be a costly mistake.

Less evident is the importance of the proper site for a service business, wholesale operation, or factory. Yet, even here, you should be concerned about several essential characteristics. Both manufacturing plants and wholesaling establishments, for instance, must have access to good transportation facilities, for bringing in raw materials or finished goods and for distributing their products. Similarly, these enterprises must often be able to count on a healthy "labor pool" in the area from which to draw machine operators, office workers, supervisory personnel, technicians, and so forth.

Yes, the requirements for different types of businesses may vary considerably. There are, however, some common areas to take into account when choosing a location, regardless of the kind of business you are setting up. In addition to such general considerations as the character of the community, the local environment, and your personal preferences, take pains to study the following:

- Accessibility to transportation
- Availability of labor
- Closeness to the company's markets
- Cost factors, such as land, construction, materials, and labor
- Local ordinances and regulations
- Quality of local services (police and fire protection, and so on)
- Residency factors (climate, quality of schools, places of worship, recreational facilities, and so forth)
- Sewers, water supply, power, and other utilities
- Space for future expansion
- Tax structure

Determining Facility Needs

Our nation's manufacturing companies purchase raw materials, semiprocessed goods, and/or components. In their factories, they utilize these elements in the fabrication of other products designed for both consumer and nonconsumer markets.

Obviously, then, there may be several other location requirements for the manufacturing facility (in addition to many of the factors listed at the end of the preceding section). For example, the new factory may need to be erected on a sizable parcel of land. Because of the high cost of space in most American cities, many of today's plants are situated in more rural areas, where land costs are relatively low. Preferably, too, the plant should be convenient to necessary distribution facilities—a major highway, if truck transport is commonly used, or a railroad spur, if outgoing goods are destined for distribution by train. Still another requirement may be the ready availability of sufficient local labor, since the company may need to employ a considerable number of workers.

The typical wholesaling company has need of ample warehouse facilities to store the large quantities of goods it must purchase all during the year for eventual resale to industrial accounts and/or retail firms. Like the manufacturing plant, the wholesale operation requires bays and docks for handling incoming and outgoing shipments as well as ready access to one or more of the major transportation modes. Still another similarity between today's warehouse and the modern factory is that both types of buildings are often found in rural or suburban areas where the cost of land is not too high. More often then not, the modern warehouse facility occupies a flat, one-story building rather than the older, multistory type commonly seen in the downtown sections of many cities. Within these single-level structures, forklifts and other equipment can move pallets and skids of merchandise about rather easily.

As mentioned above, with a retail store operation, a good location is often the primary requisite for success. Retailers need to open stores where the traffic that passes by is brisk. They look for a "trading area" that is extensive, carefully investigate the demographic and other characteristics of consumers in the area, check into their competitors' strengths and weaknesses, and seek ample parking facilities. (These and other location criteria for retail operations are treated in greater detail later on in this chapter.)

As to the service sector, it's evident that in many different types of service enterprises, the business premises often play a significant role. An obvious illustration can be found in the lodging industry. Certainly, the hotel, motel, or inn that aspires to more than modest success has need of a location that is convenient to traffic, along with an attractive entrance and building, and appropriate furniture and decor.

In much the same way, theaters, beauty salons, dry cleaning establishments, dance studios, and the like require locations that are convenient to large numbers of consumers—and premises that will contribute toward building continued patronage.

THE RETAIL LOCATION

The majority of new businesses spawned each year are retail stores. These outlets are particularly vulnerable to failure due to the wrong location. Consequently, the subject of store location is treated here in more detail.

Success in a retail store depends to a large extent on the quantity and the quality of the traffic passing by. Most often this is pedestrian traffic, though in some cases, the number of passing automobiles and available parking facilities can be of vital significance. In addition to the need for sufficient space for the display and sale of merchandise and for work room and storage, consider these factors:

- The extent of the store's "trading area"
- The demographics of the population in the area (see chapter 3, "Demographic Segmentation")
- The nature of the competition
- The compatibility of neighboring stores
- Parking facilities
- The availability of public transportation
- The volume of traffic (pedestrian and vehicular)
- The store building itself
- The storefront

In cities, you also need to weigh the benefits of a corner location against those of a spot within a block, and determine whether you have selected the "right" side of the street.

The Trading Area

If you plan to open a retail shop, become familiar with both the *trading area* concept and the various types of locations that are available to you. The trading area is the area surrounding a particular store (or group of stores) from which it draws most of its shoppers. For the average, small "in-city" shop that sells convenience goods and impulse items, the trading area may only extend for a few blocks in one or two directions and for even less in the other directions. The trading area can be far larger for a high-image specialty goods store that caters to an elite clientele. Discount houses, department stores, and the larger planned shopping centers may pull shoppers from many miles away.

Types of Retail Locations

Let's consider the different kinds of shopping areas that make up the retail structure of a typical city. We may arbitrarily assign the various types into two categories: the older, in-city (and largely unplanned) retail areas and the newer, planned shopping centers. Those in the first category consist of the central business district (CBD), secondary business districts, neighborhood shopping streets, and a few other types.

The Central Business District. This is the "downtown" or "center-city" section where a large number of stores are concentrated. Traditionally, the CBD is a bustling area with office buildings, banks, theaters, restaurants, and many types of retail stores. Sizable window frontage and floor space characterize these outlets. The main branches of department stores and large units of the major chains are usually found here, along with shops offering specialty merchandise and shopping goods (articles that consumers are willing to expend time and effort comparing with competing merchandise as to price and quality) as well as convenience items. Although the "downtown" sales picture has become bleaker over the years as the population mix in many cities has shifted to a less economically advantaged clientele, many locations in the central business district still enjoy brisk sales. Rents, however, have increased at a prodigious rate. This fact, along with the deteriorating "quality of life" in many of these sections, has lead many business owners to react negatively toward CBD locations.

Here and there across the country, though, we have seen some successful instances of revitalized downtown areas. Some notable examples are Hawthorne Plaza in Los Angeles, Faneuil Hall Marketplace in Boston, and Canal Place in New Orleans.

Secondary Business Districts. Found along the major arteries leading out of downtown districts, secondary business districts often present a more attractive situation than CBDs. Most cities have several of these sections; major metropolitan areas may have many more. Rents here, too, are comparatively high, but area residents favor these shopping areas because they can buy just about anything in this concentration of stores. Traffic can be quite heavy, especially during the afternoons and on Saturdays. As a retailer, don't be put off by a high rent—all too often low monthly rent means low monthly sales.

Neighborhood Shopping Streets. In most cities, there are a good number of areas where brisk retail sales are registered. Dependent for the most part on the density of residents in the vicinity, neighborhood shopping streets may extend from one or two city blocks in length to as many as eight or more. The typical shopping area presents a well-balanced assortment of store types: small branches of chain store operations (supermarkets, variety stores, fast-food outlets, and so forth); a liberal sprinkling of specialty stores; and a much larger number of shops that sell convenience merchandise. Here you find bakeries, hardware stores, dry cleaners, meat and fish stores, bars and luncheonettes, pharmacies, shoe stores, and the like. Rents in the section are usually moderate. Business failures are relatively rare, and empty stores are quickly grabbed up.

Clusters and Freestanding Stores. Woven throughout the residential areas of large cities are numerous small clusters of shops. Generally, the stores are located on or near the corner of a single city block. You may also find an occasional freestanding retail outlet with its own parking facilities. More often than not, this type of store is positioned at a major intersection or along a highway.

Planned Shopping Centers. Often situated on the outskirts of cities and in the suburbs are the relatively new retail developments—the so-called *planned shopping centers.* Three distinct types of these store groupings can be seen: the neighborhood, community, and regional shopping centers.

Neighborhood Centers. The smallest of the three types is the *neighborhood shopping center.* It usually consists of a row of stores, which complement each other. For this reason, it's also known as a *strip center,* even though many of them have been erected in the shape of an L or a U. Frequently, its main attraction (or *anchor store*) is a supermarket or large variety store. Parking space is available for a limited number of automobiles. When situated in areas that are still being built up, neighborhood center locations can be attractive for many types of retail businesses. Their drawing power generally extends for a few miles around.

Community Shopping Centers. The trading area of the *community shopping center* is much larger. There may be twenty or thirty stores in the center and parking for hundreds of cars. Often, the cornerstone retailer is a junior department or discount store of the K Mart or Zayre's type.

Regional Centers. Today's typical *regional shopping center* is a huge, one-stop shopping complex thirty to fifty or more acres in size. It contains department store branches, restaurants, banks, theaters, chain store units, and independent retailers. Here, consumers are able to shop in a leisurely fashion for merchandise and services of just about every conceivable kind—from impulse products and convenience items to shopping goods and specialty merchandise. Most of the successful regional centers around the country today are completely enclosed, all-weather malls. This type of center draws shoppers from villages and towns as far as an hour away by car. Often, its parking facilities can handle a thousand or more vehicles.

These locations have their good and bad points. If you rent a store in a shopping center, you're assured of some customers, especially in the evenings and on Saturdays. The majority of shoppers are, of course, attracted by the department store(s). Many, however, like to stroll through the rows of other stores in the mall. Consumers enjoy the frequent shows, demonstrations, exhibits, and other public relations gestures put on by the shopping center association. The general atmosphere, the security, maintenance, and group sales promotions are all typically well managed. However, as a tenant, you're limited in your display and promotion approaches. Many centers, for example, don't permit a retailer to display a banner on the surface of the store window. You might be compelled to keep your store open in accordance with the shopping center's hours, even on days—or at times—when you do very little business and can't really afford to keep on help. You'll also be required to join the mall association and pay your proportion of the dues.

If you're considering a shopping center location, you should visit a number of centers and talk to various store owners. Discuss the pros and cons with real estate people before deciding on this type of location. Keep in mind, too, that the location *within* the center can be especially important to the success of a retail store.

A PLAN FOR CHOOSING YOUR LOCATION

This section presents an organized, step-by-step procedure designed to widen your horizons and to help you make your location decision. The plan presumes you'll conduct your location hunt at a leisurely pace. Above all, avoid the temptation to rush into business. Adopt a leisurely, investigative stance!

Here are the recommended steps:

1. Convince yourself that you should not limit your choice of location to any one area before taking this entire list into consideration.

2. Remind yourself that there are fifty states to choose from. (Trying your hand—and luck—in a foreign country might be more complicated than you would care to attempt at this stage of the game.)

3. Draw on your personal storehouse of information: What have friends, relatives, and co-workers told you about other places? What have you learned about the states from your own travels or through reading?

4. Narrow your thoughts down to two or three states where you would like to live and, more specifically, where you feel an excellent opportunity exists for the type of business you have in mind.

5. Read everything you can about these states. Write away for information about the climate, the local economy, the per capita income, the characteristics of the population, the industry, and so forth. Try to narrow down your preferences to one state.

6. Next, survey the one state you have targeted on for half a dozen areas that seem attractive. Preferably, these should be growing areas—and places where the quality of life seems to jibe with your own values.

For help at this point, you can contact the state development agency and city planning commissions, chambers of commerce, utility companies, local banks, and so forth. The latest Census of Business also provides details about the types of businesses in those areas.

7. Now the difficult work begins. You'll need to select carefully criteria by which you can evaluate the various locations and make your final decision. Judging each location by this list enables you to rank them in order from "most promising" to "least promising" for your new enterprise.

Read once more through the location factors treated in the first few pages of this chapter. Choose the criteria most appropriate for your particular business. Jot them down on a sheet of paper. You may be able to add one or two of your own that have not been listed. For example, you may decide that an important consideration for you is the quality of life in the particular community (in light of your personality, personal goals, and leisure-time preferences). Add the phrase *quality of life* to your list.

8. Prepare a chart like the one shown in exhibit 6–1 to rate or score the locations you're considering.

9. Use a simple rating scale: for example, a scale of 1 to 5 with 1 signifying a rating of "poor," as follows:

EXHIBIT 6–1. LOCATION RATING SHEET FOR A MANUFACTURING PLANT

Criteria	A	B	C	D
Accessibility to transportation				
Availability of labor				
Closeness to company's markets				
Competition				
Cost factors				
Demographics of community				
Parking facilities				
Quality of life for me				
Quality of local services				
Trading-area size				

Alternative Locations:

Source: Compiled by the author.

1 Poor
2 Fair
3 Good
4 Very good
5 Excellent

Take care to work out the rationale behind your ratings so you understand the numbers you use. For instance, in rating "Trading-area size," you would assign a 1 to a location with a limited trade area of one or two blocks around, while an extensive area might earn a 4 or 5 rating. Where competition might interfere substantially with your business in a particular location, assign a score of 1; where competition is weak or nonexistent, give a rating of 5.

10. Now rate each of the possible locations, A, B, C, and so on, working on one criterion at a time. After all criteria have been considered, total up the columns. Obviously, the location with the highest score would be the one to select. Or, so it would seem. However, there is one more step to consider.

11. In any set of criteria, some are always more important than others to you. As an example, if you're contemplating opening a retail shop, the volume of pedestrian traffic that passes by is likely to be of great importance to your business success. The demographics of the neighborhood (population mix, income characteristics, and so forth) might be much more significant than many of the other criteria on your list. If so, some of the criteria ought to be *weighted* in order to take their relative importance into account.

To accomplish this, you would assign a weight factor of 2 or 3 to one or more of the criteria (depending on their value to you) and then multiply your earlier ratings by 2 or 3 across the various locations you're considering. According to the criteria you have selected and the assigned weightings you have given them, location D in exhibit 6–2 should be your first choice, locations E and C your second and third choices.

But you're still not ready to make your final decision. Once you have ranked the six locations, you then need to consider several other aspects, such as the comparative rents you'll have to pay for the three top locations, the availability of suitable living quarters for yourself in those areas, local living costs, and so on. In other words, any one of the three might be a good choice; now you must narrow it down to the one location best suited to your needs.

BUILD, RENT, OR BUY?

Having set your sights on the best location for your proposed business, you'll now face still another major decision area: Should you build, rent, or buy the facilities you need?

EXHIBIT 6–2. Weighted Rating Sheet for Retail Locations

Criteria	Weights	Alternative Locations:					
		A	B	C	D	E	F
Competition	2	6	6	6	10	8	4
Demographics of community	3	6	3	9	12	3	9
Parking facilities	1	2	5	3	4	3	1
Quality of life for me	3	12	3	9	12	15	6
Space for future expansion	1	1	3	4	4	3	2
Trading-area size	1	3	3	1	2	4	3
Volume of traffic	3	9	3	9	12	6	12
Total Scores:		39	26	41	56	42	37

Source: Compiled by the author.

Here are just a few of the possibilities:

- There may not be a location readily available. In this case, you might consider buying out someone else's business.
- Premises—a building or a store—may indeed be available, either for rent or for sale. There's a good chance, however, that the premises may not be suitable for your purposes. A substantial and costly remodeling job might be necessary.
- If you're thinking about building, you may discover nothing more than a vacant lot (or small piece of land) obtainable in the area. This situation might require you to have suitable premises erected on the spot. Furthermore, time and cost factors must be weighed carefully.

To Build or Not to Build?

The ideal solution is to construct premises of the exact dimensions, type, architectural style, and materials that meet your every need, down to the most minute specification, with an exacting eye to the future and eventual expansion.

Among the advantages to this approach are a considerable depreciation allowance to help you curtail your tax liability each succeeding year; the benefit of being able to secure a mortgage on your property when you need to improve your cash position; and the delight of anticipating a probable, sizable capital gain when you finally dispose of the building, years later.

Of course, the big negative here is that you'll need to invest a significant chunk of capital at the very beginning. This is the time when you can least afford such an investment. There are also some real problem areas in constructing your own place of business. Experts and specialists must be consulted and closely involved every step along the way.

Why Not Rent?

Renting your business premises is comparatively easy on your firm's "pocket-book." Other than the necessity of putting down a deposit as security and paying a month or two of rent in advance, your capital remains relatively untapped. Moreover, with the help of your attorney and a cooperative landlord, you might arrange a favorable lease. As long as you continue to pay your rent regularly and live within the terms of your agreement, you'll have few problems and you'll avoid unnecessary headaches. Your landlord worries about paying insurance premiums, meeting property tax liabilities, and repairing, heating, or air conditioning the premises.

Yet, the fact that you remain a tenant does leave you vulnerable to some extent. When your lease expires, your landlord may opt for a sharp rise in your rent (unless you anticipated this situation in the wording of the original lease). You may even discover that you've lost the location to some other bidder, even though you may have built up the location over years of persistent effort.

Should You Buy?

On the other hand, if you decide to purchase the property, some of the disadvantages of renting will be eliminated. You need not worry about losing the location or about an unexpected rent increase. You will have to take into account increases in real estate taxes as time goes by. Increasing labor and maintenance costs can also put a dent in profits.

Although buying your premises necessitates a large initial investment, you can reap tax benefits through depreciation. And—as with building your own place—you can always mortgage the premises when you need cash or sell them for a healthy profit.

YOUR PREMISES—GENERAL CONSIDERATIONS

The style, construction, and overall external appearance of your business building are vital factors in the formulation, over time, of your "company image." A modern, well-maintained building has a far more favorable impact on customers, suppliers, and the general public than a seedy-looking façade.

Entrances and exits should be clearly indicated and kept free of litter. Walkways should be kept clean and in excellent repair. Lawns, hedges, shrubbery, and the like must be kept neatly trimmed and healthy looking. If at all possible, steps should be avoided. Though they may be needed because of different levels between buildings and sidewalks, steps present a psychological barrier to many people. Naturally, an attractive place of business is important to the retail enterprise because it relies heavily on passersby.

The Interior

Visualize the inside of your premises as a well-lined box or series of boxes. Walls, ceilings, and floors need to be covered by paint or other materials.

Walls serve two functions: that of lending some support to the building itself, and, more importantly, that of dividing the inside area into separate compartments for specific business activities, such as the offices and selling floor. Consequently, their thickness and composition are determined by both structural and acoustic factors. Any columns or pillars necessary to the building structure must remain intact; walls must be built around them, or else they must be incorporated into the walls.

With regard to ceilings, an attentive eye is needed for considerations like good acoustics, space requirements, proper lighting, and the like. Low ceilings convey the impression of tight, confining quarters which, in turn, can psychologically hamper employee productivity. On the other hand, high ceilings create an open, roomy environment.

Selecting proper lighting for the premises calls for the advice of a specialist. There are basically two types of lighting: fluorescent and incandescent. Both have advantages and disadvantages. Fluorescent lighting provides a high level of light intensity, does not generate much of a heat load in a room, and is relatively inexpensive in its consumption of electricity. Yet, colors often appear different under such lighting—a fact of considerable significance in a women's dress shop, for instance. Incandescent lighting, like the bulbs you burn in your table lamps at home, reveals warm, lifelike tones in clothing and other merchandise or when used to highlight special displays.

As to the flooring, consider its load-bearing capability (as in the case of a factory containing heavy machinery), its resistance to chemicals, nonskid surfaces to avoid accidents, its wearability, and so forth. Sometimes, leaving the floor totally uncovered may be more prudent. Or painting might be the solution, with a stone or cement floor in a plant or with a well-made wooden floor in a retail shop. Floor coverings range from linoleums and carpeting of many qualities and shades to an abundant variety of tiles and other materials.

SOME NOTES ON LAYOUT

In addition to the more obvious construction features mentioned above, premises planning must include staircases and stairwells, aisles, elevators, conveyors, and the like—all of which facilitate the flow of people, supplies, and merchandise. Moreover, attention must be paid to plumbing, air conditioning, heating, and sanitary facilities as well.

The critical factor in setting up a business operation is the understanding that different activities must be performed under one roof. With regard to the proper layout of your premises, this means that internal layout is largely dictated by the functions to be performed. The natural temptation is to fulfill only your immediate requirements because space always seems to be at a premium. Forgo that temptation. Even at this early stage, good business administration looks to the future—and to growth. For this reason you should consider hiring, at the outset, the services of an architect experienced in your particular field of business.

Factories and Warehouses

Most manufacturing plants and warehouses have certain activities in common. Special areas are usually needed for receiving incoming deliveries of materials (or merchandise) and supplies, for storage or stockkeeping, for performing office-type activities, and for shipping out goods. A factory must also incorporate space for production machinery and equipment, an area for cleaning materials and tools (a maintenance shop), perhaps temperature-controlled rooms for certain types of materials or goods, and so on.

In the ideal factory or wholesaler's warehouse, activities are arranged in as straight a line as possible in order to minimize the flow of materials throughout. The receiving department should be at one end of the building, where the raw materials/finished products are brought in. Here, one or more bays are needed for trucks to draw up and unload. There should also be an unloading platform and a checking area where incoming deliveries can be checked off against their bills of lading. At the building's other end, one would expect to find the shipping department where, again, bays and loading platforms are required. In between the two ends, space should be allocated to the warehoused stock (and to machinery in the case of a factory), with special areas sectioned off for office work, machine shop, loading and handling equipment, and other necessary goods and activities.

An alternate layout might be the common U shape, where both shipping and receiving departments are located at the same end of the building. This setup enables the company to avail itself of a single (or double) bay and dock. In this type of layout, stocks and supplies are stored down the center of the U.

In the final analysis, the internal layout of a manufacturing plant depends heavily on the production flow pattern used: whether the firm employs job, batch, or mass production methods. The type of production approach determines how the machinery should be arranged.

Retail Stores

In the case of the retail store, layout becomes even more important because of its direct impact on sales. Again, function largely determines the internal arrangement and contents. At the same time, you should also strive to project not only a particular "store image" but also a "merchandising environment" that will contribute effectively to sales. Proper interior design and decor can be used to create the desired setting. Thus, we may find plush carpeting, rich wall colors, and expensive chandeliers in a high-quality shoe store—or a charming Oriental decor in a Japanese restaurant.

The larger portion of the premises is usually devoted to selling activities, with additional space for workrooms and storage. Among the more important considerations here are an ample entrance, aisles that comfortably permit customer traffic (and store merchandise) to flow freely, store fixtures and displays located for maximum shopper exposure, good lighting, and an attractive decor.

The entrance should open into an unobstructed view of the selling area.

Interior design often encompasses the *grid layout,* where in-store traffic is compelled to follow a prearranged path (often, one that calls for making right-angle turns) as shoppers pass more deeply into the store. This type of setup can be readily seen in a typical supermarket or self-service drugstore or variety store. An example of the grid layout can be seen in exhibit 6–3.

Many retailers prefer this layout approach because it maximizes shopper exposure to many different products carried by the store.

Another possibility is the *free-form layout.* Here, no attempt is made to direct the flow of traffic. Shoppers can proceed in any direction. They are also able to pause easily in front of any one display for leisurely examination. Aesthetically, this type of layout is also more pleasing to consumers. Department boundaries are usually curved or irregular in shape, rather than straight, as is the case with the grid layout. (See exhibit 6–4.)

Some stores, of course, combine the basic elements of both approaches to layout.

EXHIBIT 6-3. A GRID LAYOUT

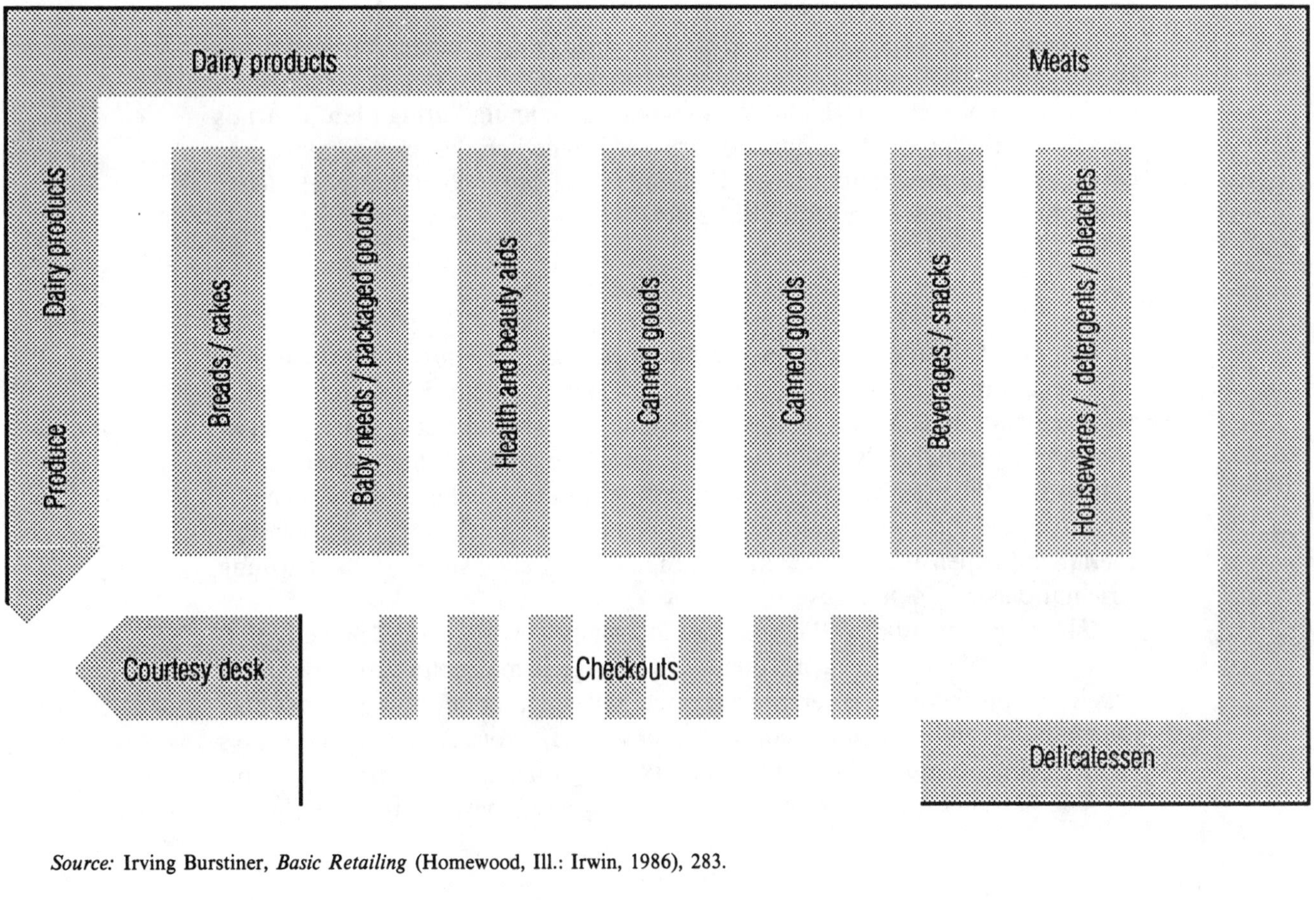

Source: Irving Burstiner, *Basic Retailing* (Homewood, Ill.: Irwin, 1986), 283.

EXHIBIT 6-4. A FREE-FORM LAYOUT

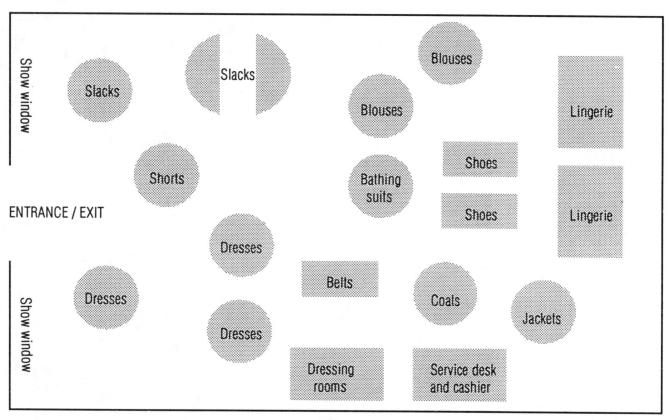

Source: Irving Burstiner, *Basic Retailing* (Homewood, Ill.: Irwin, 1986), 285.

FOR FURTHER INFORMATION

Books

Apple, James M., ed. *Plant Layout and Materials Handling,* 3d ed. New York: Wiley, 1977.

Mechlenburgh, J. C. *Process Plant Layout.* New York: Halsted Press, 1985.

Thompkins, James A., and John A. White. *Facilities Planning.* New York: Wiley, 1984.

White, John A., and Richard L. Francis. *Facility Layout and Location: An Analytical Approach.* Englewood Cliffs, N.J.: Prentice-Hall, 1974.

Pamphlets Available from the Small Business Administration

MANAGEMENT AIDS

MA 2.002—"Locating or Relocating Your Business"

MA 2.017—"Factors in Considering a Shopping Center Location"

MA 2.021—"Using a Traffic Study to Select a Retail Site"

III

MANAGING THE BUSINESS ORGANIZATION

7

An Introduction to Small Business Management

A vital component of human rationality, which distinguishes humankind from the beast, is the faculty for making order out of chaos. People must organize innumerable pieces of knowledge into usable wholes in order to function effectively in their environment. Organizing involves arranging, classifying, and systematizing, as well as thinking and planning. These processes are characteristic of individuals and of groups. Every organization or institution reflects these processes because they are established and administered by human beings. Moreover, since people are so incredibly diverse, we find that their groupings and institutions reflect countless variations in both form and substance.

THIS BUSINESS OF BUSINESS

On a purely philosophical plane, it would seem that all living things are motivated by two basic goals: the programmed will to maintain their existence (to continue to live, to protect, to defend, and when necessary, to repair themselves) and the instinct to grow, to perpetuate their kind.

Plants, animals, the tiniest of microscopic organisms, and we humans as well all possess these two essential motivations. Furthermore, all human groups display these same drives, whether they be families or social groups, religious denominations or political associations, small villages or sprawling nations.

A new business is just such a grouping, engaged in a purposeful activity and endowed with a spirit and vitality that stem from those built-in goals. It's a curious mixture of people, things, and activities. It's ideally so ordered, so arranged and woven into an intricate network, so purposeful and coordinated, that it's able to strive toward those two overriding objectives like a single, though complex, organism. Operating like a complicated piece of machinery, your new firm will be a system of individual pieces, parts, cogs, and wheels all working together toward a common endeavor: to continue its existence and to grow.

Every business is also a society in miniature with its own body of rules and regulations, its ways and customs. As in society at large, its "citizens" play out their assigned roles. A business is also a stratified—that is, a grouped and subgrouped—society that designates expected behavior for each person according to status, class, and other criteria.

To demonstrate this, think about the traditional department store organization with its hundreds of employees distributed throughout a hierarchy of power and authority. Top management includes the board of directors, its chairperson, and the corporation's president. Next is the operating management, generally a committee of assorted vice presidents heading up specialized functions of store operations, merchandising, personnel management, and others. Then there are various levels of middle and lower management including the merchandise managers, floor and department managers, buyers, salesclerks, and cashiers.

Within this society in miniature, there are two kinds of people: the leaders, who use their power and authority, skills and techniques to influence the others; and the rest, the larger number of helpers who collectively push the organization toward its objectives.

Yes, the structure and organization of your company will be integrated into a total master plan that you design to accomplish your goals. This network places people into niches, and each niche becomes a vital link in the overall effective operation of this dynamic system.

THE MEANING OF ADMINISTRATION

To administer any activity (or, for that matter, any business or institution) is to run it, to direct it, or, more simply, to manage it. From giant multinational corporations to tiny, one-person operations, *every* enterprise needs an astute administration to direct and integrate all the components: the people, the equipment, the practices and techniques applied in daily functioning, the financial aspects, and so forth.

The words *administrator, executive, leader,* and *manager* all connote similar functions, as illustrated in the following example:

> A seasoned army general is preparing for a major battle. Together with his staff officers, he first sets his objectives and then prepares a comprehensive battle plan designed to garner victory. Subsequently, he gathers, arranges, and coordinates all his *matériel de guerre:* intelligence reports; troops and their officers; tanks, guns, and ammunition; gasoline, food, and medical supplies; air cover and other support systems. (Here we see the military leader exercise two of the four basic management functions: *planning* and *organizing.*)
>
> Once the master plan has been fully devised and all elements coordinated, the general then puts the plan into action. He directs the activities as the plan

unfolds, supervising the details and evaluating the results as events occur. He does this carefully, so that any deviations from the planned outcome can be confronted as they happen, and contingency measures can be taken to bring things back into line and on target. (Here are the other two management functions in action: *directing* and *controlling.*)

With relation to your business, *you* are the general, the directing force. To administer your business successfully, you'll find that you must be continually exercising one or more of those four functions: *planning, organizing, directing,* and *controlling.*

The Management Task

You need to operate on a two-dimensional front. In the impersonal dimension you'll be engaged in activities such as setting priorities, allocating resources, scheduling, decision making, and the like. On the personal side you'll need to motivate people, train and develop their skills, counsel them, and so forth.

Both dimensions involve particular *skills* and *behavior.* All of chapter 9 is devoted to the skills of "Leadership in Management." Over the next few pages, however, the four management functions are discussed in some detail.

PLANNING

Effective management begins with planning, which in turn implies setting goals. Planning is the most important function of all in establishing and maintaining a business.

No doubt about it. Planning is hard work; it involves thinking, and thinking is always hard work. In essence, planning is problem solving and decision making: speculating on the future (both near and far), setting objectives (long- and short-range), considering alternatives, and making choices.

Planning for the future necessitates flexibility to cope with the unexpected, setting timetables, establishing priorities, and deciding on the methods to be used and the people who will be involved. As administrator you must analyze the existing situation, formulate targets, and apply both logic and creativity to all the details in between.

Owners of small-scale enterprises are typically so busy running their operations that they often shunt planning to the sidelines. Yet, its importance cannot be overemphasized! As the owner of a small business, you *must* plan for it even more intensively than the head of a large corporation because you don't have the large financial resources to cover a serious mistake. Poor planning can put you out of business.

Planning: An Introduction

Here's a list of preliminary planning activities for small business managers:

1. Explore diligently your firm's "mission," or *raison d'etre,* and clarify the purposes for which you have established it.

2. After careful discussion of these purposes, formulate your overall, long-term company goals.

3. Examine these goals, one by one, and then make a list of specific objectives to be accomplished over, say, the next five years.

4. Designate specific goals for each subdivision within your firm (such as marketing, production, finance, and personnel).

5. Decide on policies for each department, making sure they conform with those objectives.

6. Finally, outline strategies for reaching the objectives, using the available company resources.

Planning Isn't Easy

Talk to any business executive. Chances are that he or she is usually far too busy trying to surmount day-to-day problems to spend much time at all on planning. If you follow an administrator throughout the day, you'll see that person spending a great deal of time and effort doing things like visiting employees at their daily chores, chatting with them, making suggestions, and providing assistance. That's probably because it's far easier to do something of a physical nature than to think. Thinking requires lots of concentration and plenty of mental effort.

Some people are a bit suspicious about planning because they realize it has to do with the future, not the present, and the future is really unpredictable. So, they think, why bother? Furthermore, many people have never been taught how to plan and don't have the foggiest idea how to proceed. Maybe they resist the need for imposing self-discipline or don't have enough confidence in themselves. Perhaps they're reluctant to think on a conceptual plane. Perhaps they've never mastered the art of establishing priorities.

Whatever the reasons, planning is often deferred to the future. Yet, planning gives purpose and direction to daily business activities. Without it, such activities are aimless and uncoordinated.

Types of Plans

Long-term and *master* plans are set up by top management to give overall direction to company efforts. Strategic in nature, long-term plans are needed to cope with an ever-changing environment. *Operational* plans design day-to-day work details. *Single-use* plans are formulated for specific situations. *Standing* plans, on the other hand, are set up for repeated use over a longer period of time.

Company policies are examples of standing plans. They serve as guidelines for management and employees, imparting a solidarity and dependability to company operations. These policies exist in all areas of a well-administered business: in production, pricing, distribution, personnel, finance, and the like. To illustrate, consider these few examples of production policies:

- We shall manufacture only those products that enjoy a brisk sales volume (that is, over 10,000 units a month).
- We intend to add to the product line up to three new items each year.
- We shall produce only items requiring raw materials that can be purchased domestically (or from several different sources).

Budgets are plans that have been translated into dollars-and-cents projections and that are the culmination of a great deal of careful analysis. In effect, they're both guides to follow and targets to shoot for. Materials budgets and sales budgets, labor budgets, and budgets for capital expenditures—all become standards for management action. Good budgeting is needed to direct internal activity and to assign responsibility.

A Step-by-Step Approach to Planning

Using the outline offered below, plan for two or three separate events; this exercise will help you internalize the method rapidly. Practice, after all, makes perfect! It's helpful to plan for something concrete the first time around, such as a major promotion for the spring.

1. Assess the present state of affairs, external (the economy, your competition, and so on) as well as internal.

2. Set the target date for the activation of the plan.

3. Make a forecast of the future state of affairs (at the target date and thereafter, for the duration of the plan-to-be).

4. List specific objectives that are both reasonable and attainable.

5. Develop methods for reaching the objectives.

6. Work out the details by using the "Five Ws" (Who? What? Where? When? Why?)—and How? Determine your resources and structure your plan with a time schedule.

7. Commit the details to paper.

8. Set up a control system to monitor the plan's operation and to make adjustments for deviations from planned outcomes.

9. As the plan unfolds, make the necessary changes to compensate for such deviations.

Some Comments on Forecasting

Planning is disciplined thinking, which is based on the present and oriented to the future. Plans begin with an analysis of the way things are and with a forecast of the way things will (or should) be. Of course, predicting future events based on an extrapolation of current—and incomplete—information can never be entirely accurate.

Begin any major forecasting effort with a full consideration of the general state of the economy. Then move down to the next level and appraise conditions within the industry of which your firm is a member. After that, evaluate the state of the company itself.*

Among the variables affecting your forecast are such uncontrollable factors as the Gross National Product (present and future), employment and unemployment levels, productivity indexes, population trends, government policies, and the like. When you make predictions, watch the various business indicators and project accordingly: stock prices, corporate profits, wholesale price levels, and others.

Not only should you use such indexes and study trends but you should also gather opinions and interpretations from other people. You must also exercise personal judgment; for example, when you make projections for next year's sales, you should not only use the available statistics but also evaluate the capabilities of your sales force and sales manager.

ORGANIZING YOUR ORGANIZATION

As your business grows, you'll discover that along with increasing volume come additional duties and responsibilities. Eventually, you'll reach the point where you have to seek assistance so you can allocate your energies and time more beneficially to your business.

At that point, the seeds of your new organization have sprouted. Now you must pay heed to management principles like *specialization* and the *division of work.*

As each new employee is hired, he or she must be placed in an appropriate niche and assigned a specific set of duties. As the business administrator, your task is to define those niches and then locate the right people to fill them. Essentially, you must match people with jobs.

Exhibit 7–1, for example, describes some of the activities that need to be performed in a small retail business in its preorganization or one-person-operation stage. According to this chart, the owner must allocate time to three activity areas: buying, selling, and controlling finances. In addition, however, each work cluster or category involves a number of specific tasks. Buying

---

*For additional information about forecasting, see: Earl H. Anderson, "Probabilistic Forecasting for the Small Business," *Journal of Small Business Management* 17 (January 1979), 8–13; Robert S. Sobek, "A Manager's Primer on Forecasting," *Harvard Business Review* 51 (May–June 1973), 6–28; John G. Wacker and Jane S. Cromartie, "Adapting Forecasting Methods to the Small Firm," *Journal of Small Business Management* 17 (July 1979), 1–7.

merchandise for resale, for example, would include seeking out and visiting sources of supply, viewing potential items to carry in the store, negotiating prices and terms, arranging for delivery, and so forth.

At first, all these necessary functions are performed by one individual. Then, as sales increase, there's more work to be done. When the first employee, or helper, is hired, business owners are inclined to delegate very few tasks. They won't permit the newcomer to do the buying, for example, simply because experience is needed before a person can do the purchasing job well. Moreover, buying the right goods at the right prices is a major factor in the firm's profit picture, and an owner is understandably reluctant to relinquish control over this vital area.

For similar reasons, the entrepreneur usually resists turning over any of the major financial aspects of the business to the new employee. So, in most cases the employee in the typical small store is assigned to the selling function, thus affording the proprietor more time to do a better job at both purchasing and controlling finances.

The chart in exhibit 7–2 depicts the work responsibilities of a small retail company with four employees. A breakdown of the functions that may be seen in a growing manufacturing enterprise is shown in exhibit 7–3.

Over time, a company's management is increasingly challenged by the task of coordinating the activities of daily operations. Each business depends on the people within who, interlocked and strategically deployed in some structural arrangement, perform all the functions necessary for the total system to accomplish its objectives. This framework or structure called *organization* represents,

EXHIBIT 7-1. A TYPICAL SMALL RETAILER ORGANIZATION CHART

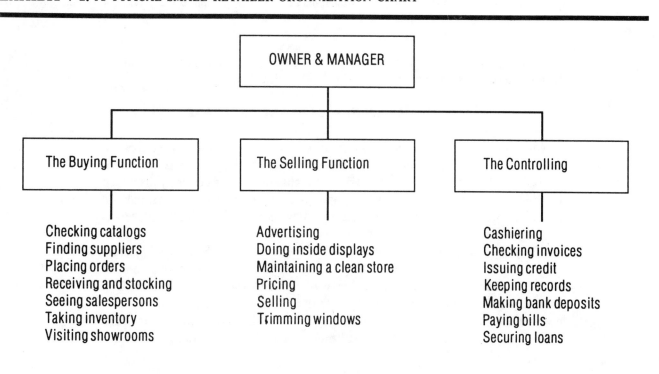

The Buying Function	The Selling Function	The Controlling
Checking catalogs	Advertising	Cashiering
Finding suppliers	Doing inside displays	Checking invoices
Placing orders	Maintaining a clean store	Issuing credit
Receiving and stocking	Pricing	Keeping records
Seeing salespersons	Selling	Making bank deposits
Taking inventory	Trimming windows	Paying bills
Visiting showrooms		Securing loans

EXHIBIT 7-2. ORGANIZATION CHART OF A SMALL RETAIL COMPANY

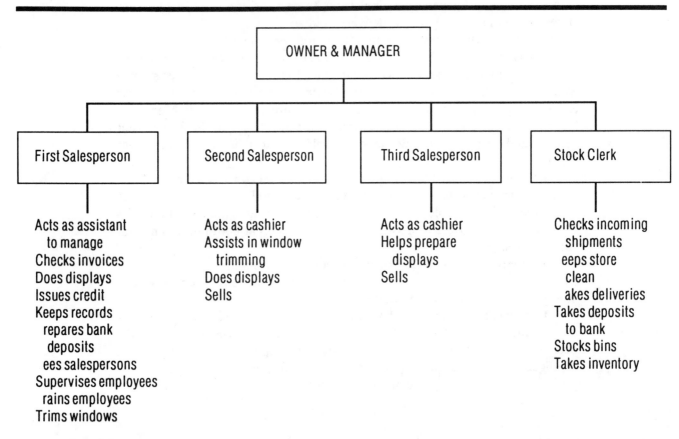

Owner can now devote more time to the buying and control functions. In addition, he or she must now oversee all the employees The owner begins to rely more heavily upon the first employee to train and supervise the others.

in actuality, the overall strategic design for operating the business. A positive, forward-looking structure, it is a unified plan of action.

Some Basics from Organization Theory

Organization is not and cannot be an exact science; theories of organization cannot specify wholly "right" answers. Nevertheless, the small business manager ought to be familiar with the dimensions that are most frequently discussed by organizational theorists. Some examples are conflict between individual and organizational goals, departmentalization, line and staff positions, flat versus tall organizations, and unity of command.

Employee Goals Can Be at Odds with Company Goals. You should recognize at the outset that people working in your organization are there primarily to satisfy their own needs. Perhaps they want security and income or the feeling that they have a place within a group, or they need to be recognized as somebody important, and so on. Although they'll work willingly toward your firm's objectives, this will happen only if their personal aims remain attainable

EXHIBIT 7-3. ORGANIZATION CHART OF A SMALL, GROWING MANUFACTURING COMPANY

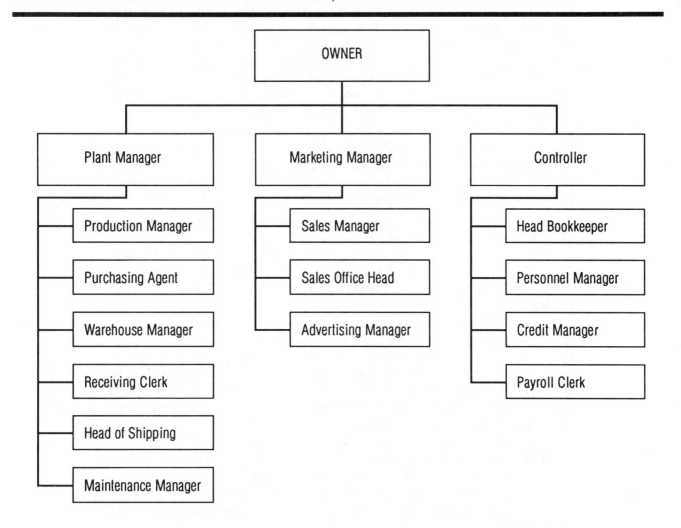

through employment with you. Their goals and yours are not identical; at times, differences between individual and group goals will result in conflict. For the sake of internal harmony, you must concentrate on reconciling any differences that arise.

The Need for Departmentalization. As anyone in business knows, a wealth of activities need to be performed by your employees. Handling these myriad tasks is made easier by classifying the many work details into departments. Departments are segments of the business whose work functions are interrelated and so can be grouped together under the supervision of a single specialist. In addition to the sales, production, and bookkeeping departments, other departments commonly seen in business include purchasing, shipping, receiving, payroll, and advertising.

Line and Staff Personnel. Most organizations have been arranged according to the *line-and-staff* concept. Line people both give and receive orders along the chain of command from the head of the company down to the lowest-level worker. People in staff positions, on the other hand, are outside this chain of command. They are present to aid and support the line personnel. Examples of these staffers include administrative assistants, legal advisors, personnel department employees, and other supportive service workers. These people possess a much more limited kind of authority. Within their own specialized areas of responsibility, of course, they direct their own department personnel.

Should Your Organization Be Flat or Tall? As a business grows, the organizational structure shows layers of authority: top, middle, and lower (supervisory) management. Communication barriers tend to form between the layers. People at the top of the hierarchy tend to have little contact with people at the bottom. In the traditional "tall" structure, people become relatively confined within their own specialized positions, and dissatisfaction begins to emerge from persons in middle and lower positions. Broadly interpreted, their feeling is that they're not really making a significant contribution to the business. This attitude spreads or deepens, and decisions tend more and more to be made at the top and filtered down to the bottom levels.

Furthermore, management positions multiply. The organization gradually becomes laden with many chiefs and high salaries. A kind of rigidity sets in that mitigates against creative problem solving and results in an overabundance of red tape.

In the "flat" type of organization, on the other hand, there are only one or two levels of management. The supervisory leadership exercised by the executives is of a more personal nature, with more face-to-face contact. People in lower management niches take on more responsibility for their efforts and make more decisions. The fact that these individuals are closer to the action than higher management and are permitted to make decisions on the spot makes for increased initiative and higher morale.

One Boss or More? The *unity of command* principle is one policy that should seldom be violated. Most workers would agree that no employee, indeed no executive, should have to answer to more than one superior. Having more than one supervisor can cause confusion, as, for example, where an employee working within a partnership arrangement is given two opposing directives by the partners.

How Many Subordinates Can You Handle? The principle here is referred to as *span of management* (or *span of control*). The average manager finds it relatively easy to oversee one to several workers on the job: to watch over them, train them, direct them, and guide them. As the number of subordinates increases, it becomes more and more difficult for the supervisor to devote enough attention to each person.

How many people a supervisor can oversee depends on several factors: the supervisor's capabilities; the abilities and characteristics of the subordinates; and the nature of the work being performed. The greater the span of management (that is, the number of individuals under one superior), the fewer the number of supervisors and departments necessary. A narrow span, however, enables supervisors to work more closely with their people.

The average small business owner can often manage up to six or eight subordinates before things become too unwieldy.

Decentralization. As a business grows, the mass of work details increases.

Yet it's hard for the entrepreneurial personality to delegate, to let go of the responsibilities so far handled alone, and to assign them to people who he or she fears are less capable and less motivated!

Some managers keep a firm grasp on everything. They maintain home offices where power, authority, and tight supervisory controls are centralized. Others decentralize to the point where a capable group, to a large degree autonomous, manages each major division of the business. This concept of decentralization—organizing a firm around self-governing "profit centers" banded together in a loosely controlled federation—maximizes individual initiative, ensures localized decision making, and facilitates the pinpointing of responsibility.

A Method for Delegating Work

Eventually the very existence of your business will depend on relinquishing some of the details to assistants. You'll be faced with the problem of delegation. Here are some guidelines suggested by the Small Business Administration to assist owners in delegating work:

- Do it slowly.
- Give your employees facts to work with.
- Share your knowledge.
- Add responsibility gradually.
- Keep a loose rein.
- Give authority.
- Tolerate mistakes.
- Train your employees well.

DIRECTING

After you've prepared the plan and organized the necessary components (personnel, finances, methods and procedures, materials, and so on), you're ready to put the plan into action and direct it. Directing really tests the mettle of the operating executive. This is the "hands-on" point. Until now the administrative activity has been mostly in the mind of the planner(s). Now you're involved in a one-to-one "contact sport." The people in your organization must be motivated, persuaded, led, coordinated, encouraged, and so on. Involved here are concepts like teamwork, supervision, and productivity. For the most part, these concepts constitute the subject matter of chapter 9, so little more needs to be said about them at this point.

CONTROLLING

An analysis of the controlling function would seem to indicate the need for measuring results all along the way while the plan is unfolding, as well as the necessity for making adjustments where and when needed. Logically, the control function cannot be separated from the planning function; they are interdependent, much like the two sides of the same coin.

Controlling is a process that includes analysis, setting standards, monitoring, securing feedback, and taking corrective action. (See exhibit 7–4.)

1. *Analysis:* Study and compare, for quantity and quality, the output of people and machines, the products made, the systems employed, and so forth. Examine everything with a careful eye to standards and decision making.

2. *Setting Standards:* As a result of analysis, establish acceptable standards of performance in all areas. In turn, these standards become control valves, quantitative and qualitative measurements for future performance, guidelines for projecting cost, time, and sales.

3. *Monitoring:* You need regular inspection and performance checks to note exceptions to the standards you've set and possible reasons for the deviations.

4. *Securing Feedback:* A foolproof system for reporting deviations from standards must be established so that the proper people are notified regularly and promptly.

5. *Corrective Action:* Finally, all exceptions to the established standards must be acted on. Adjustments need to be made promptly so that contingent outcomes are brought back on target.

EXHIBIT 7-4. Controlling: the process

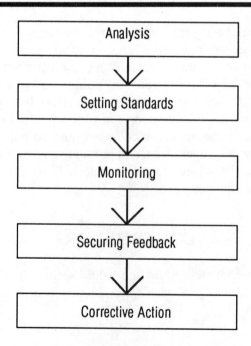

All areas of a business must be subject to this control function. You might think quite readily of inventory control, order processing, quality control, and production control. Yet controls are just as necessary in the personnel area (for example, in performance evaluation); in the financial end of things (where ratios can be used to investigate a variety of problems); in the long-term planning of projects; and so forth.

For control is, in essence, self-discipline.

THE ROLE OF COMMUNICATION

Businesses run on communication. Prospective customers are located, contacted, and persuaded to buy products and services through communication. Similarly, employees are found, hired, trained, and directed; departments are managed; machines are manned and operated. Communication is the oil that lubricates the various gears and cogs in the free-enterprise system.

Let's examine the process of communication in business. There are a number of components involved. Indeed, communication in business appears to be a closed system with all parts interacting in synergistic fashion. The major elements may be seen in exhibit 7–5, which simplifies a company's external communications with its customers.

Some essential parts of the communication system are

- *Source:* the sender or originator of the messages
- *Messages:* information emitted by the source and directed to the receivers

EXHIBIT 7-5. EXTERNAL COMMUNICATIONS DIAGRAM

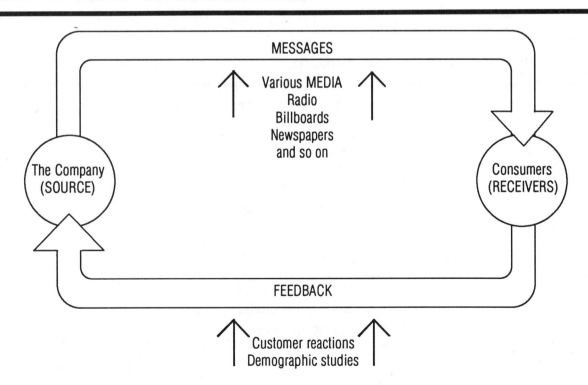

- *Media:* the various carriers or transmitters of the messages (such as radio, newspapers, billboards, and so on)
- *Receivers:* those for whom the messages are intended
- *Feedback:* customer reactions, demographic information, and other facts returned by or drawn back from customers to assist management in its decision making

Improvements within any of these areas—for example, in the quality of messages sent or the refinement or elaboration of the feedback process—improve the productivity of the entire communication system.

Applied to a firm's internal organization, the communications picture looks something like the diagram in exhibit 7–6. Messages (orders, instructions, and the like) are passed down from the top to lower levels, through verbal and written communications. Feedback moves upward, completing the system. Of course, the effectiveness of this internal system also depends on unimpeded horizontal communication on each individual level.

Unfortunately, poor communication is commonly observed within organizations, perhaps due to the pressures of day-to-day details, which often make communicating on a one-to-one, face-to-face basis nearly impossible.

As a business owner, you should make certain that all messages to employees are couched in terms that can be clearly understood and that convey your (or your supervisors') exact meaning. To accomplish this, learn to look at things from the employees' point of view and become familiar with their vocabulary. Moreover, good listening skills constitute an important asset in communication; half-hearted listening interferes considerably with effective management. Encourage your employees to listen, too. Make sure they understand your instructions, and encourage them to ask questions.

As a final point, train all your supervisory personnel to be effective communicators, too.

EXHIBIT 7-6. INTERNAL COMMUNICATIONS DIAGRAM

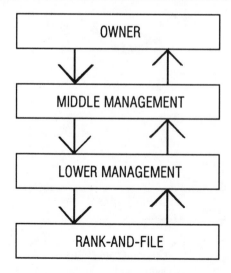

FOR FURTHER INFORMATION

Books

Adelstein, Michael E., and W. Keats Sparrow. *Business Communications.* San Diego, Cal.: Harcourt Brace Jovanovich, 1983.

Albrecht, Karl. *Successful Management by Objectives.* Englewood Cliffs, N.J.: Prentice-Hall, 1978.

Donnelly, James H., Jr., James L. Gibson, and John M. Ivancevich. *Fundamentals of Management: Functions, Behaviors, Models,* 5th ed. Plano, Tex.: Business Publications, 1984.

Lawless, David J. *Organizational Behavior: The Psychology of Effective Management,* 2d ed. Englewood Cliffs, N.J.: Prentice-Hall, 1979.

Mescon, Michael H., Michael Albert, and Franklin Khedouri. *Individual and Organizational Effectiveness.* New York: Harper & Row, 1985.

Reitz, H. Joseph. *Behavior in Organizations,* rev. ed. Homewood, Ill.: Irwin, 1981.

Stoner, James A. *Management,* 3d ed. Englewood Cliffs, N.J.: Prentice-Hall, 1986.

Terry, George R., and Stephen G. Franklin. *Principles of Management,* 8th ed. Homewood, Ill.: Irwin, 1982.

Williams, J. Clifton. *Human Behavior in Organizations,* 2d ed. Cincinnati: South-Western, 1982.

———, Andrew J. Du Brin, and Henry Sisk. *Management and Organization,* 5th ed. Cincinnati: South-Western, 1985.

Pamphlets Available from the Small Business Administration

MANAGEMENT AIDS

MA 2.004—"Problems in Managing a Family-Owned Business"
MA 2.007—"Business Plan for Small Manufacturers"
MA 2.008—"Business Plan for Small Construction Firms"
MA 2.010—"Planning and Goal Setting for Small Business"
MA 2.020—"Business Plan for Small Retailers"
MA 2.022—"Business Plan for Small Service Firms"
MA 3.010—"Techniques for Problem Solving"
MA 5.009—"Techniques for Productivity Improvement"

Booklets Available from the Superintendent of Documents

S/N 045-000-00185-7—*Job Analysis, Job Specifications, and Job Descriptions*—$4.50.
S/N 045-000-00186-5—*Recruiting and Selecting Employees*—$4.50.

8

The Management of
Human Resources

In the beginning, the prudent entrepreneur operates alone, perhaps with the assistance of one or two family members. New business owners are usually apprehensive about adding employees, realizing that to do so would add substantially to the overhead costs that they are trying so hard to hold down. Indeed, when the situation finally does demand additional help, often the entrepreneur's immediate reaction is to hire part-timers.

Employees are, of course, a major resource of a firm. Hiring the right people—and training them well—can often mean the difference between scratching out the barest of livelihoods and steady business growth.

Incidentally, personnel problems do not discriminate between small and big business. You find them in all businesses, regardless of size. Usually, new entrepreneurs have had little prior experience with any personnel activities. Staffing, for example, is often done on the combined bases of personal judgment and intuition. New business owners have also probably had little exposure to good supervisory practices unless, by chance, they were fortunate enough to have worked under an excellent supervisor in some past position. Most likely, they're totally unfamiliar with such things as personnel recordkeeping, labor legislation, and union relations (from an employer's point of view). Exhibit 8–1 offers a basic overview of the modern personnel function.

In small-scale enterprises, a closeness often develops rapidly between owners and their employees. This is natural. In time, employers get to know each worker fairly well. Dependency relationships on the employees' part may develop. However, when a company grows to the point where, for instance, there are eight or ten employees "on the books," these relationships have usually multiplied so tremendously that much of the initial owner-employee contact and closeness have begun to fade. Indeed, by this time, owners may have

EXHIBIT 8-1. ACTIVITIES IN THE PERSONNEL ADMINISTRATION AREA

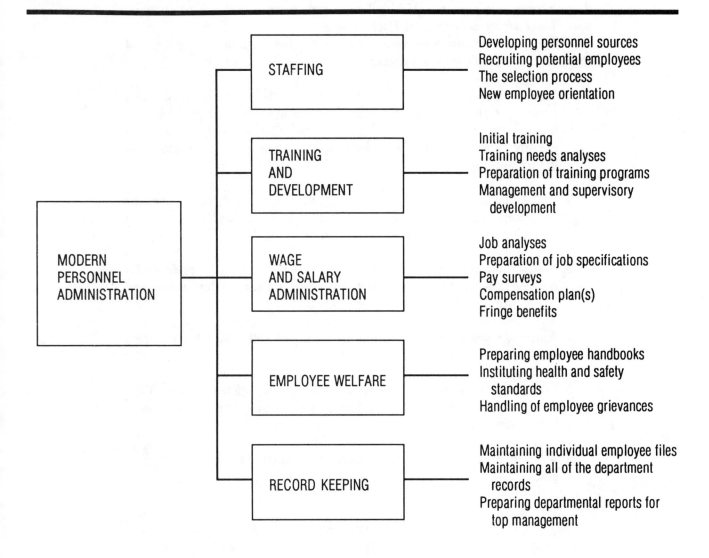

interposed one or two layers of intermediate management between them and their rank and file.

HUMAN RESOURCES PLANNING FOR THE SMALL COMPANY

Like any other phase of your business, the human resources dimension requires your top management skills. You need to set goals, to plan and organize, and so on. At the heart of your personnel planning will lie considerations such as how to allocate your human resources to maximum advantage and how to control total labor costs.

When the firm is new and small, there's little immediate need for long-range thinking about personnel. Add people slowly, at least for the first year or so of operation. Thereafter, as soon as you can, you should devise a system for human resources planning (HRP). Nowadays, many companies of all types have successfully implemented HRP programs.

When the time comes for integrating such a system into your business, I recommend the following approach:

1. Take an inventory of your current employees. Set down on paper their present job titles and descriptions. Review and assess past performance, listing both their strengths and weaknesses. (This analysis can help you identify those who show promise and can, some day, be promoted to higher positions.)

2. Determine the organizational changes your business will require over the next few years. Project the types and numbers of people you'll need to fill all niches in the organizational structure.

3. Match these positions with the people you have on hand. Decide which positions you can fill with your own employees (when the time is ripe) and which will have to be filled by new hires.

4. Anticipate some degree of employee turnover and adjust future needs accordingly.

5. Bear in mind that people have to be "phased in" to new positions. They must be trained for some time before they can be expected to perform at a satisfactory level.

6. At all times, keep a careful watch over recruitment, selection, and training costs.

The Turnover Problem

One fact of life you'll have to live with is employee turnover. Every business has it. Some firms lose people at a faster rate than others, but whatever the turnover rate, it always hurts to lose a good employee (financially, as well as psychologically).

There are initial costs involved in locating, interviewing, hiring, and training an employee to the point where he or she reaches full potential. Then, there are intermediate costs of doing without that person until a replacement is found. Still more expenses are incurred in acquiring the replacement.

People leave their jobs for a variety of reasons. Some leave unexpectedly and for unavoidable reasons: ill health, death, marriage, relocation, and deliberate terminations for due cause. Some losses are avoidable. They may be caused by poor supervisory practices on the part of owners or middle managers, by internal friction and personality clashes, by management's failure to provide proper incentives or an opportunity to move up the ladder, and so forth.

When any employee leaves, an exit interview should be conducted and the results recorded. A review of the findings will be useful to management in taking corrective action to reduce the turnover rate. This step becomes more valuable as the company grows.

SETTING PERSONNEL POLICIES

Few small enterprises can afford even a fledgling personnel department during the first few years of business operation. Nevertheless, a large mass of personnel forms and data generally accumulates rather rapidly from the very beginning. To hold problems to a minimum, specific personnel policies should be established as early as possible. These become useful guides in all areas: recruitment and selection, compensation plan and employee benefits, training, promotions and terminations, and the like. All attendant systems and paperwork should be carefully designed and personnel files set up to hold application forms, testing and medical records, evaluation forms, changes in status, and so forth.

One practical activity that can help in setting policy is the preparation of job descriptions for all positions in your firm. Analyze each position in detail and then set down on paper the specific job title, the duties and responsibilities assigned, the relationships with other segments of the business, and any other relevant details. (This information will help you write up job specifications for every opening that comes up.) In addition to the information already mentioned, add the special qualifications needed by the jobholder, such as the levels of education and experience required, familiarity with special equipment, minimum physical requirements (if these are pertinent), and so on.

A sample job description can be seen in exhibit 8–2.

THE STAFFING PROCESS

Broadly interpreted, the staffing process includes any activities pertinent to the recruitment and selection of employees. Pinning down details and correct procedures in advance prevents errors later on that can cause trouble and expense.

Personnel Sources

You need to explore and develop the potential of a variety of sources for future employees. Here's a listing of the more common avenues for you to pursue:

- Advertising through classified and display advertisements in newspapers, radio advertising
- Advertising through posted announcements, window signs, and other "point-of-need" methods
- Recommendations (referrals) from others: friends, employees, acquaintances, and the like
- Schools and universities: vocational, academic, technical, business
- Employment agencies: public, private

EXHIBIT 8-2. A SAMPLE JOB DESCRIPTION

JOB TITLE:	SERVICE AND SAFETY SUPERVISOR		
DIVISION:	Plastics	D.O.T. CODE:	889.133–010
DEPARTMENT:	Manufacturing	EEO-1 AAP CATAGORIES:	1/2
SOURCE(S):	John Doe	WAGE CATAGORY:	Exempt
JOB ANALYST:	John Smith	VERIFIED BY:	Bill Johnson
DATA ANALYZED:	5/26/83	DATE VERIFIED:	6/5/83

JOB SUMMARY

The SERVICE AND SAFETY SUPERVISOR works under the direction of the IMPREGNATING & LAMINATING MANAGER: **schedules** labor pool employees; **supervises** work of gardeners, cleaners, waste disposal and plant security personnel; **coordinates** plant safety programs; **maintains** daily records on personnel, equipment and scrap.

JOB DUTIES AND RESPONSIBILITIES

1. **Schedules** labor pool employees to provide relief personnel for all manufacturing departments: **prepares** assignment schedules and **assigns** individuals to departments based on routine as well as special needs in order to maintain adequate labor levels throughout the plant; **notifies** Industrial Relations Department weekly about vacation and layoff status of labor pool employees, contractual disputes, and other employment-related developments.
2. **Supervises** the work of gardeners, cleaners, waste disposal and plant security personnel; **plans** yard, clean-up, and security activities based on weekly determination of needs; **assigns** tasks and responsibilities to employees on a daily basis; **monitors** progress or status os assigned tasks; **disciplines** employees as necessary in accordance with labor contracts.
3. **Coordinates** plant safety programs: **teaches** basic first-aid procedures to security, supervisory, and lead personnel in order to maintain adequate coverage of medical emergencies; **trains** employees in fire fighting and hazardous materials handling procedures; **verifies** plant compliance with new or changing OSHA regulations; **represents** division during company-wide safety programs and meetings.
4. **Maintains** daily records on personnel, equipment, and scrap: reports ammount of waste and scrap to cost accounting department; updates personnel records as necessary; **reviews** maintenance checklists for towmotors.
5. **Performs** other miscellaneous duties as assigned.

JOB REQUIREMENTS

1. Ability to apply basic principles and techniques of supervision.
   a) Knowledge of principles and techniques of supervision.
   b) Ability to plan and organize the activities of others.
   c) Ability to get ideas accepted and to guide a group or individual to accomplish a task.
   d) Ability to modify leadership style and management approach to reach a goal.
2. Ability to express ideas clearly both in written and oral communications.
3. Knowledge of recent Red Cross first-aid procedures.
4. Knowledge of OSHA regulations as they affect plant operations.
5. Knowledge of labor pool jobs, company policies, and labor contracts.

MINIMUM QUALIFICATIONS

Twelve years of general education or equivalent; and one year supervisory experience;
and first-aid instructor's certification.

OR

Substitute 45 hours classroom supervisory training for supervisory experience.

JOB SPECIFICATIONS

1. KNOWLEDGE: Knowledge of supervisory principles/techniques; knowledge of first-aid procedures sufficient to teach others; familiarity with federal safety regulations.
2. Mental Application: Applies effective principles of supervision to direct and motivate employees.
3. Accountability: Directly supervises the work of up to 25 laborers and security personnel; responsible for insuring proper towmotor maintenance.

- Agencies that provide temporary help
- People who just drop by or write in for positions
- Unions

The Selection of Personnel

Among the tools available to help you decide who to hire and who to reject are the employment application, the employment interview, the reference check, tests, and the probationary or tryout period for new employees.

The Employment Application. Ask prospective employees to complete an employment application. Standard application forms are available at your local business stationery store; they accommodate the applicant's name, address, and telephone number, a history of prior work experiences, educational preparation, health and financial information, and personal data. Or, you can devise your own form by thinking through the kinds of information you need.

Generally, you can save both time and expense by using a preliminary "short form," or "screening" application. This is a modified version of the larger application form, often a small, 4-by-5-inch printed slip with room for only a few pertinent details: the applicant's name and address and the mandatory job specifications you've outlined in advance for a particular position. Assume, for instance, that you've run a classified ad in the local paper announcing a single opening at your place, and the ad draws twenty to twenty-five applicants. You can have them complete the shorter form quite easily since it only requires several minutes to fill out. You can then make a quick decision as to who does or does not have the qualifications you seek. This way you rapidly narrow down the crowd to just a few persons who can remain for interviews. If one of the requirements is, for example, two years of previous experience in a similar position, it's simple to accomplish this preselection quickly.

Short-form applications can also serve as a resource list for you; that is, a source of future employees if openings develop for which these individuals are more suited.

The Employment Interview. An interview is usually the next step. The employment interview is one of the major tools in the processing of job applicants. Essentially, it has two aims: (1) to elicit information to supplement the facts submitted on the application form; and (2) to gain useful insights into the appearance, behavior, and personality of the prospective employee.

Because it's comparatively easy for an interviewer to be overly influenced by an outstanding characteristic of an applicant, it's wise to develop and use an interview rating form that touches on all important areas. This will help you objectify your assessment of an individual. Of course, the more you interview people—and the more you read about how to interview in books on human resources administration—the better you'll be at it!

Interviews can be patterned and directive. This means you plan out your approach in advance—that is, the kinds of questions you intend to ask, the order in which you'll ask them, what in particular you'll be looking for, and so forth. Interviews can also be nondirective: Here, the basic approach is to refrain from doing much talking and to encourage the interviewee to speak at length.

Well-trained personnel interviewers often look for "knock-out factors," the presence of certain undesirable characteristics or symptoms that in and of themselves are sufficient cause for turning down an applicant. Among the more commonly employed "knock-out factors" are

- Evidence of frequent job-hopping in the past
- Excessive indebtedness
- Poor communicative ability
- Poor emotional control
- Too high a standard of living
- Unexplained gaps in the employment record*

Reference Checks. As a general rule, you should make it your business to check personally all references offered by job applicants. A simple form letter and questionnaire can be devised to cover the major points in which you are interested. Or you can contact former employers and other references by telephone. This method is often preferable, not only for quicker results but also because many people are reluctant to put negative comments down in writing. At times, telephone checking is useful in that any hesitancy about the person in question can be discerned quite readily and probed diplomatically during the conversation.

Tests. On the whole, most smaller companies do not test job applicants except when a position requires special skills. Measures of typing speed and accuracy (or stenographic skill), arithmetic and spelling tests for clerical employees, tests of manual dexterity for certain occupations, and demonstrations of ability to run specialized equipment (such as lathes) all come under this classification.

Some firms make use of a variety of paper-and-pencil tests to aid in their selection processes. These range from intelligence tests and general knowledge measures to personality batteries, tests of selling ability, and so forth. These tests are expensive to use and are generally not recommended until a business has grown to a substantial size. Their most valuable contribution is probably in screening out applicants with personality defects or below-average intelligence.

However, many managements shy away from testing because of anxiety over conforming to the intent of equal employment opportunity laws. Tests used must be demonstrably both valid and reliable.

Medical Examinations. These can, of course, be helpful, especially where a position requires frequent physical effort. In some localities, such examinations are mandated by law. (Food handlers, for example, must be licensed.) However, when paid for by the employer, these tests can be quite expensive, especially if the number of employees is considerable.

Orientation. The first few days on the job are crucial to the newly hired person. This is when favorable or unfavorable work-related attitudes are formed and when the employee is either turned on or off. Of course, when you

*Irving Burstiner, "Current Personnel Practices in Department Stores," *Journal of Retailing* 51 (Winter 1975–76), 8–9.

assign an individual to his or her section, you must make sure the person receives some initial instruction—namely, about the company itself, the particular department, and the nature of the work. In addition, it is helpful to appoint an experienced member of the department to coach the new employee.

In this same context, a well-prepared employee handbook can be extremely valuable. The "Sample Table of Contents" in exhibit 8–3 presents a range of topics that you could include in your firm's handbook.

Probationary Period. Actually, the final phase of the selection process (once an individual has been assigned to a post) should be a probationary or tryout period of a few weeks or months. This trial period is a valuable step; it will ensure that you haven't made an erroneous decision. During this time, the new worker should be observed and frequently rated. It's far more difficult to discharge a below-average performer after many months have elapsed, especially if your company has been unionized.

TRAINING

An estimated \$30 billion to \$40 billion are spent annually for employee training in both the public and private sectors.* The training function is a vital, ongoing activity that requires your attention as the owner of a small business. Employees need and want training not only to perform their jobs satisfactorily but also as preparation for eventual promotion. Indeed, you owe it to yourself even more than to your employees to make sure they are well trained. Proper training alleviates a good many unnecessary headaches.

Here are a few of the advantages that can result when people are well trained:

- Better employee morale
- Increased sales
- Less waste
- Lower turnover rate
- Increased productivity
- Reduced operational costs
- Speedier employee development

Often, a new employee receives adequate initial training but is thereafter expected to "go it alone." In a healthy business operation, training should be continuous. No clerical worker, salesperson, machine operator, or bookkeeper ever attains 100 percent efficiency or output at his or her job; there's always room for improvement. Moreover, every worker should have the opportunity to move up the ladder; this implies training for a new and higher position. Frankly, there's a substantial difference between satisfactory performance and performance that is outstanding. We're not necessarily talking here about a 5 percent or 10 percent difference; in some cases, productivity can be doubled or

---

*Robert L. Craig and Christine J. Evers, "Training for Small Business," *Small Business Bibliography No. 86* (Washington: Small Business Administration, October 1981 reprint), 2.

EXHIBIT 8-3. A SAMPLE TABLE OF CONTENTS FOR AN EMPLOYEE HANDBOOK

Employee Handbook
SAMPLE TABLE OF CONTENTS

1 - WELCOME MESSAGE

2 - HISTORY OF THE COMPANY

3 - THIS IS YOUR BUSINESS

4 - YOU AND YOUR FUTURE

5 - WHAT YOU NEED TO KNOW

> **Working hours**
> **Reporting to Work**
> **"Time Clock"**
> **Rest Periods**
> **Absence from Work**
> **Reporting Absences**
> **Employment Record**
> **Pay Period**
> **Shift Premiums**
> **Safety and Accident Prevention**
> **Use of Telephones**
> **How to Air Complaints**

6 - THESE ARE YOUR BENEFITS

> **Vacations**
> **Holidays**
> **Group Insurance**
> **Hospitalization & Surgical Benefits**
> **Free Parking**
> **Training Program**
> **Christmas Bonus**
> **Savings Plan**
> **Profit-sharing Plan**
> **Suggestion Awards**
> **Jury Duty**
> **Military Leave**
> **U.S. Old Age Benefits**
> **Unemployment Compensation**
> **Equal Employment Opportunity**

7 - THESE SPECIAL SERVICES ARE FOR YOU

> **Credit Union**
> **Education Plans**
> **Medical Dispensary**
> **Employee Purchases**
> **Company Cafeteria**
> **Monthly Magazine**
> **Annual Outing**
> **Bowling League**
> **Baseball Team**

8 - INDEX *or* TABLE OF CONTENTS

Reproduced from "Pointers on Preparing an Employee Handbook," *Management Aid No. 197* (Washington, D.C.: Small Business Administration, 1975), 3.

even tripled. As a case in point, there are always a few star performers in any sizable sales force who far outstrip the others in the production of sales.

In a small new enterprise, most training occurs on the job; that is, the immediate supervisor is held responsible for training the worker. But as a business grows, the need for more thorough and professional training becomes evident. It's never too early to begin making plans for better training in the future, if only to fill additional niches as they open up in the organizational hierarchy. This is preferable to hiring supervisors and managers from the outside, usually at a higher cost.

A careful *needs analysis* of your organization and all the people in it should be the first step in coordinating your training efforts.

A Checklist for Your Training Program

The Small Business Administration recommends taking the following steps when establishing a major training program:

1. Make a needs assessment of your company on a departmental, section, and unit basis.
2. Set the objectives to be accomplished through your training efforts.
3. Determine the curriculum (subject matter). Make certain you include not only product, company, and customer knowledge but also skills development and personal adjustment training.
4. Select the types of training that best serve your purposes.
5. Select the training methods to be used.
6. Set up a timetable and schedule for your program.
7. Select the instructor(s).
8. Watch your costs.

Training Methods and Techniques

A wide variety of training methods and techniques are available for your purposes. Among the more frequently used approaches are lectures, small-group discussions, seminars, conferences, case analyses, programmed instruction, committee work, and role-playing. Of course, the most commonly found method is on-the-job training; variations of this approach include apprenticeships and internships.

For employees pegged for eventual promotion to management levels, there are still other useful techniques: job rotation, in-basket methods (exercises to help one learn how to set priorities among various tasks), special project assignments, management games, sensitivity training, outside training (at local universities or by trade associations), and so on.

WAGE AND SALARY ADMINISTRATION

Wage and salary administration is another significant segment within the human resources management sphere. This area involves setting up and then overseeing the operation of a comprehensive compensation plan to cover all of your employees.

As a point of information only, the term *wages* is usually applied to payment for employee services rendered on an hourly, daily, or piecework basis. It's often used in connection with the earnings of day laborers, other manual workers, and workers on factory production belts. On the other hand, *salary* generally refers to compensation paid out on a weekly (or semimonthly, monthly, and so on) basis, and describes the earnings of office personnel, supervisors, and other "white-collar" employees.

An employee's pay depends, of course, on the levels of education and experience, the skills, and the knowledge needed to do the job. In a large organization, all positions are generally grouped according to different types and levels of work and then arranged in a hierarchy according to levels of authority and responsibility. The jobs are then compared with similar positions in the particular industry. Pay scales are then set at the average prevailing rates for those positions. In a new small business, however, the prevalent approach is simply to "meet the competition" (which, if you think about it, is much the same thing!).

As we know, people do expect to earn more over time. Every worker wants an occasional raise. It's therefore a good idea to establish a fixed compensation range for each and every position in the company—that is, a minimum or starting rate, and a maximum (or *cap*). It is also helpful to initiate a personnel evaluation program whereby all employees are reviewed periodically and pay increases are contingent on satisfactory performance.

Compensating Employees

To pay your employees, you can choose from the three basic compensation plans commonly seen in industry: the regular (or "straight") salary approach, the commission-only plan, and the combination plan.

Regular Salary Plan. This is by far the most popular compensation approach. Under this plan, you pay the employee a stated amount each and every week (or on some other regular basis). Most employees like this kind of arrangement because they appreciate the sense of security derived from a steady income to pay for their food, rent, and so on.

Management, too, usually prefers the regular salary plan because of its simplicity and because it enables them to know their labor costs in advance and budget accordingly. On the negative side, paying a steady salary does little to encourage above-average effort. When a person's salary remains the same regardless of the amount of work performed (or sales produced), there obviously exists little incentive to "try harder." (Of course, if an employee is *too* far under par, the possibility of losing the job does provide some motivation to work at an acceptable level!)

Commission-Only Plan. Some companies follow the philosophy that their salespeople should be paid only if they deliver sales. Under the commission-only plan, the employee receives a specified percentage of the sales dollars he or she brings in. The rate of commission paid is dependent on (among other things) the type of industry and the nature of the selling job required.

The major advantage of the commission-only approach is that it provides a substantially high level of motivation for many sales employees. While sales costs tend to fluctuate with economic conditions and with productivity, paying more dollars in commission can only mean that the firm is earning higher profits simultaneously. Expressed as a percentage of the sales volume, this cost remains a constant.

Top sales producers seem to like this method. Indeed, many of them do not want to work on any other basis. Of course, there are drawbacks to be considered as well. When earnings depend entirely on sales productivity, people on a commission-only basis sometimes tend to sell more aggressively, possibly generating unfavorable customer reactions. Under this plan, too, a company may find it more difficult to get its sales representatives to perform other necessary, nonselling activities.

More properly classified as a *combination plan,* a variation of the commission-only approach is the *guaranteed-draw-against-commission* approach. Under this compensation method, the firm is willing to advance several hundreds of dollars each week to a salesperson as an advance against future commissions in order to meet daily expenses.

Combination Plans. These plans are designed to incorporate the more desirable features (from management's point of view) of both the regular salary and the commission-only approaches, in an attempt to have the best of both worlds. Although there are a number of variations, the most common is the *salary-plus-commission* method: The company furnishes a basic, steady salary each week that is designed to meet the employee's needs, and then a small percentage of actual sales is earned as a commission. Often, this latter amount is paid monthly. This combination approach guarantees the salesperson some funds for paying current expenses and provides some type of override that will induce the employee to try harder.

Fringe Benefits

All the "extras" that firms have added to the basic compensation of their employees over the years amount to a sizable cost factor today. For the average company, these financial "fringe benefits," which are now expected by employees, can add another 30 percent or more to wages and salaries. (Note that we're not discussing those costs required by law, such as the firm's contribution to the Social Security system.) Small firms are cautioned against adopting these fringe benefits too quickly and too freely. Some are almost mandatory if an organization is to compete effectively for personnel against other firms in the industry. Other fringe benefits, while perhaps desirable, should be postponed until the company is in a strong, healthy position.

Some of these benefits are listed below, in no particular order:

vacation with pay	health insurance
paid holidays	retirement plan
pay for jury duty	awards and prizes
emergency loans	recreational activities
life insurance	medical examinations
severance pay	profit sharing
employee lunchroom	accident insurance

performance bonuses	use of company car
uniforms	tuition reimbursement
employee discounts	social events

FEDERAL LABOR LEGISLATION

Since the mid-1930s, a number of important federal laws have been enacted on behalf of employees. As a result, business owners need to make certain that all facets of personnel administration within their organizations conform to existing regulations.

A list of the more important federal acts appears in table 8–1.

TABLE 8–1. FEDERAL LABOR LEGISLATION

Year	Title	Major Thrust
1935	The National Labor Relations Act (also called the Wagner Act)	Designed to counter unfair practices on the part of employers (in the Depression years) and to reduce industrial unrest, this law gives employees the right to organize and to engage in collective bargaining. It also established the National Labor Relations Board.
1938	The Fair Labor Standards Act (once known as the Federal Wages and Hours Law)	This act established federal regulation of wages and hours, a minimum wage, provision for overtime pay, and constraints on child labor. A notable exemption here is administrative and executive personnel.
1947	The Labor-Management Relations Act (also known as the Taft-Hartley Act)	This law banned the closed shop and created the Federal Mediation and Conciliation Service.
1963	The Equal Pay Act	This act established the premise of equal pay for men and women who do the same work. It prohibits discrimination against employees on the basis of sex.
1964	The Civil Rights Act	This piece of legislation created the Equal Employment Opportunity Commission. Along with subsequent amendments, it prohibits discrimination among employees on the basis of race, religion, sex, or national origin in hiring practices, compensation levels, or advancement opportunities.
1967	The Age Discrimination in Employment Act	Similar to the Civil Rights Act in its intent, this law bars discrimination in businesses engaged in interstate commerce against persons between the ages of forty and sixty-five on the basis of age. (A subsequent amendment raised the top age to seventy.)
1970	The Occupational Safety and Health Act (OSHA)	This act seeks to assure safe working conditions for employees. Businesses must comply with safety and health standards and keep accurate

TABLE 8–1. (*Continued*)

Year	Title	Major Thrust
		records pertinent to this area. They are also subject to inspections designed to monitor compliance with the provisions of this act.
1972	The Equal Employment Opportunity Act	An amendment to the Civil Rights Act of 1964, this legislation extended its provisions to include employees of local and state governments, educational institutions (both public and private), and others.
1973	The Vocational Rehabilitation Act	Along with subsequent amendments, this act outlawed employment discrimination against handicapped persons who are able to fulfill their work responsibilities.
1974	The Employee Retirement Income Security Act (ERISA)	Designed to protect the retirement income rights of employees, this act assures vesting rights and specifies the proper funding of retirement plans.
1978	The Mandatory Retirement Act	This legislation eliminated the practice of requiring a worker's retirement at age sixty-five.
1983	The Job Training Partnership Act	This law replaced the earlier "CETA" (Comprehensive Education and Training Act) of 1978 and provides grants to individual states for the training of unemployed and economically disadvantaged persons.

Source: Compiled by the author.

MANAGING UNION RELATIONS

Like it or not, unions are a fact of life—a fact that you may need to face, sooner or later.

It's true that small business owners typically look askance on the unionization situation. Indeed, many entrepreneurs are suspicious of and resent employees who seek union affiliation, feeling that these people are ingrates and even disloyal, at the very least.

This kind of attitude can probably be traced to the belief that any unionization initiative will encroach on an owner's absolute control over a business. This does appear to pose a threat. A visit by the union local's business agent carries with it the weight of an organization far more powerful than the one the entrepreneur administers. Moreover, small business owners are at a total disadvantage in that they usually have little knowledge of unions and of management-union relations.

You need to understand, however, that employees have the legal right to organize. Furthermore, if this does take place, you do *not* lose control of your business. The right approach for you to adopt is that both company management and union will work together to help your business grow.

Estimates have placed the number of union members today (excluding agricultural workers) at about one-fifth of the nation's labor force. Most locals are affiliated with either a national or international labor organization. The majority of these are tied into (and backed by) the giant AFL-CIO. So, the power is certainly there!

A small-scale enterprise may be able to continue operating for some time before attracting the attention of a union. It helps, too, if you pay your employees decently and treat them well. When a union representative does finally make a call, however, he or she will want to talk with your employees about representing them in labor negotiations. At that time, any resistance on your part can lead to unpleasant action. Imagine the effects of a line of people parading to and fro in front of your building entrance and chanting, "Pass them by! Pass them by!" Imagine them carrying posters that read, in bold black letters, "Do Not Patronize! This Is a Nonunion Shop!"

Collective Bargaining

A healthy attitude to maintain toward union endeavors is one of understanding and tolerance. Unions do have a place in our economy. Workers (as well as employers) do have the right to organize. Consequently, there can be no logical reason for any hostility on your part. In today's climate, management-union relations can be open and aboveboard, businesslike and even friendly, and mature. Bear in mind that the union has almost as much at stake in the continued prosperity and growth of your business as you do.

What happens eventually is that the local representing your employees will want to negotiate a labor contract with you. The process by which the contract is agreed upon is called *collective bargaining*.

Activities during contract negotiations resemble the kind of dickering and bargaining that take place when a firm or an individual attempts to sell an expensive property to a shrewd buyer. Each of the two sides approaches the bargaining table well prepared. Each has a clear idea as to what it's prepared to offer and what it's looking for. Each has plotted its strategy and its tactics in advance.

A period of give and take almost always characterizes the preagreement phase. The completed contract spells out all the agreed-upon details: the new wage agreement; paid holidays; a listing of the conditions under which the union members will be expected to work; the procedure for handling employee grievances; a no-strike pledge; the length of time the contract will be in effect; and the like. Today, most contracts also include an *escalator clause* that guarantees a wage increase when the cost-of-living index goes up by a specified percentage.

FOR FURTHER INFORMATION

Books

Beach, Dale S. *Personnel: The Management of People at Work,* 5th ed. New York: Macmillan, 1985.

Chruden, Herbert J., and Arthur W. Sherman. *Managing Human Resources,* 7th ed. Cincinnati: South-Western, 1984.

Douglass, John, Stuart Klein, and David Hunt. *The Strategic Management of Human Resources.* New York: Wiley, 1985.

Flippo, Edwin B. *Personnel Management,* 6th ed. New York: McGraw-Hill, 1984.

Fossom, John A. *Labor Relations: Development, Structure, Process,* 3d ed. Plano, Tex.: Business Publications, 1985.

French, Wendell L., and Cecil H. Bell, Jr. *Organization Development: Behavioral Science Interventions for Organization Improvement,* 3d ed. Englewood Cliffs, N.J.: Prentice-Hall, 1984.

Halloran, Jack. *Personnel and Human Resource Management.* Englewood Cliffs, N.J.: Prentice-Hall, 1986.

Ivancevich, John M., and William F. Glueck. *Foundations of Personnel: Human Resource Management,* 3d ed. Plano, Tex.: Business Publications, 1986.

Pigors, Paul, and Charles A. Myers. *Personnel Administration: A Point of View and a Method,* 9th ed. New York: McGraw-Hill, 1981.

Sloane, Arthur, and Fred Witney. *Labor Relations,* 5th ed. Englewood Cliffs, N.J.: Prentice-Hall, 1985.

Strauss, George, and Leonard R. Sayles. *Personnel: The Human Problems of Management,* 4th ed. Englewood Cliffs, N.J.: Prentice-Hall, 1980.

Werther, William B., Jr., and Keith Davis. *Personnel Management and Human Resources,* 2d ed. New York: McGraw-Hill, 1985.

Pamphlets Available from the Small Business Administration

MANAGEMENT AIDS

MA 2.004—"Problems in Managing a Family-Owned Business"
MA 5.001—"Checklist for Developing a Training Program"
MA 5.007—"Staffing Your Stores"
MA 5.008—"Managing Employee Benefits"

Booklets Available from the Superintendent of Documents

S/N 045-000-00020-6—*An Employee Suggestion System for Small Companies*—$3.50.
S/N 045-000-00149-1—*Management Audit for Small Retailers*—$4.50.
S/N 045-000-00165-2—*Managing the Small Service Firm for Growth and Profit*—$4.25.
S/N 045-000-00151-2—*Management Audit for Small Manufacturers*—$4.25.
S/N 045-000-00186-5—*Recruiting and Selecting Employees*—$4.50.
S/N 045-000-00189-0—*Managing Retail Salespeople*—$4.75.
S/N 045-000-00191-1—*Training and Developing Employees*—$4.50.
S/N 045-000-00196-2—*Employee Relations and Personnel Policies*—$4.50.
S/N 045-000-00203-9—*Management Audit for Small Service Firms*—$4.50.

9

Leadership in Management

Y ou can't be a leader unless you have someone to lead. This is self-evident. Equally true is the corollary: Where there's a leader, there are followers (at least *one*). Consequently, *your* business leadership skills won't truly flourish until you've hired your first employee.

THE DYNAMICS OF LEADERSHIP

Social psychologists tell us that leadership is a process involving certain types of interpersonal behavior. Acts of leadership exert influence upon other people. Verbs usually associated with leadership—*guiding, instructing, motivating, encouraging,* and the like—imply a sense of purpose, of movement, of action.

Studies of work groups in action suggest that much of the behavior of leaders falls into one of two categories:

- The behavior is oriented toward completing the work group's assigned tasks.
- The behavior shows consideration for and support of the members of the group.

The first type of behavior is practical and involves getting a job done; the second is more personal, involving the care and nurturing of human needs. Together, these two dimensions define the job of the manager: *The manager works with people and with things to get the job done.*

LEADERSHIP STYLES

Leadership involves interaction. It's a way of behaving—of persuading and inducing, of guiding and motivating. A totally rounded leadership form calls for a mastery of certain skill areas, the creation of the right climate within which the work group can function properly, and the direction and control of group activities.

Leadership style is often a reflection of personality. However, a single, consistent type of behavior may not always be applicable or desired. What works well with one person (or group) may not necessarily work at all with the next. Individuals as well as groups are extremely varied. Consequently, effective leadership requires an eclectic approach, taking into account the three-way match among leader, group members, and the situation at hand. Most people, over the long pull, tend to rely on the style that yields the best results.

The Autocratic Leader

At one end of the leadership continuum is the authoritarian type. He or she tends to rule with absolute power, commanding obedience through domination, intimidation, and threats. This person insists on complete compliance with orders, yields no authority to anyone else, and makes decisions alone. Usually, this type of individual is production-oriented in thinking (that is, people exist for the sake of performing the required work).

This is the "boss" type of leader. Some people, for various reasons, both need and want this kind of leader. Perhaps they had a domineering parent, or became conditioned to autocratic bosses in past jobs, or for some other reason put up with an autocratic supervisor. These employees are usually reluctant to shoulder responsibility. They like to be told what to do, preferring the kind of boss who is an exacting taskmaster, gets things done, protects workers against outsiders, yet can mete out punishment when warranted.

Undoubtedly, autocratic leadership behavior can occasionally be of value, as when coping with impending peril or in emergencies. Nevertheless, an autocratically run group will eventually show evidence of some undesirable types of behavior, such as demonstrations of aggression and internal conflict within the group. This kind of employee behavior probably stems from unanswered, ongoing frustrations and from the stifling of individual creativity.

Some autocrats exhibit parental behavior. They infantilize their subordinates, treating them in the same way some fathers and mothers raise young children. Depending on the circumstances, this type of boss wavers from being indulgent and permissive to being firm and unyielding. Such treatment of adults can weaken individual initiative and make workers ever more dependent on their leader.

The Democratic Leader

The democratic leader obviously possesses a broader view of the leadership role. He or she realizes that workers are needed to help get the job done and accepts the fact that they are people, not machines. Moreover, he or she realizes that people have separate and distinct personalities, needs, wants, and drives that must be met if they are to function well. This leader's overall attitude centers on ways to create a climate wherein all do their best to meet both group and company objectives. A democratic-type supervisor knows that the most successful approach is to develop employees over time to the point where they can function ably on their own. Consequently, this person exhibits an openness at all times, remains accessible, and is eager to communicate freely with others. This wise leader keeps employees informed about ongoing conditions and about any impending changes that may affect them. Decisions are arrived at with the group's input. For the most part, the carrot-and-stick principle is dropped out of respect for the individuals; they are encouraged to exercise self-direction and make decisions on their own.

More than any other leadership stance, this type of administration produces workers who are motivated self-starters. As a result of continued democratic leadership, cooperative endeavor is encouraged and productivity should edge upwards.

The Laissez-faire Leader

Still a third type of executive, far less often encountered in the business sector than either the autocrat or democrat, is the *laissez-faire* leader. In truth, managers of this type do not display the kinds of behavior we would customarily expect from business leaders. They practice what is tantamount, more or less, to a "hands-off" policy with regard to their subordinates. Typically, they abstain completely from such leadership acts as guiding, directing, training, or even extending encouragement to the members of their groups. Their basic philosophy, which they often confuse with a democratic approach to leadership, can be summed up in the phrase, "I'll let my subordinates take care of things."

Characteristics of Leaders

Many of us are guilty of holding stereotypical notions about leaders. We tend to believe that a good leader is one who commands respect, who electrifies the atmosphere when entering a room, who is, without a doubt, aggressive, domineering, able at manipulation, a skilled communicator, an extrovert, and so on. Our concepts even go beyond personality to physical attributes; we think that a good leader is usually taller and heavier (and more attractive) than the rest of us.

Oddly enough, some of the greatest leaders in world history, and many capable managers of major corporations, have been quiet, unassuming, introspective, short, and thin people. In fact, leaders can be just like you and me—or anyone else. Management experts have often theorized about the kinds of personal traits necessary for effective performance in the role of leader. Studies have compared the qualities evinced by top executives with those demonstrated by unsuccessful leaders in order to uncover the characteristics that differentiate the two. Yes, several distinguishing attributes keep showing up—but bear in mind that leadership has three dimensions: the leader, those who are led, and the individual situation. Consequently, whether you rate high or low in these attributes does not necessarily make you a good (or bad) leader.

Perhaps you'll find it helpful to review the following list of personal traits that can be valuable in dealing with others:

adaptability	open-mindedness
alertness	optimism
communication skills	patience
confidence	persuasive powers
creativity	poise
curiosity	resourcefulness
dependability	sensitivity to others
drive	supportiveness
enthusiasm	teaching ability
evaluation skills	tolerance
flexibility	warmth
human relations skills	willingness to listen
maturity	willingness to take chances

Inasmuch as leadership activity also has a task-oriented, impersonal dimension, certain additional skills need to be developed. Among these are

- The ability to establish priorities
- A capacity for giving credit when due
- Skill at planning and scheduling
- Proficiency in problem solving
- A willingness to delegate responsibility to others

UNDERSTANDING YOUR EMPLOYEES

People are complex. This statement, of course, doesn't surprise you at all! Yet, it's so important to bear in mind in your relationships with your employees. Each individual is multifaceted; among his or her many sides are the intellectual, the physical, the emotional—and the economic, social, political, and moral as well. So it's not surprising that people's behavior can be as complex and as difficult to interpret as people are themselves.

Acquire a Knowledge of Psychology

Over the next few pages, we offer a few facts derived from basic adult psychology and from social psychology (the psychology of people in groups), which can help you in your role as leader. But first, let's review three basic points:

1. *People hold values.* Values are concepts we come to accept over the years as we interact with others and with our environment.

2. *People form attitudes.* Attitudes serve as vehicles for organizing knowledge, for adjusting to the world around us, for shielding us from confusion and pain, and for orienting us toward things that are pleasurable.

3. *People develop response traits.* We have habitual ways of responding to and dealing with others.

Personality is an amalgam of values, attitudes, and interpersonal response traits.

You might prepare yourself by reading a basic psychology textbook, which will give you many insights into what makes people tick. In turn, this could lead to an increased capability on your part to motivate and direct your employees.

What Motivates People

Motives are the energizing forces that drive all of us and are behind most behavior. Many of our actions result from the interplay of several motives. Some motives are largely rational; this means that they are based on logic. For example, you probably avoid speeding in your automobile because (1) it might involve you in an accident that could endanger your vehicle or your life; and (2) you might receive a speeding ticket. These two motives are clearly logical.

On the other hand, many motives are of an emotional (or nonrational) nature. Consider the urge to place a $10 bet on a particular horse in the third race at the track. Logically, your chances of winning are far less than fifty-fifty, yet you have a "feeling" you might win.

The line of demarcation between rational and emotional motives is rather hazy. You might avoid speeding because of an emotional motive: *fear* of being ticketed, or of having an accident, and so on. Similarly, there could be a rational motive for the gambling situation; for example, if you needed considerably more money for a vital purpose than you had in your pocket at the time.

Furthermore, what motivates one person does not necessarily budge the next. The same motive can lead to varied behaviors in different people. The same behavior in different people can result from different motives.

All of us are driven by many motives: economic motives, safety motives, social motives, and so forth. Some of our motives derive from inborn drives like hunger, thirst, the need for sleep, and sex. The majority of our motives, however, are learned—those that we develop as we interact with our environment.

Levels of Human Needs

One way to understand better the subject of human needs and wants is to review a notable theory proposed many years ago by the eminent psychologist Abraham Maslow.* He maintained that people are animals who are continually wanting and that human needs can be arranged on different levels according to their "potency" for influencing behavior. He postulated that all of us are constantly struggling upwards to attain higher rungs on this "pyramid of

---

*A. H. Maslow, "A Theory of Human Motivation," *Psychological Review* 50 (1943), 370–96. Copyright © 1943 by The American Psychological Foundation. Adapted by permission of the publisher and author. See also: Abraham H. Maslow, *Motivation and Personality,* 2d ed. (New York: Harper & Row, 1970).

needs" until we reach its pinnacle. From time to time, most people are restrained from proceeding up the hierarchy or may be knocked down to lower levels by outside conditions (or, perhaps, by inner forces).

Needs at the lowest level—and therefore the most powerful of all—are the ones Maslow describes as the *physiological,* or *bodily, needs.* These include hunger, thirst, and sex. Once these needs have been largely satisfied, the human being will want still more and will move up to the next level of the pyramid, to the *safety needs.* On this level, people think of their safety: of gaining shelter from the elements and protection from accidents and other threats to well-being. If a person can provide for these needs, other wants soon develop; these Maslow termed the *love and belongingness needs.*

At this point, the individual needs love and affection and actively seeks friends, a mate, and groups for affiliation. When this level has been successfully attained, people still want (naturally!) more, and they move up to the *esteem needs.* Here, the individual wants to be respected by others, to be noticed and acclaimed, to build a reputation. By this time, the person has almost everything: income, a sense of security, family, and friends, and is acquiring a reputation and the respect of others. Yet he or she still feels an inadequacy, a sense of missing out on something, a feeling that there's still something more needed.

To the fifth—and highest—level of the pyramid of needs, Maslow affixed the name *self-actualization.* He explained this as the highest level of aspiration: to become in actuality that which an individual was designed to be. Only then was the person truly "matured." This is the supreme goal that all of us are climbing toward, all our lives.

Interpreting Maslow's Theory in Practice

Translating Maslow's concepts into modern personnel thinking, you can expect your employees to seek such things as the following:

- *Level 1 (Physiological Needs):* a decent salary—enough to keep the wolf from the door, to keep the refrigerator well stocked, and to maintain a comfortable dwelling place.

- *Level 2 (Safety Needs):* job security and safe working conditions. This need may lead to seeking life-insurance coverage for spouse and children.

- *Level 3 (Love and Belongingness Needs):* the feeling of being part of an organization and having a place in the group; acceptance by co-workers and employer; a friendly environment.

- *Level 4 (Esteem Needs):* ego satisfaction, recognition (an occasional pat on the back), authority, and status within the group; the belief that the person's work is both responsible and respected.

- *Level 5 (Need for Self-Actualization):* a chance for growth and the opportunity to demonstrate initiative; encouragement for the individual to participate and contribute to the fullest.

SUPERVISING YOUR EMPLOYEES: SOME SUGGESTIONS

It's only natural for your employees to regard you as their mentor, guide, leader, and counselor. If you set high standards for yourself as well as for them, if you continually demonstrate good human relations, and if you treat your employees as people—and not like pawns—your skills as a supervisor will be above average. To increase your leadership skills, follow the "dos" and "don'ts" suggested in exhibit 9–1.

Employee Characteristics

What should *you* be looking for in your employees? Here's a representative list of characteristics that are valuable in an employee:

- A good level of productivity
- Consistency
- Honesty
- Loyalty
- No rocking the boat
- Pleasant personality
- Promptness
- Proper behavior on the job
- Regular attendance
- Respect for authority

EXHIBIT 9–1. SOME "DOS" AND "DON'TS" FOR MANAGERS

Do:	*Don't:*
Be consistent	Be argumentative
Be fair	Be autocratic
Be honest	Be overly demanding
Build enthusiasm among your employees	Be unreasonable
Encourage them to ask questions	Conceal the truth
Encourage them to make their own decisions	Discourage initiative
Instill confidence in them	Discourage new ideas
Keep an open door	Do your thinking for your employees
Listen attentively to what they have to say	Fail to clarify your instructions
Recognize individual differences	Play favorites
Set a personal example for them	Reprimand an employee in front of others
Show consideration for the feelings of others	Think small

Source: Compiled by the author.

Some Other Thoughts on Motivation

As a potential small business owner, you may be able to glean some worthwhile insights from several other well-known management concepts.

Theories X and Y. More than a quarter century ago, management theorist Douglas McGregor investigated the attitudes of supervisors toward their employees.* His studies led him to conclude that most supervisors could be classified as belonging to one of two camps. Those who subscribe to what McGregor termed the *Theory X* approach are convinced that the average person doesn't like to work, has little if any ambition, and tries to avoid responsibility. Consequently, these supervisors feel that they need to watch workers closely and depend on the strategic application of both rewards and punishment in order to obtain satisfactory performance.

Other supervisors follow a different philosophy, the more positive *Theory Y* approach. They believe employees consider work to be as natural as play and rest, and that once committed to specific objectives, they will not only put out effort willingly but will also seek responsibility.

Theory Z. In recent years, much favorable publicity has appeared in the press with regard to Japanese management techniques. One popular book outlined the more salient attributes of the Japanese approach, dubbing the overall concept *Theory Z*—an obvious reference to McGregor's assessment of supervisory types.** Substantial delegation of responsibility, trust in each individual, and decision by group consensus are characteristically seen in Japanese companies. Of course, some of their attributes (such as lifetime employment) cannot be incorporated easily into our own economy. Still, owners of small businesses might well profit by modifying and applying other attributes to their own enterprises; for example, the participative approach to decision making and a genuine concern for one's employees.†

Job Motivators and Hygiene Factors. In the 1960s, management theorist Frederick Herzberg researched the workplace to uncover those factors that appeared to exert some influence on the job satisfaction of employees or on worker motivation.‡ He found two distinct sets of such factors: *motivators* (or *satisfiers*) and *hygiene factors (dissatisfiers)*. Herzberg maintained that motivators appeal to higher-level human needs and therefore not only motivate employees but can also increase the level of job satisfaction. Examples include recognition, responsibility, advancement, growth, and the work itself. On the other hand, some factors in the workplace that cater to people's lower needs (hygiene factors) apparently do little to encourage worker motivation. However, they can, of course, contribute to employee dissatisfaction. Salary, work-

---

*Douglas McGregor, *The Human Side of Enterprise* (New York: McGraw-Hill, 1960), 31–44, 47–48.

**William Ouchi, *Theory Z* (Reading, Mass.: Addison-Wesley, 1981).

†Matthew C. Sonfield, "Can Japanese Management Techniques Be Applied to American Small Business?" *Journal of Small Business Management* 22 (July 1984), 18–23.

‡Frederick Herzberg, *Work and the Nature of Man* (New York: Thomas Y. Crowell, 1966), 71–91. See also: Frederick Herzberg, "One More Time: How Do You Motivate Employees?" *Harvard Business Review* 46 (January-February 1968), 53–62.

ing conditions, company policies, and relations with one's supervisor are hygiene factors.

Obviously, then, small business owners might do well to review Herzberg's findings. More highly motivated and satisfied employees might be developed through effective management policies that lead to (among other results):

- Top-quality working conditions
- Catering to the worker's need for security
- Delegating more responsibility
- Encouraging group goal setting and decision making
- Flexible scheduling
- Job enhancement and/or redesign
- Offering a promotional ladder with the company
- Recognizing and rewarding the exceptional contribution

DECISION MAKING

In business, most management decisions are made by intuition. Owners of small enterprises especially appear to fly by the seats of their pants in much the same way that Charles Lindbergh flew over the Atlantic many decades ago—without the benefit of the vast array of intricate instruments that decorate the cockpit of today's jet aircraft.

Intuitive decision making stems partially from a lack of familiarity with problem-solving techniques and partially from the realization that extensive resources—time, energy, and funds—should only be diverted to the most serious and complex problems. Happily, these major problems don't occur very often. When they do (for example, when one is contemplating major relocation of a factory or designing a new system), the owner is often better off relying on the assistance of an experienced consultant.

Luckily, most problems in business repeat themselves, so once a satisfactory solution has been worked out (or accidentally hit upon), the entrepreneur knows how to solve the problem the next time it pops up. Only the new, infrequent, unique problems present a strong challenge.

Decision making is but one step in the problem-solving process. It's the last step, in which you choose the one alternative that seems best. When you're confronted with any problem that merits your time and energy, try applying the steps outlined in exhibit 9–2.

Of course, many more sophisticated techniques are currently in vogue for solving business problems. For the most part, these approaches are used by the larger companies and not by the small firm. There are methods that take into account chance or probability, those that use mathematics and statistics, those that require computer programming, and so on. You may have read or heard about some of the following techniques: game theory, decision theory, queuing theory, decision matrices, simulation, and linear programming. All of these methods (and others, too) lie well outside the scope of this book. If, at a later date, you become interested in learning more about them, a number of good books are available on the topic of decision making in business and industry.

EXHIBIT 9–2. STEPS IN THE PROBLEM-SOLVING PROCESS

1. *Diagnose the problem.* On a sheet of paper, write down a clear statement of the problem's "essence;" this will help you keep the pinpointed problem clearly in mind as you begin to work toward its solution. Many problems are quite complex; often, you need to go further and break down the original problem statement into its major parts. Each part should then be summarized and written down as a "subproblem" statement. Another useful trick is to draw a simple diagram of the problem situation, making certain you put in all the elements involved.

2. *Gather information.* Hunt for pertinent information to help you solve the problem. (Facts are not only available from internal records, external sources of data, and primary research; they are also readily obtained from people.)

3. *Generate alternative solutions.* Develop a number of alternative solutions to the problem. (Creative thinking can help here. See chapter 12 for approaches to use in generating ideas.)

4. *Evaluate the alternatives.* Rate the alternatives according to each of several criteria; for example, cost, time, judged effectiveness or payoff, effect on you, and so on. Use a simple numerical rating scale, such as 0 = Poor, 1 = Fair, 2 = Good, 3 = Very Good, and 4 = Excellent. If some criteria are more important to you than others, then accord more weight to those in your analysis.

5. *Select the best alternative(s).* At this juncture, you make your decision.

6. *Translate your decision into action.*

Source: Compiled by the author.

FOR FURTHER INFORMATION

Books

Boyd, Bradford B. *Management-Minded Supervision,* 2d ed. New York: McGraw-Hill, 1984.

Chung, Kae H., and Leon C. Megginson. *Organizational Behavior.* New York: Harper & Row, 1983.

Du Brin, Andrew J. *Contemporary Applied Management,* 2d ed. Plano, Tex.: Business Publications, 1985.

Fulmer, Robert M. *Practical Human Relations,* rev. ed. Homewood, Ill.: Irwin, 1983.

George, Claude S., Jr. *Supervision in Action,* 4th ed. Englewood Cliffs, N.J.: Prentice-Hall, 1985.

Haimann, Theo, and Raymond Hilgert. *Supervision: Concepts and Practices of Management,* 3d ed. Cincinnati: South-Western, 1982.

Halloran, J., and G. Frunzi. *Supervision: The Art of Management,* 2d ed. Englewood Cliffs, N.J.: Prentice-Hall, 1986.

Keys, Bernard, and Joy Henshall. *Supervision.* New York: Wiley, 1984.

Kossen, Stan. *The Human Side of Organizations,* 3d ed. New York: Harper & Row, 1983.

Mosley, Donald C., and Paul H. Pietri. *Supervisory Management: The Art of Working With and Through People.* Cincinnati: South-Western, 1985.

Portnoy, Robert A. *Leadership: What Every Leader Should Know About People.* Englewood Cliffs, N.J.: Prentice-Hall, 1986.

Preston, Paul, and Thomas Zimmerer. *Management for Supervisors,* 2d ed. Englewood Cliffs, N.J.: Prentice-Hall, 1983.

Reece, Barry L., and Rhonda G. Brandt. *Effective Human Relations in Organizations,* 2d ed. Boston: Houghton Mifflin, 1984.

Sartain, Aaron, and Alton W. Baker. *The Supervisor and the Job,* 3d ed. New York: McGraw-Hill, 1978.

Steinmetz, Lawrence L., and Ralph H. Todd, Jr. *First-Line Management: Approaching Supervision Effectively,* 3d ed. Plano, Tex.: Business Publications, 1983.

Warrick, D. D., and Robert Zawacki. *Supervisory Management.* New York: Harper & Row, 1983.

Pamphlets Available from the Small Business Administration

MANAGEMENT AIDS

MA 2.004—"Problems in Managing a Family-Owned Business"
MA 2.010—"Planning and Goal Setting for Small Business"
MA 5.008—"Managing Employee Benefits"
MA 5.009—"Techniques for Productivity Improvement"

Booklets Available from the Superintendent of Documents

S/N 045-000-00185-7—*Job Analysis, Job Specifications, and Job Descriptions*—$4.50.
S/N 045-000-00186-5—*Recruiting and Selecting Employees*—$4.50.
S/N 045-000-00189-0—*Managing Retail Salespeople*—$4.75.
S/N 045-000-00191-1—*Training and Developing Employees*—$4.50.
S/N 045-000-00196-2—*Employee Relations and Personnel Policies*—$4.50.
S/N 045-000-00206-3—*Managing for Profits*—$4.50.

IV
PRODUCTION MANAGEMENT

10

Production: Processes and Plant

Here's a sampling of small businesses, all of which have one thing in common:

- Manufacturing cleaning compounds
- Glass-cutting for windows
- Dressmaking
- Assembling pocket radios
- Printing circulars and business cards
- Handcrafting beaded flowers
- Molding plastic toys
- Building houses
- Tool and die making

The common thread that binds together these different types of enterprises is *production.* Production is an activity that converts materials into useful forms. A great deal of activity must take place in order to produce useful things. Management must plan, organize, direct operations, and control the overall situation. The materials involved may be raw materials, semiprocessed or semi-finished goods, or even finished products. Machinery and equipment, methods, and processes are the basic elements of production.

Traditionally, there are four types of manufacturing processes:

- *Analysis.* The breaking down of raw materials, such as crude petroleum, into their components.

- *Extraction.* The removal of substances from other materials, as in the extraction of copper from ore.

137

- *Fabrication.*   Changing the form of materials in some way such as by pressing, weaving, cutting, and the like. Examples include the manufacture of clothing, shoes, metal bolts, and so forth.

- *Synthesis.*   Combining materials to form new products, as in the manufacture of glassware, metal products, synthetic fibers, and so on. Another kind of synthesis is *assembly,* whereby various fabricated parts are placed together to form a new product (as in the manufacture of automobiles).

Among small businesses, synthesis and fabrication are by far the most common types of manufacturing.

PRODUCTION PROCESSES

Production can be either continuous or intermittent. In *continuous production,* materials are brought uninterruptedly to the machines, the equipment runs smoothly for long periods of time, and standard products roll off the machines to be stored in the warehouse as reserves against future orders. This process is often called *flow production.* Good illustrations of factories in continuous production are television assembly plants and automobile plants. Of course, a completely automated factory is ideal for this type of production.

Intermittent production is often referred to as *job* or *job lot production* (and where less intermittent, as *batch production*). This kind is typical of most small manufacturing enterprises. Machinery (or hand labor) "runs" are characteristically short—*interrupted*—as opposed to continuous. The materials flow varies; that is, frequent changes in setting up, dismantling, or changing the equipment are necessary. The products turned out are usually custom-made items. A printing shop is an excellent example of intermittent production.

PRODUCTION METHODS

Before the advent of factories, early manufacturing processes combined manual skills with small hand tools to produce useful objects. Although handcrafted items are still with us, production today is more machine-oriented than ever, and this tendency toward automation becomes more pronounced with each passing decade. Today, we have machines that

stamp	melt	carry	pour
heat	lift	roll	mix
sift	cut	weld	mill
chop	affix	blow	press
sort	turn	shape	depress

Nowadays, there are machines designed to duplicate nearly every imaginable function formerly performed by hand. Moreover, the use of robots to assist production has been increasing steadily.

A factory, though, is more than its machinery. The typical plant could be compared to a large, activity-choked arena. To run this arena profitably, all the major resources of the firm must be drawn together in a logical, businesslike way: management, capital, human resources, machinery, materials, and methods. Brief comments regarding several of these resources follow.

Management. One or more layers of management are needed to set objectives and then to formulate plans in line with those objectives; to marshal and organize all the other resources in order to accomplish those objectives; to direct operations; and to control all the elements of this giant jigsaw puzzle.

Human Resources. A human resources support system is required to operate not only the machinery but *all* production activities. In any factory there are many specialized functions to manage. This leads to the principle of *specialization of labor* and to the setting up of an organizational structure designed to accomplish the various jobs. Consequently, both semiskilled and skilled workers may be needed as well as a variety of functional departments, such as purchasing, receiving, production, stockkeeping, and quality control.

Machinery. This includes power equipment and tools (both those that are permanently positioned and those that are portable), hand tools and equipment, and auxiliary equipment such as dies, gauges, jigs, and fixtures. In addition to running the machines, important activities here include purchasing, maintaining, and replacing equipment.

Methods. Because of the intricate nature of the production process, methods and systems used in factory settings are many and varied. Some examples include methods for production planning and production control, the setting of detailed procedures, the fixing of standards, and the designing of layouts.

PRODUCTION SCHEDULING

The Small Business Administration maintains the following:

> Some small manufacturers take production schedules for granted because bottlenecks are few and far between. Minor problems are easily ironed out, and orders are delivered to customers on time.
>
> Other small manufacturers are not as fortunate. Scheduling in their plants is complicated by the nature of the process, the complexity of the products, and frequent changes in quantity requirements.*

The SBA also suggests that the small-plant production scheduler should be familiar with these important factors before lining up production: production layout, factory workload, factory capability and versatility, and existing standards, systems, and procedures. Before actual scheduling begins, everything that needs to be done must be spelled out:

> *Product Description.* The product description describes individual parts as well as the finished product. One part of this is the bill of materials. It lists all of

*John B. Kline, "Pointers on Scheduling Production," *Management Aid No. 207.* (Washington: Small Business Administration, June 1977 reprint), 2.

the items needed to produce a part, or in total, the final product. Prints and drawings depict the parts, showing much detail as to their physical characteristics. Specifications describe in detail the allowable tolerances in dimensions, sizes, and finishes.

Process Description. The process description is concerned with the steps needed to produce individual parts of the complete product. It will list the operations sequences, the machines to be used, the amount and kind of labor, and the estimated time involved. Additional data may include machine set-up instructions and inspection instructions.

Another phase of the process description is the *route sheets.* These are operation sequence outline forms with an allowance for set-up times and for movement of the job from one operation to the next. If your production is divided into departments, route sheets can be used by a department to schedule the time for a particular job, to monitor a series of jobs, and to tell where the part will go next.*

FUNCTIONAL DEPARTMENTS WITHIN THE PLANT

In addition to the primary production function, there are a number of other major functions that must be performed in a factory. These include purchasing, receiving, shipping, quality control, research and development (R & D), maintenance, and stockkeeping. In the smallest manufacturing firms, of course, such functions are shared among the owners and a few employees. As the firm grows larger, specialists are eventually sought to manage those areas, and departmental divisions soon follow.

Purchasing

In plant operations, the *purchasing* function has to do with the procurement of all raw materials, components, machinery, equipment, supplies, and necessary services. Eventually, this area comes under the direction of a purchasing agent. Responsibilities assigned to this department include cultivating of sources of supply for all items to be purchased; placing purchase orders (after securing quotations and working out prices and terms); following up on goods ordered; comparing invoice after receipt of goods with purchase order; and approving and forwarding invoices to the accounts payable department. The purchasing agent maintains a close liaison with the receiving department and is kept abreast of stock levels of all materials and supplies. (The agent must keep a perpetual running inventory if there is no stockkeeping department.)

Receiving

All purchases of raw materials, semiprocessed goods, equipment, supplies, and the like come into the plant through the receiving department. Activities generally in the receiving category are described on the following page.

*Ibid., 4.

1. Receiving onto the unloading platform all incoming materials, goods, and supplies, including returns from customers

2. Checking all incoming merchandise for quantity, price, quality, and so forth against both the packing slip and the accompanying bill of lading. Further, checking each delivery against a copy of the original purchase order issued from the plant

3. Routing and transporting all materials to the proper department or assigned area(s) of the warehouse

4. Keeping records of various types, ranging from the receiving register *(log)* where all pertinent details of each shipment are recorded, to the invoices submitted to the purchasing department for payment

Shipping

The shipping department is similar to the receiving department except that it lies at the other end (figuratively if not literally) of plant activities.

As with the receiving department, the importance of maintaining tight internal control along with the necessary paperwork cannot be overemphasized. Some of the major activities that take place in the shipping department are

- Order processing
- Order picking
- Order assembly
- Order checking
- Special packing (where required)
- Routing shipments
- Scheduling shipments
- Following up on damage claims

Quality Control

This area of specialization is an essential phase of good factory management. The quality-control function ensures that established standards are observed and that what is produced by the plant indeed conforms to customer (and company) specifications.

In the small production facility, this function is often vested in a single individual who may also have other duties. However, where the products or the manufacturing processes are more complicated, a small department may be needed to inspect products and maintain effective control. An efficient factory operation regularly checks not only its output but also all incoming merchandise (whether raw materials, semifinished components, or finished goods such as supplies).

Generally speaking, quality control involves sampling products from time to time, running tests, using measuring devices, and even statistical methods.

The goal is to detect inferior or substandard products early in the game and then take steps to correct these deviations from the norm.

Research and Development

A separate and distinct R&D facility is characteristic only of large corporations. Rarely does a small manufacturer have an individual, let alone a section or department, dedicated to researching and developing new products, methods, machinery, and the like. Even among the larger firms, the research and development function is most often found within companies that are committed to industry leadership and a policy of "being first in their field."

Consequently, this R&D function isn't at all organized in a small manufacturing company but is spread among the various people who comprise the firm. Results, therefore, emerge only occasionally and in a serendipitous fashion rather than from deliberate, planned effort. In the typical small firm, development comes about largely through trial and error.

Maintenance

Usually, a well-organized factory is quickly placed under the capable administration of a skilled plant engineer. This is a logical step, because the breakdown or interruption of a machine, a boiler, a transformer, or any other important piece of equipment can rapidly bring activities to a virtual standstill. Plant engineers must frequently have at their disposal other specialists, such as electricians, machinists, plumbers, and carpenters.

The maintenance shop or section is responsible for keeping all machinery and equipment in top-notch operating condition, constructing new facilities when needed within the plant, moving machines from one location to another, assembling newly purchased equipment, and so forth. It's extremely important to schedule any major maintenance efforts so as to avoid interfering in any way with the flow of production. Likewise, good plant maintenance is *preventive* in the sense that all equipment is inspected on a regular, scheduled basis to avoid a slowdown or stoppage.

Stockkeeping

Materials supply is of paramount importance in the efficient operation of every stage of the manufacturing cycle. Raw materials must be readily available for scheduled production runs. Semifinished and fabricated components need to be in place when called for. Finished products have to be warehoused as ready stocks until drawn against the customer orders.

So, overseeing substantial quantities of materials is a major, ongoing effort within the plant. Often, this job is under the direction of a "storekeeper." In actuality, stockkeeping is the part of the overall inventory control system that deals with specifics like organizing and maintaining the storage area, placing and moving about the stored goods, protecting the materials, issuing merchandise from the storage area, and doing the necessary paperwork.

FOR FURTHER INFORMATION

Books

Adam, E., Jr., and R. Ebert. *Production and Operations Management: Concepts, Models, and Behavior,* 3d ed. Englewood Cliffs, N.J.: Prentice-Hall, 1984.

Fogarty, Donald W., and Thomas R. Hoffman. *Production and Inventory Management.* Cincinnati: South-Western, 1983.

Greene, J. *Operations Management: Productivity and Profit.* Englewood Cliffs, N.J.: Prentice-Hall, 1984.

Hax, A., and D. Candia, Jr. *Production and Inventory Management.* Englewood Cliffs, N.J.: Prentice-Hall, 1984.

Heinritz, S., and P. Smith Farrell. *Purchasing: Principles and Applications,* 7th ed. Englewood Cliffs, N.J.: Prentice-Hall, 1986.

Laufer, A. C. *Production and Operations Management,* 3d ed. Cincinnati: South-Western, 1984.

Lee, Lamar, Jr., and David N. Burt. *Purchasing and Materials Management: Text and Cases,* 4th ed. New York: McGraw-Hill, 1984.

Mayer, Raymond E. *Production and Operations Management,* 4th ed. New York: McGraw-Hill, 1982.

Monks, Joseph G. *Operations Management: Theory and Problems,* 2d ed. New York: McGraw-Hill, 1982.

Plossl, G. *Production and Inventory Control: Principles and Techniques,* 2d ed. Englewood Cliffs, N.J.: Prentice-Hall, 1985.

Schonberger, Richard J. *Operations Management: Productivity and Quality,* 2d ed. Plano, Tex.: Business Publications, 1985.

Sumanth, David J. *Productivity Engineering and Management.* New York: McGraw-Hill, 1984.

Pamphlets Available from the Small Business Administration

MANAGEMENT AIDS

MA 2.005—"The Equipment Replacement Decision"
MA 2.007—"Business Plan for Small Manufacturers"
MA 2.011—"Fixing Production Mistakes"
MA 2.014—"Should You Lease or Buy Equipment?"
MA 2.027—"How to Get Started with a Small Business Computer"
MA 3.010—"Techniques for Problem Solving"
MA 5.009—"Techniques for Productivity Improvement"

Booklets Available from the Superintendent of Documents

S/N 045-000-00146-6—*Decision Points in Developing New Products*—$4.25.
S/N 045-000-00162-8—*Cost Accounting for Small Manufacturers*—$6.00.

S/N 045-000-00167-9—*Purchasing Management and Inventory Control for Small Business*—$4.50.

S/N 045-000-00181-4—*Purchasing for Manufacturing Firms*—$4.75.

S/N 045-000-00182-2—*Inventory Management—Manufacturing/Service*—$4.75.

S/N 045-000-00183-1—*Inventory and Scheduling Techniques*—$4.75.

S/N 045-000-00185-7—*Job Analysis, Job Specifications, and Job Descriptions*—$4.50.

11

Manufacturing: Inventory and Materials

As we learned in chapter 10, the production function involves the processing, or conversion, of materials into useful forms. Four different kinds of manufacturing approaches were discussed: analysis, extraction, fabrication, and synthesis. We may therefore define *production management* as the planning, organizing, directing, and controlling of the production function. Among the primary areas of concern for the production manager are estimates of product demand, production layout, labor requirements, the machinery and equipment to be used, inspection and control systems, materials management, maintaining product quality, inventory control, and plant maintenance.

PRODUCTION PLANNING

It is useful to regard the production process as a closed system that consists of three significant dimensions: (1) inputs; (2) operations; and (3) outputs. Items 1 and 3 require only a brief note of explanation. The second calls for a somewhat more detailed discussion.

Inputs and Outputs

Into this production "system," we enter our *primary* inputs—the raw materials and/or semiprocessed goods and components (parts) we may need to manufacture our products. In addition, we must also avail ourselves of additional resources, which we may regard as inputs required for the system to operate. These include labor, capital, machinery, equipment, and supplies.

The outputs are, of course, the products we manufacture in our plant.

OPERATIONS MANAGEMENT

Much of the activity within any manufacturing plant lies within the operations area. Operations may be defined as the processing, or conversion, of inputs into outputs.

Functions in Operations Management

As you will recall from the last chapter, a bill of materials for each product is worked up during the product description phase. This bill is a written list of all materials needed to manufacture the particular item. It is at this point that operations management takes over. During the next phase (process description), management charts the production process, selects the machines to be used, determines sequences to be followed and labor needs, outlines setup instructions, and so forth. Plans are made for the following processing stages: routing, loading, scheduling, dispatching, and follow-up. (See exhibit 11–1.) Here's what these terms mean:

> *Routing.* This is initiated once the bill of materials for the product has been prepared and the process description completed. Each individual operation as a component of the total product is planned; a sequence of steps is indicated; time and labor are apportioned to the various steps in the progression; and work stations, machines, and departments are spelled out. Route sheets and flow charts are used.

> *Loading.* This function involves computing the amount of time required for each operation and adding that to work already planned for each machine or work station. This results in a *machine load chart* (traditionally, a bar chart).

> *Scheduling.* This production phase deals with the timing of production in order to meet deadlines and delivery requirements. It involves determining when each operation is to be performed, starting and completion times, and so forth. The operation and flow processes charts, the machine load chart, and the network Program Evaluation and Review Technique (PERT) chart are the principal charts used for scheduling.

> *Dispatching.* This involves the authorization of operations in the shop through work orders (instructions).

> *Follow-up.* Also called *reporting,* this function is normally the bailiwick of the dispatcher, whose job it is to supply information about work in progress. The reporting of delays and other problems can lead to rapid corrective action.

EXHIBIT 11-1. PROCESSING STAGES

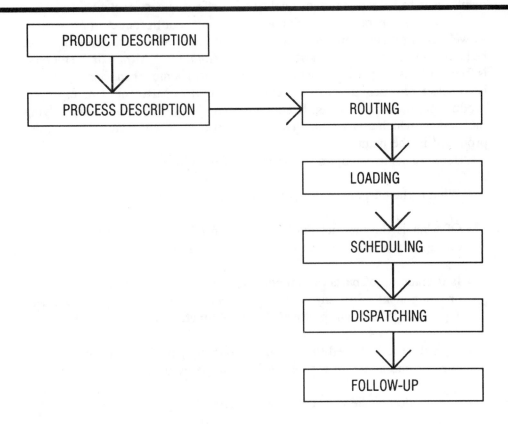

MAINTAINING PRODUCT QUALITY

The small manufacturer who struggles to build a profitable business should realize that success over the long term can be assured only by emphasizing product quality (for the price, of course). To maintain the proper quality levels in all goods produced at a plant, serious and continuous attention needs to be paid to the following product aspects:

- Performance
- Features
- Reliability
- Conformance
- Durability
- Serviceability
- Aesthetics
- Perceived Quality*

*Reprinted from "What Does 'Product Quality' Mean?" by David A. Garvin, *Sloan Management Review* 26 (Fall 1984), 29–30, by permission of the publisher. Copyright © 1984 by The Sloan Management Review Association. All rights reserved.

At the same time, for the operation to remain profitable, production management needs to balance product quality with effective cost control.

Production operations can be refined to bring about product improvement as well as to reduce manufacturing costs. One interesting technique that can be helpful in accomplishing these goals is *value analysis.* * Although the method is frequently used by a single person within the firm, a more beneficial approach is to select representatives from several different departments (for example: production, sales, purchasing, R&D). They can be quickly trained in applying the method, which basically involves asking probing questions about every item produced in the plant.

Here are some examples of the kinds of questions asked:

- What is the purpose of this product? What is it supposed to do, or be for?

- Of what is the product made? Can we produce it by using some other (cheaper, more readily available) materials or substances?

- Is it made up of parts or components? What is the purpose of each part or component? Can any of them be replaced with others that are less expensive or that will perform the same function as well or better?

- Does the product need to be made of so many parts? Can we reduce their number and come up with essentially the same product?

- Can we design the item differently? Better?

Another worthwhile approach is for management to encourage the formation and participation of one or more *quality circles* within the company.** These are "small groups of volunteers who meet regularly to identify, analyze and solve quality-related problems in their area of responsibility."† Not only do these groups facilitate plant operations, but the results of their efforts can be better product quality as well as greater output. Other likely benefits are increased job satisfaction and higher employee morale.

Two other methods the manufacturing firm can use to build a healthy organization, reduce expenses, ensure continued product quality, and improve decision making in general are to adopt a *participative management* stance and

---

*See: Vincent G. Reuter, "What Good Are Value Analysis Programs?" *Business Horizons* 29 (March-April 1986), 73–79.

**For background information, see: C. Philip Alexander, "A Hidden Benefit of Quality Circles," *Personnel Journal* 63 (February 1984), 54*ff;* Larry R. Smeltzer and Ben L. Kedia, "Knowing the Ropes: Organizational Requirements for Quality Circles," *Business Horizons* 28 (July-August 1985), 30–34; David N. Landon and Steve Moulton, "Quality Circles: What's in Them for Employees?" *Personnel Journal* 65 (June 1986), 23–26; Philip C. Thompson, *Quality Circles: How to Make Them Work in America* (New York: AMACOM, 1982).

†Sandy J. Wayne, Ricky W. Griffin, and Thomas S. Bateman, "Improving the Effectiveness of Quality Circles," *Personnel Administrator* 31 (March 1986), 79.

to create an internal *task team* to wrestle with company difficulties. The first is a "managerial philosophy that subordinates should be permitted to be more involved in the decisions and actions that will affect them."* The second involves appointing a few employees to a special task force, charging them with investigating problem areas across various departments and functions within the business, and recommending solutions to those problems.**

INVENTORY MANAGEMENT AND CONTROL

There should be little difficulty in understanding the significance of the inventory control concept in the manufacturing enterprise. Its purposes are simply to manage and control two varieties of inventories: (1) the *materials inventory* necessary to the production process; and (2) the finished *merchandise inventory*, which is stored for eventual customer orders.

By logical extension, then, effective inventory management calls for thorough attention to such activities as the acquisition of materials required for plant production (which involves both the purchasing and receiving functions); the handling, internal movement, and storage of materials (the stockkeeping function); and the physical distribution of materials and manufactured goods (the shipping function).

Sales objectives are first translated into the types and quantities of products to be manufactured. Based on production needs (as defined by the various bills of materials), the purchasing department will seek to order the required materials so that they arrive in time and in sufficient quantities to enable production to keep up with its schedules. After they are brought into the receiving section and checked off, the materials are then assigned to the appropriate departments, sections, and so forth.

Stockkeeping is charged with the handling, internal movement, and storage of materials, as well as with the finished goods inventory. The shipping department handles the distribution of the plant's product, along with the attendant recordkeeping.

A firm's inventories represent a substantial financial investment, not only because of the initial costs of purchasing the materials required for production but also for the many additional processing costs (labor, machines, electricity, and overhead expenses) and storage. Consequently, this phase of the business requires nearly continuous and responsible planning: working up projections, determining desirable inventory levels, ascertaining lead times for timely ordering, setting into position effective inventory methods and control systems, and other details. Here, the twin objectives seem to be (1) to meet the needs of plant

---

*Joseph T. Straub, *Managing: An Introduction*. (Boston: Kent, 1984), 303. See also: Peter R. Richardson, "Courting Greater Employee Involvement Through Participative Management," *Sloan Management Review* 26 (Winter 1985), 33–43.

**Helpful suggestions regarding the creation of task forces may be found in: William J. Altier, "Task Forces—An Effective Management Tool," *Sloan Management Review* 27 (Spring 1986), 69–76.

and customers alike, and simultaneously (2) to hold down inventory levels to their minimums, commensurate with those needs.

Among the more important requisites for effective control are

- Setting up a good perpetual inventory system (which may be maintained manually, mechanically, or electronically)
- Taking occasional physical inventory counts
- Establishing minimum/maximum levels for all items inventoried
- Strategically using buffer or reserve stocks
- Knowing the details of all pertinent costs

Recordkeeping is extensive in this area, and a great deal of direction for management can be derived from all this paperwork. Management can study, item by item, the *movement* or sales figures for all merchandise carried by the firm. Indeed, the need for small business owners to plan and evaluate their inventory investments cannot be overemphasized. One survey of small-scale enterprises (including manufacturing, construction, distributive trades, and service businesses) revealed that these firms tend to rely on *simple controls* and *management judgment* rather than on the kinds of quantitative techniques used by large companies.*

Descriptions of three different inventory control systems suitable for small business that can be implemented on a micro- or minicomputer are offered in a 1983 issue of the *Journal of Small Business Management.* ** Additional information regarding the management and control of inventories (including ABC analysis) can be found in chapters 23 and 24 of this book.

MATERIALS MANAGEMENT

Basically, the materials management function sees to it that the right raw materials, semifinished products, and components are brought into the plant at the right times and in sufficient quantities to meet all production requirements. Although manufacturers generally purchase the materials they require from suppliers, management may occasionally decide to fabricate some of these goods (or parts) within the plant itself. The pros and cons of each "make-or-buy" situation are weighed, and appropriate decisions are made.

Materials Requirement Planning

One of the most difficult—and continuous—tasks that confronts plant management is that of estimating the types and quantities of materials required for their production needs. Happily, the price of a microcomputer now lies well within

---

*B. J. Grablowsky, "Financial Management of Inventory," *Journal of Small Business Management* 22 (July 1984), 59–65.

**John H. Blackstone, Jr., and James F. Cox, "Inventory Management Techniques," *Journal of Small Business Management* 23 (April 1983), 27–33.

the reach of most small firms. For this reason, more and more small business owners seem to be resorting to a helpful materials planning system. Known as "Materials Requirement Planning" (or MRP), it is especially useful for companies with yearly revenues in excess of $2 million to 3 million.* This system offers production management the opportunity "to plan in the face of inaccurate forecasts and to react quickly and effectively to the unexpected."**

Among the benefits that MRP offers are a reduction in inventory levels, speedier purchasing, and improved scheduling of production runs.†

MRP has been described as:

> . . . an integrated computer-based information system designed for the ordering and scheduling of dependent demand items such as raw materials, components, subassemblies, and parts. The requirements for the finished products (end items) generate the requirements for the respective components by using lead time information to determine the amount and timing of such orders. The planning horizon is broken into time brackets (e.g., weeks, months, etc.), so that scheduling for the end items and their components can be fulfilled in a timely fashion.‡

FOR FURTHER INFORMATION

Books

Adam, E., Jr., and R. Ebert. *Production and Operations Management: Concepts, Models, and Behavior,* 3d ed. Englewood Cliffs, N.J.: Prentice-Hall, 1984.

Fogarty, Donald W., and Thomas R. Hoffman. *Production and Inventory Management.* Cincinnati: South-Western, 1983.

Greene, J. *Operations Management: Productivity and Profit.* Englewood Cliffs, N.J.: Prentice-Hall, 1984.

Hax, A., and D. Candia, Jr. *Production and Inventory Management.* Englewood Cliffs, N.J.: Prentice-Hall, 1984.

Laufer, A. C. *Production and Operations Management,* 3d ed. Cincinnati: South-Western, 1984.

Lee, Lamar, Jr., and David N. Burt. *Purchasing and Materials Management: Text and Cases,* 4th ed. New York: McGraw-Hill, 1984.

Mayer, Raymond E. *Production and Operations Management,* 4th ed. New York: McGraw-Hill, 1982.

---

*Dale G. Sauers, "MRP for Small Business," *Journal of Small Business Management* 22 (July 1984), 1–8.

**Ibid., 2.

†Charles H. Davis, Feraidoon (Fred) Raafat, and M. Hossein Safizadeh, "Production and Inventory Information Processing: Material Requirements Planning," *Journal of Small Business Management* 21 (July 1983), 26.

‡Ibid., 26–27.

Monks, Joseph G. *Operations Management: Theory and Problems,* 2d ed. New York: McGraw-Hill, 1982.

Plossl, G. *Production and Inventory Control: Principles and Techniques,* 2d ed. Englewood Cliffs, N.J.: Prentice-Hall, 1985.

Schonberger, Richard J. *Operations Management: Productivity and Quality,* 2d ed. Plano, Tex.: Business Publications, 1985.

Sumanth, David J. *Productivity Engineering and Management.* New York: McGraw-Hill, 1984.

Pamphlets Available from the Small Business Administration

MANAGEMENT AIDS

MA 2.011—"Fixing Production Mistakes"

MA 2.027—"How to Get Started with a Small Business Computer"

MA 3.010—"Techniques for Problem Solving"

MA 5.009—"Techniques for Productivity Improvement"

SMALL BUSINESS BIBLIOGRAPHIES

SBB # 75—"Inventory Management"

SBB # 85—"Purchasing for Owners of Small Plants"

SBB # 88—"Manufacturing Management"

SBB # 90—"New Product Development"

Booklets Available from the Superintendent of Documents

S/N 045-000-00146-6—*Decision Points in Developing New Products*—$4.25.

S/N 045-000-00162-8—*Cost Accounting for Small Manufacturers*—$6.00.

S/N 045-000-00167-9—*Purchasing Management and Inventory Control for Small Business*—$4.50.

S/N 045-000-00181-4—*Purchasing for Manufacturing Firms*—$4.75.

S/N 045-000-00182-2—*Inventory Management—Manufacturing/Service*—$4.75.

S/N 045-000-00183-1—*Inventory and Scheduling Techniques*—$4.75.

V
MARKETING BASICS

12

Marketing and Product/Service Management

Regardless of the nature of your new enterprise, the managing of the marketing function will demand more creativity and more astute judgment than any other single phase of the business. Your warehouses may be jammed to the rafters with inventory, your new machines may be churning out thousands of merchandise units each day, your store's shelves may be crammed with goods, yet all can come to naught if sales are not consummated. The end purpose of all this activity and preparation is the accomplishment of those exchange transactions called "sales," where your firm receives customer dollars in exchange for its products.

THE MARKETING CONCEPT

In contrast to the old-fashioned accent on production that characterized American business only a few decades ago, today's healthy small firm is one that is, first and foremost, oriented toward the customer. This contemporary "marketing concept" approach is simple to learn:

1. Identify your intended customer groups.
2. Find out all you can about their needs and wants.
3. Try to satisfy them with the right products and/or services, supported by the right promotion, and available at the right time and location.

Under this modern marketing concept, an alert entrepreneur designs the firm's organizational structure so as to give the marketing component its deserved prominence. The marketing function is fully integrated with other traditional divisions of the business such as finance and production, and placed in a position to coordinate them. The company's marketing strategies and tactics are purposeful, well organized, and projected years into the future. Moreover, within a marketing-oriented firm, planning responds to sociocultural and even natural environmental changes, and displays abundant flexibility.

In directing your company's marketing efforts, bear in mind that there is little you can do about certain elements of the environment. Two examples are the legal framework within which your firm must operate and the general business conditions of the economy. Only four factors are truly within your control, and you must learn to manipulate them skillfully to compete successfully in the marketplace. These controllable elements are *products, pricing, promotion,* and *distribution.* Together, they are commonly referred to as the *marketing mix.*

Each of these major factors in marketing decision making is sufficiently important to be treated in a separate chapter. This chapter deals with products—the first of the four elements. The next three chapters are devoted to in-depth presentation of the other elements.

PRODUCT MANAGEMENT

Of the four constituent elements in the marketing mix, products probably present the major challenge facing your company. The other three ingredients are usually only support activities which, when carefully planned, will facilitate the movement of your goods into the hands of your customers. Products are the items that you *produce* (if you are a manufacturer) or *select and buy* (in wholesaling and retailing) to fulfill the needs and wants of your customers.

To manufacturers and intermediaries alike, effective management of the product sphere is crucial. Product-line management involves many things: finding and selecting the proper items to carry; determining how wide or narrow a line to offer; deciding when to discard or retain an item, when to add new products to the line, and so forth.

What is a Product?

To the layperson, the word *product* generally signifies the actual, physical object offered for sale. Modern marketing, however, approaches the product as much more than a simple, three-dimensional object. It's as though this "thing" designed to satisfy customer needs were surrounded by an intangible, invisible aura (or *frame of reference*). Contained within this aura are other attributes not so easily discerned: the reputation of the producer or seller, the style of the packaging, past messages conveyed by advertisements of the product, other people's impressions and opinions about the item, and so on.

A product, then, is much more than an object. It's an intricate mental concept, rich in connotations. It reflects an image that literally comprises a *total package of satisfactions* for the intended user.

Products do not exist by themselves, frameless and within a vacuum. A pair of Florsheim shoes, an electric toaster emblazoned with the Proctor-Silex or

General Electric label, a Gucci handbag, a tube of Crest toothpaste, or a Chevrolet Caprice—each of these articles is positioned within a frame of reference that differentiates it from competitive products.

CLASSIFYING PRODUCTS

You may find it useful to learn how marketing practitioners assign products to categories, since these classifications provide an orderly basis for product management. The following are common approaches to product classification:

- Industrial and consumer goods
- Necessities and luxuries
- Durables and nondurables
- Convenience, shopping, and specialty goods
- Staples and fashion items

These labels by no means exhaust the possibilities. They are, however, sufficient to provide a basic grasp of product classification. Each sample category is discussed briefly below.

Industrial and Consumer Goods

This classification scheme is based on the user for whom the products are intended. The merchandise used by industry, commerce, government, and intermediaries of all types in the ordinary conduct of their operations is referred to as *industrial goods.* Partially finished as well as completely finished products may be included in this category, along with lumber, industrial chemicals, tools, machines, supplies, and the like. *Consumer goods* are the finished products intended for use by the final consumer. Clothing, household furnishings, automobiles, fishing tackle, and groceries are some examples.

Necessities and Luxuries

This grouping classifies products according to the urgency or lack of urgency people show in their buying habits. This type of consumer behavior is tied to the concept of *discretionary purchasing power.* Obviously, categorization in this manner is sometimes misleading in that one person's luxury might be another's necessity. A new electronic typewriter purchased by a salesclerk, high school student, or automobile mechanic is most likely considered a luxury good, yet the identical machine is probably a necessity to a writer of fiction, a college professor, or a business executive.

Durables and Nondurables

The word *durable* means "of a lasting quality." Products that last a long time (and are consequently purchased less often), such as pocket calculators, clothing, television sets, and pots and pans, are called *durable goods.* The contrasting term, *nondurable goods,* refers to items that provide temporary satisfaction: Foodstuffs and many services come under this category.

Convenience, Shopping, and Specialty Goods

Here again, products are looked at from the standpoint of the consumer, taking into consideration the time and effort expended in shopping for the items. People generally spend almost no time shopping for items like chewing gum, sugar, and butter, and so these are designated *convenience goods.* Such merchandise is readily available at many locations; there's little *product* difference but often substantial differentiation of one *brand* from the next.

Furniture, jewelry, fashionable clothing, carpeting, and the like are called *shopping goods* because they require more time and effort by the shopper. Here, the consumer usually wishes to compare the item with other similar offerings with regard to price, quality, and style before making a choice.

Prospective buyers expend even greater effort before purchasing *specialty goods* such as custom-made products, special brands, better-quality clothes, and the like. Of course, there could be some overlapping here, depending on individual consumer motivation and "search behavior." A convenience item for one person may be a shopping good or even a specialty item for the next.

Staples and Fashion Items

Staple goods are those that enjoy a widespread and generally continuous demand over time. Examples include men's socks, razor blades, fresh eggs, and butter. When demand is erratic and subject to wide fluctuations, as with nonstaple merchandise (men's shirts, women's shoes and sportswear, and the like), the products are referred to as *fashion goods.*

MANAGING THE PRODUCT LINE

The first requirement in product management is to reach a consensus on specific product objectives, which are then followed as guidelines. Among those commonly encountered in business are increasing sales, enlarging the company's market share, fully utilizing manufacturing capacity, matching new or improved products of competitors, and changing methods of distribution. Before deciding on such objectives, management should do some diligent soul-searching and ask questions like these:

- What kind of business are we in?
- Which segments of the general market are we catering to?
- Which new segments can we service in the future?
- How well do our current products meet the needs of our customers?
- Are there other items we ought to be carrying?
- Are there items in our line we should drop?
- What new products can we add to replace those we discard?
- Is each of our items compatible with the other products in our line?

THE PRODUCT LIFE CYCLE CONCEPT AND ITS IMPLICATIONS

The *Product Life Cycle* (PLC) concept is of special importance in the first steps of market strategy development and has been well publicized over the years in the marketing literature. (See exhibit 12–1.) The concept attempts to describe the performance of any successful new product from the point at which it is first introduced into the marketplace through its final demise. Except for fashion merchandise and fads, most products appear to pass through four stages before reaching obsolescence. These are the *introductory, growth, maturity,* and *decline* stages of the PLC.

Introductory Stage

When a new product is introduced into the marketplace, it is unknown to most of its targeted purchasers. Obviously, some groundwork has to be prepared for the "launching." During the introductory stage of the PLC, the innovating firm must invest substantial funds in promotional activities of the "pioneering" type in order to carry the "product story" to prospective buyers. Once it has provided the product information, the company must ensure that people will be able to purchase the item at convenient locations. So, manufacturers need to consider what distribution channels to employ in order to reach those prospects.

For the innovating company, this first stage is a costly one. The producer must absorb the initial costs involved in designing the product, in gearing up the machinery and internal systems for its manufacture, in promoting the item, and in securing enough initial distribution points to generate product viability in the marketplace.

EXHIBIT 12-1. THE LIFE CYCLE OF A TYPICAL NEW PRODUCT

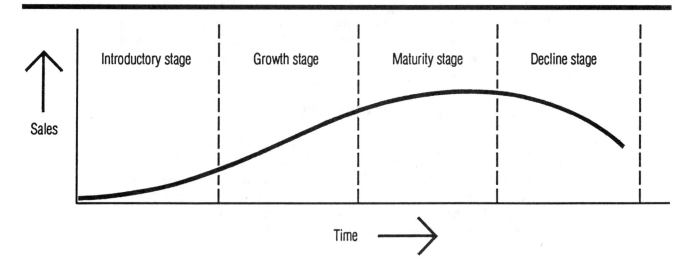

Often, the manufacturer seeks to recover much of this investment by placing a higher-than-ordinary price tag on the item. Or, the company might seek mass distribution instead, by pricing the product somewhat "below-the-market" in order to secure a strong foothold. In either case, little or no profit is usually accrued during this introductory stage. Frequently, the manufacturer encounters losses, sometimes severe.

Both wholesalers and retailers are cautious about adding to their regular lines an article of merchandise that is obviously in its introductory phase. They realize that most of their regular customers are likely to be unfamiliar with the product and that it may therefore be difficult for them to sell. Consequently, these distributors may ask the supplier for such extras as free point-of-purchase signs and other materials, cooperative advertising dollars, full return privileges, and the like. The large-scale retail firm may even request exclusive distribution in its trading area.

Growth Stage

Provided these initial efforts result in gradual customer acceptance, more and more people will learn of the new product, try it, and (if satisfied) continue purchasing and using the item. During the growth stage of the PLC, greater effort is exerted in distribution so that merchandise becomes increasingly available at more locations. Sales volume starts to climb. After the start-up costs are substantially absorbed by sales, the additional revenues resulting from more market penetration lead to a sharp rise in company profit. For the manufacturer, this stage generally bears the highest profit margin. During this stage, too, manufacturing methods are generally refined as production gears up to meet demand. This, in turn, results in even lower per-unit costs.

Advertising is increased to support product growth, but now a broader sales base exists which supports advertising expenditures. For the new small company, it might be advantageous at this juncture to expand the number of purchase points, simply to keep costs within a reasonable range.

Wholesalers and retailers who handle the new product begin to enjoy the fruits of expanding demand. They order more heavily as they experience a higher stockturn rate. The manufacturer may launch additional product variations—new sizes, new colors, or new materials. It should be noted that, even at this comparatively early point in the product life cycle, when profits peak, competition begins to enter the picture, seeking to emulate the evident success of the pioneering manufacturer.

Maturity Stage

Eventually, the ascending growth curve begins to level off (although this might not occur for years). By the time the successful product has entered the maturity stage of the PLC, it has found widespread consumer acceptance, and a number of competitors offering similar products have appeared on the scene. For the originating firm, the environment is then a highly competitive one and competitors' prices are sometimes much lower. The producer is frequently compelled to step up promotional efforts in an attempt to differentiate the product from those of competitors, thus protecting the initial advantage and market share so assiduously cultivated. Naturally, such tactics tend to force costs upward. In turn, profits begin to shrink. At best, efforts like these constitute a delaying action, although they can occasionally extend this particular stage for a long period of time. (The majority of products now in the marketplace are most likely in the maturity stage of their respective life cycles.)

Both retail and wholesale distributors take advantage of the competition for their business among suppliers of the same types of goods. These merchants ask their sources of supply for better terms, more extended warranties (where available), more frequent deliveries, money for cooperative advertising, and so on. They also seek to drop and replace those suppliers with whom they have not been happy.

Decline Stage

In the face of declining sales and profits, manufacturers sometimes make last-ditch efforts to resuscitate the item. These include approaches like new packaging, special promotions, new versions, price changes, and so on. Although it is often difficult to discard a product, sooner or later, as sales continue to decline, the decision has to be faced. In this final decline stage, appropriate steps include planning to phase out the item, tapering down gradually on inventory, working out equitable arrangements with intermediaries so they do not suffer losses along the way, and disposing of excess inventory.

With products that are clearly in their decline stage, distributors will begin to reduce the number of variants they carry, cut back on reorders, and gradually start phasing out the merchandise. They may even mark down their goods in order to close them out.

THE "EIGHTY-TWENTY PRINCIPLE"

A practical rule of thumb you can apply in a variety of ways to your marketing planning is the *eighty-twenty principle*. For example, if a manufacturing company lists all of its accounts according to their annual purchases, chances are that the firm will discover as much as 80 percent of its total annual sales coming from about 20 percent of its customers.

Similarly, a firm maintaining a sales force of around fifty salespeople can analyze each employee's sales productivity according to this same principle. More likely than not, management will learn that the major portion of sales has been brought in by as few as nine or ten star performers.

The eighty-twenty principle can also be applied to product-line management. One company, a wholesaler of janitorial chemicals and supplies, maintained a huge inventory of more than 8,000 items in order to service hundreds of regular customers. Sales results for a two-year period were analyzed by computer, on an item-by-item movement basis. Management was surprised to learn that 1,700 items accounted for more than 75 percent of their annual sales volume. Needless to say, the product line was drastically reduced by more than 50 percent over the next few months. This resulted in a savings of $250,000 in capital formerly tied up in inventory. Although sales initially dropped by 4 percent, fewer salespeople could thereafter devote more time to fewer products (and the firm's mail-order catalog accented the more popular merchandise), resulting in an overall sales increase of more than 15 percent by the end of the year.

NEW-PRODUCT DEVELOPMENT

From time to time, the progressive small company introduces one or more new products into its line. Many factors can spur such a move: a desire to enhance the firm's reputation as an innovator in its industry; the need to stimulate sales, replace products in a decline, or outperform a serious competitor; or, more simply, a desire to take advantage of occasional special deals.

The New-Product Development Process

For the manufacturing company, the new-product development process involves a logical sequence:

1. The emergence of the "raw" idea
2. A "screening" procedure whereby the idea is evaluated, along with others, against previously established criteria
3. The tedious research and development period during which the idea is gradually refined, a prototype of the item is made, cost analyses are worked up, production methods are devised, marketing factors such as price and packaging are considered, and estimates are made of demand and expected profits
4. The testing stage wherein the product's performance in one or several areas is carefully watched
5. Full-scale introduction on the market

The criteria mentioned in stage two above may include the following: the size of market for the item, the product's potential contribution to company profits, the uniqueness of the item and its effect on other products in the line, and the ease with which it can be integrated into the total production load.

Generally, the expenditures required to develop a single new product are substantial, to say the least. This fact, coupled with the recognition that most new products fail, is a serious warning to the recently established small business to think twice (or more) before embarking on this path. Until the firm is well established, management would be wiser to consider a different strategy in its product-line management: waiting until a competitor has had a substantial degree of success with an item and then producing its own improved version (thus "riding on the bandwagon").

Perhaps there is more sanity and less risk in striving to be second than in being first!

Where to Find New Products

Ideas for new products come from a variety of sources: the company's suppliers and their sales representatives, customers and prospective customers, company personnel, trade journals and general publications, and competitors.

Of course, the bulk of ideas for new products or services can and should be generated internally, especially if the organization has a product development section or committee. In an "open" organization, where all employees are encouraged to come up with helpful ideas, there should be no lack of new product ideas. Certainly, a simple suggestion-box system, reinforced by efficient follow-through procedures, will be of considerable value. For the retailer, a "want-slip" system can serve the same purpose.

Creative Thinking Approaches

The employee or internal team in charge of generating new product ideas can be quickly indoctrinated in some of the more popular "creative thinking" techniques. These include brainstorming, attribute listing, "running the alphabet," and checklists. Each of these approaches is described below in brief detail.

Brainstorming. Although commonly encountered as a group procedure, brainstorming can be used by individuals as well. Generally enjoyed by participants, it provides group members with the benefits of a highly motivating atmosphere. The group, usually small, meets for the purpose of coming up with ideas in quantity within a short time span—perhaps ten or fifteen minutes. There are no holds barred; participants are encouraged to let their imaginations run wild, while at the same time, all criticism or judgment is withheld. Ideas flow so fast at times that the use of a tape recorder is recommended. Over the following two or three days, ideas generated from the "brainstorm" can be typed up for thoughtful analysis. A set of previously established criteria is then applied, and the more promising alternatives are selected.

Research has demonstrated conclusively that significantly more good ideas are produced through brainstorming procedures (either individually or in groups) than through more customary approaches to idea generation.

Attribute Listing. As its name suggests, this technique involves preparing a list of the significant characteristics of a product that, combined, will differentiate it from other products. Let's say your company is in the business of manufacturing ordinary pencils and you are hunting for new, unique products to add to your line. You begin by describing the basic pencil itself: its color(s), its size and shape, its substances and constituent materials, and its function(s)—to write, and perhaps to erase. Each of these characteristics then becomes a logical candidate for change or variation.

For example, the color *yellow* could be changed to dozens of other colors or to *striped, polka-dotted,* or *transparent.* Other attributes, such as size, shape, material, function, texture, odor, and taste, can be used to originate hundreds of variations. Changing the function of a pencil, for example, from *to write* to something else, like *to play with, to eat,* or *to use as a weapon* (or myriad other possible functions) might lead to pencil-shaped objects that are toys, or made of chocolate, or designed for self-defense.

The manufacturer of luggage, giftware, or small appliances can employ the same approach to develop new product ideas.

Running the Alphabet. Also known as the *ABC method,* this approach borrows liberally from the word association techniques of psychologists. Essentially, it consists of preparing in advance a list of words beginning with the letter *A,* then *B* words, and so on through the alphabet until forty or fifty words have been listed. From a practical point of view, it's desirable to work mostly with nouns. The words selected are then used to "mine" for ideas. (Of course, once you have gained practice with the technique, there's little need to follow the ABCs studiously. There is no reason why you can't begin anywhere in the alphabet, say, with words starting with *G*s, *L*s, *P*s, or *S*s.)

Here's a hypothetical example of the technique in action:

A canned soup manufacturer wanted ideas for new soups in order to increase the company's market share. A sampling of the list prepared under this creative approach follows:

abalone	ball	camera
Africa	banquet	carousel
alligator	blossom	circus
apple	bronze	cognac
apricot	Brooklyn	crystal
Aquarius	bubble	cup
aspirin	cabana	
badge	calliope	

The manufacturer considered the words one by one and came up with many new ideas, including: abalone soup (and, by extension, many other fish soups), fruit soups, soups for medicinal purposes, and so on. Edibles such as fruits, vegetables, meats, fish, and so forth, are rather amenable to the "soup" concept.

In this respect, then, the ideas may not be all that original or new. More likely than not, some competitive firm already succeeded in linking several of the more likely concepts to new soup possibilities. Indeed, the competitor may be on the verge of launching the new product in the marketplace.

It's in the "mental manipulation" of the "nonedibles" on this list (for example, *Aquarius, blossom,* or *cabana*) that the true worth of this technique would emerge. It's easy to see how ideas generated *via* these unorthodox associations can result in truly innovative suggestions.

Consider, for instance, the word *Aquarius.* One immediately conceives of a soup designed specifically for consumers born under this sign, and, by logical extension, a dozen items in a new line of "astrological soups." If you can't imagine what could be included in such products, you could begin with (at the very least) the more familiar alphabet soup—replacing the letters with miniature symbols of the zodiac.

Of course, this technique (like brainstorming and attribute listing) can be applied to a variety of business problems, ranging from artwork and copy for advertising to choosing a packaging style, planning major promotions, and producing names for new products. For example, in hunting for ways to motivate your salespeople, you might come across the *B* words *badge* and *ball.* These stimuli could trigger ideas like issuing merit badges (or, by extension, certificates) to outstanding performers of the month or quarter, instituting an annual ball for employees who surpass their quotas (or an outing at a ball park), and so on.

Checklists and Other "Pump-Primers." Checklists are used daily in business for purposes of measurement and/or control, and sometimes to ensure thoroughness in planning. A checklist is also a valuable device for triggering the imagination, although it's seldom used in this creative capacity.

Consider, for example, the familiar "five *W*s" of the journalist: *Who? What? Where? When? Why?* (A sixth question—*How?*—is usually added to this mini-checklist.) The "five *W*s" can be of extraordinary value in investigating and analyzing many types of business problems, such as declining sales, loss of market share, the proper deployment of company resources, and the like. They are also useful in planning for promotion campaigns, expansion, and so on.

One famous checklist in the so-called creativity literature was devised by Alex Osborn, the "father of brainstorming." It is essentially, a series of nine groups of questions all designed for the purpose of generating new product ideas from existing products. Some examples are "How can this product be adapted to other uses? What else can we add to (or subtract from) it? Can we rearrange any of its components? Can the item be enlarged or reduced?"*

In addition to checklists, other "pump-primers" exist that can prod our imaginations. The classified telephone directory, for instance, can be used as a source of leads (new prospects for a salesperson to pursue). The daily newspapers and business publications are also excellent sources of ideas for your day-to-day business activities.

PACKAGING AND BRANDING

Along with the development of a new item, the manufacturer must think about *packaging:* enclosing the product in some type of package or container for purposes of protection. Of course, the item must be packaged so that it can be easily handled, placed in cartons, shipped, stored, and eventually placed on shelves or on display, all with an eye to avoiding damage to the contents. Furthermore, the modern package helps to sell the merchandise it contains through a combination of factors that include design, color, and materials used. Moreover, the package usually identifies the originating company.

Some retailers and wholesalers, of course, will package goods themselves. In this respect, the selection and subsequent popularization of a brand name, trademark, or other identifying device can be of substantial importance to the company seeking to differentiate its merchandise from competitors'. Over time,

*See Alex F. Osborn, *Applied Imagination,* 3d rev. ed. (New York: Charles Scribner's Sons, 1963), 286–87.

the *brand name* will establish a vital "sales personality" for the product. Hence, care should be exercised at the outset in the selection of a name. A simple name is preferable; it should be easy for the consumer or industrial buyer to spell and to pronounce. It also should be easy to recall.

Often, the name chosen is simply the firm's name, like General Electric, Heinz, Timex, Budweiser, Black & Decker, Atari, or Remington. At times, brand names reflect the benefits promised to users of the product or imply its important qualities. Consider the following, for example: Pepsi Free, Beautyrest, Ivory soap, and One-A-Day vitamins.

As a general rule, unless the new company has based its entire marketing effort on a single innovative product (which is rarely the case), the choice of brand name is relatively unimportant. In the long run, the popularization of a company name is more significant. In time, the firm's name can be successfully used to "brand" its products.

THE MARKETING OF SERVICES

Marketing practitioners who work for companies that offer services for sale often proceed in much the same manner as do their counterparts in organizations that market products. Yet there are sharp differences between the kinds of approaches that are needed to market services and traditional product marketing methods. Certain distinctive features of services make them more difficult to market than products: intangibility, perishability, inseparability from the service provider, and variability in quality.*

As an illustration, let's consider that first quality of *intangibility.* Products are real, not abstract. Because they are concrete objects, prospective buyers can see, touch, feel, and examine them before arriving at a purchase/no purchase decision. For example, the consumer (or organizational buyer) who is shopping for a suitcase is able to look over and compare a number of different styles and brands; determine the quality of the materials of which it is made, the hinges, and the closures; make an estimate of its durability; and so forth.

On the other hand, the person who is interested in a service—for example, a complete medical examination, a Caribbean cruise, or World Series tickets—remains at a comparative disadvantage because: "A service is rendered. A service is experienced. A service cannot be stored on a shelf, touched, tasted or tried on for size."**

Because of the distinctive characteristics of services, certain aspects of marketing them take on added importance. Two of the more important are the capabilities of the people who perform or deliver the service (knowledge, training, skill, good customer relations, and so on) and the premises or other

---

*Joel R. Evans and Barry Berman, *Essentials of Marketing* (New York: Macmillan, 1984), 452.

**G. Lynn Shostak, "Breaking Free from Product Marketing," *Journal of Marketing* 41 (April 1977), 73.

environment in which service performance or delivery takes place.*

More information about the marketing of services is offered in chapter 25—"Improving Results in Your Service Business."

FOR FURTHER INFORMATION

Books

Assael, Henry. *Marketing Management: Strategy and Action.* Boston: Kent Publishing, 1985.

Cunningham, William H., Isabella C. M. Cunningham, and Christopher M. Swift. *Marketing: A Managerial Approach,* 2d ed. Cincinnati: South-Western, 1987.

Evans, Joel R., and Barry Berman. *Marketing,* 2d ed. New York: Macmillan, 1985.

Hartley, Robert F. *Marketing Fundamentals.* New York: Harper & Row, 1983.

Kotler, Philip. *Marketing Essentials.* Englewood Cliffs, N.J.: Prentice-Hall, 1984.

McDaniel, Carl, Jr. *Marketing: An Integrated Approach,* 2d ed. New York: Harper & Row, 1982.

Mentzer, John T., and David J. Schwartz. *Marketing Today,* 4th ed. San Diego: Harcourt Brace Jovanovich, 1985.

Nickels, William G. *Marketing Principles,* 2d ed. Englewood Cliffs, N.J.: Prentice-Hall, 1982.

Pessemier, Edgar A. *Product Management: Strategy and Organization,* 2d ed. New York: Wiley, 1982.

Reibstein, David J. *Marketing: Concepts, Strategies, and Decisions.* Englewood Cliffs, N.J.: Prentice-Hall, 1985.

Shaw, Roy, and Richard J. Semenik. *Marketing,* 5th ed. Cincinnati: South-Western, 1985.

Stanton, William J. *Fundamentals of Marketing,* 7th ed. New York: McGraw-Hill, 1984.

Webster, Frederick E., Jr. *Industrial Marketing Strategy,* 2d ed. New York: Wiley, 1984.

Pamphlets Available from the Small Business Administration

MANAGEMENT AIDS

MA 1.018—"Checklist for Profit Watching"
MA 2.007—"Business Plan for Small Manufacturers"

---

*See, for example: Valarie A. Zeithaml, A. Parasuraman, and Leonard L. Berry, "Problems and Strategies in Services Marketing," *Journal of Marketing* 49 (Spring 1985), 33–46; Leonard L. Berry, Valarie A. Zeithaml, and A. Parasuraman, "Quality Counts in Services, Too," *Business Horizons* 28 (May-June 1985), 44–52; G. Lynn Shostak, "Service Positioning Through Structural Change," *Journal of Marketing* 51 (January 1987), 34–43.

MA 2.013—"Can You Make Money with Your Idea or Invention?"
MA 2.020—"Business Plan for Retailers"
MA 2.022—"Business Plan for Small Service Firms"
MA 2.028—"The Business Plan for Homebased Business"
MA 4.012—"Marketing Checklist for Small Retailers"
MA 6.005—"Introduction to Patents"

Booklets Available from the Superintendent of Documents

S/N 045-000-00146-6—*Decision Points in Developing New Products*—$4.25.

13

The Management of Prices

The pricing area is of no less, and possibly greater, weight than the other ingredients of the marketing mix. It requires consummate managerial skill on your part. How a firm handles its pricing frequently spells the difference between marketing success and failure. Business survival and growth depend upon proper pricing practices.

THE MEANING OF PRICE

Clearly, the price concept is closely associated with products (and product management). Indeed, these two *P*s are often handled in tandem, although this shouldn't be the case. Price, you see, has many facets:

- Price facilitates the buying and selling process.
- Price is affected by the interplay of supply and demand.
- Price is a useful tool in promotion.
- Price can help—or hinder—sales.
- Price ties into methods of distribution.
- Price can affect your bottom-line figure for better or for worse.
- Price is related to costs and profits.
- Price can be a valuable tool when used as a competitive weapon.
- Price can be manipulated strategically from one stage of the product life cycle to the next.

To the consumer, the price of a product (or service) represents nothing more than the seller's interpretation, expressed in monetary terms, of the

169

product's utility value: its ability to satisfy a buyer's wants or needs. Consequently, shoppers regard the price of an item as "fair" (congruent with their own perceptions of its worth in dollars and cents) or pegged higher or lower than "fair." If they consider the price too high, consumers resist purchasing the item. If the price is considered low, then it becomes a "bargain" (although a low price can cause shoppers to doubt the quality of the product).

So for most products there appears to be an acceptable *price range* instead of a specific and exact *price point.* Bear this in mind when pricing your goods.

To manufacturers, price is a more complex affair. Indeed, most producers regard their *manufacturer's price* as a composite designed to cover, at the very minimum, all of the following: the cost of the raw materials that went into the product, the cost of labor required for manufacture, part of the production overhead and the administrative and selling expenses, plus a margin of profit to make it all worthwhile.

Wholesalers and retailers approach pricing in much the same way, except that the *cost of goods purchased* is substituted for materials and other manufacturing expenses.

Most small businesses use this *cost-plus* approach to pricing. Nevertheless, prices shouldn't be formulated solely in this manner. The perceptive small businessperson sees a built-in inconsistency here: the method pays no attention whatever to the *demand* for the product. When the demand for an item is heavy and people are clamoring for it, the majority of consumers will tolerate an increase in the regular (list) price. While some people will refuse to purchase the item, most will buy it anyway, and the resulting sales will generate a good deal more profit overall. Further, when demand is light, maintaining the usual price of an article may lead to a decrease in sales volume.

You should also take into consideration other pertinent factors:

- Competitors' prices
- Desired return on your investment
- Economic conditions
- Level of demand
- Location of your business
- Market factors
- Product factors
- Seasonal factors
- The *price/quality relationship* (and other psychological factors)

SETTING PRICES FOR GOODS AND SERVICES

Business organizations often find it quite difficult to arrive at the right selling prices for their goods and/or services. In actual practice, companies may approach the price-setting problem from several distinctly different vantage points. Three of the pricing bases most commonly found in industry are those of *demand, competition,* and *cost.*

Theoretically, an item's price tends to fluctuate in direct proportion to customer demand for that item. As demand intensifies, the price is apt to rise;

as demand falls, we may expect the price to begin to fall. In following a *demand-oriented pricing* approach, management will strive to determine both the current demand level and the price that customers appear willing to pay for the item. The firm may proceed to work up estimates of the different levels of demand that might be expected at various selling prices—in order to determine the one price that should yield the highest sales volume and/or profit.

In *competition-based pricing,* little or no attention is paid to actual demand. Instead, the firm reviews the prices set by its major competitors before making its own pricing decisions. The company may then decide to (a) maintain parity with its competitors, (b) set its prices above those of its competition (usually to project an above-the-average image), or (c) undersell its competition.

By far the most popular approach of all, though, is that of *cost-oriented pricing.* It's logical to assume that any selling price should cover all pertinent costs and also produce some profit for the business enterprise.

The next section offers more details about cost-based pricing.

THE "COST-PLUS" APPROACH

Business costs are traditionally broken down into *fixed* and *variable* expenses (although some firms go further in their accounting procedures and use terms like *semivariable* costs). The term *fixed costs* encompasses all costs that remain approximately the same whether, for example, ten pieces or ten thousand pieces of Item X are produced each day in the plant. In other words, these expenses do not vary along with the ebb and flow in the production rate. The fixed-costs category includes such expenses as rent, heat, insurance, depreciation, executive salaries, interest on loans, and property taxes.

Expenses that *do* vary along with output are labeled *variable costs.* These include the cost of raw materials (or semiprocessed materials and components if used), wages earned by the production workers (direct labor), warehousing and shipping costs, and sales costs (commissions).

When setting prices by means of a cost-plus approach, management typically takes into consideration total variable expenses per unit as well as a per-unit share of the firm's fixed costs. Also built into the price structure is the amount of profit desired (per unit, of course). By far the most common cost-plus approach, this method is known as *full-cost pricing.*

PRICING POLICIES

Work out in advance, and to your own satisfaction, a number of specific pricing policies for every aspect of your company's marketing activity. For example, mull over the best pricing strategy to employ with relation to your competition.

In addition to the three basic pricing strategies discussed above, other marketing areas for establishing a pricing policy include

- The marketing channels employed (setting manufacturer's, wholesaler's, retailer's, and consumer's prices)

- The stage of the product life cycle. (For example, in the introductory stage, a company has the choice of adopting a *skimming* policy whereby the price is set high in an attempt to "skim the cream" of the market; or a *penetration* policy whereby the price is set low in order to establish a strong foothold within short order in the marketplace)

- The promotion mix area (the use of such devices as specials, cents- or dollars-off sales, leader items, and the like)

- Discounting, arranging terms of payment, and so on

MARKUPS (OR MARKONS)

When you set the selling price of any item, you should not only cover all relevant per-unit costs but also tack on an appropriate amount so that you end up with some profit for your firm.

Take the situation where the owner of a small gift shop purchases two dozen decorative ashtrays from a jobber at $30.00 a dozen. Individually, the ashtrays have cost $2.50. The retailer decides to put them on display at $4.50, thus asking $2.00 more than the original cost. Is this amount all profit? Not really, if you're thinking in terms of *net* profit, for a store proprietor must also consider operating expenses: rent, electricity, insurance, labor, advertising costs, and the like. So the $2.00 is really a *contribution* toward overhead. Hopefully, that figure also contains some profit as well.

The $2.00 represents the retailer's *markup*. Markup is the difference between the cost of an item and its selling price—the amount of *gross* profit earned on the article of merchandise when it is sold. Markup is usually expressed as a percentage—either of the selling price (usual in retail businesses) or of the cost (usual in manufacturing and wholesaling). *Markon* is another term used fairly interchangeably with *markup*, because the gross profit margin is *marked on* to the cost to arrive at the selling price.

Although this difference in terms could be regarded as hair-splitting, we ought to relegate markons to the manufacturing and perhaps wholesaling spheres and leave markups to the retailers. The manufacturer generally approaches the pricing of products by totaling each item's direct costs and then *marking on* a fixed percentage of the costs as a contribution to overhead and profit. The knowledgeable retailer, on the other hand, thinks first in terms of the overall percentage of sales needed to cover operating expenses and to yield the planned (net) profit margin, and then adds on this percentage to the costs of the hundreds of items brought in at different costs.

Let's attempt to work this through by way of an example. Assume that an item costs the manufacturer $1.00 to produce. This cost figure is arrived at by combining the cost of materials per unit ($.55) with the direct labor cost ($.45). Seeking $.60 as a contribution toward other expenses and toward profits, the producer decides to offer the item at $1.60 per unit to wholesalers. This represents a desired *markup on cost* of 60 percent ($.60 divided by $1.00.)

After buying the article at $1.60, the wholesaler prices it for sale to retailers at $2.08, apparently looking for a markup (again, on cost) of 30 percent. This percentage covers expenses and profit for performing wholesaling services as the goods travel along the marketing channel toward the final consumer. (See the section on "Marketing Channels in the Economy" in chapter 15.)

Markups in Retailing

The majority of small retailers approach the pricing problem in the same way. Jewelry stores, for instance, traditionally use a *keystone* markup in pricing merchandise: They simply double their costs. If a gold wedding band costs a jeweler $120, the item is usually offered to the consumer at a selling price of $240. This earns the retailer a 100 percent markup (or markon) on the cost.

A better approach to pricing is the following: You can follow the pricing procedures of department stores and large chain store organizations. Well in advance of each season, these retail companies set their merchandise plans. Along with sales projections, they plan their inventory requirements, expenses, profits, and so forth. Their planned sales figures form the basis for their calculations; all other areas are then tied in—expressed as some percentage of the sales volume.

Of course, while a department store carries literally thousands of different items, the small retail shop might offer only a hundred or two. It's difficult for the small store owner to keep abreast of all the separate costs, especially since the cost of a single item may vary throughout the year and from one supplier to the next. However, by maintaining all paperwork (inventory records, accounting statements, and the like) on a *retail,* rather than a cost-valuation basis, the small store proprietor can use this information for decision making as skillfully as department store management. For example, by using the net sales figure atop the past year's income statement, a retailer can readily calculate the firm's total operating expenses as a percentage of sales. Then, when making plans for the following year, the merchant can build both expected operating expenses and a planned profit target into the pricing of store merchandise.

To demonstrate this point, let's return to the earlier illustration of the item that costs $1.00 to manufacture and ends up being offered to the retailer (by the wholesaler) at a cost per unit of $2.08. Suppose you are the store merchant in this case, and you have calculated that your operating expenses total 34 percent of sales. You would like to shoot for an 8 percent profit goal for the year before taxes. Putting the two percentages together, you now have a 42 percent-of-sales figure that must be "covered" over and above the original cost of your merchandise. Since you need an overall markup of 42 percent of sales on goods sold during the year, you try to price most items you buy for resale with that figure in mind. The item that costs you $2.08, then, should sell at about $3.59. (*Note:* To obtain the proper selling price, divide the cost price by the *complement of the markup.* This is what you have left after you subtract the markup, whatever it may be, from 100 percent. In this case, we have 100 percent — 42 percent = 58 percent. If you divide $2.08 by .58, you'll come up with that $3.59 figure).

Of course, this figure may not seem quite right for a retail selling price—and so the merchant will probably peg the price at $3.50 or $3.95 (either of which seems, psychologically, like a better figure).

Also, the selling prices for individual items may vary somewhat from the prices derived from that 42 percent markup. Some merchandise can be sold for more money because of its appeal, while other articles may have to be placed on sale for less. What's important here is that the retailer attains the targeted 42 percent (at least) on an overall, *maintained markup* basis.

BREAK-EVEN ANALYSIS

The *break-even point* is a vital concept that you should understand completely before your business even gets off the ground. It's the point at which the sales you are able to generate cover all costs. If sales do not reach that level, your firm will find itself "in the red." However, once that point has been passed, your profits will start to mount.

If you own a small factory that manufactures a single product, you may also want to know just how many units of that item must be sold before you can reach your break-even point. Here's the way to find out:

1. Bear in mind that at the break-even point, there is neither profit nor loss; costs are exactly equaled. This indicates that whatever approach we use to arrive at a break-even figure, all costs must be taken into account. Hence, we can use the following formula:

$$\frac{\text{Break-even Point}}{\text{(in units)}} = \frac{\text{Total Fixed Costs}}{\text{Per-unit Contribution Toward Fixed Costs}}$$

2. Let's assume you have estimated that your total fixed expenses for the year will be $110,000. You have pegged your variable costs on a per-unit basis at $.88, and your unit price to wholesalers will be $2.70. This means that every unit you sell will make its tiny contribution of $1.82 ($2.70 − .88) toward your fixed expenses.

3. Substituting those amounts for the terms in the formula above, we have:

$$\frac{\text{Break-even Point}}{\text{(in units)}} = \frac{\$110,000}{\$1.82} = 60,440 \text{ (approx.)}$$

In short, you'll need to produce approximately 60,440 units before you reach your break-even point. After that, profits should start coming in.

4. To determine the sales volume you must reach in order to attain your break-even point, simply multiply the number of units required to be sold by the selling price. In this particular situation, the needed sales volume is $163,188 (60,440 × $2.70).

The manufacturer will often experiment with break-even analysis by considering what the various break-even points would be at different selling prices. This analysis aids in determining how to price products.

Another Approach to Calculating Break-even Points

Assume you're thinking about launching a retail business such as the Two Sisters' Dress Shoppe discussed in chapter 5. You can figure your break-even point right from the pro forma income statement you prepared for your first year of operation. Simply follow the procedure below:

1. Add up all your expected operating expenses, both fixed and variable, for the year. (Let's say this totals $45,000.)

2. Decide on the average retail markup you can expect to maintain during the year, expressed as a percentage of the sales. (For example, if we assume a 40 percent markup, then what we're really saying is that forty cents out of every dollar taken in will be gross profit, and that the balance of that dollar will be paid out for the merchandise you purchase for resale.)

3. Divide the total expenses (No. 1 above) by the *per-dollar gross profit* figure (No. 2 above) to find your breakeven point. (In this case, it amounts to $45,000 divided by $.40—which is $112,500.)

4. You might want to go further and find out what your store must produce in sales in order to break even on a *monthly* basis. One way is simply to divide the yearly figure by twelve. Of course, you ought to bear in mind that some months (like December) are busier than others, and so you can only discuss the "average" month in this situation.

5. If you want to calculate your *daily* break-even figure, count up the number of days your store will be open during the month, and divide the monthly figure (No. 4 above) by this number.

PROMOTIONAL PRICING

When establishing prices for their goods and/or services, companies can resort to a variety of promotional pricing strategies in order to boost sales, increase shopper traffic, or otherwise facilitate the selling process. This is especially true of wholesalers and retail firms.

Some of the more popular promotional pricing techniques are briefly described below:

Bait pricing. An illegal promotional practice whereby a retailer prices an item at a bargain price (with no intention of selling the item) and then advertises the offer in order to bring people into the store.

Bait-and-switch pricing. The "follow through" on the bait-pricing technique mentioned above. Once the seeker of the advertised "bargain" is in the store, the merchant attempts to switch the shopper to another, higher-priced brand or type.

Leader pricing. A favorite technique of retailers, this involves lowering the customary selling price of one or more popular articles in order to attract consumers to the store. Although the firm will earn a lower-than-ordinary markup on the merchandise it sells in this manner, it will still enjoy some gross margin dollars.

Loss leader pricing. A variant of leader pricing, whereby the selling price of an item is reduced even more drastically, to the point at which the retailer offers it at below original cost. The technique, illegal in many states where unfair sales-practice laws are in effect, may be employed occasionally for a dual purpose: to clear out stock while simultaneously increasing in-store traffic.

Multiple pricing. A promotional pricing technique designed to induce the shopper to purchase two or more units of a product at one time by affording some savings, such as "three for $2.50."

Odd-and-even price endings. A pricing concept with psychological ramifications. Despite the fact that research in this area has been inconclusive, many retailers prefer to use prices that end in odd figures, such as $1.89, $6.49, or $19.95. On the other hand, there are some who prefer even-figure price endings or even-dollar amounts and price their merchandise accordingly.

Prestige pricing. A technique whereby a company deliberately sets higher-than-customary prices for its offerings in order to differentiate its image from those of its competitors. This has the psychological effect of inducing people to regard the merchandise (and the firm) as better in quality.

Price lining. A technique that seeks to make it easier for shoppers to select merchandise and, at the same time, simplifies stock planning for the retailer. Here, the number of choices made available to the consumer is reduced by grouping similar items within a few, rather than many, price lines. For example, a menswear store might group its neckties at $6.50, $12.75, and $19.95, depending on quality and appearance of the goods.

Psychological pricing. A term applied to any of several pricing tactics employed by companies to create buyer interest in the product or service by appealing to certain beliefs that people hold; for example, prestige pricing or the use of odd-price endings.

In addition to the promotional pricing techniques described above, many other pricing terms are in common use in the business world. A few of these are explained on the following page:

Advertising allowance. A contribution made by a manufacturer or distributor toward the costs incurred by another channel member to induce the latter firm to advertise the former's products.

Bid pricing. Estimating, then setting the price for, an individual job to be performed (as in construction work) in order to bid against competitors for the work.

Brokerage allowance. The fee or commission earned by a broker for the role played in bringing buyer and seller together.

Geographical pricing. Any of several distribution-oriented approaches to price determination designed to encompass solutions to the freight problem. Among them are zone, FOB-factory, and uniform delivered pricing.

Guarantee against price decline. A tactical management decision designed to contribute to good channel relationships. For example, a manufacturing company will try to protect its distributors against falling prices in industries (or commodities) when prices fluctuate excessively during the year.

List price. The price customarily quoted for a particular article. Also known as the *basic list price.*

Penetration pricing. A marketing tactic most often used at the introductory stage of a low-priced product's life cycle. Here, management deliberately sets a low price to assure ready acceptance and to gain extensive distribution.

Uniform delivered pricing. A form of geographical pricing whereby all customers are charged the same price even though they may be located in different geographical areas. Here, the company has calculated in advance the effects of differing freight charges and "built them in" to the price through some overall adjustment for freight.

Zone pricing. A form of geographic pricing whereby, for example, a firm sells a product at one price to all purchasers east of the Mississippi and at another price to those located west of the Mississippi. (An excellent example of zone pricing is that engaged in by the U.S. Postal Service in its handling of parcel post.)

DISCOUNTS

One of the most important aspects of pricing is the area of discounts. A discount is a reduction from the regular selling price (or list price) of a product or service, usually expressed in terms of a percentage of the selling price. For example, many retail firms offer their personnel an employee discount as part of the total compensation package. This discount may run from 10 or 15 percent "off" the retail price of merchandise bought in the store to as much as 25 or 30 percent and more.

Here are some other important types of discounts:

Cash discount. A reduction in price granted to encourage early payment of an invoice.

Introductory discount. A reduction in the regular price to induce intermediary institutions (wholesalers, retailers) or final consumers to buy a particular (usually new) product.

Quantity discount. A reduction in the normal selling price of an item to induce purchasers to buy in quantity.

Seasonal discount. A reduction in selling price offered to encourage customers to purchase products in advance of a forthcoming season.

Trade discount. Any reduction from the regular list price of goods that is offered to intermediary firms as compensation for the functions they perform along the channel structure. Usually expressed as some percentage off the quoted price as, for example, $144 per dozen, less 45 percent.

FOR FURTHER INFORMATION

Books

Hirshleifer, J. *Price Theory and Applications,* 3d ed. Englewood Cliffs, N.J.: Prentice-Hall, 1984.
Marshall, A. *More Profitable Pricing.* New York: McGraw-Hill, 1980.
Monroe, Kent B. *Pricing: Making Profitable Decisions.* New York: McGraw-Hill, 1979.
Oxenfeldt, Alfred R. *Pricing Strategies.* New York: AMACOM, 1982.
Symonds, Curtis W. *Pricing for Profit.* New York: AMACOM, 1982.

Pamphlets Available from the Small Business Administration

MANAGEMENT AIDS

MA 1.019—"Simple Breakeven Analysis for Small Stores"

Booklets Available from the Superintendent of Documents

S/N 045-000-00137-7—*Guides for Profit Planning*—$4.50.
S/N 045-000-00192-0—*The Profit Plan*—$4.50.
S/N 045-000-00195-4—*Understanding Costs*—$3.25.

14

Promotion Management

An apt synonym for *promotion* is *persuasive communication.* It is through well-planned and coordinated promotional activities that consumers are attracted to your products or informed about your services, persuaded to try them, and ultimately become your regular customers.

The purpose of this chapter is to bring the esoteric world of account executives and Madison Avenue down to a more practical level in order to help you to run this phase of your business with the same professionalism you need in other areas.

PROMOTIONAL OBJECTIVES

While promotional activities may be varied and subject to change, they do have to be congruent with the firm's long-range objectives. They must also be flexible enough to admit occasional tactical maneuvering and, less frequently, allow broad changes in strategy as your company copes with competitors' moves and environmental dynamics. Some common promotional objectives are

- Attracting new customers
- Establishing brand differentiation
- Enhancing the firm's image
- Increasing store traffic
- Introducing new products
- Obtaining additional distributors
- Opening up new territories
- Selling products or services
- Supporting the company's salespeople
- Sustaining brand loyalty

THE BUDGET FOR PROMOTION

Typically, setting the annual expenditure for promotion represents a complex challenge. There's no one pat approach here; management is generally unable to assess the consequences of allocating X dollars to next year's promotional activity. Most budget decisions in this area are quite subjective. Often, they're preceded by an investigation (generally unscientific) that raises questions like:

- How much can we afford to allocate to promotion?
- Can we learn from our competitors? How much do they spend annually, on the average?
- What was the total dollar amount we spent last year, and how did it help our sales?
- Would we be better off putting some of our promotion dollars into new equipment or machinery? Office help? Additional salespeople?
- Are there particular promotion areas that need to be beefed up?

In planning the promotion budget, companies follow diverse strategies, perhaps gravitating from one to another every two or three years. A few of these approaches are discussed below:

Percentage-of-sales. Allocating a small percentage of overall sales volume, usually matching the trend within the particular industry

Meet the competition. Going overboard for one year in order to match the estimated promotional expenditure of a leading competitor

Objective-and-task. Defining the job that needs to be done and then estimating how much is required to accomplish the job

Status-quo. Holding down next year's budget to the amount that will be spent during the current year (or, perhaps, making a minuscule adjustment in the percentage, upward or downward)

Multibudget. Preparing several alternative budgets (low, medium, high), then forecasting the expected return on investment for each, and selecting the most promising one

THE PROMOTION MIX

Promotion's first objective is to initiate demand for the company's products and services. Here, the small business owner should think in terms of planning the blend or mixture of several basic ingredients, much like mixing a cocktail. This deliberate *promotion mix* always encompasses three major ingredients (although the proportions vary depending on the nature of the job): personal selling, advertising, and sales promotion—with a dash of publicity.

As can be seen in exhibit 14–1, the promotion-mix "blends" will differ from one type of company to another.

PERSONAL SELLING

For the small manufacturer or wholesaler, there's no doubt that energetic *personal selling* efforts constitute the most critical aspect of promotion. This is also true for the retail firm, though to a lesser degree. Retail selling differs radically from other forms of personal selling in that there's little need to

EXHIBIT 14-1. POSSIBLE PROMOTION-MIX BLENDS FOR VARIOUS TYPES OF SMALL COMPANIES

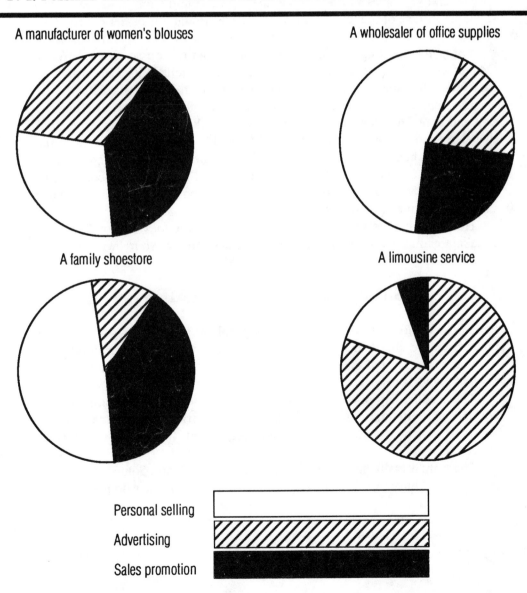

"prospect" for customers in the usual sense, much less call on them to promote your wares. Good selling practices are brought into play once the shopper enters the store. This section, then, addresses the manufacturer and wholesaler rather than the retailer.

Partnerships are frequently formed in which one partner has experience in plant operation and the other in sales. In such cases, the sales-oriented partner makes the necessary contacts and visits. More commonly, however, the young manufacturing company contracts with a *selling agent* to sell its particular product or product line. This agent works closely with the company, under contract, and is charged with selling the plant's entire output.

Manufacturers' agents (or *reps*) are intermediaries in the channels of distribution. They offer the small firm quick entry into a territory by providing an experienced sales staff and ready-made customers. These sales representatives can bring in orders for your company shortly after you sign up with them.

Generally, a sales rep is compensated on a commission basis, earning a small percentage of the total billings facilitated through his or her efforts. This approach enables you to calculate your sales costs with comparative ease.

For help in locating suitable agents, contact your trade association, MANA (Manufacturers' Agents National Association) of Laguna Hills, California,* or the National Council of Salesmen's Organizations in New York City.**

Engaging a sales rep to promote your product offers obvious advantages in cost and time. However, there are several drawbacks as well. Your representative also assists other clients, making it impossible to work 100 percent of the time on your behalf. In addition, if you fail to renew your agreement when it expires, your rep may take some of your customers along to your competitor. Moreover, you might find your selling expenses running rather high if your sales volume increases substantially.

However, as sales volume continues to expand, you may eventually decide to take a giant step forward and initiate a sales force of your own.

SALES-FORCE MANAGEMENT

Once this decision is reached, a number of problems have to be resolved. These range from the kind and number of salespeople required, through developing training programs and plans for compensating salespeople, to methods of deployment and supervision.

The productivity of the small company's salespeople is of paramount importance in its attempt to secure a foothold in the marketplace. The salespeople are its battle troops directly on the firing line; in fact, they're the very lifeline of the business.

There are literally hundreds of kinds of selling positions. Some require little in the way of ingenuity or sales ability, like that of the route salesperson who,

*P. O. Box 3647, Laguna Hills, CA 92654

**225 Broadway, New York, NY 10007

while making rounds, routinely notes orders for milk, pretzels, potato chips, and other items onto a preprinted order form. Other selling jobs are more demanding, requiring a high level of skill and creativity. Examples include the selling of life insurance, group pension plans, swimming pools, and retirement condominiums.

Personnel Aspects

Evidently, good selling is more of an art than a science. The expert practitioner needs to possess not only good communication skills but also a thorough understanding of the psychological processes underlying human interactions. Salespeople are not born with these capabilities; such skills are developed and enhanced through practice and training.

Few star sales performers are out of work. Consequently, it's difficult for the small company to locate unemployed top salespeople, much less hire them. It generally makes more sense for the young firm to hire "green troops"— potential sales representatives—and then develop that potential through training. The company should search for individuals who display characteristics commonly found in successful salespeople: good communicative ability, empathy, drive, good appearance and posture, emotional balance, and so forth.

Before initiating a brand-new sales force to promote the product line, a company should make a careful appraisal of the characteristics and needs of its targeted prospect groups. In so doing, the firm will gain insights into the type and caliber of salespeople needed to do the job well. (For details on the recruitment, training, compensation, and supervision of employees, see chapters 8 and 9.)

Organizational Structure

Sales forces are usually structured according to geographical requirements, along product lines, by customer type, or some combination thereof. Of course, the right kind of internal organization is affected by a number of variables, most importantly: the product line, the amount of capital, the desired scope of sales activity, and the nature of the customers. In the earlier stages, the salespeople should be directed by the owner(s) of the business; later on, management may consider adding a sales manager to the organization for better results.

It is essential for outside salespeople to be backed up by an efficient inside sales office, a fail-safe order-processing and delivery system, diligent credit supervision, competent management, and good two-way communication.

What to Do about Travel Expenses

Outside salespeople incur expenses while traveling from one account to the next. Included are the costs involved in traveling by rail, air, or automobile; meals on the road; overnight lodging; and telephone calls. In the majority of instances, such expenses are reimbursed by the company.

Some firms, however, arrange to have their sales representatives pay their own expenses without reimbursement, usually by setting them up in a self-employed "independent contractor"–type of relationship. Automobiles may be purchased or leased by the firm for their salespeople's use. Other companies require their sales personnel to use their own vehicles. Either approach has its benefits and drawbacks. Your accountant, who knows your business, can give you advice in this area.

In establishing an expense-reimbursement plan, you should have your salespeople report their expenses to you on a regular basis, preferably weekly. Check these expense reports carefully to ensure that they seem reasonably accurate. Your position ought to be that your people will neither gain nor lose.

As a general rule, salespeople on the road should not expect to stay overnight at exclusive luxury hotels (with certain exceptions: specific industries, higher-level sales representatives, and so on). Neither should they be expected to stay at rundown rooming houses. Indeed, the same type of accommodations are called for as if the salesperson were traveling for personal reasons. Likewise, reasonableness should be the keynote for dining out. These days, a daily "cap" of $35 for meals is ample. (Of course, this does not refer to taking prospects to dinner. That is *entertainment!*)

Deploying Your Troops

If you have the usual type of sales organization, you should consider assigning your salespeople to "manageable" territories. This approach permits you to pare travel costs substantially and to cover each area more intensively, thereby ensuring better service to your firm's accounts. This arrangement also lends itself quite well to the fixing of responsibility; you'll find it easier to hold your people accountable for both sales production and sales expenses.

In the selling game, a lot of time is frittered away on traveling to, from, and between accounts; waiting in outer reception areas until purchasing agents can be seen; doing paperwork and keeping records; and so forth. Proper attention to the scheduling and routing of your salespeople can reduce much of these wasted efforts.

Training Your Salespeople

In a healthy sales organization, training is a continuous function, with initial training when the employee first joins the company, and follow-up or refresher training later on. The content of beginning training programs should encompass topics like the history of the firm, the product line, pricing, the demographics and other characteristics of the company's clientele, internal systems, and sales instruction. More advanced training is often oriented toward improving sales performance: methods of prospecting, how to make more effective presentations, ways of handling objections, how to close a sale, and the like. Available training methods run the gamut from formal classroom lectures to programmed instruction and self-study. Included here are small-group discussions, role playing, demonstrations by top sales performers, films and other audio-visual material and equipment, attending classes in selling at local universities, and so forth.

Assessing Sales Performance

Evaluations of sales personnel have at least two primary purposes: (1) to provide management with information for decision making in this particular promotion area, and (2) to improve the performance of salespeople over time. While continuous training for people in the selling operation is admittedly essential—not only for improving sales skills but also for teaching self-management—the gathering of comparative data does enable supervisory management to pinpoint deficiencies and correct below-par performance.

Both subjective and objective approaches should be used to assess selling performance. Subjective criteria include the salesperson's extent of company knowledge and product knowledge, his or her familiarity with competitive organizations and their offerings, the ability to communicate effectively, good personal appearance and proper attire, and steady work habits. Objective evaluation mainly consists of comparing the "input-output" statistics of the entire sales force. Among the more useful ratios and indexes in this connection are the number of orders secured each month related to the number of calls made, the average sales volume per order, and the number of new accounts landed per the number of visits made.

Exhibits 14–2 and 14–3 contain useful suggestions for measuring and improving salesperson performance.

EXHIBIT 14-2. MEASURING PERFORMANCE

SOUND CRITERIA FOR MEASURING PERFORMANCE

Which of the following are sound criteria for measuring the performance of salesmen?

1. Volume of sales in dollars.
2. Amount of time spent in office.
3. Personal appearance, for example, clothes, style of haircut, cleanliness, and neatness.
4. Number of calls made on existing accounts.
5. Number of new accounts opened.
6. Completeness and accuracy of sales orders.
7. Promptness in submitting reports.
8. Dollars spent in entertaining customers.
9. Extent to which salesman sells his company.
10. Accuracy in quoting prices and deliveries to customers.
11. Knowledge of the business.
12. Planning and routing of calls.

Source: "Measuring the Performance of Salesmen," *Management Aid No. 190* (Washington, D.C.: Small Business Administration, 1975), 6.

EXHIBIT 14-3. IMPROVING PERFORMANCE

GUIDE FOR IMPROVING A SALESMAN'S PERFORMANCE

One goal of measuring a salesman performance is to help him improve. The three steps in bringing about improvement, when, an if, it is needed are: planning, measuring, and correcting.

PLANNING

- Get the salesman's agreement about what he is to obtain or exceed for the next year:

    1. Total profit contribution in dollars.
    2. Profit contribution in dollars for:
        Each major product line.
        Each major market (By industry or geographical area).
        Each of 10–20 target accounts (for significant new and additional business).

- Get the salesman's agreement about expense within which he is to stay for the next year:

    1. His total sales expense budget in dollars.
    2. His budget in dollars for: travel, customer entertainment, telephone,
        and other expenses.

- Have the salesman plan the number of calls he will make to accounts and prospects during the next year.

MEASURING

- Review at least monthly the salesman's record for:
    1. Year-to-date progress toward his 12-month profit contribution goals.
    2. Year-to-date budget compliance.

CORRECTING

Meet with the salesman if his record shows that he is 10 percent or more off target. Review with him the number of calls he has made on each significant account plus what he feels are his accomplishments and problems. In addition, you may need to do some of the following to help him improve his performance:

- Give the salesman more day-to-day help and direction.
- Accompany salesman on calls to provide coaching.
- Conduct regular salesmeetings on subjects which salesman want covered.
- Increase sales promotion activities.
- Transfer accounts to other salesmen if there is insufficient effort or progress.
- Establish tighter control over price variances allowed.
- Increase or reduce selling prices.
- Add new products or services.

Source: "Measuring the Performance of Salesmen," *Management Aid No. 190* (Washington, D.C.: Small Business Administration, 1975), 7.

ADVERTISING

For many small manufacturers, advertising constitutes the bulk of the total promotional effort. In contrast to personal selling, advertising is simply paid communication designed to influence prospects and customers en masse.

Effective management of this area of your business requires attention to specifics like selecting and then researching market segments; setting advertising objectives; conceptualizing plans; constructing messages and advertisements; and selecting the media for reaching your targets.

One basic principle to follow here is to reach as much of your "preselected" audience as you can at as low a cost as possible. This may be accomplished through a variety of media: newspapers, magazines, radio, television, billboards, subway and bus cards, direct mail, circulars, and the like. Of course, it's difficult (if not impossible) to assess the effectiveness of your firm's advertising. Mail order and direct-mail advertising are exceptions: Responses to your advertisements can be keyed or couponed and some evaluation made of results.

Types of Advertising

Depending upon how you look at it, advertising may be classified in a number of ways:

- According to the company's position along the channel of distribution, either *manufacturer, wholesaler,* or *retailer advertising.* (Where the cost of advertising is shared by two channel members, this is referred to as *cooperative advertising.*)

- According to the planned geographical coverage, that is, *national, regional,* or *local advertising*

- By what is being advertised, that is, *product, brand,* or *institutional* (company, industry) *advertising*

- By the media employed, either *television, radio, print* (newspaper, magazine), *outdoor* (billboard), *car card* (subway, bus), *direct mail,* or *mail-order advertising*

The Media

Where should you advertise? Companies depend on the advertising media (newspapers, magazines, radio, television, and so forth) to carry their promotional messages to prospective and actual customers.

Proper media selection is a difficult task for the entrepreneur. For optimum yield, specialized knowledge is a must. If you envision a moderate-sized advertising budget for your new business, I strongly urge you to enlist the services of a small advertising agency willing to take on your account and grow along with you.

Some factors to take into consideration in making media choices are the appropriateness and size of each medium's audience or readership, comparative media costs, production costs, and the relative rapidity of results you can expect. Each medium has its own particular attributes, negative as well as positive.

Where speedy action is wanted, the air media (radio and television) and the daily newspaper lead all other media. Reaction to advertising in these three is almost immediate: 70 to 80 percent (if not more) of the results will be in within the first week.

Newspapers. In small towns, the local newspaper is a valuable medium for most retail store operations. In a metropolitan area, however, much of the newspaper's circulation is "waste" simply because a substantial number of readers live or work miles away from the location in question. Unless the "pulling power" of the advertisement is exceptional, it's doubtful that many of those consumers would visit the premises. On the other hand, weekly area newspapers—or small-space classified advertisements used on a regular basis—can be of value to most types of enterprises.

You should know that newspapers can assist you in preparing copy as well as layout for your purposes. Often they're able to furnish standard illustrations or cuts for a more effective presentation.

Magazines. Magazines and trade journals can be effective media when used for expanding your distribution, securing additional dealers for your products or services, recruiting salespeople in different territories, or selling goods by mail order. Advertisers may expect to "pull" results for a long time, simply because these publications may lie around the office or home for many months. For this reason, too, the advertiser can count on multiple readership. Photographs reproduce well in magazines, and full-color reproduction is usually available when needed.

There are, of course, a few drawbacks to this medium. For one thing, considerable "lead time" is required: Copy and art for your ad must be submitted months in advance of the publication date to ensure getting into the particular issue. For another, the cost of space can be rather high.

Radio and Television. Both of the air media are characterized by fast results, short lead time, and flexibility. Because it reaches large audiences and appeals to two senses, rather than one, television has both tremendous impact and extensive reach. Nevertheless, it is used only occasionally by the smaller firm. Air time is expensive, and the cost of preparing even a thirty-second commercial can be extremely high.

Local radio is generally more feasible for the small company and is of value in reaching specific segments of the market or for offering special "deals" or promotions. Of course, radio copy can be written for you by your local station representative.

One disadvantage of the air media is that messages conveyed by either are short-lived. Moreover, radio announcements are limited in that they depend on sound alone, rather than sight and sound. Another problem is that in any one area of the country—and at any one time—a number of radio stations are likely to be broadcasting. Thus, listeners are, in reality, "fragmented" into a number of separate audiences, each listening to a different station. This means that your announcement being aired over one station will not reach any of the other groups.

Other Media. Often, a company will utilize one or more additional vehicles to carry its promotional messages to its target prospects or customers. Among these are direct mail, the position media (outdoor and transit advertising), the Yellow Pages, and handbills. Direct mail is an exciting medium and one that has been growing in popularity by leaps and bounds over the past two decades. These days, American business spends more each year on direct mail than for either radio or magazine advertising. The medium ranks third highest in annual advertising expenditures, after newspapers and television (in that order).

An extremely versatile medium, direct mail is capable of reaching nearly every conceivable target group: plumbers or restaurant owners, mathematics teachers or physicians, hardware manufacturers or golf club members, stamp collectors or ham radio operators, ceramic tile wholesalers or government officials, and so forth. It's also a powerful and persuasive medium; like personal selling, it conveys a sales message directly from the seller to the potential buyer. Moreover, complete information can be presented—something that is often not possible when using other media because of the high cost of additional space or air time.

Two disadvantages of the direct-mail medium, though, are the high cost per M as compared to newspaper and magazine ad costs and the "junk-mail problem" (that is, that many recipients just toss direct mailings into the wastebasket without reading the material).

Table 14–1 summarizes some of the advantages and disadvantages of the major advertising media.

Before ending this section, we should stress the importance of handbills. For retailers especially, the handbill (or flier) is a relatively inexpensive, yet often effective, medium. For maximum value, be sure to avoid distributing simplistic printed announcements. Instead, offer well-conceived and imaginative messages aimed at motivating shoppers to visit the location.

Here's a case in point:

A young technician completed an excellent training course in television repair and servicing and then opened a small repair shop in a large city. His was an "off-main-street" location, one that carried a low monthly rental. However, the area was saturated with block after block of apartment houses. For a rather inconsequential investment, he printed up 2,000 handbills, which he managed to distribute personally to the occupants of these buildings. Because the circular offered a service call (at no charge) and suggested that the apartment dwellers keep the flier handy "just in case," he was able to build a substantial clientele within a few months.

Messages

Any advertising you use for your company should be designed primarily to inform people about your products and/or services and to persuade them to buy. Hence, whatever the medium you select, each "message" should

TABLE 14–1. MAJOR ADVERTISING MEDIA: SOME ADVANTAGES AND DISADVANTAGES

Medium	Advantages	Disadvantages
Print Media		
Newspapers:		
	Short lead time	Competition from other ads, news stories
	Low cost per M	Waste circulation
	Flexibility	
	Extensive coverage of market	
Magazines:		
	Long life of ad	Long lead time
	Multiple readership	Lack of flexibility
	Market selectivity	Waste circulation
	Good reproduction of photographs	Higher cost per M than newspapers
	Availability of color	
Air Media		
Radio:		
	Fast results	Short message life
	Short lead time	Limited to one sense
	Flexibility	Fragmentation of audience (many stations compete for listeners)
	Relatively inexpensive	Relatively inexpensive
	Market selectivity	
	Substantial audience loyalty	
Television:		
	Fast results	High cost of air time
	Impact	High cost of producing commercials
	Extensive reach	Short life of message
	Scheduling flexibility	
Other Media		
Direct Mail:		
	Most persuasive medium	High cost per M
	Can reach specific target groups	"Junk-mail" problem

Source: Compiled by the author.

- Be clear, and couched in the targeted customers' vocabulary
- Provoke interest
- Appeal to people's wants and needs
- Stress desirable features of the product or service
- Sound believable
- Motivate people to buy
- Tell them where they can buy

In addition to the message copy, artwork and layout are also essential elements in preparing newspaper advertisements. Artwork and layout complement and reinforce the copy and at the same time attract the attention of more readers. For this reason, large black type (or unusual typefaces), borders around the advertisement, illustrations, and halftones (photographs) will not only contribute to the total message but also result in expanded readership. Yes, a picture may be worth a thousand words (or more!).

As a general rule, doubling the size of an advertisement does not by any means trigger an automatic 100 percent increase in the number of readers. Often, only an additional 10 or 15 percent readership can be expected. Given the erratic, though perfectly normal, behavior of the fallible human memory, there's far more value in designing and using an *advertising campaign* than in scheduling a single, one-shot advertisement, no matter how large, in the newspaper. Preferably, one ought to think in psychological terms: the reinforcement of learning that takes place in the regular reader's mind as a result of *frequency of exposure.*

SALES PROMOTION

Sales promotion is a composite of activities that round out the personal selling and advertising components of a company's promotion mix. The primary aims of sales promotion are to stimulate sales at the point of purchase (when selling consumer goods and services through retail stores and service shops) and to assist the intermediaries (wholesalers and retailers) as they move these products toward the targeted purchasers. In addition, sales promotion aids both the manufacturer and the distributor handling industrial goods and services.

Among the sales promotion aids often employed by firms are catalogs, reprints of advertisements, special displays and display fixtures, banners and signs, exhibits and trade shows, and premiums. Their major contribution is in the areas of training, supporting, and otherwise helping along the efforts of the salespeople involved.

Promotion at the Point of Purchase

A few of the more popular sales promotion tools wielded by modern marketers are listed below:

contests	premiums
coupons	PMs ("Push
demonstrations	Money")
displays	sales events
endorsements	sampling
exhibits	tie-in
fashion shows	promotions
games	trade shows
giveaways	trading stamps

In the list above, *displays* are the single most significant category for the retail store. The majority of retail firms rely on window displays to attract the attention of passersby, to hook their interest, and to induce them to enter the store. Once inside, shoppers can be persuaded to make purchases through effective selling on the part of the salesclerks, aided by additional (interior) displays.

While a detailed treatment of this important area is beyond the scope of this chapter, exhibit 14-4 offers some basic pointers to provide general directions for window displays.

EXHIBIT 14-4. SOME THOUGHTS FOR WINDOW DISPLAYS

- Shoppers will regard your storefront and show window as the "face" of your retail business. Therefore, the window treatments should always convey the impressions of quality, style, and distinctiveness that you would like to project.

- Displays should be kept clean and neat in appearance at all times. A crowded display contributes nothing but clutter; instead, use air (or "breathing") space between merchandise groupings.

- Whether you engage the services of a professional window trimmer or do the displays yourself, your windows should be changed frequently. At least ten to fifteen changes each year are recommended. (Hint: You might be able to hire someone with display training from a local high school's distributive education program.)

- Window displays are generally more effective when built around a single, unifying theme (Back-to-School, Mother's Day, Christmas, Springtime, Vacation Fun, Travel, and so forth).

- Merchandise, materials, display stands, mannequins (if required), and signs or posters should be carefully selected and prepared ahead of time so that the window can be completely trimmed without incident within a few hours' time.

- In selecting appropriate merchandise to put into the window, pay careful attention to the seasonality factor, to product sales appeal, and to individual gross markups.

- Color is an essential ingredient of display. The color combinations used in the window should be attractive and harmonious.

- Window bases (platforms) are usually covered with appropriate materials which contribute to the overall effect of the display—satins, netting, burlap, paper, artificial grass mats, and so forth. The retailer should build up a stock of such materials, over time.

- All point-of-purchase materials, such as sign tickets, posters, banners, and the like, should look professional and be kept perfectly clean.

- Special effects, such as motion, lighting, and sound, can be used profitably in connection with your display to draw attention to your window. As a simple example, motion can be imparted to a section of your display through the use of a small electric (or battery-operated) turntable or ceiling turner.

Source: Compiled by the author.

A WORD OR TWO ABOUT PUBLIC RELATIONS

The phrase *public relations* is a catchall sort of term. Narrowly interpreted, it can mean little more than a stream of news releases, emitted by a company over time, that manage to find their way into print—or over radio or television. Such an interpretation leads many business executives to consider "P.R." as tantamount to free, unpaid advertising. Actually, news releases of this type are more in the realm of *publicity* than of public relations.

More properly defined, *public relations* (P.R.) comprises a wide range of activities expressive of the firm's attitudes toward others. In the main, it consists of meaningful two-way communication between the company and its many publics: internal (employees, stockholders) as well as external (customers and prospective customers, suppliers, competitors, government agencies, and so on).

Every company has public relations; the P.R. may be good, fair, or poor. A good P.R. program starts with the firm's owner(s) and is reflected throughout the organization—in good employee relations as well as in good company relationships with the outside world. Good P.R. involves observing guarantees on products, acting in an aboveboard fashion in conducting business, showing courtesy in the treatment of all, answering complaints promptly, and so forth.

The News Release

To maintain effective public relations, a company must make sure that its various publics know what it stands for—and what is going on at all times. The mainstay of a P.R. program is the *news* or *publicity release.*

News releases should be typed on an 8½-by-11-inch sheet of white paper. Ample margins should surround the double-spaced text. The organization's name and address usually appear at the top of the sheet. Also shown are the name, title, address, and telephone number of the *contact person*—the person who can be called for more details.

Type the words *For Immediate Release* above the copy. If, however, the story is to be held over for a later date, a phrase such as *Hold for Release on* . . . (time, day, date) should be substituted.

When preparing news releases, the writer should follow the principles of good journalism. Be sure to answer the "five *W*s." Use active words; avoid the passive tense. Make every word count; a news release should run only as long as is necessary to tell the complete story. If it runs to several pages in length, number them and place the word *more* at the bottom of each page except the last. To signify the end of the release, type in *30* or *# # #* below the last line of text.

FOR FURTHER INFORMATION

Books

Burton, Philip Ward. *Advertising Copywriting,* 5th ed. New York: Wiley, 1983.

Caples, John. *Tested Advertising Methods,* 4th ed. Englewood Cliffs, N.J.: Prentice-Hall, 1981.

————. *How to Make Your Advertising Make Money.* Englewood Cliffs, N.J.: Prentice-Hall, 1983.

Churchill, Gilbert A., Jr., Neil M. Ford, and Orville C. Walker. *Sales Force Management: Planning, Implementation, and Control,* 2d ed. Homewood, Ill.: Irwin, 1985.

Cohen, William. *Direct Response Marketing.* New York: Wiley, 1984.

Dalrymple, Douglas J. *Sales Management: Concepts and Cases,* 2d ed. New York: Wiley, 1985.

Futrell, Charles M. *ABC's of Selling.* Homewood, Ill.: Irwin, 1985.

Gray, Ernest A. *Profitable Methods for Small Business Advertising.* New York: Wiley, 1984.

Johnson, H. Webster, and Anthony J. Faria. *Creative Selling,* 4th ed. Cincinnati: South-Western, 1987.

Kurtz, David L., H. Robert Dodge, and Jay E. Klompmaker. *Professional Selling,* 4th ed. Plano, Tex.: Business Publications, 1985.

Norris, James S. *Public Relations.* Englewood Cliffs, N.J.: Prentice-Hall, 1984.

Nylen, David W. *Advertising: Planning, Implementation, and Control,* 3d ed. Cincinnati: South-Western, 1986.

Pederson, Carlton A., and Milburn D. Wright. *Selling: Principles and Methods,* 8th ed. Homewood, Ill.: Irwin, 1984.

Rothschild, Michael. *Advertising: From Fundamentals to Strategies.* Lexington, Mass.: D. C. Heath, 1987.

Simon, Raymond. *Public Relations: Concepts and Practices,* 3d ed. New York: Wiley, 1985.

Stanley, Richard E. *Promotion: Advertising, Publicity, Personal Selling, Sales Promotion,* 2d ed. Englewood Cliffs, N.J.: Prentice-Hall, 1982.

Storholm, Gordon, and Louis C. Kaufman. *Principles of Selling.* Englewood Cliffs, N.J.: Prentice-Hall, 1985.

Welch, Joe L., and Charles Lapp. *Sales Force Management.* Cincinnati: South-Western, 1984.

Pamphlets Available from the Small Business Administration

MANAGEMENT AIDS

MA 4.002—"Creative Selling: The Competitive Edge"
MA 4.005—"Is the Independent Sales Agent for You?"
MA 4.012—"Marketing Checklist for Small Retailers"
MA 4.015—"Advertising Guidelines for Small Retail Firms"
MA 4.018—"Plan Your Advertising Budget"

Booklets Available from the Superintendent of Documents

S/N 045-000-00133-4—*Training Salesmen to Serve Industrial Markets*—$2.50.

S/N 045-000-00152-1—*Small Store Planning for Growth*—$5.50.

S/N 045-000-00189-0—*Managing Retail Salespeople*—$4.75.

15

Distribution Management

The area of *distribution* is still another major constituent of the marketing mix. Involved here are the logistics necessary to deliver the company's products and/or services to the right places at the right time in the right quantities, and at the lowest cost. For the most part, distribution management encompasses the concept of *marketing channels* through which the merchandise moves, both the storage and transportation aspects of marketing, and the allocation of inventories.

Visualize a small factory that produces inexpensive women's slippers: The slipper manufacturer brings in raw materials and perhaps semifinished goods, slipper components, packaging materials, and other supplies, and then manufactures the finished products on the plant's machines, packages them, cartons the packages, and ships the lot off "to market." Unless the producing firm wishes to assume the burden of selling the slippers by the pair in a door-to-door canvassing operation, the services of one or more intermediaries are required. The merchandise is funneled into a kind of "pipeline" through which it is propelled to the customers. In actuality, this "pipeline" is a set of component companies, linked together to form a *marketing channel*.

MARKETING CHANNELS IN THE ECONOMY

Without a sales force of its own, the small manufacturing firm will probably resort to consigning its output to an agent for the purposes of securing distribution. The agent, in turn, might call on various local wholesalers—or operate on a more expanded scale if the output is large—to interest them in taking on the new line of products. As alternatives, the manufacturer may decide to deal directly with one large distributor that maintains a sizable sales force, or opt instead to sell directly to a number of large retail outlets in the area.

196

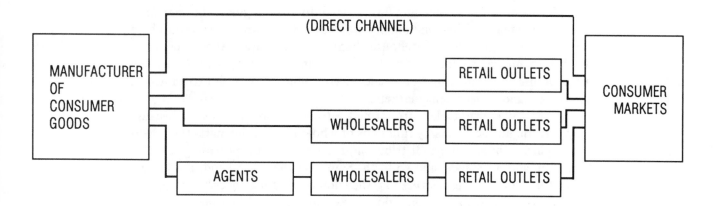

Evidently, the "more cooks who stir the broth" the less control the producer can exercise over the product line. Of course, adding intermediaries necessitates building a cost structure to compensate each of the channel members for the part it plays in the total distribution process. The small business and its management must carefully assess the benefits and drawbacks of the various alternatives, each of which may yield a different payoff for the manufacturing company. Exhibit 15–1 contains a diagram of the more customary channel choices.

SOME NOTES ON CHANNEL MEMBERS

Intermediaries are those individuals or firms that play a role within the channels of distribution between the producing company and the ultimate consumer. Most people are familiar with the role of the retailer within the economy, and so it isn't discussed in this section. Most of us, however, haven't had much contact with wholesaling institutions.

Wholesalers

Within the wholesaling sphere, several distinct categories of firms are found:

- Merchant wholesalers (*Distributor* and *jobber* are alternate terms for *wholesaler.*)
- Agents and brokers
- Manufacturers' sales branches/sales offices
- Petroleum bulk plants and terminals

Probably only the first two types are of interest to the majority of people reading this book, so the other categories are only briefly discussed here. *Manufacturers' sales branches and offices* are producer-owned and -maintained premises where potential buyers can examine the company's product line and place orders. *Petroleum bulk plants and terminals* are highly specialized facilities used to distribute petroleum products to both oil and gasoline retailers as well as to industry.

The majority of wholesaling firms fall into the "regular" or *merchant wholesaler* category. These merchant wholesalers are companies that purchase goods in large quantities, warehouse them, and then break these quantities down into smaller shipments for distribution to their customers. Many sell merchandise to retail firms for resale to consumers. Some sell to industry, commerce, and government markets.

Most regular wholesalers are termed *full-service* or *full-function* because they perform all the necessary functions of wholesalers in the marketing channel: buying, selling, storage, distribution, extending credit, providing sales information and assistance, and so forth. Some, on the other hand, are known as *limited-service* wholesalers because they don't perform all of the services that are expected. For instance, some do not extend credit to their customers but require cash on delivery. Others will not store the merchandise.

Full-Service Wholesale Firms

There are three types of full-service distributors:

General merchandise wholesaler. Much like a general store that carries a variety of different lines of goods, this type of firm provides "general merchandise" to larger and departmentalized retailers.

Single-line wholesaler. This is a firm equipped to supply its retail clients with a complete, in-depth stock in one particular line of goods, such as groceries, hardware, and the like.

Specialty wholesaler. These companies typically handle a small number of products within a particular merchandise line.

Limited-Function Wholesalers

Intermediaries in this category are far fewer in number than full-service distributors. The more common types include

Cash-and-carry wholesaler. Often a chain operation, this distributor sets up outlets at convenient locations where local retailers may come in, purchase needed merchandise with cash, and take the goods out with them. Common examples are those selling bottled/canned beverages and grocery items.

Drop-shipper. Found most frequently in the coal, lumber, and metals industries, this type of wholesale firm usually purveys raw materials or bulky products of a low-unit price to industrial users, though it's not limited to such products or markets. This type of intermediary doesn't take physical possession of the merchandise at any point, or put it in a warehouse, but rather arranges for the producer to ship the goods directly to the customer. The company (sometimes a one-person operation, commonly called a *desk jobber*) is billed directly by the producer, and in turn, sends an invoice to the customer for payment. The customer must be billed at a price high enough to incorporate a margin of profit for the wholesaler.

Mail-order wholesaler. This type of company offers retailers merchandise for resale, characteristically through the medium of printed catalogs issued periodically.

Rack jobber. This is the name given to the wholesale business involved in distributing a specialized line—soft-cover books and magazines, toys, health and beauty aids, novelties, household items, and the like—through supermarkets and other high-traffic outlets. The goods are merchandised with the aid of many types of display racks frequently placed on consignment within a store. It's the jobber's responsibility to keep the racks well stocked and fresh-looking.

Truck jobber. Commonly encountered in the grocery trade, this type of distributor services retail outlets directly from a truck with fast-moving products and perishable goods. In addition to fresh fruits and vegetables, truck jobbers handle dairy products, cookies, frozen foods, and similar items.

Agents and Brokers

These intermediaries, found in many lines of business, are mostly specialized individuals and small enterprises. Essentially, their business activity consists of buying and selling on behalf of others *(principals),* thereby earning commissions or fees. Apart from well-known types such as real estate and life insurance agents, there are two major classifications the businessperson should be familiar with: the *manufacturer's agent* and the *selling agent.* The label depends on the scope of activities the agent performs on behalf of the principal.

Manufacturers who seek distribution in specific geographical areas and who do not have their own sales forces contract with a manufacturer's agent to represent them in the selected area. Hence, the oft-employed synonym *manufacturer's representative,* or, more simply, *rep.* The rep is usually assigned an exclusive territory in which to operate. He or she handles only a portion of the total output from the manufacturer and may also represent other producers (usually with complementary lines) in the same area. Reps are asked to sell an entire "package" handed over to them by the manufacturing company; there's little or no discussion over details like prices, terms, quantities, and so forth.

On the other hand, the manufacturer gives the *selling agent* extensive authority over the details of prices, terms, customer selection, and so on. The agent is charged with selling the plant's entire production. Sometimes called a *commission agent,* this intermediary often maintains a sizable and effective sales force. The relationship between the selling agent and the principal is a close one. Indeed, it may even call for the agent to extend financial aid to the manufacturer when necessary.

Finally, the *broker* functions as an intermediary between buyers and sellers, bringing together the two parties while representing either side (not both at once, of course!).

TRANSPORTATION

Transportation is an area that involves many important decisions on behalf of both manufacturer and wholesaler. Transportation costs can range from a mere fraction of an item's selling price (as is the case with grain, coal, gravel, and other bulky commodities) to as much as 40 percent or more. Consequently, transportation (or *traffic*) management must focus on two major objectives: (1) minimizing costs and, at the same time, (2) ensuring speedy, reliable delivery of the merchandise.

Goods are moved about by land, water, or air through a variety of transportation modes employed singly or in combination, and with the assistance of several supporting agencies.

Major Transport Modes

Materials and products move overland by means of trucks, trains, and pipelines. Goods are also shipped by air (airmail, air freight) and by water (inland waterways, ocean transport). A brief overview of these five major modes of transportation follows:

Truck transport. The shipping method most favored by small business (and often by large enterprises as well) is trucking. Trucks offer faster and more frequent delivery to more destinations in the country than any other mode. They're particularly useful for short-distance shipments.

Trains. The railroads offer regular service to distant areas and are especially valuable in transporting machinery, heavy equipment, cattle and livestock, commodities, and so forth. Over their history of service to the nation, the railroads have developed a number of customer benefits that are peculiar to this mode. An example is diversion-in-transit, a service that permits shipments already en route to be redirected to another destination.

Pipelines. This method is generally confined to the movement of petroleum products.

Air. A more costly method of transporting merchandise, shipping by air is customarily of value for the rapid movement of highly perishable goods (exotic plants, seafood, and the like) and items of a high unit value, such as diamonds, jewelry, expensive drugs, and rare paintings.

Water. Moving material by barge along the nation's inland waterways is a low-cost method of transportation. Ocean transport, of course, is significant to the import and export trades.

Auxiliary Services

Some important transport services assist in the movement of goods. Among these are freight forwarders, shippers' associations, and the United Parcel Service. In addition, the U.S. Post Office forwards small shipments through their parcel post service.

WAREHOUSING

Moving goods or materials from one stop to the next along the marketing channel is one major facet of distribution. Another important aspect is the temporary storage, or warehousing, of merchandise. Many labor-saving approaches to materials handling, warehousing methods, and inventory procedures exist, all of which merit managerial attention.

Companies that require warehousing facilities must decide to either (a) maintain their own strategically located depot(s); or (b) resort to holding their goods in public warehouses. In contrast to the older, multistory structures that dot metropolitan areas around the country, today's modern warehouse is commonly a long, low, one-story building located outside a city (with access to a major highway), where land costs are substantially less. With this type of construction there's no need to install and maintain freight (and passenger) elevators or build staircases and stairwells, and no concern (or added expense) is necessary for floor load limits and the like. Furthermore, the internal flow of stock can run a straight course instead of proceeding up and down a number of levels. Goods come in at one end of the rectangular structure, are stored in the center, and then depart through the other end. Because of the excellent layout and operation of the typical modern warehouse—including wide aisles and skids (or pallets) on which cases of merchandise are stacked—heavy machinery such as forklifts can easily move the goods.

Receiving and Shipping

Ideally, then, goods are brought in through truck bays onto receiving platforms where they are accepted by the receiving department. Here, each incoming delivery is recorded in the *receiving log,* a register where information such as date and time of shipment, name of supplier, name of transporting agency, invoice number, and number of cases or cartons received are recorded. The delivery is unloaded and checked against the accompanying bill of lading for quantities, contents, possible damage, and the like. The goods received are then consigned to specific locations within the warehouse proper, as reserve stock for future shipment.

When the shipping department receives orders from the sales division, order pickers in the warehouse select the merchandise specified, assembling it in a staging area where it is shipped out. Of course, shipping times and routing are worked out in advance with an eye to transportation capability and costs.

Inventory Control

A vital phase of warehouse operation is the inventory procedure established to keep track of the merchandise. You can keep a running *book inventory* of all receipts and withdrawals, either by hand or by mechanical or electronic means. However, no method is as accurate as the taking of physical inventory on a periodic basis (weekly, monthly, quarterly, or otherwise). This involves counting directly all cases, cartons, and individual pieces of stock throughout the building, including both the receiving and shipping departments. Physical inventory is usually accomplished by a team: one individual checks out every nook and cranny of the premises, calling out the count to a second person, who enters the quantities onto a preprinted inventory sheet. Totals and extensions (translating the totals into dollar figures) are done later on in the bookkeeping section.

FOR FURTHER INFORMATION

Books

Ballou, Ronald H. *Basic Business Logistics.* Englewood Cliffs, N.J.: Prentice-Hall, 1978.

Blanchard, B. *Logistics Engineering and Management,* 3d ed. Englewood Cliffs, N.J.: Prentice-Hall, 1986.

Bowersox, Donald J. *Logistical Management,* 2d ed. New York: Macmillan, 1978.

Johnson, James C., and Donald F. Wood. *Contemporary Physical Distribution and Logistics,* 3d ed. New York: Macmillan, 1986.

Stern, L., and A. El-Ansary. *Marketing Channels,* 2d ed. Englewood Cliffs, N.J.: Prentice-Hall, 1982.

Pamphlets Available from the Small Business Administration

MANAGEMENT AIDS

MA 4.005—"Is the Independent Sales Agent for You?"
MA 7.003—"Market Overseas with U.S. Government Help"

Booklets Available from the Superintendent of Documents

S/N 003-009-00349-1—*A Basic Guide to Exporting*—$6.50.
S/N 045-000-00133-4—*Training Salesmen to Serve Industrial Markets*—$2.50.
S/N 045-000-00183-1—*Inventory and Scheduling Techniques*—$4.75.

16

Marketing Research

Marketing success is largely realized through

- Carefully and continually appraising the total environment, internal as well as external
- Setting realistic marketing objectives based on sound judgments
- Providing structures for reaching those objectives
- Assessing the results of marketing efforts so that further improvements can be made

The first step in the process implies *knowing* before *doing,* and knowing is therefore basic to marketing management. Far too often, small business is conducted by intuition, probably because the majority of problems repeat and, once solved, provide direction for decisions in the next similar situation. Nevertheless, it makes good sense to investigate new and more complex problems carefully before making decisions, and certainly before coming up with marketing plans.

Here's an illustration: Do you recall the last time you were in the market for a new automobile? Most likely, you visited a showroom where you were promptly greeted by a salesperson. Think back to that meeting; try to recall the conversation between the two of you. Isn't it true that what the sales representative talked about and did in those first few minutes with you were more attuned to "reading" you as a prospective customer than to anything else? This was important, simply because the sales presentation could then be tailored directly to you and your needs, thereby increasing the salesperson's chances of making the sale and earning a commission.

In that transaction, you witnessed the "exchange process" in action: You exchanged your money for the ownership of the car. Bear in mind, too, that communication was involved, on a one-to-one basis (the most persuasive way to communicate).

It's no different with any company that seeks to sell its products or services. Remember: The primary purpose behind a firm's promotional activities is to make sales. Again, this is done through communication, whether on a one-to-one basis as in personal selling, or indirectly through advertising and/or sales promotion. The key concept here is the following: The more a company knows about its intended prospects, the better it can tailor its messages to reach those prospects and induce them to become customers.

At any event, it should now be clear to you that attempts to "read" or "research" prospective customers can be of help to you in your own business.

THE NATURE OF MARKETING RESEARCH

Marketing research is a collective term; it embraces all the activities that assist management in reaching marketing decisions. In reality, it's nothing more or less than a logical, orderly approach to fact finding. Marketing research reduces unknowns to knowns, thereby reducing risks, and enables management to make more rational choices among alternatives.

It should be understood from the outset that no planning is 100 percent infallible. No one can predict the future with certainty. To put it differently, all that research can do (if done properly) is increase your chances of coming up with better decisions. Don't think of it as a substitute for business acumen but simply as an additional managerial tool for you to use.

To the small business owner, marketing research appears to be a "frill"— something that only the larger corporations can afford to pursue. Rarely do entrepreneurs get involved in this form of activity. What holds most of them back, apparently, are (1) a lack of familiarity not only with the methods and techniques of research but even with its purposes, (2) the realization that outside research services are costly, and (3) an inability to evaluate the costs in concrete terms, such as return on investment.

When you get right down to it, all business executives conduct research on occasion, usually without realizing that is what they're doing. Comparing yesterday's sales figures with those of the same day or date last year and drawing conclusions (which may be correct or erroneous) falls into the research category. Some additional examples of simple business research are telephoning a sampling of your customers to ask their opinions about a new product or service you're offering; carefully checking through the rate schedules and readership data of various magazines in order to determine the best place for your one-column advertisement; and studying the "production" ratios of your six sales representatives (number of calls made per day, number of sales per 100 calls, and so on) for the purpose of discovering which ones may need more training or assistance.

Like any other form of activity, research can be performed in a careless, slipshod manner or in a more disciplined fashion. Of course, the way you conduct it influences the extent to which you will find the results useful.

Of course, the large-scale, formal types of study cannot be undertaken on a regular basis in the small company; there just isn't enough room in the operating budget. However, both the brand-new and the established small business need to carry on simple research from time to time in such vital areas as sales, market analysis, and company growth.

A SIMPLE APPROACH TO FOLLOW

If you've had any military training in your past, you're more than familiar with the "by-the-numbers" learning technique. It is a simple approach to use when you need to gather information to help you solve a business problem:

1. Try to clarify the problem in your mind by attempting to put down on paper a clear-cut statement of it, preferably in the form of a question. Some examples of common problems might be: "What method can I use to control my inventory?" "How can we increase sales by 10 percent in Illinois?" "Through what channels should we distribute our products?" "How can we motivate our sales employees?"

2. Next, do some investigating: Examine past records of your company that may pertain to the problem at hand, speak with knowledgeable people who might be able to shed some light on the subject, and try to find out if any information has been published in the particular area you're investigating. During this "searching" stage you may encounter several possible solutions to your problem. If one or more of these seem applicable, you need go no further.

3. Should you decide you need more details, and if it's worth the time, effort, and the expense involved, then you can proceed to a more sophisticated level. You may want to design a simple questionnaire, to be mailed out to your customers, your suppliers, or to specific groups in the general population, depending upon the nature of your problems. For faster results, you can query some of these people over the telephone. (Both of these approaches are treated at greater length in a later section of this chapter.)

4. Finally, for an occasional problem that resists your best efforts at solving, you might consider hiring a research firm to handle the project, provided it's worth the expense involved. Turn things over to specialists who are thoroughly familiar with suitable research designs, selection of sample populations, data collection, and statistical analysis of the findings.

Later on in this chapter is a section entitled "A Simple, Inexpensive Research Tool for the Small Business." You can use this model to tap the opinions, attitudes, likes, and dislikes of customers about your company, your products and prices, your promotional efforts, and so forth. In brief, it can produce effective "customer-oriented" facts for making decisions in business. It also has a good many other applications.

TYPES OF MARKETING RESEARCH

Here's a convenient classification of the more common types of studies used in business to help managers make better decisions:

Market research. Ascertaining the needs and wants of prospective customers, assessing the potential of specific market segments, studying competitors, trading area measurement, and so forth.

Product research. Research into new product development, testing the prices of products to determine whether they're too high or too low, brand comparisons, and other investigative activities.

Promotion research. Checking the effectiveness of displays or advertising copy, comparing different newspapers and magazines as to costs involved and numbers of readers reached, measuring advertising recall, and similar studies.

Sales research. Evaluating the performance of salespeople, studying sales expenses and sales, territory analyses, and the like.

Company research. Checking business trends for the industry and the firm, investigating the firm's "image," studying employee morale or facility locations, and so on.

HOW TO GATHER INFORMATION

In the process of collecting information for decision making, it's helpful to think in terms of two general categories of information, or data: *primary* and *secondary.* Primary data are those facts that are not readily available and that therefore require considerable initiative and effort on the part of the investigator. The term *secondary data* encompasses facts that are normally available, although they may necessitate some searching around. The trick with secondary data is to know the sources you can tap—how and where to locate the information desired.

Chances are that most of the "fact finding" you'll be doing in your small business will involve secondary data; hence, this category is discussed first.

Secondary Data

When acquiring secondary data, bear in mind the following:

- The reliability of the source
- The possibility of bias on the part of the collecting agent
- The fact that the information is dated
- The applicability of the information to your specific problems (since the facts may originally have been gathered for a completely different purpose)

Among the many sources of secondary information are internal company records of all kinds, government compilations of statistics, trade associations, public and university libraries, research organizations, business and scholarly journals, and reference works such as encyclopedias. In the majority of cases, the two most fruitful sources for solving your business problems will be the internal records of your company and government statistics.

Company Records. In the established firm, abundant records of every type are available. These include historical sales data on a daily, weekly, and monthly basis; records of inventory levels and flow; financial statements; purchasing records; and personnel files. Often, what's involved here is rearranging or reordering the facts to make sense out of them, and then applying the findings to the problem at hand.

Let's assume, for example, that you own a menswear store and that it reflects a departmentalized layout: sport jackets in one section, slacks in another, shirts and ties in a third, and so forth. Assume further that you would like to investigate the sales of these various merchandise classifications, perhaps so you could organize a more effective store layout. "After all," you reason, "if I do 20 percent of my business in sport jackets, perhaps I should devote about that percentage of my store's selling area to that particular classification."

Obviously, you need to ascertain the sales volume enjoyed by each class. You must "attack" your in-house records by merchandise classification. Further, you might want to analyze these categories not only by total dollar sales volume but also by the number of units sold. This study of company records will provide further insights to help you in thinking through your decision.

Government Statistics. The government is a formidable supplier of information of every type and description for the business world. The Department of Commerce is probably the most important government source at the federal level. This department compiles statistical data obtained periodically through its Bureau of the Census (*Census of Population, Census of Manufactures, Census of Business, Census of Agriculture,* and so on). In addition, the department issues an annual summary of the economy in its *Statistical Abstract of the United States.* This can be found in most public libraries. On a monthly basis, it publishes the *Survey of Current Business,* which offers data on both sales and inventories as well as statistics on commerce and industry.

Other departments, such as the Department of Labor (with its *Monthly Labor Review*) and the Department of Agriculture, issue reports periodically.

Other Sources. A good many other sources of information exist for the alert business manager. These include newsletters and occasional reports issued through a number of organizations including the Federal Reserve Banks, the Federal Communications and Federal Trade Commissions, and various state and county agencies. Familiarize yourself with the indexes usually available in the public library, such as the *Business Periodicals Index,* the *Wall Street Journal Index,* and the *New York Times Index.* Other indexes are available in fields such as personnel administration, psychology, chemistry, and sociology.

Then there are the trade directories and other reference works that are valuable to business enterprises, including those issued by Dun & Bradstreet, the *Thomas' Register of Manufacturers,* and other trade books. Such periodicals as *Dun's, Forbes, Fortune, Business Horizons,* the *Harvard Business Review,* and various academic journals (the *Journal of Marketing,* the *Journal of Retailing,* the *Journal of Business,* and the like) make for additional worthwhile reading.

Primary Data

The collecting of primary information in marketing research usually involves one of three approaches: (1) asking people (the *survey method*), (2) watching people (the *observation method*), or (3) setting up an experimental situation (the *experimental method*).

Survey Method. Because surveys are relatively inexpensive and are adaptable to a wide range of problems, they seem to be by far the most popular device for gathering primary information. The survey method essentially seeks answers to specific questions through personal interviews, telephone interviews, or mail questionnaires. In one form or another, the technique can be of value in gathering information for any of the five types of research listed earlier in this chapter.

The preparation of a useful interview guide or questionnaire is difficult. It requires good thinking and planning. Consideration should be given to the wording and sequencing of questions, how easily the results can be tabulated, the validity of the questions themselves, and so forth. Mail and telephone surveys are generally less expensive than personal interviews. Of the three types, the telephone survey will produce the most immediate response. Of course, there's no substitute for the personal interview (when conducted by a competent interviewer) to extract the maximum amount of information from the person interviewed and to probe specific areas in depth.

Observation Method. As the name suggests, this method involves watching people's behavior, such as their facial expressions or movements in reaction to something presented to them; for example, observing or filming customers in the act of making a purchase. In this kind of study, mechanical equipment such as cameras (often hidden from view) and tape recorders are used to gather information needed to solve the problem at hand. The major flaw with these techniques is that we can only observe *behavior.* We cannot ascertain what goes on within people's minds.

Experimental Method. The experimental approach involves the deliberate setting up of an experiment under well-controlled circumstances. As an illustration, a chain store retailer might wish to try out a new gift item at several different selling prices before deciding on the price that would yield the best possible combination of unit volume and gross profit. The merchant might then try to locate among his or her retail outlets three stores that are roughly equivalent in terms of store size, clientele, type of neighborhood, and monthly sales volume. The retailer is attempting here to "control" some of the other factors that might affect the outcome of the experiment; in other words, he or she is trying to keep all other things equal. Identical displays of the new item are set up in each store and put on sale on the same day in all three locations. There's one difference from store to store, however: At Store A, the price tag reads *$4.50;* at Store B, *$4.95;* and at Store C, *$5.50.* At the end of two or three weeks, a comparison of the sales data on the item from store to store should prove illuminating!

Of course, there are many other ways to set up experiments, or *experimental designs* as they are called. Further discussion of such designs, however, is beyond the scope of this book. (For more information, refer to the books on marketing research listed at the end of this chapter.)

A SIMPLE, INEXPENSIVE RESEARCH TOOL FOR THE SMALL BUSINESS

One variation of the survey method that appears to be very useful for the small firm is known as *the semantic differential.* It's an easy-to-use research tool that can be employed to tap people's impressions of, opinions about, or attitudes toward objects, concepts, or things.

Basically, the semantic differential consists of a number of pairs of adjectives and/or short phrases printed on a sheet of paper. These pairs, called *polar* words or phrases, are opposite to each other in meaning. Examples include *good/bad, high-priced/low-priced,* and *cold and businesslike/warm and neighborly.* The two opposites that form a pair are set off from each other by a number of dashes. The entire line thus formed is referred to as a *semantic differential scale.*

To ascertain a person's opinion about a particular object, you ask the individual to check off the one position on each of the several scales that most nearly coincides with the way the person feels about the object.

A sample of a semantic differential containing eight separate scales of this type is shown in exhibit 16–1. The form asks for people's impressions about a particular company. The individual who feels that the ABC Company is an *extremely progressive* firm would place a check mark over the dash in column 1. On the other hand, a person who believes that the same firm is *very backward* would check column 6. The fourth column represents a neutral position.

Once shown how to enter opinions onto the form, the average person should need no more than two or three minutes to complete a sheet that contains up to fifteen scales.

To illustrate the use of this technique, let's take as an example a wholesaler of giftware who wishes to gather information regarding the attitudes customers (retailers) hold toward the company. The distributor can use the semantic differential presented in exhibit 16–1, substituting the correct firm name for the *ABC Company.* The distributor then prepares a mailing to all customers which includes the semantic differential sheet, a letter of explanation, and a stamped (or metered) return envelope. To ensure that the customers will indicate their true feelings toward the company, they're advised in the letter to return the sheet *anonymously.*

In the event that this wholesaler has a lengthy customer list, the cost of the research can be reduced by limiting the mailing to 10, 20, or 30 percent of the customers. This is often done when conducting a survey. In such cases, it's wise to try to select the sample on a *random* basis so that every firm on the list has an equal chance of being selected. An easy approach is to choose every third, fifth, tenth, etc. name from the entire list and mail to those selected names only.

Tallying up the responses for any number of people is relatively simple. Each scale (the two opposite words or phrases plus the spaces in between) is treated separately. You add up the total number of individuals who have checked off Column 1, Column 2, and so on. Then, you multiply the number of individuals per column by *the number at the top of the column* to obtain a *total* score. This total score is then divided by the total number of people who have responded in order to obtain an *average* score for the entire group.

This may sound somewhat complicated, so let's use a concrete example: the 100 returns received by the giftware distributor mentioned above. The following distribution of check marks was observed on the first scale, *progressive/ backward:*

Number of Column	Number of People Checking Column
1	2
2	3
3	12
4	9
5	31
6	26
7	17

The first step in analyzing the results is to obtain a total score by multiplying the number of individuals who have checked off each column by the number of the column. In brief, we must multiply 2 by 1, which yields 2; then 3 by 2, yielding 6; next, 12 by 3, to obtain 36; and so on to the last entry. Then, total all the sums. In the distribution above, the total score amounts to 510. Then, divide this total by the number of people who responded to the scale. In this case, it was one hundred. Dividing 510 by 100, we come up with an average rating of 5.1 for the entire group. This would indicate that, as a whole, the one hundred respondents regarded the giftware firm as being *somewhat backward.*

It's just as easy to translate these average (or *mean*) scores into pictorial form so that management can readily grasp their significance. Take a blank sheet containing the semantic differential and mark off for each scale the approximate position where the group's mean score falls. Then, connect all of the marks with straight lines. What then emerges is a *profile* or *image* of the group's collective response to the various scales of the semantic differential.

By way of illustration, exhibit 16–2 shows the profile of customer reactions to the salesclerks of a medium-size store.

Not only is this procedure valuable for obtaining insights into people's attitudes toward your business but it can also be useful in ascertaining their opinions about your competition. All you need do is repeat the process, asking

EXHIBIT 16-1. A SAMPLE SEMANTIC DIFFERENTIAL INSTRUMENT

QUESTION: *What are your impressions of the ABC Company?*

	(1) Extremely	(2) Very	(3) Somewhat	(4) DON'T KNOW	(5) Somewhat	(6) Very	(7) Extremely	
Progressive	___	___	___	___	___	___	___	Backward
Cold and businesslike	___	___	___	___	___	___	___	Warm and neighborly
Reliable	___	___	___	___	___	___	___	Unreliable
High-priced merchandise	___	___	___	___	___	___	___	Low-priced merchandise
Poor credit policies	___	___	___	___	___	___	___	Good credit policies
Wide variety	___	___	___	___	___	___	___	Little variety
Poor customer relations	___	___	___	___	___	___	___	Good customer relations
Little-known company	___	___	___	___	___	___	___	Well-known company

EXHIBIT 16-2. A PROFILE OF CUSTOMER REACTIONS

QUESTION: *What are your impressions of our salesclerks?*

	(1) Extremely	(2) Very	(3) Somewhat	(4) DON'T KNOW	(5) Somewhat	(6) Very	(7) Extremely	
Friendly	___	X	___	___	___	___	___	Unfriendly
Of little help to customers	___	___	___	___	X	___	___	Of great help to customers
Courteous	___	___	X	___	___	___	___	Discourteous
Lazy	___	___	___	X	___	___	___	Hardworking
Know little about selling	___	___	___	___	X	___	___	Know how to sell
Familiar with merchandise	___	X	___	___	___	___	___	Unfamiliar with merchandise

211

others to rate your major competitor. (Of course, the proper way to conduct this kind of survey is to make certain that the people you survey do not know who is behind the survey. This way, you're more likely to receive unbiased opinions!)

By placing the two profiles side by side on a single page, you will be able to view rather graphically your company's strengths and weaknesses vis-à-vis those of your competitor. This can lead to your taking steps to bolster your weak points, and to publicize your strong ones to greater avail.

There is one problem with the semantic differential: the difficulty of selecting the right adjectives or phrases to fit your particular needs. To help you, three lists of suggested scales are offered in exhibit 16–3 for use by small manufacturers, wholesalers, and retailers. These are not meant to be all-inclusive. However, they should provide enough material to yield some useful information for your business.

EXHIBIT 16–3. SCALE SUGGESTIONS FOR VARIOUS TYPES OF ENTERPRISES

FOR THE SMALL MANUFACTURING COMPANY:

progressive . . . backward
cold and businesslike . . . warm and neighborly
wide variety of products . . . little variety of products
unreliable firm . . . reliable firm
low prices . . . high prices
good customer relations . . . poor customer relations
fast deliveries . . . slow deliveries
poorly advertised . . . well advertised
excellent product quality . . . poor product quality
hard to deal with . . . easy to deal with
excellent service . . . poor service
unpopular styles . . . popular styles
liberal credit policies . . . stringent credit policies

FOR THE SMALL WHOLESALING ENTERPRISE:

(*Note:* Use these in addition to many listed above for the small manufacturer.)
salespeople are helpful and "low key" . . . salespeople are aggressive and pushy
good adjustment policies . . . poor adjustment policies
too many "out-of-stocks" . . . merchandise is readily available
salespeople are unfamiliar with product line . . . salespeople are knowledgeable about products
provides excellent help with advertising . . . does not provide advertising help

FOR THE SMALL RETAILING FIRM:

(*Note:* Use these in addition to many listed in the above category.)
attractive displays . . . unattractive displays
quite a shabby place . . . store is spotlessly clean
poor store layout . . . excellent store layout
convenient store hours . . . store hours are inconvenient
a comfortable place to shop . . . an uncomfortable place to shop
sensitive to customer needs . . . insensitive to customer needs

EXHIBIT 16–3. (*Continued*)

slow checkout . . . speedy checkout
easy return privileges . . . strict return privileges

FOR THE SMALL SERVICE BUSINESS:
(*Note:* Use these in addition to many listed in the above category.)
a dependable company . . . company is not dependable
offers top-quality service . . . offers poor-quality service
competent personnel . . . incompetent personnel
service carries a superior guarantee . . . service is not guaranteed

Source: Compiled by the author.

FOR FURTHER INFORMATION

Books

Gorton, Keith, and Isobel Carr. *Low-Cost Marketing Research: A Guide for Small Businesses.* New York: Wiley, 1983.

Hartley, Robert F., George Prough, and Alan B. Flaschner. *Essentials of Marketing Research.* New York: Macmillan, 1983.

Kinnear, Thomas C., and James R. Taylor. *Marketing Research: An Applied Approach,* 2d ed. New York: McGraw-Hill, 1983.

Luck, David J., and Ronald S. Rubin. *Marketing Research,* 7th ed. Englewood Cliffs, N.J.: Prentice-Hall, 1987.

Tull, Donald S., and Del I. Hawkins. *Marketing Research: Measurement and Method,* 4th ed. New York: Macmillan, 1987.

Weiers, Ronald M. *Marketing Research.* Englewood Cliffs, N.J.: Prentice-Hall, 1984.

Pamphlets available from the Small Business Administration

MANAGEMENT AIDS

MA 4.019—"Learning About Your Market"

VI

FINANCIAL MANAGEMENT OF THE SMALL FIRM

17

Managing the Company's Finances—I

In our frontier days, trappers and Indians brought furs and animal skins to the local trading post where they bartered them for foodstuffs and other products proferred by the settlers. Finished goods imported from Europe also found their way into these earliest retail outlets.

But bartering as a way of American life has, for the most part, long since vanished—except to reveal itself on occasion in "trading" situations wherein, for example, a person might exchange a ten-year-old electric typewriter for someone else's used (and rusted!) bicycle. We may also find an occasional firm that will exchange, or barter, some of its products for those of another company—products of equivalent value, of course.

Today, all business organizations, even the nonprofit type, run on money. Indeed, money is the fuel that fires up the business engine.

The inability to interpret and control the financial factor effectively is one of the prime causes of business failure. Efficiency in production, dynamic sales delivery, top-notch human resources management, and adroit handling of other phases of the business—all of these activities take a distant second place to the consummate skill needed for managing a company's finances.

This brings us to the whys and wherefores of *accounting*.

SOME ACCOUNTING FUNDAMENTALS FOR THE SMALL BUSINESS OWNER

Every company needs a systematic approach to money management: an accounting system that helps the owner(s) keep track of all business transactions and other financial information. Inputs must be fed into the system, and outputs must be registered so that a state of equilibrium can be maintained. Further, it's obvious that all the entries in and out of the system must be classified in a sensible, useful fashion so they can be "worked"—that is, added up, subtracted, and compared. Accounting isn't bookkeeping; bookkeeping is simply a necessary part of a firm's accounting system.

Here are some of the things an accounting system enables us to do:

- Interpret past performance
- Measure present progress
- Anticipate and plan for the future
- Control operations
- Uncover significant trends
- Compare results with similar firms and within the particular industry
- Make decisions
- Comply with government regulations

Your firm's accounting system is based on a simple, balanced equation:

$$\text{Assets} = \text{Liabilities} + \text{Net Worth}$$

A second important concept with which you need to become familiar is the *profit equation*. It's important to every profit-oriented business:

$$\text{Profit} = \text{Sales} - \text{Costs}$$

You've already run across these two basic equations—in different form—in chapter 5. For the sake of convenience, we reproduce here the two major accounting statements presented in that chapter. (See exhibits 17–1 and 17–2.)

Check the balance sheet for the ADG-Tenafly Manufacturing Company (exhibit 17–1). Note how it's divided into two major sections: (1) assets; and (2) liabilities + capital (net worth). Both sections total up to $87,950. Notice that the sections conform to each other.

Now, refer to the income statement in exhibit 17–2 for The Two Sisters' Dress Shoppe. This is, in fact, a detailed expansion of the profit equation.

RATIO ANALYSIS

The two major accounting statements—the balance sheet and the income statement—contain a great deal of information about the results of company operations and the current state of the firm's finances. Company management can manipulate this information in ways that yield meaningful insights for decision making. One of these ways is *ratio analysis*. Using this technique, you juxtapose one item of information against another, thereby forming a ratio. (A ratio is a proportion that expresses or implies some kind of relationship between two numbers.) For example, consider this statement: "Your chances of losing in this game are about one out of three." The ratio implied in that statement can be expressed as 1 in 3, $\frac{1}{3}$, or simply 1:3.

A ratio is like a fraction—a numerator placed over a denominator. It's often

EXHIBIT 17–1. A SAMPLE YEAR-END STATEMENT

ADG-TENAFLY MANUFACTURING COMPANY
Balance Sheet
December 31, 1987

Assets			Liabilities		
CURRENT ASSETS			CURRENT LIABILITIES		
Cash on hand	$300		Accounts payable	$4,700	
Cash in bank	7,150		Notes payable within one year	1,400	
Accounts receivable, less allowance for bad debts	9,720		Accrued payroll taxes	1,960	
Merchandise inventory	11,880				
Total current assets		$29,050	Total current liabilities		$8,060
FIXED ASSETS			LONG-TERM LIABILITIES		
Land	$7,560		Note payable, due 1993	$3,000	
Building, less depreciation	33,330		Note payable, due 1996	7,000	
Equipment, less depreciation	12,060				
Furniture and fixtures, less depreciation	5,950				
Total fixed assets		58,900	Total long-term liabilities		10,000
Total Assets		$87,950			
			Capital (Net Worth)		
			Capital, December 31, 1987		69,890
			Total Liabilities and Capital		$87,950

Source: Compiled by the author.

EXHIBIT 17–2. A SAMPLE P&L

THE TWO SISTERS' DRESS SHOPPE
Profit and Loss Statement
May 1987

GROSS SALES FOR MAY	$19,700		
Less returns and allowances		420	
Net Sales			$19,380
COST OF GOODS			
Merchandise inventory, May 1		11,550	
Purchases during month		6,100	
Freight charges		115	
Total merchandise handled		17,765	
Less inventory, May 31		6,315	
Cost of goods sold			11,450
Gross profit (margin)			7,930

EXHIBIT 17–2. (*Continued*)

OPERATING EXPENSES		
Salaries	3,100	
Utilities	420	
Rent	1,000	
Stationery and printing	140	
Insurance	260	
Advertising and promotion	245	
Telephone	140	
Travel and entertainment	65	
Dues and subscriptions	40	
Bad debts	220	
Depreciation	820	
Total operating expenses		6,450
Operating profit		1,480
OTHER INCOME		
Dividends	90	
Interest on bank account	60	
Total other income		150
Total income before taxes		1,630
Less provision for income taxes		560
Net Income (or Loss)		$1,070

Source: Compiled by the author.

and easily converted to a percentage by first dividing out the fraction and then multiplying the result by 100 percent.

As an example, assume your company earned $400,000 in sales last year, that your total labor costs were $100,000, and that the rental for your premises came to $48,000. Two helpful ratios can easily be constructed here—namely, a *labor-to-sales* ratio and a *rent-to-sales* ratio:

$$\text{Labor/Sales} = \frac{\$100,000}{\$400,000} = \frac{1}{4} = 25\%$$

$$\text{Rent/Sales} = \frac{\$48,000}{\$400,000} = \frac{12}{100} = 12\%$$

You can now determine (from putting the figures together in a meaningful way) that last year you paid out one dollar in labor for every four you took in ($\frac{1}{4}$, or 25 percent of sales); and twelve out of every hundred dollars in sales ($\frac{12}{100}$, or 12 percent) went for rent. You can literally track your progress, or lack of it, from one year to the next by comparing these ratios and others. Of course, businesspeople often find it more helpful to compare percentages over time, since they're easier to work with.

Now we can get on to the business of learning about more of the useful ratios that you can obtain from your basic accounting statements.

Liquidity Ratios

Here we're interested in finding out just how "liquid" our company appears to be. Comparing *liquidity ratios* over a period of years is helpful in determining whether things are improving or deteriorating. A firm is said to be liquid when it has enough in assets to pay all its debts and still has some funds left over.

The Current Ratio. Current assets divided by current liabilities gives you the *current ratio.*

Check the balance sheet of the ADG-Tenafly Manufacturing Company once more. The firm's current assets are listed as $29,050 and its current liabilities as $8,060:

$$\text{Current Ratio} = \frac{\$29,050}{\$8,060} = 3.6{:}1$$

As a general rule of thumb, a current ratio of at least 2:1 (twice as much in current assets as in current liabilities) is desirable. This reflects a fairly sound financial situation for most firms. However, the safe current ratio will vary by industry, and it might be wiser to compare the current ratio with that of other companies similar to yours. Also, if your current ratio decreases over time, you may have a developing problem that you should look into.

The Quick Ratio. Also called the *acid test ratio,* the *quick ratio* is a more significant indicator than the current ratio of a firm's ability to liquidate its debts. It's similar to the current ratio, except that the valuation of the merchandise inventory is omitted:

$$\text{Quick Ratio} = \frac{\text{Cash} + \text{Negotiable Securities} + \text{Accounts Receivable}}{\text{Current Liabilities}}$$

Here's the quick ratio for the ADG-Tenafly Manufacturing Co.:

$$\text{Quick Ratio} = \frac{\$17,170}{\$8,060} = 2.13{:}1$$

As with the current ratio, the higher this ratio the better. The quick ratio should be at least 1:1. If it's less than this, the company may be headed for financially troubled waters. Again, it would be fruitful not only to compare your quick ratios for several years to watch for trends in direction but also to compare your ratios to those of other firms in your industry.

Profitability Ratios

Profitability ratios let you know how profitable (or unprofitable) your company's operations are. Of course, profits may be lined up and measured against a variety of data, such as sales, net worth, assets, and so forth. Generally, profitability ratios are expressed as percentages rather than proportions or fractions.

The Profit-to-Sales Ratio. If you examine the data furnished on the P&L

statement of The Two Sisters' Dress Shoppe, you can see that for the month of May the store earned a net profit after taxes of $1,070 on a net sales volume of $19,380. Here's how you calculate the *profit-to-sales ratio* for this store:

$$\text{Profit/Sales} = \frac{\text{Net Profit (after taxes)}}{\text{Net Sales}} \times 100\%$$

$$= \frac{\$1,070}{\$19,380} \times 100\%$$

$$= 5.5\%$$

This means that for every dollar of sales during May of 1987, the retailer earned 5.5 cents. You must remember that this particular ratio varies from one month to the next, because retail businesses will not enjoy the same dollar sales nor the same expenses each month. December sales, for instance, may increase dramatically while the store's outlay for labor, advertising, and other expenses may constitute a less-than-usual percentage of sales. Generally, the true picture is reflected more accurately by semiannual or yearly computations of this and other profitability ratios. The month-to-month fluctuations wash out over time.

Incidentally, for the majority of small retail firms, the annual profit-to-sales ratio runs about 2 to 5 percent (higher or lower in individual cases).

Other Indications of Profitability. Additional ratios may be computed similarly. Here are two others frequently used by businesspeople:

$$\text{Profit/Net Worth} = \frac{\text{Net Profit (after taxes)}}{\text{Net Worth}} \times 100\%$$

$$\text{Return on Assets} = \frac{\text{Net Profit (after taxes)}}{\text{Assets}} \times 100\%$$

Other informative ratios that can indicate profitability and are especially useful to retail companies include sales/square foot of selling space, average sale/customer, and sales-to-inventory.

Inventory turnover—or *stockturn*—is not a direct profitability ratio, but business owners make good use of it to ascertain how fast (or slow) their inventory is moving and to help them in ordering goods. Three different stockturn ratios are used:

$$\text{Stockturn (in Units)} = \frac{\text{Number of Units Sold}}{\text{Average Inventory in Units}}$$

$$\text{Stockturn (at Cost)} = \frac{\text{Cost of Goods Sold}}{\text{Average Inventory at Cost}}$$

$$\text{Stockturn (at Retail)} = \frac{\text{Retail Sales}}{\text{Average Inventory at Retail}}$$

In all three instances, we derive the figure for *average inventory* by averaging the inventory listings by dollar valuation or by unit count. For example, if a physical inventory is taken on January 1 and then again on December 31 (or on January 1 of the following year), there would be two listings. In this case, the value of both (or their total number of units) would be added together and then divided by 2 to obtain the average inventory. Where management regularly takes inventory at the end of each month, thirteen listings would be used to calculate the average inventory.

YOU CAN AVOID CASH-FLOW PROBLEMS

At one time or another during the year, an acute shortage of cash seems to plague many firms. At times the business is extremely "tight" for operating capital; it may temporarily lack the funds to purchase raw materials or merchandise, to buy supplies, or to pay various bills.

To maintain good financial control of your business, managing the cash flow is imperative. The "ebb and flow" of ready cash within the year can actually be plotted out in advance with a simplified *funds-flow* form, such as the one in exhibit 17–3. Details are, of course, filled in from the monthly profit and loss statements you have developed.

RECORD KEEPING FOR YOUR COMPANY

Keeping books properly is essential to your firm's accounting system. Before you start your operation it's generally advisable to have an accountant set up your books according to the specific needs of your company. Thereafter, you can maintain your own books until the business can afford to pay for a full-time or even part-time bookkeeper. Another approach is to use the services of a firm in the "bookkeeping systems" business. For a fee, they will maintain your books for you. Note, though, that the Small Business Administration advises that you will need to maintain (at the very minimum) four basic types of records, regardless of whether you or someone else keeps your books.* These are

- Sales records
- Cash receipts
- Cash disbursements
- Accounts receivable

If you decide on a "do-it-yourself" approach, there are simplified, one-book systems available at most business stationery stores. However, I'd still recommend that you seek the assistance of a qualified accountant. This person can set you up with a tailor-made approach designed not only to meet your accounting needs but also to provide information over time to help you make decisions.

---

*John Cotton, "Keeping Records in Small Business," *Small Marketers Aids No.155* (Washington, D.C.: U.S. Small Business Administration, 1974), 2.

EXHIBIT 17-3. A FUNDS-FLOW STATEMENT

ESTIMATED CASH FORECAST

	JAN.	FEB.	MAR.	APR.	MAY	JUN.	JUL.	AUG.	SEP.	OCT.	NOV.	DEC.
(1) Cash in Bank (Start of Month)												
(2) Petty Cash (Start of Month)												
(3) Total Cash—Add (1) and (2)												
(4) Expected Cash Sales												
(5) Expected Collections												
(6) Other Money Expected												
(7) Total Receipts—Add (4), (5) and (6)												
(8) Total Cash and Receipts—Add (3) and (7)												
(9) All Disbursements (for Month)												
(10) Cash Balance at End of Month. In Bank Account and Petty Cash—Subtract (9) from (8)*												

*This balance is your starting cash balance for the next month.

Source: "Business Plan for Retailers," *Small Marketers Aid No. 150* (Washington, D.C.: Small Business Administration, 1970), 17.

As an overall guide, every transaction should be entered in a journal on a daily basis. If this is done—if you keep copies of all bills, receipts, canceled checks, checkbook stubs, and so on—your bookkeeper will be able to make sense of it all.

How Long to Keep Records. It's customary to keep business tax records for at least six years and your basic journals of original entry for about the same length of time. General ledgers, corporate minutes, leases, contracts, copyrights and patents, and other important documents should be kept indefinitely. It's also advisable to keep employee payroll records for at least five years (sometimes longer, depending on the requirements of the state in which your company is located).

Receiving documents, purchase orders, sales records, and other internal records are typically kept for three years or so. You can usually discard job tickets upon completion of the job; production orders, though, should be held for a few months.

FOR FURTHER INFORMATION

Books

Hartley, W. C., and Yale Meltzer. *Cash Management: Planning, Forecasting, and Control.* Englewood Cliffs, N.J.: Prentice-Hall, 1979.

Horngren, Charles T. *Introduction to Management Accounting,* 6th ed. Englewood Cliffs, N.J.: Prentice-Hall, 1984.

Hylsop, D., and I. Place. *Records Management: Controlling Business Information.* Englewood Cliffs, N.J.: Prentice-Hall, 1982.

Keith, L., and R. Keith. *Accounting: A Management Perspective,* 2d ed. Englewood Cliffs, N.J.: Prentice-Hall, 1985.

Kolb, Burton A. *Principles of Financial Management.* Plano, Tex.: Business Publications, 1983.

Krevolin, N. *Records/Information Management and Filing.* Englewood Cliffs, N.J.: Prentice-Hall, 1986.

Lynch, Richard M., and Robert W. Williamson. *Accounting for Management: Planning and Control,* 3d ed. New York: McGraw-Hill, 1983.

Neveu, Raymond. *Fundamentals of Managerial Finance,* 2d ed. Cincinnati: South-Western, 1985.

Pamphlets Available from the Small Business Administration

MANAGEMENT AIDS

MA 1.001—"The ABC's of Borrowing"
MA 1.011—"Analyze Your Records to Reduce Costs"
MA 1.016—"Sound Cash Management and Borrowing"
MA 1.017—"Keeping Records in Small Business"
MA 1.018—"Checklist for Profit Watching"

Booklets Available from the Superintendent of Documents

S/N 045-000-00137-7—*Guides for Profit Planning*—$4.50.
S/N 045-000-00142-3—*Financial Recordkeeping for Small Stores*—$5.50.
S/N 045-000-00150-4—*Ratio Analysis for Small Business*—$4.50.
S/N 045-000-00162-8—*Cost Accounting for Small Manufacturers*—$6.00.
S/N 045-000-00208-0—*Handbook of Small Business Finance*—$4.50.

18

Managing the Company's Finances—II

*B*udgets are detailed plans that represent set objectives against which to measure results. They are valuable management tools: In effect, they are blueprints that enable you to anticipate what will be, establish specific objectives, and chart the right course to help you attain those objectives.

Additionally, by monitoring what happens as your firm passes through the budget period, you'll be in a position to make the necessary adjustments that will keep your plan on target. While budgets may be reviewed semiannually or quarterly, a monthly budget review should be much more productive.

BUDGETING FOR PLANNING AND CONTROL

Despite their value as both planning and control devices, though, budgets are not found all that often in small-scale enterprises. This is especially true for small retail organizations. Conjecturing as to the possible reasons behind the lack of "budget orientation," I can only surmise that (a) budgeting is an activity that runs contrary to the entrepreneurial personality; (b) the typical small business owner is not conversant with budgeting techniques; and/or (c) the preparation of budgets for various phases of a business consumes an inordinate amount of time (a commodity that the entrepreneur feels must be dispensed most frugally).

Although budgets can be prepared for any time period, a good way to initiate the budgeting process for your firm is to devise an *overall* or *master* budget for the coming year. Once you have worked your way through your first annual budget, you might then consider the preparation of overall budgets for each quarter of the year.

You'll need to start construction of your master budget with a realistic estimate of the sales volume you expect to realize. This projection of future sales will enable you to construct not only your sales budget but also budgets for every other area of your business: your production, labor, selling expenses, overhead expenses, and so forth. You'll even be able to prepare budgeted operating statements and balance sheets.

At this point, let's take a look at a basic sales budget. Assume that you manufacture and sell three different products and that your sales representatives cover four states. Your sales budget might then look like table 18–1.

Starting with your sales budget, you can then begin to work up other useful budgets: for the amount of units to produce, materials to be purchased, cost of goods sold, selling expenses, administrative expenses, and so on. When you have established budgets for all segments of the business, you can then use this information to prepare your two basic accounting statements.

As an example, table 18–2 is the proposed production budget for Product A for the small manufacturing business discussed above, based on a quarterly approach. Note that individual budgets need to be prepared for each of the three products made.

CAPITAL BUDGETING

Budgeting today, of course, is a way of business life. In a healthy firm, budgets are strategically employed in every phase of the enterprise, for both planning and control purposes.

TABLE 18–1. A BASIC SALES BUDGET

	Projected Sales for Next Year, by Units:			
State	Product A	Product B	Product C	Total Units
Ohio	$ 17,000	$ 12,500	$ 8,600	$ 38,100
Michigan	14,800	9,700	13,400	37,900
Illinois	25,600	14,300	12,600	52,500
Indiana	5,200	15,000	6,100	26,300
Totals:	$ 62,600	$ 51,500	$ 40,700	$154,800

	Projected Sales for the Year, by Dollars:			
State	Product A	Product B	Product C	Total Dollars
Ohio	$ 76,570	$ 75,000	$ 28,380	$179,950
Michigan	66,600	58,200	44,220	169,020
Illinois	115,200	85,800	41,580	242,580
Indiana	23,400	90,000	19,830	133,230
Totals:	$281,770	$309,000	$134,010	$724,780

Source: Compiled by the author.

TABLE 18–2. A PROPOSED PRODUCTION BUDGET

Production Budget (in Units)—Product A:				
Needed for:	First Quarter	Second Quarter	Third Quarter	Fourth Quarter
Planned Sales	$12,000	$14,400	$20,000	$16,000
End-of-Quarter Inventory	3,600	4,400	5,000	3,900
Total Needs for Period	15,600	18,800	25,000	19,900
Less Beginning of Quarter Inventory	2,500	4,700	6,000	2,800
Need to Manufacture	$13,100	$14,100	$19,000	$17,100

Source: Compiled by the author.

Capital budgeting involves setting aside moneys each year for large investments that might need to be made. Throughout the lifetime of your business, you will occasionally be confronted with major decisions involving your company's finances. A few common examples are purchasing costly equipment or machines, expanding or relocating your business premises, instituting a complete internal reorganization, developing and launching a new product. Consequently, you need a logical method to follow in planning and evaluating budgetary alternatives.

In this context, there are some important "money concepts" to keep in mind:

- A firm's capital is always limited.
- Money borrowed for capital expenditures will cost more money.
- Today's dollar is worth one dollar-plus, in the sense that it can be held in a bank account and draw interest.
- Tomorrow's dollar will probably be worth one dollar-minus.
- Money assigned to capital expenses may sometimes be put to different, more productive, uses.

Capital Spending Decisions

Capital investments are made for two basic reasons: (1) to lower operating costs, or (2) to increase sales. Any major commitment of your firm's funds warrants due caution and consideration on your part. Indeed, a common mistake of many small enterprises is to put too many dollars into capital assets, thereby precipitating a cash crisis that can immobilize operations and even cause bankruptcy.

Of course, such investments can be made directly from the company treasury through borrowed or equity capital and long-term leasing. Whatever the approach (or combination thereof), you will find the following procedure of value in making decisions of this nature:

1. List all of the alternatives on a sheet of paper. Remember also to list the one alternative that's always present in such situations: Do nothing.

2. Work up all the costs involved for each of the choices. Be sure to include estimates of details like the cost of borrowing additional sums of money if you don't have enough, and the value of leaving your firm's current dollars untouched and earning interest in a savings account.

3. Estimate the most likely results (outcomes), in dollars and cents, of each of the alternatives.

4. Select the best alternative—for example, the one with the greatest payoff (after subtracting the total costs from the most likely results).

Capital Budgeting Is a Serious Process

Needless to say, any financial commitment that will involve a substantial portion of your capital must be regarded as a major move. Because the resources of most small businesses are quite limited, their owners need to devote serious thought to the capital budgeting process.

When faced with the need to consider such moves, you should begin by preparing several alternative budgets to help you make the buy/don't buy decision. These budgets must, of course, take two significant aspects into consideration: (1) the total cost of the purchase (or "outlay"); and (2) how much time it will take for you to repay your treasury through the "inflow" of net income attributed to the capital item.

The two most popular approaches to resolving such problems are the *payback period method* and the *net present value method*. When using the first method, you work out the length of time it will take to recover the cost of the purchase from earned net income (after taxes, of course). As an example, let's suppose you're thinking of replacing an old machine with a newer model. Your total cost for the new machine, installed in your plant, will amount to $28,000. You're convinced, though, that it should help you turn out about 30 percent more units per week than the old machine. After working up all the necessary figures, you reach the conclusion that the additional production should bring you—annually, after taxes—about $9,200 in additional profit. By dividing the cost ($28,000) by the annual earnings ($9,200), you can assume that the original outlay will be repaid in a little over three years. Chances are, then, that you would decide to purchase the new machine. On the other hand, had you calculated that your annual earnings would be only $3,000, you might well pass up the opportunity to buy the machine. Rather than wait nine years or longer to recoup your investment, you would be better off placing that money in, say, a long-term savings account at a good rate of interest.

The net present value method is preferable to the payback period method because it recognizes that, over time, the value of money depreciates (in the face of inflation). It calls for adjusting the expected inflow of income according to value tables that show the discounting of one dollar at different specified rates over the expected number of "payback years."

EXPENSE MANAGEMENT

Three areas of internal activity can be found within any company involved in the manufacturing or distribution of goods and/or services: (1) production—or buying for resale, (2) selling, and (3) the financial aspects of operating the business. By tackling one area at a time and applying sound business judgment, you should be able to increase your net profits over time.

Essentially, there are only two ways to make more money in business. Either you increase sales while holding down costs; or lower costs while holding up sales. Expense management deals with the second approach: lowering costs in every segment of your business.

Types of Business Expenses

Most small firms use what is called a *natural classification of expenses,* assigning each cost incurred in operating the enterprise to a particular debit account. Below is a categorization of business expenses that is suitable for the average small company:*

salaries and wages	insurance
contract labor	interest
payroll taxes	depreciation
utilities	travel expenses
telephone	entertainment
rent	advertising
office supplies	dues and
postage	contributions
maintenance	miscellaneous expenses

If you scan the above list, you will quickly see that many of the expenses lie within your control, that some of them are *fixed* (that is, they continue whether your sales volume increases or decreases), and that most of them seem to be *variable* in nature and fluctuate along with sales.

To hold down costs, your challenge is to work out a delicate balance between sales and expenses all along the way, and in all areas of variable costs. Consequently, it's wise to bear in mind at all times the basic accounting formulas mentioned earlier in the book:

$$\text{Assets} = \text{Liabilities} + \text{Net Worth}$$

and

$$\text{Profits} = \text{Sales} - \text{Costs}$$

*John Cotton, "Keeping Records in Small Business," *Small Marketers Aid No. 155* (Washington, D.C.: U.S. Small Business Administration, 1974), 6.

Many management tools are available to assist you in your endeavors, among them: ratio analysis; operational techniques (such as time and methods study, work simplification, value analysis, critical path method, and so forth); and budgeting. All of these approaches are quite useful in making comparative analyses of information, so arranged that you can compare the present period with past periods—that is, make projections (based on trend extrapolation) into the future.

CREDIT MANAGEMENT

Manufacturers and wholesalers find it imperative to offer credit terms to their customers along the marketing channels, simply in order to survive. Retailers and many service firms, on the other hand, generally operate on a cash basis. Nowadays, however, even these latter types are more and more frequently extending credit to customers. Indeed, some of our larger department stores today boast that as many as 70 percent (or more) of their clients are charge-account customers.

There are two basic types of credit: *trade credit* and *consumer credit*. In either case, a firm that offers credit is engaged in more than a simple service; credit is a deliberate marketing strategy designed to stimulate business and give a firm a competitive edge.

Companies extend trade credit to give their customers some leeway in operating. A retailer who purchases goods for resale from a wholesaler might simultaneously owe substantial amounts of money to other wholesalers and to other creditors, such as the telephone and electric companies, the insurance company, and the landlord. This retailer simply does not have enough cash on hand to pay all of the business's bills upon receipt of goods or services and is extended credit by the wholesale supplier.

This is not too different from the shopper to whom consumer credit has been extended: He or she must wait until the next paycheck before being able to pay various bills.

In the case of trade credit, a wholesaler ships goods to a retail firm, sending along with the shipment an invoice indicating the terms of payment. One common example is *2/10, net 30*. This means that the retailer is permitted thirty days of credit from the date of the invoice. Further, if the bill is paid promptly—that is, before ten days have passed—the retailer is entitled to deduct 2 percent from the face amount of the bill. Naturally, this kind of savings can mount up over the course of a full year.

Extending Credit

Each company, of course, must determine its own credit policy. While credit is a must for both manufacturer and wholesaler, other types of firms need to weigh the advantages and disadvantages of credit extension. Obviously, there are risks attached to the strategic deployment of credit as a sales-generating tool. Credit is an area of business operations that cannot be taken lightly.

Indeed, it merits a well-thought-out approach, careful and continuous monitoring, and occasional reappraisal.

Generally, a firm's credit approach involves

1. Setting policies, including standards for measuring each applicant
2. Devising a credit application form to be completed by the person or firm applying for credit
3. Checking on the data provided on the application form
4. Evaluating, then approving, the application
5. Setting a credit limit for the applicant
6. Monitoring credit usage carefully
7. Establishing a collection policy for delinquent accounts

The Three Cs of Credit

A decision to extend credit to any specific client is generally based on what is called the *three Cs of credit.* These are the following:

Character. Since an individual's character—in the sense of personality or behavior patterns—is extremely difficult to appraise, much less define, *character* is usually translated to mean the applicant's willingness to pay bills when they are due. Hence, records must be studied to determine what kind of behavior was evidenced by the applicant in the past with respect to debts.

Capacity. This criterion refers to a person's (or firm's) ability to pay debts out of current income.

Capital. Another indication of the credit applicant's ability to pay is, of course, his or her financial resources (or net worth, in the case of a business firm).

The information provided in the application form is then checked carefully by mail or telephone, and/or with a credit bureau or mercantile agency, such as Dun & Bradstreet.

Consumer Credit

Often, a retail enterprise tries to avoid unnecessary risk by signing up with one or more of the major credit card entities, such as Visa, MasterCard, American Express, or Diner's Club. While it is true that a credit card arrangement requires the business firm to yield a small percentage of sales volume to the agency (a fee often between 3 and 6 percent), offering such a service to customers generally results in an overall sales increase that more than compensates for the agency fee.

When retailers extend credit to consumers, it usually takes one of several basic forms described on the following page.

Open credit. Also referred to as *open account, open book,* or *regular* credit, this form extends short-term credit to customers without requiring any down payment and without adding either interest or carrying charges to the bill. It is usually extended for a thirty-day period.

Installment credit. Here, a customer is required to place a down payment on merchandise and then pay up the balance in full over a period of time in regular installments. Most often, the buyer signs a conditional sales contract and is charged for the service (for example, 1½ percent per month on the unpaid balance).

Option-terms credit. This type of credit permits a customer to charge up to a limit and pay (if he or she so desires) within thirty days of the billing date without penalty. A firm can assign a carrying charge for any amount not paid within that time period and release additional credit (up to the limit) as payments are made. Thus, the features of both open credit and *revolving charge* credit are combined in one plan. (The latter refers to the continuous releasing of credit to the credit ceiling as payments are made.)

Collections

No matter how tightly supervised your credit activities may be, there will still be some customers who pay their bills late and others who won't pay them at all. The structuring of a good collection procedure helps to reduce "delinquency" to an appreciable degree. A working policy might include the following steps:

1. Institute some kind of "red flag" bookkeeping technique to alert you when an account is tardy in payments.

2. Mail a duplicate invoice—stamped *past due, second notice,* or some similar phrase—to the customer shortly after discovering an amount overdue.

3. After several weeks elapse without your receiving a response, send out the first in a series of form letters. (Prepare these long in advance.) The first letter should be pleasant in tone and suggest that the customer may have accidentally overlooked payment of such-and-such an amount. (You might consider placing a telephone call in between the first and second letters to find out what has been happening.)

4. If you hear nothing further, send out the other letters, each of which becomes progressively stronger. These should be spaced so that they reach the addressee about every ten days or two weeks. Your last letter in the series should emphasize the fact that you're about to turn the delinquent account over to your attorney.

5. Turn the matter over to your attorney.

FOR FURTHER INFORMATION

Books

Hartley, W. C., and Yale Meltzer. *Cash Management: Planning, Forecasting, and Control.* Englewood Cliffs, N.J.: Prentice-Hall, 1979.

Hobbs, James B., and Carl L. Moore. *Financial Accounting,* 3d ed. Cincinnati: South-Western, 1984.

Horngren, Charles T. *Introduction to Management Accounting,* 6th ed. Englewood Cliffs, N.J.: Prentice-Hall, 1984.

Keith, L., and R. Keith. *Accounting: A Management Perspective,* 2d ed. Englewood Cliffs, N.J.: Prentice-Hall, 1985.

Kolb, Burton A. *Principles of Financial Management.* Plano, Tex.: Business Publications, 1983.

Lynch, Richard M., and Robert W. Williamson. *Accounting for Management: Planning and Control,* 3d ed. New York: McGraw-Hill, 1983.

Neveu, Raymond. *Fundamentals of Managerial Finance,* 2d ed. Cincinnati: South-Western, 1985.

Pamphlets Available from the Small Business Administration

MANAGEMENT AIDS

MA 1.001—"The ABC's of Borrowing"
MA 1.004—"Basic Budgets for Profit Planning"
MA 1.011—"Analyze Your Records to Reduce Costs"
MA 1.015—"Budgeting in a Small Service Firm"
MA 1.016—"Sound Cash Management and Borrowing"
MA 2.014—"Should You Lease or Buy Equipment?"

Booklets Available from the Superintendent of Documents

S/N 045-000-00137-7—*Guides for Profit Planning*—$4.50.
S/N 045-000-00162-8—*Cost Accounting for Small Manufacturers*—$6.00.
S/N 045-000-00175-0—*Asset Management*—$2.75.
S/N 045-000-00176-8—*Managing Fixed Assets*—$4.75.
S/N 045-000-00180-6—*Credit and Collections: Policy and Procedures*—$4.75.
S/N 045-000-00193-8—*Capital Planning*—$4.50.
S/N 045-000-00208-0—*Handbook of Small Business Finance*—$4.50.

19

How to Protect Your Business

Every new business venture represents a gamble, for it is difficult to predict the future. Even with a well-conceived business plan, adequate financing, and managerial experience in the same field, you'll still find the chances for success hovering around the fifty-fifty mark at best. The odds are no different from those you face in flipping a dime and calling "Heads!" or "Tails!" The risk present in this situation is two-directional: either you win or you lose.

Many of us willingly embrace *speculative risk* where, although we might lose, it is also possible to win—at times a substantial sum. Indeed, the psychological excitement of gambling is a well-known phenomenon. Witness the thousands who place bets at the race track, buy lottery tickets, or play poker. Small business owners, too, are quite familiar with this type of risk; it characterizes the new product development process, the selection of a second or third location, the installation of a major piece of machinery, and the like.

In some situations, the risk might run in only one direction, that of loss. Should a fire, for example, suddenly envelop your home or apartment, the expected outcome can only involve loss, not gain. This kind of risk is called *pure risk.* Insurance exists primarily to protect individuals and organizations against loss caused by damage to property, life, or limb in such situations.

Yes, accidents can happen. Disaster can strike without warning. Furthermore, there's no way any business, much less any individual, can be exempted from such calamities. A serious fire can put you out of business overnight—or in an hour. A lesser blaze could cause considerable property damage, forcing you to close down your operation for weeks. A lawsuit seeking to hold you accountable for negligence that resulted in injury can threaten not only your business but also your personal assets (if your business isn't incorporated).

To protect your business, it's imperative that you not only accept the existence of pure risk but also learn how to live with it, and manage it.

236

HOW TO APPROACH
THE RISK-MANAGEMENT PROBLEM

Managements adopt a variety of positions on the problem of handling risk. These range from doing nothing at all, thereby consigning their chances to fate, to attempting to cover just about every possible calamity with some kind of insurance policy.

If you don't want to join the thoroughly illogical "do-nothing" school, here are some common ways to approach risk management:

- *Set up risk-reduction programs* to reduce the possibility of property damage or loss and accidental injuries within your place of business.*

- *Transfer your risk to insurance companies,* especially the major perils such as fire and casualty.

- *Assign risk to third parties,* where possible, as in the case of the retailer who requests product liability coverage from the manufacturer in order to be protected from possible litigation.

- *Set aside as large a contingency fund* as you can manage, to cover potential losses, thus adopting a self-insurance posture.

Basic Pointers

Here are a few helpful suggestions for protecting your company from risk:

- *Think in terms of a well-planned program* that you need to set up initially and then maintain throughout the life of your business. Risk management consists of more than a set of insurance policies, even though such coverage will play a substantial role in the program.

- *Seek professional help at the outset.* You are certainly not an expert in this field. Your most valuable asset here is a knowledgeable and capable insurance representative. This agent or broker can tailor a program to your precise needs, place your insurance with responsible companies, help you in negotiating claims, and advise you when you are in doubt.

    List your risk priorities: Write down the various perils that could affect your business, consult with the professional, and then arrange them in order from most to least serious in their potential for damaging your business. Obviously, insurance protection against a catastrophe should find itself toward the top of your list. Included in this category are property, casualty, and workers' compensation insurance. At the tail end of the list

---

*See the list under "Protection Means More Than Insurance" later in this chapter.

should be less significant risks that would involve the loss of smaller amounts of money. These risks you may elect to transfer or not; examples include plate glass insurance, credit insurance, and rent insurance.

- *Hold down excessive costs*   in several ways: Set up internal risk-reduction programs; talk frankly with your representative about policy terms and conditions; compare insurance coverages and companies where premiums might be exorbitant or where the loss value incurred would be small; and use deductibles. Finally, it's a wise move to investigate the advantages of package policies.

- *Keep accurate records*   not only of your various coverages but also of all insured property. For example, in the event of a claim for property destroyed by fire, the insurance company will require a complete listing, down to description, age, cost or replacement value, and so forth. Photographs are extremely useful. In this respect, "a picture is worth a thousand words!" Nowadays, many business owners prefer to record their property on videocassettes. Put these, along with your detailed descriptions, in your vault, or give them to your insurance agent. Update your records each year.

- *Adapt your insurance policies to changing conditions.*   Keep your eye on both internal (within the firm) and external conditions. Be sure you have sufficient coverage at all times. It's wise to review your risk-management program annually and make necessary changes to ensure the vitality of your business.

PROTECTING YOUR PROPERTY: FIRE INSURANCE

No business should be initiated without insuring against fire. Although chances are good that your plant or store will never burn down, the fact that it *could* happen—that your machinery, equipment, fixtures, or inventory could be damaged, if not destroyed, by fire—should convey the urgency of such coverage.

A fire insurance policy will put you back where you were prior to the loss. It's also important for credit reasons. Unless your place is insured against fire, you'll find it just about impossible to obtain a mortgage on it.

While a basic fire policy insures only against damage from fire or lightning, most business owners extend the scope of coverage to include additional perils, such as smoke, windstorm, hail, explosion, and riot. Protection against possible damage from vandalism and malicious mischief can also be included in your fire policy. The cost of adding these various coverages to the fire premium itself is relatively small.

A fire policy will *exclude* coverage for other types of items, such as cash, stock certificates, bonds, and property deeds. To cover these, additional *floater* policies might be required.

The premium you pay will be based on several factors, including the location of your business (the town it's in, the neighborhood, the surrounding buildings, and so forth), the condition and maintenance of your premises, and the structure and type of your building.

When you first apply for this type of coverage, it's wise to set the overall amount based on what's referred to as the *actual cash value.* This is the replacement cost of the property at current market prices less depreciation. The alternative is to use the purchase cost. Bear in mind, however, that when your insured amount has been based on initial cost, an allowance for depreciation over several years could bring down the covered sum considerably. A piece of equipment that originally cost you $6,000 might now be valued at less than $4,000.

Coinsurance

The concept of *coinsurance,* often misunderstood by the small business owner, merits some explanation. It's designed to spread the cost of fire insurance more equitably among users. In effect, it grants lower premium rates to those who insure their property more fully. The insured firm agrees to maintain coverage on its property at a stipulated percentage of its current value; the most commonly used percentage is 80 percent. Should this agreed-upon figure not be continued and a loss occur, then the firm suffers a penalty in proportion to the deficiency.

For example, companies X and Y have each taken out a policy on their respective properties—valued in each case at $200,000. Firm X has arranged for 80 percent coinsurance; its policy carries a face amount (for total loss) of $160,000. It pays about $3,000 annually in premiums. Firm Y's management feels that the chances of a total loss due to fire are rather remote and wants to "save" on its premium payments. Firm Y thus secures a policy in the amount of $100,000 and finds that its annual cost is about $1,900—or $1,100 less than the cost to firm X. Assume, now, that both companies have fires, and the damage in both instances totals $20,000. Firm X can then expect to receive the full $20,000 that it claims. However, firm Y is penalized because it was "underinsured." Because it had been insured for only half of the actual value ($100,000, instead of $200,000), only half of the claim value is paid—$10,000.

LIABILITY INSURANCE AND OTHER COVERAGES

There is always the possibility that you may become embroiled in legal actions brought by individuals who suffer injuries and then seek to attribute them to negligence on your part. This is an ever-present threat, one that can have serious (even fatal) consequences to a small business. Unfortunately, courts and juries in recent years have more often favored the claimant than the defendant in such cases. Moreover, the amounts of judgments awarded in these lawsuits have skyrocketed. These actions not only cover medical, surgical, disability, and funeral expenses but are also designed to include compensation for "loss of future earnings" to dependents, the costs of defending the action, and the like.

In this context, you may be sued by anyone: customers or passersby, messengers and delivery people, employees, and even, peculiarly enough, trespassers. Court action can follow such common situations as these: someone breaking a capped tooth on a piece of shell in a bowl of soup or on a chocolate-covered filbert; a person tripping over a broken tile or slipping on a highly waxed floor; or an individual being knocked down by another while entering through the doorway of your store or plant.

Moreover, the accident doesn't have to take place on your business premises. One of your employees, on the way to the bank to make a deposit, may accidentally injure another person—who may promptly initiate a suit against your employee and you. According to both common and statutory law, you can be held accountable for negligence that causes personal injury. Consequently, you need liability insurance for protection in this area. These policies generally cover such things as the costs of defending lawsuits, the medical and surgical expenses incurred, and judgments awarded. They also contain specified limits.

It's important to realize that the amount of liability coverage can usually be increased substantially with a small increase in premium. On the basis of the actual, unfortunate experiences of a good many small companies, it is prudent to seek greater, rather than lesser, coverage in this area.

Automobile Insurance

Generally, a business firm insures its automobiles, trucks, and other vehicles against the possibility of physical damage and theft, as well as against bodily injury to others. To this end, they purchase commercial vehicle insurance, including collision insurance. Rates vary considerably from one locale to another. The rates depend not only on the particular area involved but also on the type and age of the vehicles, the distances traveled, the ages of the drivers, and so forth.

Some Other Types of Insurance to Think About

A good many other kinds of business situations that involve pure risk can be covered by insurance. Some of the more common risks are listed in this section. Of course, not every one is necessarily applicable to your business, nor would they all be advisable to have. You should discuss your particular needs in depth with your insurance agent or broker.

Business Interruption Insurance. In the event that your premises suffer a serious fire, the insurance policy you carry covers your direct losses in merchandise, equipment, the plant itself, and so forth. However, you may sustain other, indirect losses. You might not be able to get back into operation for weeks or months after extensive fire damage. This setback would mean that little or no income would be forthcoming for some time. Yet you might want to continue paying salaries to your key people in the interim. At the same time, you might have to pay your monthly utility bills, meet payments on loans, send in insurance premiums that fall due, and so on.

Business interruption insurance will compensate you for the fixed expenses that ordinarily have to be paid out while your business is interrupted.

Fidelity and Surety Bonds. Fidelity bonds are obtained from insurance or bonding companies. They are designed to protect a business against loss due to dishonesty on the part of its employees. Such bonds are available on an individual or group basis. They are especially useful where employees have access to large sums of money or inventory. Surety bonds are of a similar nature, except that they are generally issued to guarantee performance by contractors.

Glass Insurance. Through a comprehensive glass policy, your business can be insured against damage to glass panes, doors, showcases, counter tops, signs, and the like.

Crime Insurance. The small business owner seldom links the possibility of loss through robbery, burglary, or theft to the concept of insurance coverage. Yet, it has been estimated that the total amount of business property damaged each year by fire might, in fact, be *less* than losses due to criminal acts.

Robbery insurance covers you against property loss by force or by threat of violence; burglary insurance covers property stolen by someone who leaves visible signs of forced entry. The "Storekeeper's Burglary and Robbery Policy" is a special form of insurance available to retailers.

Comprehensive crime policies will cover both of these perils as well as other types of property theft, disappearance, or destruction. Crime insurance may not be readily available in high-risk areas. In such cases, the entrepreneur can seek coverage under the Federal Crime Program. (Your agent or broker can provide you with details.)

Water Damage Insurance. Property may be insured against accidental damage caused by water in various forms: escaping steam, overflows from refrigeration and air conditioning equipment, melting snow that leaks through roofs or basement walls, and the like.

Boiler and Machinery Insurance. Some small business owners find this type of insurance of considerable interest. (It's also called *power-plant insurance.*) It protects a firm against loss due to the explosion of boilers, furnaces, engines, and similar equipment.

Group Health Insurance. This popular type of insurance policy covers you and your employees for sickness, injury, or accidental death. Three classes of coverage are usually offered: a basic medical plan, including hospitalization and surgery; a major medical plan that provides for the high cost of physician and nurse expense both in and out of the hospital; and a disability income plan that compensates for lost earnings due to accidental injury or an illness.

WORKERS' COMPENSATION INSURANCE

Under common law you must, to the best of your ability, provide for your employees an environment free from the possibility of accidental injury (or occupational and radiation diseases). Responsibilities include safe working conditions; adequate servicing and maintenance of machinery, tools, and equipment; and work procedures that prevent accidents on the job. You're even required to exercise care in hiring, selecting, and assigning workers in your business.

One of the most important features of workers' compensation laws is that employees are made eligible for benefits regardless of whether you, as an employer, are guilty of negligence or not. Compliance with state law is usually accomplished by acquiring a workers' compensation insurance policy. This insurance provides benefits to injured employees in the form of medical expense reimbursement and replacement of lost wages.

Your premium is based on the size of your payroll and on the kinds of jobs within your organization. The extent of the hazards faced in your type of business is also a factor. Your premium could range from as little as 1 percent of your payroll to as much as 20 percent or more. You can lower your premium, over time, through internal safety measures that reduce the accident rate in your place of business below the average for that particular type of business.

LIFE INSURANCE

Why Purchase Business Life Insurance?

Few mature individuals need to be convinced of the benefits offered by personal life insurance. As responsible people, they're prone to seek protection from life's uncertainties by purchasing one or more life insurance policies in addition to their homeowners' and automobile policies. Yet many business owners are reluctant to think in terms of *business* life insurance, feeling this is a luxury they cannot afford.

This is a shortsighted attitude. Indeed, business life coverage may be something you cannot afford to be without! Think of the long-range possibilities. When you die, or if you become disabled, what will happen to that successful business you have built? How will your family manage? If the business must be liquidated, who will take care of this? Or, if yours is a partnership, and a partner passes away, how can you protect your share of ownership?

With the help of your insurance representative (and your attorney and accountant), you can tailor your business life insurance to your specific needs. Business life policies can be written to protect owners and their families against financial loss due to death or serious injury. Prearrangements can be made to assure the business continues in this event. With life insurance to provide necessary cash and a properly prepared "buy-and-sell" agreement, the deceased's share of ownership may be returned quickly and fully to the heirs, and the surviving owners will be able to carry on the business without interruption.

Key-person insurance provides a similar kind of protection. The untimely death of a valuable employee (for example, a top salesperson, the production manager, or a chief designer) can seriously affect the performance of a firm. The insurance proceeds from key-person coverage can be used by your business to offset a loss in profits or to pay for the cost of hiring and training a replacement.

Incidentally, an important benefit of business life insurance lies in the fact that the cash accumulation in the permanent-type policy is available as a reserve fund for contingencies, or even for retirement.

The basic types of life insurance are described in exhibit 19–1.

EXHIBIT 19–1. TYPES OF LIFE INSURANCE

Whole Life. This is also known as *ordinary* or *straight* life. You are covered for the face amount of the policy throughout your lifetime. The premium, too, is calculated to be paid over the course of your lifetime. This type of policy carries a limited cash surrender value as well as loan privileges and other nonforfeiture values.

Limited Payment Life. A variation of whole life insurance, the limited policy requires the payment of premiums for a set number of years (fifteen, twenty, or more). At the end of this period, no more premiums are paid; the policy is then fully paid up. Thereafter, the insured remains covered for the rest of his or her life. Since the premiums are higher than those paid for a whole life policy, this type has a substantial cash surrender and loan value.

Endowment Life. This form of insurance has many provisions similar to the limited payment life policy in that the policy owner continues to pay premiums for a designated number of years until the policy is fully paid up. At this point, the accumulated cash value equals the face amount and is paid out in a lump sum *(endowment)* to the policy owner. Other provisions for payment are also available.

Term Life. Generally, this requires the lowest dollar outlay for life insurance because the premiums paid are completely used up for the sole purpose of insurance protection. Because of this, the policy does not accumulate a cash reserve for the insured and, consequently, has no cash surrender value or loan possibilities.

Source: Compiled by the author.

PROTECTION MEANS MORE THAN INSURANCE

Even though insurance coverage is available to protect your business against nearly every kind of threat, relying on insurance alone is foolhardy. You can take many steps to help reduce risk. Consider carefully the various kinds of risk and how to guard against them, and you will keep your losses down.

Some Ways to Avoid Property and Casualty Losses

You can also take many preventive measures to safeguard your business against fire or accidental injury. Here are a few examples:

- Place approved fire extinguishers in selected spots around the facility. Check them on a regular basis. See to it that your employees know of their locations.
- Hold fire drills periodically until everyone in your place knows exactly what to do and where to go in case of fire.
- Store flammable materials in proper, closed containers, and keep those containers in a cool area.

- Install a sprinkler system. Use smoke alarms in storage rooms.
- Make sure that fire doors and exits are clearly marked.
- Keep aisles, passageways, and stairwells free from all encumbrances.
- Maintain all equipment and machines in good condition. Place guardrails and other protective devices around machinery with moving parts. Train employees thoroughly in the proper handling of all equipment.
- Practice good housekeeping. Do not permit trash to accumulate on the premises.

REDUCING THEFT

Every business is vulnerable to loss through criminal activity. Theft is a blanket term: It includes shoplifting, embezzlement, and employee pilferage as well as the more "professional" crimes of burglary and robbery.

Shoplifting. Retail stores are particularly susceptible to larceny by shoplifters, amateurs as well as professionals. Unfortunately, assaults upon the retail merchant's profit picture are so prevalent these days that department stores, discount houses, and other large retailers maintain their own private security forces, in addition to employing every imaginable type of security device. Generally, small-scale retailers can't afford this kind of expense.

Employee Theft. Employees can steal small, inexpensive articles (pens, typewriter ribbons, staplers, and the like) and they can take home larger merchandise, too. Occasionally, an employee who is in a position of substantial trust steals money from the cash drawer or juggles the books to conceal theft.

Ways to Reduce Losses from Theft. The business owner can take many steps to hold down losses from criminal acts. (See exhibit 19–2 for some useful suggestions along these lines.)

EXHIBIT 19–2. SUGGESTIONS FOR REDUCING LOSSES FROM THEFT

Your Employees Can Help

- In hiring new people, make certain your selection and screening procedures are good. Make it known from the beginning that you expect honesty in all your employees, and set a personal example with your own behavior at all times.

- Train your personnel to be calm and cooperative in the event of a holdup. A life is a precious thing that no amount of money can replace.

- If possible, always schedule at least two individuals to open up in the morning and close at night, and to make bank deposits.

- Train your employees to be alert: to watch people who enter your store with coats over their arms or carrying shopping bags or bulky packages; to keep an eye on those who look or act suspicious; to wait promptly on customers.

- Try to maintain adequate floor coverage by adding extra salespeople during busy hours.

EXHIBIT 19–2 (*Continued*)

Tighten Up on Procedures and Policies

- Keep good records in accordance with good accounting procedures.

- If possible, sign all checks yourself. Never sign blank checks to leave behind when traveling or on vacation.

- Make certain all cash disbursements have your personal approval.

- Try to reconcile all bank statements throughout the year. Review all canceled checks and their endorsements.

- Keep close watch over the shipping and receiving functions. This includes setting up tight recordkeeping systems within both departments, supervising the loading and unloading of trucks, and even fencing off the two areas from other departments.

- Always remove excess cash from the cash register and place it in the safe. Bank frequently and at different times from day to day. Leave the cash drawer empty and open at night (to avoid possible forced entry that might damage the equipment).

- Keep all keys locked up when not in use, and issue as few as you have to, in order to avoid unnecessary duplication.

- Prosecute any shoplifter who is apprehended and any employee caught stealing. (If there's any doubt whatsoever in a particular incident, it might be wiser to avoid prosecution because of the possibility of a lawsuit for false arrest.)

- To prevent salesclerks from pocketing change or bills from the register, insist on issuing register receipts to all customers. An even better arrangement is to make out sales slips for each and every sale.

What to Do with the Premises

- Install a good alarm system, preferably a central system, on the premises. In high-risk areas, consider additional safeguards, such as gratings and a private patrol service.

- Protect all doors and entrances with properly installed, pin-tumbler-type cylinder locks and deadbolts.

- Safes should be of high quality, fire resistant, and fastened to the building itself.

- Your business premises should be adequately illuminated at night. This applies to the area around the building or store (front/sides/back) as well as inside.

- In a retail store, place small, expensive items in locked showcases. Tie down merchandise on display wherever practical.

- Use antishoplifting signs around the premises to discourage petty larceny.

EXHIBIT 19–2. (*Continued*)

- Locate your check-out stand or cash register near the store's exit. If you can afford to, station a guard at the exit as well.

- Equip your store with convex wall mirrors, two-way mirrors, and closed-circuit television cameras that move to encompass a view of a wide area (even if these are only dummies!).

Source: Compiled by the author.

FOR FURTHER INFORMATION

Books

Crane, Frederick G. *Insurance Principles and Practice,* 2d ed. New York: Wiley, 1984.

Greene, Mark R., and James S. Trieschman. *Risk and Insurance,* 6th ed. Cincinnati: South-Western, 1984.

Mehr, Robert I. *Fundamentals of Insurance,* 2d ed. Homewood, Ill.: Irwin, 1986.

Riegel, Robert, Jerome S. Miller, and C. Arthur Williams, Jr. *Insurance Principles and Practices: Property and Liability,* 5th ed. Englewood Cliffs, N.J.: Prentice-Hall, 1980.

White, Edwin H., and Herbert Chasman. *Business Insurance,* 5th ed. Englewood Cliffs, N.J.: Prentice-Hall, 1980.

Williams, C. Arthur, Jr., and Richard M. Heins. *Risk Management and Insurance,* 4th ed. New York: McGraw-Hill, 1981.

Pamphlets Available from the Small Business Administration

MANAGEMENT AIDS

MA 3.006—"Reducing Shoplifting Losses"

VII

LEGAL ASPECTS AND TAX POINTERS FOR THE SMALL COMPANY

20

Legal Aspects for the Small Firm

Like societies everywhere, our own society is governed by myriad laws. Of necessity and for our common good, we live and function within a vast and extremely complex framework of rules, regulations, customs, practices, ordinances, and the like. These exist at every level of government: federal, state, and local. They are enforced through our court system. If we are to avoid unnecessary risk or penalty, we need to see to it that our behavior conforms to "the law."

While we are, of course, familiar with much of our legal environment, certain aspects are of particular interest to the business world. Instances of "business law" in operation include the choice of legal form under which to operate an enterprise (discussed in chapter 4); the dissolution of partnerships and the formation of corporations; agency law; contract law; the law of torts; and "commercial law" (embracing sales and the transfer of title, warranties, commercial paper, and the like).

Some of the more significant aspects for the businessperson are briefly addressed in this chapter. A detailed discussion of the legal environment lies, of course, well beyond the scope of this book. However, table 20–1 presents a summary of the major federal legislative acts that may affect the business enterprise. For additional, in-depth information regarding this entire area, you may wish to refer to the books on business law listed in the bibliography at the end of the chapter.

COMMON LAW AND STATUTORY LAW

Basically, our American legal system rests on two distinct bodies of law: *common law* and *statutory law.*

TABLE 20–1. FEDERAL LAWS OF SIGNIFICANCE TO THE SMALL BUSINESS OWNER

Year	Legislation	Major Thrust of Law
1890	Sherman Antitrust Act	Prohibited combinations, trusts, and conspiracies that restrain trade.
1906	Pure Food and Drug Act	Banned the adulteration or misbranding of foods and drugs sold in interstate commerce. Created the Food and Drug Administration (FDA).
1914	Clayton Act	Further strengthened the Sherman Act. Barred tying contracts and price discrimination that tends to reduce competition.
1914	Federal Trade Commission Act	Prohibited unfair methods of competition. Created the Federal Trade Commission (FTC).
1935	National Labor Relations Act (Wagner Act)	Gave workers the right to organize and engage in collective bargaining. Created the National Labor Relations Board (NLRB).
1936	Robinson-Patman Act	Barred sellers from offering buyers goods of like grade and quality at different prices in order to lessen or injure competition. Declared that promotional allowances offered must be made available on proportionately equal terms to all buyers.
1938	Food, Drug, and Cosmetic Act	Broadened the authority of the FDA, adding cosmetics and therapeutic devices to foods and drugs.
1938	Fair Labor Standards Act (Federal Wages and Hours Law)	Established wage and hour regulations, minimum hourly wage, and conditions for minors who work.
1938	Wheeler-Lea Act	Banned deceptive packaging; expanded FTC authority to include false or misleading advertising.
1939	Wool Products Labeling Act	Required specific information to be placed on labels attached to products made of wool.
1951	Fur Products Labeling Act	Established label requirements for fur products, including type of fur and country of origin.
1953	Flammable Fabrics Act	Prohibited interstate shipment of apparel that contains flammable goods. Later amended to include fabrics, materials, and home furnishings.
1960	Hazardous Substances Labeling Act	Mandated that warning notices be affixed to household products that contain poisonous, corrosive, or otherwise dangerous substances.
1963	Equal Pay Act	Required employers to give men and women equal pay for the same work.
1964	Civil Rights Act	Outlawed discrimination in employment practices because of race, religion, sex, color, or national origin. Created the Equal Employment Opportunity Commission (EEOC).
1966	Fair Packaging and Labeling Act	Required that the ingredients be disclosed on many packaged products or on labels attached to them.

TABLE 20–1. (*Continued*)

Year	Legislation	Major Thrust of Law
1967	Age Discrimination in Employment Act	Prohibited employment practices aimed at discriminating against persons between the ages of forty and sixty-five. (Subsequently amended to age seventy.)
1968	Consumer Credit Protection Act (Truth in Lending Act)	Mandated that terms and interest charges be fully disclosed to persons who buy on credit.
1969	Child Protection and Toy Safety Act	Banned harmful or dangerous toys from the marketplace.
1970	Fair Credit Reporting Act	Required that credit reporting agencies keep accurate records and provide interested consumers with access to their records.
1970	Occupational Safety and Health Act	Required employers to provide their workers with a safe work environment. Established the Occupational Safety and Health Administration (OSHA).
1972	Equal Employment Opportunity Act	Widened the scope and authority of the EEOC.
1972	Consumer Products Safety Act	Prohibited the sale of harmful products. Created the Consumer Product Safety Commission (CPSC), empowered to set product safety standards.
1974	Employee Retirement Income Security Act	Designed to protect and regulate employee pensions.
1975	Equal Credit Opportunity Act	Barred discrimination against credit applicants because of sex or marital status. (Later amended to prohibit discrimination on the basis of age, religion, race, or national origin.)
1975	Fair Credit Billing Act	Aimed at shielding consumers from unfair credit billing practices.
1975	Magnuson-Moss Warranty Act	Required full disclosure of warranty terms in clear language.
1977	Fair Debt Collection Practices Act	Banned the use of deception, harassment, and other unreasonable tactics in attempts to collect past-due accounts.

Source: Compiled by the author.

Common Law

The existing body of common law that underlies our legal system is also called *customary* or *unwritten* law. We can trace its origins back to colonial times and, beyond that, to England. Our early colonists were quick to adopt for their own use the extensive system of laws and constraints by which the English people were then being governed. Of course, that impressive legal environment that defined the duties, responsibilities, and behavior of individuals was itself the end result of an evolutionary process that took place over centuries. Rooted for the most part in custom, the British legal system was continuously being modified and refined by decisions made in their nation's courts.

Statutory Law

A statute is a law that has been passed by a legislature. *Statutory law,* then, is the term we apply to laws that governments—again, at all levels—have enacted. Thus, we are subject to federal, state, county, municipal, and town statutes. As you might suspect, the collective body of statutory law in the United States is far greater than the common law.

THE LAW OF AGENCY

Of critical importance to the business world is the *law of agency.* The term *agency* can be defined as "a contractual relationship involving an agent and a principal, in which the agent is given the authority to represent the principal in dealings with third parties.*

Agency situations call for a mutual agreement to be reached by two parties (persons, organizations): the principal and the agent. Typically, the principal authorizes the agent to act on his or her behalf. Thus, the agent is an authorized representative of the principal. The agreement may be in the form of a written contract, or it may be simply an oral agreement.

THE LAW OF CONTRACTS

The *law of contracts* has been called "the basic foundation of business law."** Each of the following instances calls for the signing of a contract:

- A homeowner selects carpeting to be installed in her six-room house.
- A consumer puts a down payment on a new Chevrolet sedan and then arranges to repay the balance over a period of three years.
- A manufacturer arranges with a salesperson to "represent" the company in three southern states.
- A construction firm offers to build a second warehouse for a large wholesaler.
- The comptroller of a large consumer service company enlists the aid of an office machine repair firm to service the company's equipment.
- A chain-store retailer hires a maintenance firm to polish the brass on its storefronts on a monthly basis.

A contract has been defined simply as "a mutual agreement between two or more people to perform or not perform certain acts."† For a contract to be

---

*John Jude Moran, *Practical Business Law* (Englewood Cliffs, N.J.: Prentice-Hall, 1985), 332.

**Ibid., 48.

†John A. Reinecke and William F. Schoell, *Introduction to Business: A Contemporary View,* 4th ed. (Boston: Allyn and Bacon, 1984), 594.

legal and enforceable in a court of law, it must meet the following requirements:

- An offer or a proposal must have been made by one party to another.
- The purpose of the offer/proposal must be legal.
- The offer/proposal must be accepted by both parties.
- Acceptance must be voluntary; intimidation, coercion, or threat cannot be used.
- "Consideration" must be present—that is, each party must give the other something of value.
- Parties to the contract must be competent—that is, of legal age and mentally sound.

THE LAW OF TORTS

The *law of torts* deals with private, or civil, wrongs—as contrasted with public wrongs such as criminal acts. A tort is a wrongful act committed by one person or organization against another or against that other's property or reputation. If a tort has been committed, the wronged party can seek redress in court.

Two types of torts can be distinguished: intentional and unintentional torts. "Intentional torts include assault, battery, conversion, defamation, fraud, false imprisonment, invasion of privacy, interference with business relations, malicious prosecution, nuisance, strict liability, and trespass. Unintentional torts include negligence, products liability, and misrepresentation."*

THE LAW OF PROPERTY

The *law of property* deals with all those materials, goods, and other things of value that people or organizations own. This body of law obtains in an extensive variety of situations that range from real estate transactions and tenant-landlord relationships to mortgages, wills, bankruptcy, and so forth. It applies to real property as well as to personal property. Real property consists of land, homes, and other buildings that are permanently affixed to land.

PROTECTING PATENTS AND COPYRIGHTS

Patents are granted by the federal government to those who have designed innovative products and submitted the required paperwork. If granted a patent, you have the exclusive right to manufacture and market your invention for a period of seventeen years. All other individuals and organizations are barred from producing or selling the item.

If you have invented something and wish to obtain a patent for your own

*Moran, *Practical Business Law*, 32.

protection, be sure to enlist the services of a patent attorney.* This specialist will conduct a patent search to determine if the item is patentable—that is, whether or not a similar invention has already been registered. The cost of this procedure may run to a few hundred dollars. You then need to prepare an application, submit the required filing fee, and register the product with the Commissioner of Patents and Trademarks, Washington, DC 20231.

Trademarks**

A *trademark* is a letter, word, mark, symbol, sound, or device—or some combination of these—that is used by a manufacturer or seller to identify a product or service. Companies develop trademarks, brand names, and logos (logotypes) in order to differentiate their organizations, products, and services from those of competitors. As they are publicized over time, these distinguishing marks can grow to be of considerable marketing importance.

Copyrights

A *copyright* is the legal right to reproduce and sell an original work or composition, such as a poem or essay, an article or short story, a book, a musical composition, a painting or illustration, or a photograph.

Any original work that is written, typed, recorded, taped, photographed, illustrated, or otherwise fixed in a tangible form of expression belongs to its creator. Under the Copyright Act of 1976, the author or creator owns the work for the length of his or her lifetime plus fifty years. The law applies to unpublished works as well as those that are published.

To forestall any infringement of the copyright by persons who may attempt to use the work without permission, be sure to register your ownership. The procedure entails the completion and filing of an application form, along with a small fee and two copies of the work, with The Register of Copyrights, Library of Congress, Washington, DC 20559. (For "nondramatic" literary works, ask for Form TX.)

FOR FURTHER INFORMATION

Books

Adams, Paul. *The Complete Legal Guide for Small Business.* New York: Wiley, 1982.
Cameron, George D., III, and Phillip J. Scaletta, Jr. *Business Law: Text and Cases,* 2d ed. Plano, Tex.: Business Publications, 1985.

*For more information on preparing a plan, choosing a lawyer, and other useful suggestions regarding company patents, see: Ronald D. Rothchild, "Making Patents Work for Small Companies," *Harvard Business Review* 65 (July–August 1987), 24–27*ff.*

**For some useful insights into the selection, adoption, marketing implementation, and control of trademarks, see: Dorothy Cohen, "Trademark Strategy," *Journal of Marketing* 50 (January 1986), 61–74.

Corley, Robert N., Peter J. Shedd, and Eric M. Holmes. *Principles of Business Law,* 13th ed. Englewood Cliffs, N.J.: Prentice-Hall, 1986.

Fiber, Larry Roy, and Jerry A. Weigle. *Applied Business Law.* Reston, Va.: Reston, 1983.

Purver, Jonathan M., et al. *Business Law: Text and Cases.* San Diego, Cal.: Harcourt Brace Jovanovich, 1983.

Rosenberg, R. Robert, et al. *Business Law,* 6th ed. New York: McGraw-Hill, 1983.

Wyatt, John W., and Madie B. Wyatt. *Business Law,* 6th ed. New York: McGraw-Hill, 1979.

Pamphlets Available from the Small Business Administration

MANAGEMENT AIDS

MA 6.005—"Introduction to Patents"

21

Taxation and Your Business

It has been said that nothing is as certain as death and taxes. This is unfortunately a truism, and your new business is no exception to the rule.

Your enterprise is subject to taxes at all three levels of government: federal, state, and local. This alone ought to convince you that you're in dire need of as much professionalism in the tax management area as in all segments of your business—production, sales, personnel, and so on. Because of the complexities of tax law, frequent new rulings, changing regulations, and difficulties of interpretation, it's nearly impossible to adopt a do-it-yourself stance in this field.

The Internal Revenue Service offers assistance in the form of the comprehensive *Tax Guide for Small Business (Publication 334)*. Its scope ranges from a treatment of the different forms of ownership, to a description of accounting periods, procedures, and recordkeeping, as well as instructions for completing the proper tax forms and information returns. Contact your local IRS office for a copy. (*Note:* Even if you obtain this publication, it is still strongly recommended that you consult a tax advisor.)

What taxes do you face? Let's first consider those imposed by the federal government.

FEDERAL TAXES

The major tax bite taken by Uncle Sam is in the form of income and social security taxes. Incidentally, new responsibilities accompany your transition from worker to business owner. Not only are you taxed on your earnings but you're also automatically conscripted into service as a deputy tax collector.

Federal Income Taxes

The legal form you have selected has a major impact on the way tax regulations apply to your new enterprise.

Sole Proprietorship. You'll recall that, for legal purposes (which of course include taxation), the individual owner and the business activity are inseparable. Consequently, if you have chosen this form, you're required to file your annual federal tax return on the familiar Form 1040 ("Individual Income Tax Return"). This is the same form you completed as an employee.

In addition, you need to complete and submit, attached to your Form 1040, both a separate Schedule C ("Profit or Loss from Business or Profession—Sole Proprietorship"), and Form 4562 ("Depreciation and Amortization"). A sample of each is shown in exhibits 21–1a and 21–1b, respectively.

On this schedule, you must furnish details about your business activity for the year just ended: your sales, the cost of goods sold (and how you arrived at the figures), the resulting gross profit, your business expenses and other deductions, explanations of such items as depreciation, and your net profit. This last figure is added to other income you earned during the year and put on your Form 1040.

As sole proprietor, you're also required to calculate what your expected income tax will be for the coming year. Submit Form 1040ES ("Declaration of Estimated Tax for Individuals") along with your Form 1040. The IRS provides you with instructions, a worksheet on which you can work out your estimated tax, and four declaration vouchers. Each of these vouchers must be mailed, in turn, before the fifteenth of April, June, September, and January. Part payment of your estimated tax must accompany each voucher.

Partnership. As with the sole proprietorship, tax liability is assessed only for the earned incomes of the individual partners involved and not against the business directly. Each partner files a tax return on Form 1040, where his or her distributive share of the business profits is noted. In addition, you're required to submit a report of your business operation on Form 1065 ("U.S. Partnership Return of Income"). This is only an information report; no tax payment accompanies its submission. A sample of Form 1065 is included in exhibit 21–2a. Report gains or losses during the year on Schedule D (see exhibit 21–2b). You must also file Schedule K–1 ("Partner's Share of Income, Credits, Deductions, etc."); an example is shown in exhibit 21–2c. And, as with the sole proprietor, each partner also files an estimated tax.

Corporation. If you elected this form of ownership, your tax reporting problems are more complicated. As an employee of the firm, you report your earnings (and other income) as well as dividends from the corporation during the taxable year on Form 1040. As a separate entity, the corporation must file its own return as well; for this purpose, use Form 1120 ("U.S. Corporation Income Tax Return").* If the firm operates on the calendar year basis, the

---

*You may file Form 1120-A ("U.S. Corporation Short-Form Income Tax Return") instead, providing the firm's gross receipts, total income, and total assets are all under $250,000, and you meet several other requirements. (See exhibit 21–4.)

EXHIBIT 21-1(a). SCHEDULE C (FORM 1040)

SCHEDULE C (Form 1040)

Department of the Treasury
Internal Revenue Service

Profit or (Loss) From Business or Profession
(Sole Proprietorship)

Partnerships, Joint Ventures, etc., Must File Form 1065.

▶ Attach to Form 1040, Form 1041, or Form 1041S. ▶ See Instructions for Schedule C (Form 1040).

OMB No. 1545-0074

1987

Attachment Sequence No. **09**

Name of proprietor	Social security number (SSN)
Susan J Brown	111 00 1111

A Principal business or profession, including product or service (see Instructions) *Retail, ladies apparel*

B Principal business code (from Part IV) ▶ 3 9 1 3

C Business name and address ▶ *Milady Fashions 725 Big Sur Drive Franklin NY 18725*

D Employer ID number (Not SSN) 1 0 1 2 3 4 5 6 7

E Method(s) used to value closing inventory:
(1) ☐ Cost (2) ☑ Lower of cost or market (3) ☐ Other (attach explanation)

F Accounting method: (1) ☐ Cash (2) ☑ Accrual (3) ☐ Other (specify) ▶ ....

	Yes	No
G Was there any change in determining quantities, costs, or valuations between opening and closing inventory? (If "Yes," attach explanation.)		✓
H Are you deducting expenses for an office in your home?		✓
I Did you file **Form 941** for this business for any quarter in 1987?	✓	
J Did you "materially participate" in the operation of this business during 1987? (If "No," see Instructions for limitations on losses.)	✓	
K Was this business in operation at the end of 1987?	✓	

L How many months was this business in operation during 1987? ▶ *12*

M If this schedule includes a loss, credit, deduction, income, or other tax benefit relating to a tax shelter required to be registered, check here. ▶ ☐
If you check this box, you **MUST** attach **Form 8271.**

Part I Income

1a Gross receipts or sales	1a	397,742
b Less: Returns and allowances	1b	1,442
c Subtract line 1b from line 1a and enter the balance here	1c	396,300
2 Cost of goods sold and/or operations (from Part III, line 8)	2	239,349
3 Subtract line 2 from line 1c and enter the **gross profit** here	3	156,951
4 Other income (including windfall profit tax credit or refund received in 1987)	4	—0—
5 Add lines 3 and 4. This is the gross income ▶	5	156,951

Part II Deductions

6 Advertising	3,500	23 Repairs		1,776
7 Bad debts from sales or services (see Instructions.)	479	24 Supplies (not included in Part III)		1,203
8 Bank service charges	180	25 Taxes		5,802
9 Car and truck expenses	2,256	26 Travel, meals, and entertainment:		
10 Commissions		a Travel		
11 Depletion		b Total meals and entertainment		
12 Depreciation and section 179 deduction from Form 4562 (not included in Part III)	2,417	c Enter 20% of line 26b subject to limitations (see Instructions)		
13 Dues and publications		d Subtract line 26c from 26b		
14 Employee benefit programs		27 Utilities and telephone		3,570
15 Freight (not included in Part III)		28a Wages	63,450	
16 Insurance	950	b Jobs credit	4,400	
17 Interest:		c Subtract line 28b from 28a		59,050
a Mortgage (paid to financial institutions)		29 Other expenses (list type and amount):		
b Other	2,633	*Chamber of Commerce* 60		
18 Laundry and cleaning		*Fee Credit Card Co.* 6,000		
19 Legal and professional services		*Trash Removal* 1,600		
20 Office expense	216	*Window Washing* 238		
21 Pension and profit-sharing plans				
22 Rent on business property	12,000			7,898

30 Add amounts in columns for lines 6 through 29. These are the **total deductions** ▶	30	103,924
31 **Net profit or (loss).** Subtract line 30 from line 5. If a profit, enter here and on Form 1040, line 13, and on Schedule SE, line 2 (or line 5 of Form 1041 or Form 1041S). If a loss, you **MUST** go on to line 32	31	53,027

32 If you have a loss, you **MUST** answer this question: "Do you have amounts for which you are not at risk in this business?" (See Instructions.) ☐ Yes ☐ No
If "Yes," you **MUST** attach **Form 6198.** If "No," enter the loss on Form 1040, line 13, and on Schedule SE, line 2 (or line 5 of Form 1041 or Form 1041S).

For Paperwork Reduction Act Notice, see Form 1040 Instructions.

Schedule C (Form 1040) 1987

Source: "Tax Guide for Small Business—1987 Edition," *Publication 334* (Washington, D.C.: Internal Revenue Service, 1987), 139–40.

EXHIBIT 21-1a. (*Continued*)

Schedule C (Form 1040) 1987

Page **2**

Part III Cost of Goods Sold and/or Operations (See Schedule C Instructions for Part III)

1	Inventory at beginning of year. (If different from last year's closing inventory, attach explanation.)	1	42,843
2	Purchases less cost of items withdrawn for personal use	2	240,252
3	Cost of labor. (Do not include salary paid to yourself.)	3	– 0 –
4	Materials and supplies	4	– 0 –
5	Other costs	5	– 0 –
6	Add lines 1 through 5	6	283,095
7	Less: Inventory at end of year	7	43,746
8	**Cost of goods sold and/or operations.** Subtract line 7 from line 6. Enter here and in Part I, line 2	8	239,349

Part IV Codes for Principal Business or Professional Activity

Locate the major business category that best describes your activity (for example, Retail Trade, Services, etc.). Within the major category, select the activity code that identifies (or most closely identifies) the business or profession that is the principal source of your sales or receipts. Enter this 4-digit code on line B on page 1 of Schedule C. (Note: *If your principal source of income is from farming activities, you should file* **Schedule F (Form 1040)**, *Farm Income and Expenses.*)

Construction

Code

0018 Operative builders (building for own account)

General contractors

0034 Residential building
0059 Nonresidential building
0075 Highway and street construction
3889 Other heavy construction (pipe laying, bridge construction, etc.)

Building trade contractors, including repairs

0232 Plumbing, heating, air conditioning
0257 Painting and paper hanging
0273 Electrical work
0299 Masonry, dry wall, stone, tile
0414 Carpentry and flooring
0430 Roofing, siding, and sheet metal
0455 Concrete work
0471 Water well drilling
0885 Other building trade contractors (excavation, glazing, etc.)

Manufacturing, Including Printing and Publishing

0612 Bakeries selling at retail
0638 Other food products and beverages
0653 Textile mill products
0679 Apparel and other textile products
0695 Leather, footware, handbags, etc.
0810 Furniture and fixtures
0836 Lumber and other wood products
0851 Printing and publishing
0877 Paper and allied products
0893 Chemicals and allied products
1016 Rubber and plastics products
1032 Stone, clay, and glass products
1057 Primary metal industries
1073 Fabricated metal products
1099 Machinery and machine shops
1115 Electric and electronic equipment
1313 Transportation equipment
1339 Instruments and related products
1883 Other manufacturing industries

Mining and Mineral Extraction

1511 Metal mining
1537 Coal mining
1552 Oil and gas
1719 Quarrying and nonmetallic mining

Agricultural Services, Forestry, and Fishing

1917 Soil preparation services
1933 Crop services
1958 Veterinary services, including pets
1974 Livestock breeding
1990 Other animal services
2113 Farm labor and management services
2212 Horticulture and landscaping
2238 Forestry, except logging
0836 Logging
2279 Fishing, hunting, and trapping

Wholesale Trade—Selling Goods to Other Businesses, Government, or Institutions, etc.

Durable goods, including machinery, equipment, wood, metals, etc.

2618 Selling for your own account

Code

2634 Agent or broker for other firms— more than 50% of gross sales on commission

Nondurable goods, including food, fiber, chemicals, etc.

2659 Selling for your own account
2675 Agent or broker for other firms— more than 50% of gross sales on commission

Retail Trade—Selling Goods to Individuals and Households

3012 Selling door-to-door, by telephone or party plan, or from mobile unit
3038 Catalog or mail order
3053 Vending machine selling

Selling From Store, Showroom, or Other Fixed Location

Food, beverages, and drugs

3079 Eating places (meals or snacks)
3095 Drinking places (alcoholic beverages)
3210 Grocery stores (general line)
0612 Bakeries selling at retail
3236 Other food stores (meat, produce, candy, etc.)
3251 Liquor stores
3277 Drug stores

Automotive and service stations

3319 New car dealers (franchised)
3335 Used car dealers
3517 Other automotive dealers (motorcycles, recreational vehicles, etc.)
3533 Tires, accessories, and parts
3558 Gasoline service stations

General merchandise, apparel, and furniture

3715 Variety stores
3731 Other general merchandise stores
3756 Shoe stores
3772 Men's and boys' clothing stores
3913 Women's ready-to-wear stores
3921 Women's accessory and specialty stores and furriers
3939 Family clothing stores
3954 Other apparel and accessory stores
3970 Furniture stores
3996 TV, audio, and electronics
3988 Computer and software stores
4119 Household appliance stores
4317 Other home furnishing stores (china, floor coverings, drapes, etc.)
4333 Music and record stores

Building, hardware, and garden supply

4416 Building materials dealers
4432 Paint, glass, and wallpaper stores
4457 Hardware stores
4473 Nurseries and garden supply stores

Other retail stores

4614 Used merchandise and antique stores (except used motor vehicle parts)
4630 Gift, novelty, and souvenir shops
4655 Florists
4671 Jewelry stores

Code

4697 Sporting goods and bicycle shops
4812 Boat dealers
4838 Hobby, toy, and game shops
4853 Camera and photo supply stores
4879 Optical goods stores
4895 Luggage and leather goods stores
5017 Book stores, excluding newsstands
5033 Stationery stores
5058 Fabric and needlework stores
5074 Mobile home dealers
5090 Fuel dealers (except gasoline)
5884 Other retail stores

Real Estate, Insurance, Finance, and Related Services

5512 Real estate agents and managers
5538 Operators and lessors of buildings (except developers)
5553 Operators and lessors of other real property (except developers)
5710 Subdividers and developers, except cemeteries
5736 Insurance agents and services
5751 Security and commodity brokers, dealers, and investment services
5777 Other real estate, insurance, and financial activities

Transportation, Communications, Public Utilities, and Related Services

6114 Taxicabs
6312 Bus and limousine transportation
6338 Trucking (except trash collection)
6510 Trash collection without own dump
6536 Public warehousing
6551 Water transportation
6619 Air transportation
6635 Travel agents and tour operators
6650 Other transportation and related services
6676 Communication services
6692 Utilities, including dumps, snowplowing, road cleaning, etc.

Services (Providing Personal, Professional, and Business Services)

Hotels and other lodging places

7096 Hotels, motels, and tourist homes
7211 Rooming and boarding houses
7237 Camps and camping parks

Laundry and cleaning services

7419 Coin-operated laundries and dry cleaning
7435 Other laundry, dry cleaning, and garment services
7450 Carpet and upholstery cleaning
7476 Janitorial and related services (building, house, and window cleaning)

Business and/or personal services

7617 Legal services (or lawyer)
7633 Income tax preparation
7658 Accounting and bookkeeping
7674 Engineering, surveying, and architectural

Code

7690 Management, consulting, and public relations
7716 Advertising, except direct mail
7732 Employment agencies and personnel supply
7757 Computer and data processing, including repair and leasing
7773 Equipment rental and leasing (except computer or automotive)
7914 Investigative and protective services
7880 Other business services

Personal services

8110 Beauty shops (or beautician)
8318 Barber shop (or barber)
8334 Photographic portrait studios
8516 Shoe repair and shine services
8532 Funeral services and crematories
8714 Child day care
8730 Teaching or tutoring
8755 Counseling (except health practitioners)
8771 Ministers and chaplains
6882 Other personal services

Automotive services

8813 Automotive rental or leasing, without driver
8839 Parking, except valet
8854 General automotive repairs
8870 Specialized automotive repairs (brake, body repairs, paint, etc.)
8896 Other automotive services (wash, towing, etc.)

Miscellaneous repair, except computers

9019 TV and audio equipment repair
9035 Other electrical equipment repair
9050 Reupholstery and furniture repair
2881 Other equipment repair

Medical and health services

9217 Offices and clinics of medical doctors (MD's)
9233 Offices and clinics of dentists
9258 Osteopathic physicians and surgeons
9274 Chiropractors
9290 Optometrists
9415 Registered and practical nurses
9431 Other licensed health practitioners
9456 Dental laboratories
9472 Nursing and personal care facilities
9886 Other health services

Amusement and recreational services

8557 Physical fitness facilities
9613 Videotape rental stores
9639 Motion picture theaters
9654 Other motion picture and TV film and tape activities
9670 Bowling alleys
9696 Professional sports and racing, including promoters and managers
9811 Theatrical performers, musicians, agents, producers, and related services
9837 Other amusement and recreational services

8888 Unable to classify

EXHIBIT 21-1(b). FORM 4562 (TO BE SUBMITTED ALONG WITH SCHEDULE C)

Form **4562**	**Depreciation and Amortization**	OMB No 1545-0172
Department of the Treasury Internal Revenue Service	▶ See separate instructions. ▶ Attach this form to your return.	**1987** Attachment Sequence No. **67**

Name(s) as shown on return	Identifying number
Susan J Brown	*111-00-1111*

Business or activity to which this form relates

Retail, ladies Apparel

Part I **Depreciation** (Do not use this part for automobiles, certain other vehicles, computers, and property used for entertainment, recreation, or amusement. Instead, use Part III.)

Section A.—Election To Expense Depreciable Assets Placed in Service During This Tax Year (Section 179)

(a) Description of property	(b) Date placed in service	(c) Cost	(d) Expense deduction
1			

2 Listed property—Enter total from Part III, Section A, column (h) . . . .
3 Total (add lines 1 and 2, but do not enter more than $10,000) . . . .
4 Enter the amount, if any, by which the cost of all section 179 property placed in service during this tax year is more than $200,000 . . . . .
5 Subtract line 4 from line 3. If result is less than zero, enter zero. (See instructions for other limitations) . .

Section B.—Depreciation

(a) Class of property	(b) Date placed in service	(c) Basis for depreciation (Business use only—see instructions)	(d) Recovery period	(e) Method of figuring depreciation	(f) Deduction
6 Accelerated Cost Recovery System (ACRS) (see instructions): *For assets placed in service* **ONLY** *during tax year beginning in 1987*					
a 3-year property					
b 5-year property					
c 7-year property					
d 10-year property					
e 15-year property					
f 20-year property					
g Residential rental property					
h Nonresidential real property					

7 Listed property—Enter total from Part III, Section A, column (g). *4,300*
8 ACRS deduction for assets placed in service prior to 1987 (see instructions) . . . . , . . *440*

Section C.—Other Depreciation

9 Property subject to section 168(f)(1) election (see instructions) . . . .
10 Other depreciation (see instructions) *677*

Section D.—Summary

11 Total (add deductions on lines 5 through 10). Enter here and on the Depreciation line of your return (Partnerships and S corporations—Do NOT include any amounts entered on line 5.) *2,417*
12 For assets above placed in service during the current year, enter the portion of the basis attributable to additional section 263A costs. (See instructions for who must use.) . .

Part II **Amortization**

(a) Description of property	(b) Date acquired	(c) Cost or other basis	(d) Code section	(e) Amortization period or percentage	(f) Amortization for this year
1 Amortization for property placed in service only during tax year beginning in 1987					
2 Amortization for property placed in service prior to 1987					
3 Total. Enter here and on Other Deductions or Other Expenses line of your return					

See Paperwork Reduction Act Notice on page 1 of the separate instructions. Form **4562**

Source: "Tax Guide for Small Business—1987 Edition," *Publication 334* (Washington, D.C.: Internal Revenue Service, 1987), 141–42.

EXHIBIT 21-1b. (*Continued*)

Form 4562 (1987)   Page **2**

Part III | Automobiles, Certain Other Vehicles, Computers, and Property Used for Entertainment, Recreation, or Amusement (Listed Property).

If you are using the standard mileage rate or deducting vehicle lease expense, complete columns (a) through (d) of Section A, all of Section B, and Section C if applicable.

Section A.—Depreciation (If automobiles and other listed property placed in service after June 18, 1984, are used 50% or less in a trade or business, the Section 179 deduction is not allowed and depreciation must be taken using the straight line method over 5 years. For other limitations, see instructions.)

Do you have evidence to support the business use claimed?   ☐ Yes   ☐ No   If yes, is the evidence written?   ☐ Yes ☐ No

(a) Type of property (list vehicles first)	(b) Date placed in service	(c) Business use percentage (%)	(d) Cost or other basis (see instructions for leased property)	(e) Basis for depreciation (Business use only—see instructions)	(f) Depreciation method and recovery period	(g) Depreciation deduction	(h) Section 179 expense
USA 2805 Van	3/19/87	75%	8,667	6,500	PRE-5yrs	1,300	—0—

Total (Enter here and on line 2, page 1.) . . . .

Total (Enter here and on line 7, page 1.) 1,300

Section B.—Information Regarding Use of Vehicles

Complete this section as follows, if you deduct expenses for vehicles:

● *Always complete this section for vehicles used by a sole proprietor, partner, or other more than 5% owner or related person.*

● *If you provided vehicles to employees, first answer the questions in Section C to see if you meet an exception to completing this section for those items.*

	Vehicle 1		Vehicle 2		Vehicle 3		Vehicle 4		Vehicle 5		Vehicle 6	
1 Total miles driven during the year . . .	10,000											
2 Total business miles driven during the year	7,500											
3 Total commuting miles driven during the year.	2,025											
4 Total other personal (noncommuting) miles driven	475											
	Yes	No	Yes	No	Yes	No	Yes	No	Yes	No	Yes	No
5 Was the vehicle available for personal use during off-duty hours?	✓											
6 Was the vehicle used primarily by a more than 5% owner or related person? . . .	✓											
7 Is another vehicle available for personal use?.	✓											

Section C.—Questions for Employers Who Provide Vehicles for Use by Employees.

(Answer these questions to determine if you meet an exception to completing Section B. **Note:** Section B must always be completed for vehicles used by sole proprietors, partners, or other more than 5% owners or related persons.)

	Yes	No
8 Do you maintain a written policy statement that prohibits all personal use of vehicles, including commuting, by your employees?		
9 Do you maintain a written policy statement that prohibits personal use of vehicles, except commuting, by your employees? (See instructions for vehicles used by corporate officers, directors, or 1% or more owners.)		
10 Do you treat all use of vehicles by employees as personal use?		
11 Do you provide more than five vehicles to your employees and retain the information received from your employees concerning the use of the vehicles?.		
12 Do you meet the requirements concerning fleet vehicles or qualified automobile demonstration use (see instructions)?		

Note: *If your answer to 8, 9, 10, 11, or 12 is "Yes," you need not complete Section B for the covered vehicles.*

EXHIBIT 21-2(a). FORM 1065

Form **1065**	**U.S. Partnership Return of Income**	OMB No. 1545-0099
Department of the Treasury Internal Revenue Service	▶ For Paperwork Reduction Act Notice, see Form 1065 Instructions. ▶ For calendar year 1987, or fiscal year beginning _____, 1987, and ending _____ 19___	**1987**

A Principal business activity	Use IRS label. Otherwise, please print or type.	10-9876543 DEC87 D71	D Employer identification number
Wholesale		A&B DISTRIBUTING COMPANY	IRS
B Principal product or service		334 WEST MAIN STREET	E Date business started
Sundries		ANYTOWN MD 20904	**10 - 1 - 78**
C Business code number			F Enter total assets at end of tax year
5001			$ **44,152**

G Check accounting method: (1) ☐ Cash   (2) ☑ Accrual (3) ☐ Other

H Check applicable boxes: (1) ☐ Final return (2) ☐ Change in address   (3) ☐ Amended return

		Yes	No
I	Number of partners in this partnership ▶ **2**		
J	Is this partnership a limited partnership (see the Instructions)? . .		✓
K	Is this partnership a partner in another partnership?		✓
L	Are any partners in this partnership also partnerships? . . .		✓
M	Does the partnership meet all the requirements shown in the Instructions for Question M?	✓	
N	Was there a distribution of property or a transfer (for example, by sale or death) of a partnership interest during the tax year? If "Yes," see the Instructions concerning an election to adjust the basis of the partnership's assets under section 754		✓

		Yes	No
O	At any time during the tax year, did the partnership have an interest in or a signature or other authority over a financial account in a foreign country (such as a bank account, securities account, or other financial account)? (See the Instructions for exceptions and filing requirements for Form TD F 90-22.1.) If "Yes," write the name of the foreign country. ▶		✓
P	Was the partnership the grantor of, or transferor to, a foreign trust which existed during the current tax year, whether or not the partnership or any partner has any beneficial interest in it? If "Yes," you may have to file Forms 3520, 3520-A, or 926		✓
Q	Was this partnership in operation at the end of 1987?	✓	
R	Number of months in 1987 that this partnership was in operation ▶ 12		
S	Check this box if the partnership has filed or is required to file Form 8264, Application for Registration of a Tax Shelter . . . . . . ☐		
T	Check this box if this is a partnership subject to the consolidated partnership audit procedures of TEFRA. (See page 7 of the Instructions.) . . . . ☐		

Caution: *Include only trade or business income and expenses on lines 1a–21 below. See the instructions for more information.*

Income

1a	Gross receipts or sales $ ..**410,024**.. 1b Minus returns and allowances $ ..**3,365**.. Balance ▶	1c	**406,659**
2	Cost of goods sold and/or operations (Schedule A, line 7)	2	**267,641**
3	Gross profit (subtract line 2 from line 1c)	3	**139,018**
4	Ordinary income (loss) from other partnerships and fiduciaries (attach schedule)	4	
5	Net farm profit (loss) (attach Schedule F (Form 1040))	5	
6	Net gain (loss) (Form 4797, line 18)	6	**1,195**
7	Other income (loss)	7	
8	**TOTAL** income (loss) (combine lines 3 through 7)	8	**140,213**

Deductions *(see instructions for limitations)*

9a	Salaries and wages (other than to partners) $ ..**29,350**.. 9b Minus jobs credit $ ..**—**.. Balance ▶	9c	**29,350**
10	Guaranteed payments to partners	10	**25,000**
11	Rent	11	**9,000**
12	Deductible interest expense not claimed elsewhere on return (see Instructions) . .	12	**871**
13	Taxes	13	**2,208**
14	Bad debts	14	**2,250**
15	Repairs	15	**2,235**
16a	Depreciation from Form 4562 (attach Form 4562) $ ....**2,083**.... 16b Minus depreciation		
	claimed on Schedule A and elsewhere on return $ ....**—**.... Balance ▶	16c	**2,083**
17	Depletion (*Do not deduct oil and gas depletion.*)	17	
18a	Retirement plans, etc.	18a	
b	Employee benefit programs	18b	
19	Other deductions (attach schedule)	19	**13,947**
20	**TOTAL** deductions (add amounts in column for lines 9c through 19) . . .	20	**86,944**
21	Ordinary income (loss) from trade or business activity(ies) (subtract line 20 from line 8)	21	**53,269**

Please Sign Here

Under penalties of perjury, I declare that I have examined this return, including accompanying schedules and statements, and to the best of my knowledge and belief, it is true, correct, and complete. Declaration of preparer (other than taxpayer) is based on all information of which preparer has any knowledge.

▶ *Frank W. Able*   ▶ **4-3-88**
Signature of general partner   Date

Paid Preparer's Use Only	Preparer's signature ▶	Date	Check if self-employed ▶ ☐	Preparer's social security no.
	Firm's name (or yours if self-employed) and address ▶		E.I. No. ▶	
			ZIP code ▶	

Source: "Tax Guide for Small Business—1987 Edition," *Publication 334* (Washington, D.C.: Internal Revenue Service, 1987), 147–50.

EXHIBIT 21-2a. (*Continued*)

Form 1065 (1987)   Page **2**

Schedule A | Cost of Goods Sold and/or Operations

1	Inventory at beginning of year.	1	18,125
2	Purchases minus cost of items withdrawn for personal use	2	268,741
3	Cost of labor	3	
4a	Additional section 263A costs (see instructions)	4a	
b	Other costs (attach schedule)	4b	
5	Total (add lines 1 through 4b).	5	286,866
6	Inventory at end of year	6	19,225
7	Cost of goods sold (subtract line 6 from line 5). Enter here and on page 1, line 2	7	267,641

8a Check all methods used for valuing closing inventory:

(i) ☐ Cost

(ii) ☑ Lower of cost or market as described in regulations section 1.471-4

(iii) ☐ Writedown of "subnormal" goods as described in regulations section 1.471-2(c)

(iv) ☐ Other (specify method used and attach explanation) ▶ ....

b Check if the LIFO inventory method was adopted this tax year for any goods (if checked, attach Form 970) . . . . . ☐

c Do the rules of section 263A (with respect to property produced or acquired for resale) apply to the partnership? . . . ☐ Yes ☑ No

d Was there any change (other than for section 263A purposes) in determining quantities, cost, or valuations between opening and closing inventory? If "Yes," attach explanation . . . . ☐ Yes ☑ No

Schedule H | Income (Loss) From Rental Real Estate Activity(ies)

1 In the space provided below, show the kind and location of each rental property. Attach a schedule if more space is needed.

Property A ....

Property B ....

Property C ....

Rental Real Estate Income		Properties			Totals (Add columns A, B, C, and amounts from any attached schedule)
		A	B	C	
2 Gross Income	2				2
Rental Real Estate Expenses					
3 Advertising	3				
4 Auto and travel	4				
5 Cleaning and maintenance . .	5				
6 Commissions	6				
7 Insurance	7				
8 Legal and other professional fees	8				
9 Interest expense	9				
10 Repairs	10				
11 Taxes	11				
12 Utilities	12				
13 Wages and salaries	13				
14 Depreciation from Form 4562 .	14				
15 Other (list)					
16 Total expenses. Add lines 3 through 15.	16				16
17 Net income (loss) from rental real estate activity(ies). Subtract line 16 from line 2. Enter total net income (loss) from all properties on Schedule K, line 2.	17				17

EXHIBIT 21-2(a). (*Continued*)

Form 1065 (1987)   Page **3**

Schedule K	Partners' Shares of Income, Credits, Deductions, etc.		
	(a) Distributive share items		**(b) Total amount**

			(b) Total amount	
Income (Loss)	**1** Ordinary income (loss) from trade or business activity(ies) (page 1, line 21)	**1**	53,269	
	2 Net income (loss) from rental real estate activity(ies) (Schedule H, line 17)	**2**		
	3a Gross income from other rental activity(ies) · · · · · **3a** $			
	b Minus expenses (attach schedule) · · · · · · · · **3b** $			
	c Balance net income (loss) from other rental activity(ies) · · · · · · · · ▶	**3c**		
	4 Portfolio income (loss):			
	a Interest income	**4a**		
	b Dividend income	**4b**	150	
	c Royalty income	**4c**		
	d Net short-term capital gain (loss) (Schedule D, line 4)	**4d**	100	
	e Net long-term capital gain (loss) (Schedule D, line 9)	**4e**	200	
	f Other portfolio income (loss) (attach schedule)	**4f**		
	5 Guaranteed payments	**5**	25,000	
	6 Net gain (loss) under section 1231 (other than due to casualty or theft)	**6**	1,051	
	7 Other (attach schedule)	**7**		
Deductions	**8** Charitable contributions (attach list)	**8**	650	
	9 Expense deduction for recovery property (section 179)	**9**		
	10 Deductions related to portfolio income (do not include investment interest expense)	**10**		
	11 Other (attach schedule)	**11**		
Credits	**12a** Credit for income tax withheld	**12a**		
	b Low-income housing credit (attach Form 8586)	**12b**		
	c Qualified rehabilitation expenditures related to rental real estate activity(ies) (attach schedule)	**12c**		
	d Credit(s) related to rental real estate activity(ies) other than 12b and 12c (attach schedule)	**12d**		
	e Credit(s) related to rental activity(ies) other than 12b, 12c, and 12d (attach schedule)	**12e**		
	13 Other (attach schedule)	**13**		
Self-Employment	**14a** Net earnings (loss) from self-employment	**14a**	77,074	
	b Gross farming or fishing income	**14b**		
	c Gross nonfarm income	**14c**	77,074	
Tax Preference Items	**15a** Accelerated depreciation of real property placed in service before 1/1/87	**15a**		
	b Accelerated depreciation of leased personal property placed in service before 1/1/87	**15b**		
	c Depreciation adjustment on property placed in service after 12/31/86	**15c**		
	d Depletion (other than oil and gas)	**15d**		
	e (1) Gross income from oil, gas, and geothermal properties	**15e(1)**		
	(2) Deductions allocable to oil, gas, and geothermal properties	**15e(2)**		
	f Other (attach schedule)	**15f**		
Investment Interest	**16a** Interest expense on investment debts	**16a**		
	b (1) Investment income included on lines 4a through 4f, Schedule K	**16b(1)**	450	
	(2) Investment expenses included on line 10, Schedule K	**16b(2)**		
Foreign Taxes	**17a** Type of income			
	b Foreign country or U.S. possession			
	c Total gross income from sources outside the U.S. (attach schedule)	**17c**		
	d Total applicable deductions and losses (attach schedule)	**17d**		
	e Total foreign taxes (check one): ▶ ☐ Paid ☐ Accrued	**17e**		
	f Reduction in taxes available for credit (attach schedule)	**17f**		
	g Other (attach schedule)	**17g**		
Other	**18** Attach schedule for other items and amounts not reported above. See Instructions			

EXHIBIT 21-2(a). (*Continued*)

Form 1065 (1987)
Page **4**

Schedule L Balance Sheets
(See the Instructions for Question M Before Completing Schedules L and M.)

Assets	Beginning of tax year (a)	(b)	End of tax year (c)	(d)
1 Cash		405		8,620
2 Trade notes and accounts receivable	7,150		10,990	
a Minus allowance for bad debts		7,150		10,990
3 Inventories		18,125		19,225
4 Federal and state government obligations		1,000		1,000
5 Other current assets (attach schedule)				
6 Mortgage and real estate loans				
7 Other investments (attach schedule)		1,000		—
8 Buildings and other depreciable assets	16,000		8,900	
a Minus accumulated depreciation	4,000	12,000	5,583	3,317
9 Depletable assets				
a Minus accumulated depletion				
10 Land (net of any amortization)		500		1,000
11 Intangible assets (amortizable only)				
a Minus accumulated amortization				
12 Other assets (attach schedule)				
13 TOTAL assets		40,180		44,152
Liabilities and Capital				
14 Accounts payable		9,180		10,462
15 Mortgages, notes, bonds payable in less than 1 year		3,600		4,000
16 Other current liabilities (attach schedule)				
17 All nonrecourse loans				
18 Mortgages, notes, bonds payable in 1 year or more		14,900		14,900
19 Other liabilities (attach schedule)				
20 Partners' capital accounts		12,500		14,790
21 TOTAL liabilities and capital		40,180		44,152

Schedule M Reconciliation of Partners' Capital Accounts
(Show reconciliation of each partner's capital account on Schedule K-1 (Form 1065), Question I.)

(a) Capital account at beginning of year	(b) Capital contributed during year	(c) Income (loss) from lines 1,2, 3c, and 4 of Sch. K	(d) Income not included in column (c), plus nontaxable income	(e) Losses not included in column (c), plus unallowable deductions	(f) Withdrawals and distributions	(g) Capital account at end of year
12,500	1,000	53,719	1,101	650	52,880	14,790

Designation of Tax Matters Partner

The following general partner is hereby designated as the tax matters partner (TMP) for the tax year for which this partnership return is filed:

Name of designated TMP ▶

Identifying number of TMP ▶

Address of designated TMP ▶

265

EXHIBIT 21-2(b). SCHEDULE D (FORM 1065)

SCHEDULE D (Form 1065) Department of the Treasury Internal Revenue Service	Capital Gains and Losses ▶ For Paperwork Reduction Act Notice, see Instructions below. ▶ Attach to Form 1065.	OMB No. 1545-0099 1987

Name of partnership A + B Distributing Co.

Employer identification number 10-9876543

Part I Short-Term Capital Gains and Losses—Assets held six months or less (one year or less if acquired after 12/31/87)

(a) Description of property (Example, 100 shares 7% preferred of "Z" Co.)	(b) Date acquired (mo., day, yr.)	(c) Date sold (mo., day, yr.)	(d) Sales price (see instructions)	(e) Cost or other basis (see instructions)	(f) Gain (loss) ((d) minus (e))
1 XYZ Chemical Co. Inc. 20 shares common	12-5-86	5-1-87	2,300	2,200	100

2 Short-term capital gain from installment sales from Form 6252, line 23 or 31 . . . .

3 Partnership's share of net short-term capital gain (loss), including specially allocated short-term capital gains (losses), from other partnerships and from fiduciaries . . . .

4 Net short-term capital gain (loss) from lines 1, 2, and 3. Enter each partner's share on Schedule K-1 (Form 1065), line 4d. . . . . | 100

Part II Long-Term Capital Gains and Losses—Assets held more than six months (more than one year if acquired after 12/31/87)

5 ABC Motors 100 shares common	12-7-81	6-3-87	1,200	1,000	200

6 Long-term capital gain from installment sales from Form 6252, line 23 or 31 . . . .

7 Partnership's share of net long-term capital gain (loss), including specially allocated long-term capital gains (losses), from other partnerships and from fiduciaries . . . .

8 Capital gain distributions . . . .

9 Net long-term capital gain (loss) from lines 5, 6, 7, and 8. Enter each partner's share on Schedule K-1 (Form 1065), line 4e . . . . | 200

Source: "Tax Guide for Small Business—1987 Edition," *Publication 334* (Washington, D.C.: Internal Revenue Service, 1987), 151.

266

EXHIBIT 21-2(c). SCHEDULE K-1 (FORM 1065)

SCHEDULE K-1 (Form 1065) Department of the Treasury Internal Revenue Service	Partner's Share of Income, Credits, Deductions, etc. For calendar year 1987 or fiscal year beginning ...., 1987, and ending ...., 19....	OMB No. 1545-0099 1987

Partner's identifying number ▶ 123-00-6789	Partnership's identifying number ▶ 10-9876543
Partner's name, address, and ZIP code Frank W. Able 10 Green Street Anytown, Maryland 20904	Partnership's name, address, and ZIP code A + B Distributing Co. 334 West Main Street Anytown, Maryland 20904

A(1) Is this partner a general partner? . . . ☑ Yes ☐ No

If "yes" to Question A(1):

(2) Did this partner materially participate in the trade or business activity(ies) of the partnership? (See page 12 of the Form 1065 Instructions. Leave blank if no trade or business activities.). . . . ☑ Yes ☐ No

(3) Did this partner actively participate in the rental real estate activity(ies) of the partnership? (See page 13 of the Form 1065 Instructions. Leave blank if no rental real estate activities.). . . . ☐ Yes ☐ No

B Partner's share of liabilities

Nonrecourse. . . . . $ ....

Other . . . . $ 14,681

C What type of entity is this partner? ▶ Individual

D Enter partner's percentage of:

	(i) Before decrease or termination	(ii) End of year
Profit sharing	........%	50 %
Loss sharing	........%	50 %
Ownership of capital	........%	48.3 %

E IRS Center where partnership filed return ▶ Philadelphia

F Tax Shelter Registration Number ▶ N/A

G(1) Did the partner's ownership interest in the partnership increase after Oct. 22, 1986? . . . . . ☐ Yes ☑ No

If yes, attach statement. (See page 13 of the Form 1065 Instructions.)

(2) Did the partnership start or acquire a new activity after Oct. 22, 1986? . . . . ☐ Yes ☑ No

If yes, attach statement. (See page 14 of the Form 1065 Instructions.)

H Check here ▶ ☐ if this Schedule K-1 is for a short tax year required by section 706(b).

I Reconciliation of partner's capital account:

(a) Capital account at beginning of year	(b) Capital contributed during year	(c) Income (loss) from lines 1, 2, 3, and 4 below	(d) Income not included in column (c), plus nontaxable income	(e) Losses not included in column (c), plus unallowable deductions	(f) Withdrawals and distributions	(g) Capital account at end of year
6,500	-0-	26,860	550	325	26,440	7,145

Caution: *Refer to attached Partner's Instructions for Schedule K-1 (Form 1065) before entering information from this schedule on your tax return.*

		(a) Distributive share item	(b) Amount	(c) 1040 filers enter the amount in column (b) on:
Income (Loss)	1	Ordinary income (loss) from trade or business activity(ies)	26,635	⎱ (See Partner's Instructions for Schedule K-1 (Form 1065))
	2	Income or loss from rental real estate activity(ies)		
	3	Income or loss from other rental activity(ies)		
	4	Portfolio income (loss):		
	a	Interest		Sch. B, Part I, line 2
	b	Dividends	75	Sch. B, Part II, line 4
	c	Royalties		Sch. E, Part I, line 5
	d	Net short-term capital gain (loss)	50	Sch. D, line 5, col. (f) or (g)
	e	Net long-term capital gain (loss)	100	Sch. D, line 12, col. (f) or (g)
	f	Other portfolio income (loss) (attach schedule)		(Enter on applicable lines of your return)
	5	Guaranteed payments	20,000	⎱ (See Partner's Instructions for Schedule K-1 (Form 1065))
	6	Net gain (loss) under section 1231 (other than due to casualty or theft)	526	
	7	Other (attach schedule)		(Enter on applicable lines of your return)
Deductions	8	Charitable contributions	325	See Form 1040 Instructions
	9	Expense deduction for recovery property (section 179)		⎱ (See Partner's Instructions for Schedule K-1 (Form 1065))
	10	Deductions related to portfolio income		
	11	Other (attach schedule)		
Credits	12a	Credit for income tax withheld		See Form 1040 Instructions
	b	Low-income housing credit		Form 8586, line 8
	c	Qualified rehabilitation expenditures related to rental real estate activity(ies) (attach schedule)		
	d	Credit(s) related to rental real estate activity(ies) other than 12b and 12c (attach schedule)		⎱ (See Partner's Instructions for Schedule K-1 (Form 1065))
	e	Credit(s) related to rental activity(ies) other than 12b, 12c, and 12d (attach schedule).		
	13	Other credits (attach schedule)		

For Paperwork Reduction Act Notice, see Form 1065 Instructions.   Schedule K-1 (Form 1065) 1987

Source: "Tax Guide for Small Business—1987 Edition," *Publication 334* (Washington, D.C.: Internal Revenue Service, 1987), 152–53.

EXHIBIT 21-2(c). *(Continued)*

Schedule K-1 (Form 1065) (1987) Page **2**

	(a) Distributive share item	(b) Amount	(c) 1040 filers enter the amount in column (b) on:
Self-employment 14a	Net earnings (loss) from self-employment	46,037	Sch. SE, Part I
b	Gross farming or fishing income		} (See Partner's Instructions for Schedule K-1 (Form 1065))
c	Gross nonfarm income	46,037	
Tax Preference Items 15a	Accelerated depreciation of real property placed in service before 1/1/87		Form 6251, line 5a
b	Accelerated depreciation of leased personal property placed in service before 1/1/87		Form 6251, line 5b
c	Depreciation adjustment on property placed in service after 12/31/86		Form 6251, line 4g
d	Depletion (other than oil and gas)		Form 6251, line 5h
e	(1) Gross income from oil, gas, and geothermal properties		See Form 6251 Instructions
	(2) Deductions allocable to oil, gas, and geothermal properties		See Form 6251 Instructions
f	Other (attach schedule)		(See Partner's Instructions for Schedule K-1 (Form 1065))
Investment Interest 16a	Interest expense on investment debts		Form 4952, line 1
b	(1) Investment income included in Schedule K-1, lines 4a through 4f	225	} (See Partner's Instructions for Schedule K-1 (Form 1065))
	(2) Investment expenses included in Schedule K-1, line 10		
Foreign Taxes 17a	Type of income ____		Form 1116, Check boxes
b	Name of foreign country or U.S. possession ____		Form 1116, Part I
c	Total gross income from sources outside the U.S. (attach schedule)		Form 1116, Part I
d	Total applicable deductions and losses (attach schedule)		Form 1116, Part I
e	Total foreign taxes (check one): ▶ ☐ Paid ☐ Accrued		Form 1116, Part II
f	Reduction in taxes available for credit (attach schedule)		Form 1116, Part III
g	Other (attach schedule)		See Form 1116 Instructions
Other 18	Other items and amounts not included in lines 1 through 17g and 19 that are required to be reported separately to you		(See Partner's Instructions for Schedule K-1 (Form 1065))

	19 Properties:	A	B	C	
Property Subject to Recapture of Investment Credit	a Description of property (State whether recovery or nonrecovery property. If recovery property, state whether regular percentage method or section 48(q) election used.)	Recovery section 48(q) election			
	b Date placed in service	1-3-86			Form 4255, top / Form 4255, line 2
	c Cost or other basis	1,750			Form 4255, line 3
	d Class of recovery property or original estimated useful life	3 yr			Form 4255, line 4
	e Date item ceased to be investment credit property	2-9-87			Form 4255, line 8

Other Information Provided by Partnership:

_____

_____

_____

_____

_____

268

return is due on or before March 15th. Many corporations, however, prefer the fiscal-year basis; in such cases, the corporation tax is due by the 15th of the third month following the close of its fiscal year. A sample Form 1120 is shown in exhibit 21–3.

If you need more time for any valid reason, the corporation may file Form 7004 ("Application for Automatic Extension of Time to File Corporation Income Tax Return").

Estimated tax payments must be made by every corporation whose tax liability is expected to be $40 or more. Payments are made to an authorized commercial bank depository or to a Federal Reserve Bank. They must be accompanied by a federal tax deposit coupon and deposited according to the instructions in the coupon book.

At present, corporations are required to pay federal income tax on profits for the year according to the following three-bracket graduated rate system:*

TAXABLE INCOME	TAX RATE
Not over $50,000	15%
Over $50,000 but not over $75,000	
	25%
Over $75,000	34%

(*Note:* An additional 5 percent tax, up to $11,750, is imposed on corporate taxable income over $100,000. Corporations with taxable income of at least $335,000 pay a flat rate of 34 percent.)

With respect to accumulated earnings, the IRS cautions as follows:

A corporation is permitted to accumulate its earnings for use in possible expansion or for other bona fide business reasons. However, if a corporation allows earnings to accumulate beyond the reasonable needs of the business, it may be subject to an accumulated earnings tax.**

S Corporation. You may elect to be taxed as an *S corporation* (a small business entity) and thereby avoid being taxed as the usual type of corporation. In this case, you report your income and taxable dividends in much the same fashion as do the partners of a partnership. Certain restrictions obtain in this situation: Yours must be a domestic corporation with only one classification of stock issued; this stock must be held by no more than thirty-five shareholders; all shareholders must give their consent; the shareholders may not be nonresident aliens; and so forth.†

*Internal Revenue Service, "Tax Guide for Small Business, 1987," *Publication 334* (Washington, D.C.: Internal Revenue Service, rev. November 1987), 104.

**Ibid., 106.

†Ibid., 108.

EXHIBIT 21-3. FORM 1120

Form **1120**	**U.S. Corporation Income Tax Return**	OMB No. 1545-0123

Department of the Treasury
Internal Revenue Service

For calendar 1987 or tax year beginning .... , 1987, ending .... , 19 ....

► For Paperwork Reduction Act Notice, see page 1 of the instructions.

1987

Check if a—			
A Consolidated return ☐	Use	Name	D Employer identification number
B Personal Holding Co. ☐		10-0395674 DEC87 D71 3998	
C Business Code No. (See the list in the instructions.) **3998**		TENTEX TOYS, INC 36 DIVISION STREET ANYTOWN IL 60930	E Date incorporated **3·1·72**
			F Total assets (See Specific Instructions.)

	Dollars	Cents
$	876,628	

G Check applicable boxes: (1) ☐ Initial return   (2) ☐ Final return   (3) ☐ Change in address

Income

1a	Gross receipts or sales $2,010,000	b Less returns and allowances $20,000		Balance ► 1c	1,990,000
2	Cost of goods sold and/or operations (Schedule A)			2	1,520,000
3	Gross profit (line 1c less line 2)			3	470,000
4	Dividends (Schedule C)			4	10,000
5	Interest			5	4,500
6	Gross rents			6	
7	Gross royalties			7	
8	Capital gain net income (attach separate Schedule D)			8	
9	Net gain or (loss) from Form 4797, line 18, Part II (attach Form 4797)			9	
10	Other income (see instructions—attach schedule)			10	1,000
11	TOTAL income—Add lines 3 through 10 and enter here ►			11	485,500

Deductions (See Instructions for limitations on deductions)

12	Compensation of officers (Schedule E)			12	70,000
13a	Salaries and wages $44,000	b Less jobs credit 6,000		Balance ► 13c	38,000
14	Repairs			14	800
15	Bad debts (see instructions)			15	1,600
16	Rents			16	9,200
17	Taxes			17	15,000
18	Interest			18	27,200
19	Contributions (see instructions for 10% limitation)			19	23,150
20	Depreciation (attach Form 4562)	20	17,600		
21	Less depreciation claimed in Schedule A and elsewhere on return	21a	(12,400)	21b	5,200
22	Depletion			22	
23	Advertising			23	8,700
24	Pension, profit-sharing, etc., plans			24	
25	Employee benefit programs			25	
26	Other deductions (attach schedule)			26	18,300
27	TOTAL deductions—Add lines 12 through 26 and enter here ►			27	277,150
28	Taxable income before net operating loss deduction and special deductions (line 11 less line 27)			28	208,350
29	Less: a Net operating loss deduction (see instructions)	29a			
	b Special deductions (Schedule C)	29b	8,000	29c	8,000

Tax and Payments

Line	Description				Amount
30	Taxable income (line 28 less line 29c)			30	200,350
31	TOTAL TAX (Schedule J)			31	58,176
32	Payments: a 1986 overpayment credited to 1987				
b	1987 estimated tax payments	69,117			
c	Less 1987 refund applied for on Form 4466	( )			
d	Tax deposited with Form 7004				
e	Credit from regulated investment companies (attach Form 2439)				
f	Credit for Federal tax on gasoline and special fuels (attach Form 4136)			32	69,117
33	Enter any PENALTY for underpayment of estimated tax—check ► ☐ if Form 2220 is attached			33	
34	TAX DUE—If the total of lines 31 and 33 is larger than line 32, enter AMOUNT OWED			34	
35	OVERPAYMENT—If line 32 is larger than the total of lines 31 and 33, enter AMOUNT OVERPAID			35	10,941
36	Enter amount of line 35 you want: Credited to 1988 estimated tax ► $ 10,941 Refunded ►			36	

Please Sign Here

Under penalties of perjury, I declare that I have examined this return, including accompanying schedules and statements, and to the best of my knowledge and belief, it is true, correct, and complete. Declaration of preparer (other than taxpayer) is based on all information of which preparer has any knowledge.

► *James Q. Barclay*   Signature of officer   **3·7·88** Date   ► *President* Title

Paid Preparer's Use Only

Preparer's signature ►		Date	Check if self-employed ☐	Preparer's social security number
Firm's name (or yours, if self-employed) and address ►			E.I. No. ►	
			ZIP code ►	

Source: "Tax Guide for Small Business—1987 Edition," *Publication 334* (Washington, D.C.: Internal Revenue Service, 1987), 161–64.

EXHIBIT 21-3. (Continued)

Form 1120 (1987)
Page 2

Schedule A Cost of Goods Sold and/or Operations (See instructions for line 2, page 1.)

1	Inventory at beginning of year	126,000
2	Purchases	1,127,100
3	Cost of labor	402,000
4a	Additional section 263A costs (see instructions)	
b	Other costs (attach schedule)	163,300
5	Total—Add lines 1 through 4b	1,818,400
6	Inventory at end of year	298,400
7	Cost of goods sold and/or operations—Line 5 less line 6. Enter here and on line 2, page 1	1,520,000

8 a Check all methods used for valuing closing inventory:

   (i) ☐ Cost   (ii) ☑ Lower of cost or market as described in Regulations section 1.471-4 (see instructions)

   (iii) ☐ Writedown of "subnormal" goods as described in Regulations section 1.471-2(c) (see instructions)

   (iv) ☐ Other (Specify method used and attach explanation.) ▶ _____

   b Check if the LIFO inventory method was adopted this tax year for any goods (if checked, attach Form 970) . . . . . . ☐

   c If the LIFO inventory method was used for this tax year, enter percentage (or amounts) of closing inventory computed under LIFO . . . . | 8c | |

   d Do the rules of section 263A (with respect to property produced or acquired for resale) apply to the corporation? . . ☑ Yes ☐ No

   e Was there any change (other than for section 263A purposes) in determining quantities, cost, or valuations between opening and closing inventory? If "Yes," attach explanation . . . . ☐ Yes ☑ No

Schedule C Dividends and Special Deductions (See Schedule C instructions.)

		(a) Dividends received	(b) %	(c) Special deductions: multiply (a) × (b)
1	Domestic corporations subject to section 243(a) deduction (other than debt-financed stock)	10,000	see instructions	8,000
2	Debt-financed stock of domestic and foreign corporations (section 246A)		see instructions	
3	Certain preferred stock of public utilities		see instructions	
4	Foreign corporations and certain FSCs subject to section 245 deduction		see instructions	
5	Wholly owned foreign subsidiaries and FSCs subject to 100% deduction (sections 245(b) and (c))		100	
6	Total—Add lines 1 through 5. See instructions for limitation			8,000
7	Affiliated groups subject to the 100% deduction (section 243(a)(3))		100	
8	Other dividends from foreign corporations not included in lines 4 and 5			
9	Income from controlled foreign corporations under subpart F (attach Forms 5471)			
10	Foreign dividend gross-up (section 78)			
11	IC-DISC or former DISC dividends not included in lines 1 and/or 2 (section 246(d))			
12	Other dividends			
13	Deduction for dividends paid on certain preferred stock of public utilities (see instructions)			
14	Total dividends—Add lines 1 through 12. Enter here and on line 4, page 1. ▶	10,000		
15	Total deductions—Add lines 6, 7, and 13. Enter here and on line 29b, page 1 . . . . ▶			8,000

Schedule E Compensation of Officers (See instructions for line 12, page 1.)
Complete Schedule E only if total receipts (line 1a, plus lines 4 through 10, of page 1, Form 1120) are $150,000 or more.

(a) Name of officer	(b) Social security number	(c) Percent of time devoted to business	Percent of corporation stock owned		(f) Amount of compensation
			(d) Common	(e) Preferred	
James G. Barclay	581-00-0936	100 %	45 %	%	40,000
		%	%	%	
George M. Collins	447-00-2604	100 %	15 %	%	21,000
		%	%	%	
Samuel Adams	401-00-2611	50 %	2 %	%	9,000
		%	%	%	
		%	%	%	
Total compensation of officers—Enter here and on line 12, page 1					70,000

EXHIBIT 21-3. (*Continued*)

Form 1120 (1987)   Page **3**

Schedule J   **Tax Computation** (See instructions.)

1 Check if you are a member of a controlled group (see sections 1561 and 1563) . . . . ▶ ☐

2 If line 1 is checked, see instructions: If your tax year includes June 30, 1987, complete both a and b below.
   Otherwise, complete only b.
   a *(i)* $ .... *(ii)* $ .... *(iii)* $ .... *(iv)* $ ....
   b *(i)* $ .... *(ii)* $ ....

3 Income tax (see instructions to figure the tax; enter this tax or alternative tax from Schedule D,
   whichever is less): Check if from Schedule D ▶ ☐ . . . . | **3** | 66,606

4a	Foreign tax credit (attach Form 1118)	**4a**	
b	Possessions tax credit (attach Form 5735)	**b**	
c	Orphan drug credit (attach Form 6765)	**c**	
d	Credit for fuel produced from a nonconventional source (see instructions)	**d**	
e	General business credit. Enter here and check which forms are attached ☐ Form 3800 ☐ Form 3468 ☑ Form 5884 ☐ Form 6478 ☐ Form 6765 ☐ Form 8586	**e**	8,430

5 Total—Add lines 4a through 4e	**5**	8,430
6 Line 3 less line 5	**6**	58,176
7 Personal holding company tax (attach Schedule PH (Form 1120))	**7**	
8 Tax from recomputing prior-year investment credit (attach Form 4255)	**8**	
9a Alternative minimum tax (see instructions—attach Form 4626)	**9a**	
b Environmental tax (see instructions—attach Form 4626)	**9b**	
10 Total tax—Add lines 6 through 9b. Enter here and on line 31, page 1	**10**	58,176

Additional Information (See instruction F.)	Yes	No
H Did the corporation claim a deduction for expenses connected with:		
(1) An entertainment facility (boat, resort, ranch, etc.)? . . .		✔
(2) Living accommodations (except employees on business)? . . .		✔
(3) Employees attending conventions or meetings outside the North American area? (See section 274(h).)		✔
(4) Employees' families at conventions or meetings?		✔
If "Yes," were any of these conventions or meetings outside the North American area? (See section 274(h).) . . .		
(5) Employee or family vacations not reported on Form W-2? . .		✔
I (1) Did the corporation at the end of the tax year own, directly or indirectly, 50% or more of the voting stock of a domestic corporation? (For rules of attribution, see section 267(c).) . .		✔
If "Yes," attach a schedule showing: (a) name, address, and identifying number; (b) percentage owned; (c) taxable income or (loss) before NOL and special deductions of such corporation for the tax year ending with or within your tax year; (d) highest amount owed by the corporation to such corporation during the year; and (e) highest amount owed to the corporation by such corporation during the year.		
(2) Did any individual, partnership, corporation, estate, or trust at the end of the tax year own, directly or indirectly, 50% or more of the corporation's voting stock? (For rules of attribution, see section 267(c).) If "Yes," complete (a) through (d) . . .		✔
(a) Attach a schedule showing name, address, and identifying number. Enter percentage owned ▶		
(b) Was the owner of such voting stock a person other than a U.S. person? (See instructions.) **Note:** *If "Yes," the corporation may have to file Form 5472.*		
If "Yes," enter owner's country ▶		
(c) Enter highest amount owed by the corporation to such owner during the year ▶		
(d) Enter highest amount owed to the corporation by such owner during the year ▶		
Note: *For purposes of I(1) and I(2), "highest amount owed" includes loans and accounts receivable/payable.*		

	Yes	No
J Refer to the list in the instructions and state the principal:		
Business activity ▶ *Manufacturing*		
Product or service ▶ *Toys*		
K Was the corporation a U.S. shareholder of any controlled foreign corporation? (See sections 951 and 957.) . . .		✔
If "Yes," attach Form 5471 for each such corporation.		
L At any time during the tax year, did the corporation have an interest in or a signature or other authority over a financial account in a foreign country (such as a bank account, securities account, or other financial account)?		✔
(See instruction F and filing requirements for form TD F 90-22.1.)		
If "Yes," enter name of foreign country ▶		
M Was the corporation the grantor of, or transferor to, a foreign trust which existed during the current tax year, whether or not the corporation has any beneficial interest in it? . . .		✔
If "Yes," the corporation may have to file Forms 3520, 3520-A, or 926.		
N During this tax year, did the corporation pay dividends (other than stock dividends and distributions in exchange for stock) in excess of the corporation's current and accumulated earnings and profits? (See sections 301 and 316.). . .		✔
If "Yes," file Form 5452. If this is a consolidated return, answer here for parent corporation and on Form 851, Affiliations Schedule, for each subsidiary.		
O During this tax year did the corporation maintain any part of its accounting/tax records on a computerized system?		✔
P Check method of accounting:		
(1) ☐ Cash (2) ☑ Accrual		
(3) ☐ Other (specify) ▶		
Q Check this box if the corporation issued publicly offered debt instruments with original issue discount . . . . . . ☐		
If so, the corporation may have to file Form 8281.		
R Enter the amount of tax-exempt interest received or accrued during the tax year ▶ ...... $ 5,000		
S If you are a member of a controlled group, enter the amount of taxable income for the entire group ▶		

EXHIBIT 21-3. (*Continued*)

Schedule L Balance Sheets

Assets	Beginning of tax year (a)	(b)	End of tax year (c)	(d)
1 Cash		14,700		25,542
2 Trade notes and accounts receivable	98,400		103,700	
a Less allowance for bad debts		98,400		103,700
3 Inventories		126,000		298,400
4 Federal and state government obligations		100,000		120,000
5 Other current assets (attach schedule)		26,300		17,266
6 Loans to stockholders				
7 Mortgage and real estate loans				
8 Other investments (attach schedule)		100,000		80,000
9 Buildings and other depreciable assets	272,400		296,700	
a Less accumulated depreciation	88,300	184,100	104,280	192,420
10 Depletable assets				
a Less accumulated depletion				
11 Land (net of any amortization)		20,000		20,000
12 Intangible assets (amortizable only)				
a Less accumulated amortization				
13 Other assets (attach schedule)		14,800		19,300
14 Total assets		684,300		876,628
Liabilities and Stockholders' Equity				
15 Accounts payable		28,500		34,834
16 Mortgages, notes, bonds payable in less than 1 year		4,300		4,300
17 Other current liabilities (attach schedule)		6,800		7,400
18 Loans from stockholders				
19 Mortgages, notes, bonds payable in 1 year or more		176,700		264,100
20 Other liabilities (attach schedule)				
21 Capital stock: a preferred stock				
b common stock	200,000	200,000	200,000	200,000
22 Paid-in or capital surplus				
23 Retained earnings—Appropriated (attach schedule)		30,000		40,000
24 Retained earnings—Unappropriated		238,000		325,994
25 Less cost of treasury stock		( )		( )
26 Total liabilities and stockholders' equity		684,300		876,628

Schedule M-1 Reconciliation of Income per Books With Income per Return You are not required to complete this schedule if the total assets on line 14, column (d), of Schedule L are less than $25,000.

1 Net income per books	144,994	7 Income recorded on books this year not included in this return (itemize)		
2 Federal income tax	58,176	a Tax-exempt interest $ 5,000		
3 Excess of capital losses over capital gains	3,600	(b) Insurance Proceeds 9,500		14,500
4 Income subject to tax not recorded on books this year (itemize)		8 Deductions in this tax return not charged against book income this year (itemize)		
5 Expenses recorded on books this year not deducted in this return (itemize)		a Depreciation $ 1,620		
a Depreciation $		b Contributions carryover $		
b Contributions carryover $ 850				1,620
See Itemized Statement Attached $16,850	17,700	9 Total of lines 7 and 8		16,120
6 Total of lines 1 through 5	224,470	10 Income (line 28, page 1)—line 6 less line 9		208,350

Schedule M-2 Analysis of Unappropriated Retained Earnings per Books (line 24, Schedule L) You are not required to complete this schedule if the total assets on line 14, column (d), of Schedule L are less than $25,000.

1 Balance at beginning of year	238,000	5 Distributions: a Cash		65,000
2 Net income per books	144,994	b Stock		
3 Other increases (itemize)		c Property		
		6 Other decreases (itemize) Reserve for Contingencies		
Refund of 1986 Income Tax	18,000			10,000
		7 Total of lines 5 and 6		75,000
4 Total of lines 1, 2, and 3	400,994	8 Balance at end of year (line 4 less line 7)		325,994

EXHIBIT 21-4. FORM 1120A

Form 1120-A

Department of the Treasury
Internal Revenue Service

U.S. Corporation Short-Form Income Tax Return
To see if you qualify to file Form 1120-A, see instructions.

1235

OMB No. 1545-0890

For calendar 1987 or tax year beginning _____, 1987, ending _____, 19 ___

1987

See Instructions for list of principal business:

A Activity   Flower Sh.
B Product or service   Flowers
C Code   5995

Use IRS Name

10-2134657   DEC87   D89   5995
ROSE FLOWER SHOP, INC.
38 SUPERIOR LANE
FAIR CITY,   MD   20715

IRS

D Employer Identification number (EIN)

E Date incorporated   7/1/82

F Total assets (See Specific Instructions.)

	Dollars	Cents
$	65,987	

G Check method of accounting: (1) ☐ Cash (2) ☒ Accrual (3) ☐ Other (specify) . ▶
H Check applicable boxes (1) ☐ Initial return (2) ☐ Change in address

Income

1a	Gross receipts or sales 248,000 b Less returns and allowances 7,500 Balance ▶	1c	240,500
2	Cost of goods sold and/or operations (see instructions)	2	144,000
3	Gross profit (line 1c less line 2)	3	96,500
4	Domestic corporation dividends subject to the Section 243(a)(1) deduction	4	
5	Interest	5	942
6	Gross rents	6	
7	Gross royalties	7	
8	Capital gain net income (attach separate Schedule D (Form 1120))	8	
9	Net gain or (loss) from Form 4797, line 18, Part II (attach Form 4797)	9	
10	Other income (see instructions)	10	
11	TOTAL income—Add lines 3 through 10	11	97,442

Deductions (See Instructions for limitations on deductions)

12	Compensation of officers (see instructions)	12	23,000
13a	Salaries and wages 24,320 b Less jobs credit Balance ▶	13c	24,320
14	Repairs	14	
15	Bad debts (see instructions)	15	
16	Rents	16	6,000
17	Taxes	17	3,320
18	Interest	18	1,340
19	Contributions (see Instructions for 10% limitation)	19	1,820
20	Depreciation (attach Form 4562) . . 20		
21	Less depreciation claimed elsewhere on return . . 21a	21b	
22	Other deductions (attach schedule) . . . . (Advertising)	22	3,000
23	TOTAL deductions—Add lines 12 through 22	23	62,800
24	Taxable income before net operating loss deduction and special deductions (line 11 less line 23)	24	34,642
25	Less: a Net operating loss deduction (see instructions) 25a		
	b Special deductions (see instructions) . . 25b	25c	
26	Taxable income (line 24 less line 25c)	26	34,642
27	TOTAL TAX (from Part I, line 6 on page 2)	27	5,340

Tax and Payments

28	Payments:		
a	1986 overpayment allowed as a credit		
b	1987 estimated tax payments . . 6,000		
c	Less 1987 refund applied for on Form 4466 . ( ) 6,000		
d	Tax deposited with Form 7004		
e	Credit from regulated investment companies (attach Form 2439)		
f	Credit for Federal tax on gasoline and special fuels (attach Form 4136) . .	28	6,000
29	Enter any PENALTY for underpayment of estimated tax—Check ▶ ☐ if Form 2220 is attached . .	29	
30	TAX DUE—If the total of lines 27 and 29 is larger than line 28, enter AMOUNT OWED	30	
31	OVERPAYMENT—If line 28 is larger than the total of lines 27 and 29, enter AMOUNT OVERPAID . .	31	660
32	Enter amount of line 31 you want: Credited to 1988 estimated tax ▶ 660 Refunded ▶	32	

Please Sign Here

Under penalties of perjury, I declare that I have examined this return, including accompanying schedules and statements, and to the best of my knowledge and belief, it is true, correct, and complete. Declaration of preparer (other than taxpayer) is based on all information of which preparer has any knowledge.

▶ *George Rose*
Signature of officer

2/14/88
Date

▶ President
Title

Paid Preparer's Use Only

Preparer's signature ▶

Date

Check if self-employed ▶ ☐

Preparer's social security number

Firm's name (or yours if self-employed) and address ▶

E.I. No. ▶

ZIP code ▶

For Paperwork Reduction Act Notice, see page 1 of the Instructions.

Form **1120-A** (1987)

Source: "Tax Guide for Small Business—1987 Edition," *Publication 334* (Washington, D.C.: Internal Revenue Service, 1987), 157–58.

EXHIBIT 21-4. (Continued)

Form 1120-A (1987)

Page 2

Part I Tax Computation (See Instructions.)

Enter EIN ▶ 10-2134657

1	Income tax (See instructions to figure the tax. Enter lesser of this tax or alternative tax from Schedule D.) Check if from Schedule D ▶ ☐	1	5,340
2	Credits. Check if from: ☐ Form 3800 ☒ Form 3468 ☐ Form 5884 ☐ Form 6478 ☐ Form 6765 ☐ Form 8586	2	
3	Line 1 less line 2	3	5,340
4	Tax from recomputing prior-year investment credit (attach Form 4255)	4	
5	Alternative minimum tax (see instructions—attach Form 4626)	5	
6	Total tax—Add lines 3 through 5. Enter here and on line 27, page 1	6	5,340

Additional Information (See instruction F.)

I Was a deduction taken for expenses connected with:

(1) An entertainment facility (boat, resort, ranch, etc.)? Yes ☐ No ☒

(2) Employees' families at conventions or meetings? Yes ☐ No ☒

J Did any individual, partnership, estate, or trust at the end of the tax year own, directly or indirectly, 50% or more of the corporation's voting stock? (For rules of attribution, see section 267(c).) If "Yes," complete (1) and (2) . . . . . Yes ☐ No ☒

(1) Attach a schedule showing name, address, and identifying number.

(2) Enter "highest amount owed:" include loans and accounts receivable/payable:

(a) Enter highest amount owed by the corporation to such owner during the year ▶

(b) Enter highest amount owed to the corporation by such owner during the year ▶

K Enter the amount of tax-exempt interest received or accrued during the tax year ▶

L (1) If an amount for cost of goods sold and/or operations is entered on line 2, page 1, complete (a) through (c):

(a) Purchases ▶ 134,014

(b) Additional sec. 263A costs (see instructions) ▶

(c) Other costs (attach schedule) ▶ 9,466

(2) Do the rules of section 263A (with respect to property produced or acquired for resale) apply to the corporation? . . Yes ☐ No ☒

M At any time during the tax year, did you have an interest in or a signature or other authority over a financial account in a foreign country (such as a bank account, securities account, or other financial account)? (See instruction F for filing requirements for Form TD F 90-22.1.) . . . . Yes ☐ No ☒

If "Yes," write in the name of the foreign country ▶

N During this tax year was any part of your accounting/tax records maintained on a computerized system? . . . . Yes ☐ No ☒

O Enter amount of cash distributions and the book value of property (other than cash) distributions made in this tax year ▶

Part II Balance Sheets

		(a) Beginning of tax year		(b) End of tax year	
Assets	1 Cash	20,540		18,498	
	2 Trade notes and accounts receivable				
	a Less: allowance for bad debts	( )	( )	( )	( )
	3 Inventories	2,530		2,010	
	4 Federal and state government obligations	13,807		45,479	
	5 Other current assets (attach schedule)				
	6 Loans to stockholders				
	7 Mortgage and real estate loans				
	8 Depreciable, depletable, and intangible assets				
	a Less: accumulated depreciation, depletion, and amortization	( )	( )	( )	( )
	9 Land (net of any amortization)				
	10 Other assets (attach schedule)				
	11 Total assets	36,877		65,987	
Liabilities and Stockholders' Equity	12 Accounts payable	6,415		6,223	
	13 Other current liabilities (attach schedule)				
	14 Loans from stockholders				
	15 Mortgages, notes, bonds payable				
	16 Other liabilities (attach schedule)				
	17 Capital stock (preferred and common stock)	20,000		20,000	
	18 Paid-in or capital surplus				
	19 Retained earnings	10,462		39,764	
	20 Less cost of treasury stock	( )	( )	( )	( )
	21 Total liabilities and stockholders' equity	36,877		65,987	

Part III Reconciliation of Income per Books With Income per Return (Must be completed by all filers)

1 Enter net income per books	29,302	
2 Federal income tax	5,340	
3 Income subject to tax not recorded on books this year (itemize)		
4 Expenses recorded on books this year not deducted in this return (itemize)		

5 Income recorded on books this year not included in this return (itemize)		
6 Deductions in this tax return not charged against book income this year (itemize)		
7 Income (line 24, page 1). Enter the sum of lines 1, 2, 3, and 4 less the sum of lines 5 and 6		34,642

To gain status as an S corporation, you need to file Form 2553 ("Election by a Small Business Corporation"). Tax returns are filed on Form 1120S ("U.S. Income Tax Return for an S Corporation"). This form may be seen in exhibit 21–5. For additional information, be sure to obtain a copy of IRS Publication 589 ("Tax Information on S Corporations").

Social Security Taxes

According to the provisions of the Federal Insurance Contributions Act (FICA), your employees are covered by old age, survivors, disability, and hospital insurance. To pay for such coverage, social security (FICA) taxes are levied on both employee and employer. The employer is responsible for collecting this tax from employees by withholding it in the same way the employees' income tax is withheld.

Currently, this deduction is fixed at the rate of 7.51 percent of each employee's annual earnings, up to the first $45,000 of wages. This limit, or wage base, may be increased in the future. In addition, the firm is required to match the total amount collected from its employees, at the same rate of 7.51 percent.

FICA and withheld income taxes are reported and paid together. Within one month after the end of each calendar quarter, you need to report these taxes on Form 941 ("Employer's Quarterly Federal Tax Return"). Bear in mind, too, that you'll need to make deposits periodically to a Federal Reserve Bank or an authorized financial institution. You must accompany each deposit with a federal tax deposit (FTD) coupon. (See Publication 334 for additional details.)

Unemployment Tax

The employer is also subject to federal unemployment tax (FUTA) if he or she has paid wages of $1,500 or more during any quarter of the calendar year, or if one or more employees were working at least once each week (not necessarily for a full day) during each of twenty calendar days. In 1988 the rate of taxation may (or may not) be reduced to 6.0 percent from the 6.2 percent rate levied in 1987 on the first $7,000 of wages paid to each employee during the year. Credit of up to 5.4 percent is granted for the state unemployment tax paid; the tax rate, therefore, can be as low as 0.8 or 0.6 percent.

Deposits are required if the firm's tax liability exceeds $100 for any calendar quarter. Such deposits are made to a Federal Reserve Bank or to an authorized financial institution. They are to be accompanied by a federal tax deposit coupon. The employer must also file an annual return on Form 940 ("Employer's Annual Federal Unemployment (FUTA) Tax Return") on or before January 31.

Excise Taxes

Excise taxes are levied on the sale of certain articles, on certain types of transactions and occupations, and on the use of certain products. Such taxes are not to be included in the selling price of such items but are to be charged separately by the manufacturer or the retailer.

EXHIBIT 21-5. FORM 1120S

Form **1120S**	**U.S. Income Tax Return for an S Corporation**			OMB No. 1545-0130

Form **1120S**
Department of the Treasury
Internal Revenue Service

U.S. Income Tax Return for an S Corporation
For the calendar year 1987 or tax year beginning .... , 1987, ending .... , 19 ....
► For Paperwork Reduction Act Notice, see page 1 of the Instructions.

OMB No. 1545-0130

1987

A Date of election as an S corporation
12/01/86

B Business code no. (see Specific Instructions)
3070

Use IRS label. Otherwise, please print or type.

10-4487964   DEC87   D74   3070
ESTEX FABRICATORS, INC
482 WINSTON ST
METRO CITY   OH   43704

I R S

C Employer Identification number

D Date incorporated
3/01/72

E Total assets (see Specific Instructions)
Dollars: $ 921,714   Cents

F Check applicable boxes: (1) ☐ Initial return (2) ☐ Final return (3) ☐ Change in address (4) ☐ Amended return

G Check this box if this is an S corporation subject to the consolidated audit procedures of sections 6241 through 6245 (see instructions) . . . . ► ☐

H Was this corporation in operation at the end of 1987 (see instructions)? . . . . Yes ☐ No ☐

I How many months in 1987 was this corporation in operation (see instructions)? . . . . ►

Caution: Include only trade or business income and expenses on lines 1a through 21. See the instructions for more information.

Income	1a Gross receipts or sales 2,010,000 b Less returns and allowances 21,000 Balance ►		1c	1,989,000
	2 Cost of goods sold and/or operations (Schedule A, line 7).		2	1,520,000
	3 Gross profit (subtract line 2 from line 1c).		3	469,000
	4 Net gain (or loss) from Form 4797, line 18 (see instructions)		4	
	5 Other income (see instructions—attach schedule).		5	1,000
	6 TOTAL income (loss)—Combine lines 3, 4 and 5 and enter here . . . . ►		6	470,000
Deductions (See instructions for limitations.)	7 Compensation of officers		7	70,000
	8a Salaries and wages 44,000 b Less jobs credit 6,000 Balance ►		8c	38,000
	9 Repairs.		9	800
	10 Bad debts (see instructions)		10	1,600
	11 Rents		11	9,200
	12 Taxes		12	15,000
	13 Deductible interest expense not claimed or reported elsewhere on return (see instructions)		13	24,200
	14a Depreciation from Form 4562 (attach Form 4562).	14a 17,600		
	b Depreciation reported on Schedule A and elsewhere on return	14b 12,400		
	c Subtract line 14b from line 14a		14c	5,200
	15 Depletion (**Do not deduct oil and gas depletion. See instructions.**)		15	
	16 Advertising		16	8,700
	17 Pension, profit-sharing, etc. plans		17	
	18 Employee benefit programs		18	
	19 Other deductions (attach schedule)		19	78,300
	20 TOTAL deductions—Add lines 7 through 19 and enter here . . . . . ►		20	251,000
	21 Ordinary income (loss) from trade or business activity(ies)—Subtract line 20 from line 6		21	219,000
Tax and Payments	22 Tax:			
	a Excess net passive income tax (attach schedule)	22a		
	b Tax from Schedule D (Form 1120S)	22b		
	c Add lines 22a and 22b		22c	
	23 Payments:			
	a Tax deposited with Form 7004	23a		
	b Credit for Federal tax on gasoline and special fuels (attach Form 4136)	23b		
	c Add lines 23a and 23b		23c	
	24 **TAX DUE** (subtract line 23c from line 22c). See instructions for Paying the Tax . . . ►		24	
	25 **OVERPAYMENT** (subtract line 22c from line 23c). . . . . ►		25	

Please Sign Here

Under penalties of perjury, I declare that I have examined this return, including accompanying schedules and statements, and to the best of my knowledge and belief, it is true, correct, and complete. Declaration of preparer (other than taxpayer) is based on all information of which preparer has any knowledge.

► John H. Anders   3/9/88   ► President
Signature of officer   Date   Title

Paid Preparer's Use Only

Preparer's signature ►		Date	Check if self-employed ☐	Preparer's social security number
Firm's name (or yours if self-employed) and address ►			E.I. No. ►	
			ZIP code ►	

Form **1120S** (1987)

Source: "Tax Guide for Small Business—1987 Edition," *Publication 334* (Washington, D.C.: Internal Revenue Service, 1987), 167–70.

EXHIBIT 21-5. (*Continued*)

Form 1120S (1987)   Page 2

Schedule A   Cost of Goods Sold and/or Operations (See instructions for Schedule A.)

1	Inventory at beginning of year	1	126,000
2	Purchases	2	1,127,100
3	Cost of labor	3	402,000
4a	Additional section 263A costs (attach schedule)	4a	60,000
b	Other costs (attach schedule)	4b	103,300
5	Total—Add lines 1 through 4b	5	1,818,400
6	Inventory at end of year	6	298,400
7	Cost of goods sold and/or operations—Subtract line 6 from line 5. Enter here and on line 2, page 1	7	1,520,000

8a Check all methods used for valuing closing inventory:

   (i) ☐ Cost

   (ii) ☒ Lower of cost or market as described in Regulations section 1.471-4 (see instructions)

   (iii) ☐ Writedown of "subnormal" goods as described in Regulations section 1.471-2(c) (see instructions)

   (iv) ☐ Other (Specify method used and attach explanation) ▶ _____

  b Check this box if the LIFO inventory method was adopted this tax year for any goods (if checked, attach Form 970) . . . . ☐

  c If the LIFO inventory method was used for this tax year, enter percentage (or amounts) of closing inventory computed under LIFO . . . . |8c|

  d Do the rules of section 263A (with respect to property produced or acquired for resale) apply to the corporation? . . . ☐ Yes ☒ No

  e Was there any change (other than for section 263A purposes) in determining quantities, cost, or valuations between opening and closing inventory? (If "Yes," attach explanation.) . . . . ☐ Yes ☒ No

Additional Information Required

	Yes	No
J Did you at the end of the tax year own, directly or indirectly, 50% or more of the voting stock of a domestic corporation? (For rules of attribution, see section 267(c).)		X
If "Yes," attach a schedule showing:		
(1) Name, address, and employer identification number; **(3)** Highest amount owed by you to such corporation during the year; and		
(2) Percentage owned; **(4)** Highest amount owed to you by such corporation during the year.		
(Note: For purposes of J(3) and J(4), "highest amount owed" includes loans and accounts receivable/payable.)		
K Refer to the listing of business activity codes at the end of the Instructions for Form 1120S and state your principal: Business activity ▶ _____; Product or service ▶ _____		
L Were you a member of a controlled group subject to the provisions of section 1561?		X
M Did you claim a deduction for expenses connected with:		
(1) Entertainment facilities (boat, resort, ranch, etc.)?		X
(2) Living accommodations (except for employees on business)?		X
(3) Employees attending conventions or meetings outside the North American area? (See section 274(h).)		X
(4) Employees' families at conventions or meetings?		X
If "Yes," were any of these conventions or meetings outside the North American area? (See section 274(h).) . .		
(5) Employee or family vacations not reported on Form W-2?		X
N At any time during the tax year, did you have an interest in or a signature or other authority over a financial account in a foreign country (such as a bank account, securities account, or other financial account)? (See instructions for exceptions and filing requirements for form TD F 90-22.1.)		X
If "Yes," enter the name of the foreign country ▶ _____		
O Were you the grantor of, or transferor to, a foreign trust which existed during the current tax year, whether or not you have any beneficial interest in it? If "Yes," you may have to file Forms 3520, 3520-A, or 926		X
P During this tax year did you maintain any part of your accounting/tax records on a computerized system? . . .		X
Q Check method of accounting: (1)☐ Cash (2)☒ Accrual (3)☐ Other (specify) ▶ _____		
R Check this box if the S corporation has filed or is required to file **Form 8264,** Application for Registration of a Tax Shelter . . . . ▶☐		
S Check this box if the corporation issued publicly offered debt instruments with original issue discount . . . ▶☐ If so, the corporation may have to file Form 8281, Information Return for Publicly Offered Original Issue Discount Instruments.		
T If section 1374 (new built-in gains tax) applies to the corporation, enter the corporation's net unrealized built-in gain as defined in section 1374(d)(1) (see instructions) ▶		

Designation of Tax Matters Person

The following shareholder is hereby designated as the tax matters person (TMP) for the tax year for which this tax return is filed:

Name of designated TMP ▶	John H. Anders	Identifying number of TMP ▶	458-00-0327
Address of designated TMP ▶	4340 Holmes Parkway Metro City, Ohio 43704		

EXHIBIT 21-5. (*Continued*)

SCHEDULE K-1 (Form 1120S) Department of the Treasury Internal Revenue Service	Shareholder's Share of Income, Credits, Deductions, etc. For calendar year 1987 or tax year beginning ...., 1987, and ending ....19.... ▶ For Paperwork Reduction Act Notice, see page 1 of Instructions for Form 1120S.	OMB No. 1545-0130 1987

Shareholder's identifying number ▶	Corporation's identifying number ▶
Shareholder's name, address, and ZIP code John H. Anders 4340 Holmes Parkway Metro City, Ohio 43707	Corporation's name, address, and ZIP code Estex Fabricators, Inc. 482 Winston St. Metro City, Ohio 43704

A (1) Shareholder's percentage of stock ownership for tax year (see instructions for Schedule K-1) . . . . . . ▶ 45 %

(2) Number of shares owned by shareholder at tax year end . . . . ▶ 4500

Internal Revenue Service Center where corporation filed its return ▶ Cincinnati, OH

Tax shelter registration number (see Instructions for Schedule K-1) . . . . ▶

D Did the shareholder materially participate in the trade or business activity(ies) of the corporation? (See Instructions for Schedule K-1. Leave the check boxes blank if there are no trade or business activities.) . . . . . . ☒ Yes ☐ No

E Did the shareholder actively participate in the rental real estate activity(ies) of the corporation? (See instructions for Schedule K-1. Leave the check boxes blank if there are no rental real estate activities.) . . . . . . ☐ Yes ☐ No

F If (1) question D is checked "No" or income or loss is reported on line 2 or 3 and (2) the shareholder acquired corporate stock after 10/22/86, check here ▶ ☐ and enter the shareholder's weighted percentage increase in stock ownership for 1987 (see instructions for Schedule K-1) . . . . ▶ %

G If question D is checked "No" and any activity referred to in question D was started or acquired by the corporation after 10/22/86, check here ▶ ☐ and enter the date of start up or acquisition in the date space on line 1. Also, if an activity for which income or loss is reported on line 2 or 3 was started after 10/22/86, check the box and enter the start up date in the date space on line 2 or 3.

H If the short tax year shown above was a result of a change in tax year required by section 1378, check here . . . . ▶ ☐

Caution: *Refer to Shareholder's Instructions for Schedule K-1 before entering information from Schedule K-1 on your tax return.*

	(a) Distributive share items	(b) Amount	(c) Form 1040 filers enter the amount in column (b) on:
Income (Losses) and Deductions	1 Ordinary income (loss) from trade or business activity(ies). Date:_____	48,550	⎫ See Shareholder's Instructions for Schedule K-1 (Form 1120S).
	2 Income or loss from rental real estate activity(ies). Date: _____		
	3 Income or loss from rental activity(ies) other than line 2 above. Date: _____		⎭
	4 Portfolio income (loss):		
	a Interest	1,800	Sch. B, Part I, line 2
	b Dividends	7,200	Sch. B, Part II, line 4
	c Royalties		Sch. E, Part I, line 5
	d Net short-term capital gain (loss)		Sch. D, line 5, col. (f) or (g)
	e Net long-term capital gain (loss)		Sch. D, line 12, col. (f) or (g)
	f Other portfolio income (loss).		(Enter on applicable line of your return.)
	5 Net gain (loss) under section 1231 (other than due to casualty or theft).		Form 4797, line 1
	6 Other income (loss) (attach schedule)		(Enter on applicable line of your return.)
	7 Charitable contributions	10,800	See Form 1040 Instructions.
	8 Section 179 expense deduction (attach schedule)		⎫ See Shareholder's Instructions for Schedule K-1 (Form 1120S).
	9 Deductions related to portfolio income (loss) (attach schedule) . . .		
	10 Other deductions (attach schedule)		⎭
Credits	11a Jobs credit	2,700	Form 5884
	b Low-income housing credit		Form 8586, line 8
	c Qualified rehabilitation expenditures related to rental real estate activity(ies) (attach schedule)		⎫ See Shareholder's Instructions for Schedule K-1 (Form 1120S).
	d Credits related to rental real estate activity(ies) other than on lines 11b and 11c (attach schedule)		
	e Credits related to rental activity(ies) other than on lines 11b, c, and d (attach schedule)		
	12 Other credits (attach schedule)		⎭
Tax Preference and Adjustment Items	13a Accelerated depreciation of real property placed in service before 1987		Form 6251, line 5a
	b Accelerated depreciation of leased personal property placed in service before 1987.		Form 6251, line 5b
	c Depreciation adjustment on property placed in service after 1986 . . .		Form 6251, line 4g
	d Depletion (other than oil and gas)		Form 6251, line 5h
	e (1) Gross income from oil, gas, or geothermal properties		See Form 6251 Instructions.
	(2) Gross deductions allocable to oil, gas, or geothermal properties . .		⎫ See Shareholder's Instructions for Schedule K-1 (Form 1120S).
	f Other items (attach schedule)		⎭

EXHIBIT 21-5. (Continued)

	(a) Distributive share items				(b) Amount	(c) Form 1040 filers enter the amount in column (b) on:
Investment Interest	**14a**	Interest expense on investment debts			*1,350*	Form 4952, line 1
	b	**(1)** Investment income included on Schedule K-1, lines 4a through 4f .			*9,000*	See Shareholder's Instructions for Schedule K-1 (Form 1120S).
		(2) Investment expenses included on Schedule K-1, line 9				
Foreign Taxes	**15a**	Type of income ▶				Form 1116, Check boxes
	b	Name of foreign country or U.S. possession ▶				Form 1116, Part I
	c	Total gross income from sources outside the U.S. (attach schedule) . .				Form 1116, Part I
	d	Total applicable deductions and losses (attach schedule). . . .				Form 1116, Part I
	e	Total foreign taxes (check one): ▶ ☐ Paid ☐ Accrued				Form 1116, Part II
	f	Reduction in taxes available for credit (attach schedule)				Form 1116, Part III
	g	Other (attach schedule)				See Form 1116 Instructions.
Other Items	**16**	Property distributions (including cash) other than dividend distributions reported to you on Form 1099-DIV			*29,250*	See Shareholder's Instructions for Schedule K-1 (Form 1120S).
	17	Amount of loan repayments for "Loans from Shareholders"				

	18	Properties:	**A**	**B**	**C**	
Property Subject to Recapture of Investment Credit	**a**	Description of property (State whether recovery or non-recovery property. If recovery property, state whether regular percentage method or section 48(q) election used.).				Form 4255, top
	b	Date placed in service .				Form 4255, line 2
	c	Cost or other basis . .				Form 4255, line 3
	d	Class of recovery property or original estimated useful life .				Form 4255, line 4
	e	Date item ceased to be investment credit property				Form 4255, line 8

	19	Supplemental information for lines 1 through 18 that is required to be reported separately to each shareholder (attach additional schedules if more space is needed):
Supplemental Schedules		*Tax-exempt interest — $ 2,250*
		Nondeductible salaries and wages due to the jobs credit — $ 2,700

280

EXHIBIT 21-5. (*Continued*)

Form 1120S (1987)   Page **3**

Schedule K   Shareholders' Shares of Income, Credits, Deductions, etc. (See Instructions.)

	(a) Distributive share items		(b) Total amount	

Income (Losses) and Deductions

1	Ordinary income (loss) from trade or business activity(ies) (page 1, line 21)	1	219,000	
2a	Gross income from rental real estate activity(ies).	2a		
b	Minus expenses (attach schedule)	2b		
c	Balance: net income (loss) from rental real estate activity(ies).	2c		
3a	Gross income from other rental activity(ies)	3a		
b	Minus expenses (attach schedule)	3b		
c	Balance: net income (loss) from other rental activity(ies)	3c		
4	Portfolio income (loss):			
a	Interest income	4a	4,000	
b	Dividend income	4b	16,000	
c	Royalty income	4c		
d	Net short-term capital gain (loss) (Schedule D (Form 1120S)).	4d		
e	Net long-term capital gain (loss) (Schedule D (Form 1120S))	4e		
f	Other portfolio income (loss) (attach schedule)	4f		
5	Net gain (loss) under section 1231 (other than due to casualty or theft)	5		
6	Other income (loss) (attach schedule)	6		
7	Charitable contributions (attach schedule)	7	24,000	
8	Section 179 expense deduction (attach schedule)	8		
9	Expenses related to portfolio income (loss) (attach schedule) (see instructions)	9		
10	Other deductions (attach schedule)	10		

Credits

11a	Jobs credit (attach Form 5884)	11a	6,000	
b	Low-income housing credit (attach Form 8586)	11b		
c	Qualified rehabilitation expenditures related to rental real estate activity(ies) (attach schedule)	11c		
d	Credits related to rental real estate activity(ies) other than on lines 11b and 11c (attach schedule)	11d		
e	Credit(s) related to rental activity(ies) other than on lines 11b, 11c, and 11d (attach schedule)	11e		
12	Other credits (attach schedule)	12		

Tax Preference and Adjustment Items

13a	Accelerated depreciation of real property placed in service before 1987	13a		
b	Accelerated depreciation of leased personal property placed in service before 1987	13b		
c	Depreciation adjustment on property placed in service after 1986	13c		
d	Depletion (other than oil and gas)	13d		
e	(1) Gross income from oil, gas, or geothermal properties	13e(1)		
	(2) Gross deductions allocable to oil, gas, or geothermal properties	13e(2)		
f	Other items (attach schedule)	13f		

Investment Interest

14a	Interest expense on investment debts	14a	3,000	
b	(1) Investment income included on lines 4a through 4f, Schedule K	14b(1)	20,000	
	(2) Investment expenses included on line 9, Schedule K	14b(2)		

Foreign Taxes

15a	Type of income			
b	Name of foreign country or U.S. possession			
c	Total gross income from sources outside the U.S. (attach schedule)	15c		
d	Total applicable deductions and losses (attach schedule)	15d		
e	Total foreign taxes (check one): ▶ ☐ Paid ☐ Accrued	15e		
f	Reduction in taxes available for credit (attach schedule)	15f		
g	Other (attach schedule)	15g		

Other Items

16	Total property distributions (including cash) other than dividend distributions reported on line 18, Schedule K	16	65,000	
17	Other items and amounts not included in lines 1 through 16, Schedule K, that are required to be reported separately to shareholders (attach schedule).			
18	Total dividend distributions paid from accumulated earnings and profits contained in other retained earnings (line 26 of Schedule L)	18		

EXHIBIT 21-5. (*Continued*)

Form 1120S (1987) Page 4

Schedule L — Balance Sheets

Assets	Beginning of tax year (a)	(b)	End of tax year (c)	(d)
1 Cash		14,700		64,514
2 Trade notes and accounts receivable	98,400		83,700	
a Less allowance for bad debts		98,400		83,700
3 Inventories		126,000		298,400
4 Federal and state government obligations		100,000		120,000
5 Other current assets (attach schedule)		26,300		26,300
6 Loans to shareholders				
7 Mortgage and real estate loans				
8 Other investments (attach schedule)		100,000		100,000
9 Buildings and other depreciable assets	272,400		299,400	
a Less accumulated depreciation	88,300	184,100	105,900	193,500
10 Depletable assets				
a Less accumulated depletion				
11 Land (net of any amortization)		20,000		20,000
12 Intangible assets (amortizable only)				
a Less accumulated amortization				
13 Other assets (attach schedule)		14,800		19,300
14 Total assets		684,300		925,714
Liabilities and Shareholders' Equity				
15 Accounts payable		28,500		34,834
16 Mortgages, notes, bonds payable in less than 1 year		4,300		4,300
17 Other current liabilities (attach schedule)		6,800		7,400
18 Loans from shareholders				
19 Mortgages, notes, bonds payable in 1 year or more		176,700		265,180
20 Other liabilities (attach schedule)				
21 Capital stock		200,000		200,000
22 Paid-in or capital surplus				
23 Accumulated adjustments account			141,000	
24 Other adjustments account			5,000	
25 Shareholders' undistributed taxable income previously taxed				
26 Other retained earnings (see instructions)	268,000		268,000	
Check this box if the corporation has subchapter C earnings and profits at the close of the tax year ▶ ☐ (see instructions)				
27 Total retained earnings per books—Combine amounts on lines 23 through 26, columns (a) and (c) (see instructions)		268,000		414,000
28 Less cost of treasury stock		( )		( )
29 Total liabilities and shareholders' equity		684,300		925,714

Schedule M — Analysis of Accumulated Adjustments Account, Other Adjustments Account, and Shareholders' Undistributed Taxable Income Previously Taxed

(If Schedule L, column (c), amounts for lines 23, 24, or 25 are not the same as corresponding amounts on line 9 of Schedule M, attach a schedule explaining any differences. See instructions.)

	Accumulated adjustments account	Other adjustments account	Shareholders' undistributed taxable income previously taxed
1 Balance at beginning of year	-0-	-0-	
2 Ordinary income from page 1, line 21	219,000		
3 Other additions	20,000	5,000	
4 Total of lines 1, 2, and 3	239,000	5,000	
5 Distributions other than dividend distributions	65,000	-0-	
6 Loss from page 1, line 21	-0-		
7 Other reductions	33,000	-0-	
8 Add lines 5, 6, and 7	98,000	-0-	
9 Balance at end of tax year—Subtract line 8 from line 4	141,000	5,000	

Among the more common excise taxes are retailers' excise taxes on heavy trucks, trailers, tractors, diesel fuel, and fuels used in noncommercial aviation; manufacturers' excise taxes on tires, coal, gasoline, sport fishing equipment, and firearms; and taxes on certain transportation and communications services. Businesses liable for excise taxes must file Form 720 ("Quarterly Federal Excise Tax Return"). For more information about these taxes, secure a copy of Publication 510 ("Excise Taxes for 1989").

STATE AND LOCAL TAXES

Tax rates and other specifics vary considerably from locale to locale across the country. Prominent among such forms of taxation are the state (and sometimes the city) tax on income, real estate taxes, and sales taxes. State and local income taxes are tied in most ways to the details you provide on your federal income tax return. Real estate taxes furnish most of the revenue required for the operation of local governments and the services they provide. Sales taxes are levied by most states, many cities, and some counties on the retail prices of products (and sometimes services). Retailers are required to collect these sales taxes from their customers, keep records of what they collect, and then turn over these moneys to the appropriate taxing authorities.

Business owners may also be responsible for other, lesser taxes including unemployment and disability taxes, the corporation (or the unincorporated business) tax, and taxes on licenses and permits, among others.

HOW TO HANDLE WITHHOLDING

The federal government insists that business managers withhold from the regular paychecks of all employees a percentage of their earnings for income and social security taxes. Further, they are required to turn over such moneys to the government on a regular basis. (For instructions, refer to the section above on "Social Security Taxes.")

Consequently, you should ask all new employees to complete a W-4 form ("Employee's Withholding Allowance Certificate"). Based on the information contained therein, you withhold the required percentage of each employee's gross earnings according to tables available from the Internal Revenue Service (Publication 15—Circular E: "Employer's Tax Guide"). The tables cover different payroll periods: weekly, semimonthly, monthly, and so forth.

Thereafter, each succeeding year (before December 1) you should check every employee for changes in status. If there has been a change, ask the employee to complete a new W-4 form.

Finally, before the end of each January, you must also provide each of your employees with a completed W-2 form ("Wage and Tax Statement") for the year just ended.

DEPRECIATION

Business property with a useful life of more than one year is subject to *depreciation.* * This involves deducting, each year, some portion of that property's cost—a figure that can play an important role in determining the amount of business earnings on which you'll need to pay income tax.

Property can be tangible or intangible. Buildings, machinery, equipment, furniture, automobiles and delivery trucks, and the like are considered tangible property; they can be seen, touched, and felt. Copyrights and franchises are examples of intangible property. Land, though, is property that can never be depreciated.

To be depreciable, business property must meet three basic requirements. It must

1. Be used in business (or held for the production of income)
2. Have a determinable useful life of more than one year
3. Be something that wears out, decays, gets used up, becomes obsolete, or loses value from natural causes

How to Depreciate Your Property

According to the Tax Reform Act of 1986, you must use the *accelerated cost recovery system* (ACRS) for all tangible property placed in service after 1980, unless you're specifically prevented from using it. If you cannot use ACRS, then you need to select one of the following depreciation techniques: the straight line method, the declining balance method, or the new MACRS (modified accelerated cost recovery system).

ACRS may not be used to depreciate intangible property or for property placed in service before 1981.

Recovery periods. Under ACRS, a number of recovery periods are made available. Properties are classified as three-, five-, ten-, fifteen-, eighteen-, and nineteen-year properties according to the type being depreciated.

By way of illustration, consider the following categories:

• Three-year property: automobiles, light-duty trucks, and other items with short, useful lives
• Five-year property: most equipment, office furniture, and fixtures
• Ten-year property: manufactured homes, theme-park structures
• Fifteen-year property: real property (buildings) placed in service before March 16, 1984 (other than those designated as ten-year property)

MACRS applies to all property placed in service after the end of December, 1986. Under this method, the new classes of property are three-, five-, seven-, ten-, fifteen-, and twenty-year property.

*See: "Tax Guide for Small Business—1987 Edition," *Publication 334* (Washington: Internal Revenue Service, 1987), 38–45. For more detailed coverage of this topic area, request a copy of IRS *Publication 534,* "Depreciation."

MACRS may be useful if you wish to take your depreciation deductions over a longer period of time. For example, when considering three-year property, you can choose from three alternate recovery periods: three, five, or twelve years.

A more detailed description of MACRS and other methods of depreciation (including their applications) lies beyond the scope of this discussion. For further information, you may wish to refer to IRS Publication 534.

FOR FURTHER INFORMATION

Books

Block, Julian. *Julian Block's Guide to Year Round Tax Savings,* rev. ed. Homewood, Ill.: Dow Jones-Irwin, 1987.

Bower, James B., and Harold Q. Langenderfer. *Income Tax Procedure.* Cincinnati: South-Western, 1986.

Burke, Frank M., and Buford Berry. *Tax Practice Handbook.* Englewood Cliffs, N.J.: Prentice-Hall, 1986.

Lane, Marc J. *Taxation for Small Business.* New York: Wiley, 1982.

Lasser, J. K. *J. K. Lasser's How to Avoid a Tax Audit.* New York: Simon and Schuster, 1984.

Ruland, William. *Managers' Guide to Corporate Tax.* New York: Wiley, 1984.

Pamphlets Available from the Small Business Administration

MANAGEMENT AIDS

MA 1.013—"Steps in Meeting Your Tax Obligations"
MA 1.014—"Getting the Facts for Income Tax Reporting"

VIII

IMPROVING THE NEW BUSINESS OPERATION

22

Improving Results in Your Manufacturing Plant

As a conservative estimate, at least eight out of ten small factories operate well below their optimum capability.

Why this dire situation? For one thing, so long as a plant is producing and the operation is profitable, the factory manager is usually quite content. Handicapped by the lack of a more sophisticated level of knowledge of plant operations, this executive doesn't realize things could be better. Other factors that contribute to manufacturing inefficiency often include improper costing practices, machine operators who aren't well trained, inadequately maintained or obsolete equipment, lack of familiarity with the use of variance analysis techniques, untidy purchasing practices, and a host of other possibilities.

These days, in the face of spiraling costs and intensified competition, the name of the manufacturing game is no longer production but *productivity*.

To improve plant productivity, no magical "open sesame" need be invoked; the pathway to improvement in manufacturing is as simple as counting 1-2-3:

1. Buy better.
2. Produce better.
3. Sell better.

Actually, entries 1 and 3 are ancillary problem areas; the central problem in manufacturing is that number 2: *How to produce better.*

As we have already pointed out, effective business administration involves skillfully planning, organizing, directing, and controlling all of the elements that combine to comprise the business. In short, it calls for more efficient deployment and use of all company resources: capital, machinery, human resources, materials, and methods. Moreover, efficiency in manipulating these assets is inextricably tied to costs. Producing better (or, for that matter, buying or selling better) implies that output will be increased while cost factors representing the input will be held steady (if not reduced).

STANDARDS: THE BASES FOR IMPROVEMENT

To increase productivity, you must understand fully how your plant is operating at present, decide in a logical manner on goals that are higher than today's outputs, and then figure out ways to attain those goals. In short, *measurements* need to be taken—today, tomorrow, and beyond tomorrow. Only by recording and comparing those measurements over time can you determine whether or not plant productivity is increasing.

Such measurements are called *standards*; these are based on averages obtained through observing and recording what transpires in the factory. Of course, standards are established for control purposes and, more importantly, as points of departure for improvement. They can be set up in every division of your manufacturing enterprise, not only within the production process itself but also in purchasing, sales, and even office administration. They provide answers to dozens of questions, such as:

- How much of material A goes into each unit of product B?
- How long does it take an operator to perform task C?
- How many widgets roll off machine D each hour, each week?
- What is the yield in pounds of compound Z when fifty pounds of material X are mixed with twenty-five pounds of material Y?
- If this piece of equipment is in operation eight hours each day on a five-day-week basis, how much electricity will be used?

In the area of production, the following standards should be established:

- Direct labor cost/product unit
- Number of labor-hours needed/unit of work
- Number of machine-hours needed/operation
- Setup time/operation
- Amount of materials used/product
- Power usage/machine
- Number of products produced/day

Standards that might prove useful in the sales area include the number of new accounts opened per salesperson, the average monthly sales per salesperson, the cost of sales per sales dollar, and the gross margin contribution per territory.

Setting Standards

In efficient plant management, standards such as those mentioned above are developed and monitored regularly, perhaps with the aid of industrial engineers or consultants. These standards, of course, represent averages that are *real*. By definition, then, they are not *ideal* averages. So your next move is to work out ideal standards; in other words, strive to project the company's output if it were operating at maximum efficiency. Then, somewhere between the ideal and the real, you must find a spot where you can pinpoint an attainable level of performance that is higher than the one your plant now evidences.

Time and motion studies are techniques available to help you maximize efficiency. Time studies record the time it takes to perform each task in a factory, in order to set up time standards for every job. Motion studies analyze all movements made in accomplishing each task and arrive at the most effective sequence of motions for each.

As a final comment on standards, remember that the ratios derived from analyzing the basic accounting statements (balance sheet, income statements) serve as standards for comparison, control, and further improvement. (See the section on "Ratio Analysis" in chapter 17.)

VARIANCE ANALYSIS

Variances are differences or deviations from the norm or average. After you have worked up your initial standards, the averages you have calculated from daily plant operations will appear to fluctuate. In manufacturing, you can expect all sorts of variances: labor variances, materials variances, overhead variances, and so on. As an illustration, those standards you have developed for materials used in production can vary because of poor handling and storage, changes in the purchase price, inadequately serviced equipment, fluctuations in quality, and the like.

For each of the major cost areas (labor often being the most significant), you'll have to decide just how much tolerance, or deviation from the standard, you can permit. When variances are analyzed—compared to the standards you have decided are acceptable—those that exceed tolerable limits should be investigated thoroughly and corrective action taken at once. Often, better production planning and flow control, improved maintenance, and more training for factory personnel can be helpful here. Then, too, *network techniques* such as Critical Path Method (CPM) and Program Evaluation and Review Techniques (PERT) may occasionally prove useful.

Helpful steps for improving plant productivity include upgrading the quality of the labor component (through further training, better hiring practices, more skilled supervision); moving in the direction of semiautomation through the purchase of additional machinery and equipment (and introducing computers); and making sizable capital expenditures for plant expansion or improvement, additional personnel, and so forth.

SOME THOUGHTS ON UPGRADING PLANT PRODUCTIVITY

Production

In a healthy factory operation, production planning is accomplished well in advance. Better planning means increasing the accuracy of your sales forecasting. Devote lots of good thinking to this thorny problem; involve your best people in the process. It is worth your while to learn about the more popular methods companies depend on for developing their sales forecasts.*

Forecasting Techniques. Both qualitative and quantitative techniques are available. Among the qualitative approaches—which, incidentally, are frequently referred to as *judgmental* or *naive* methods—are

- *The jury of executive opinion*—a technique that involves asking your company's executives for their opinions
- *The Delphi method*—a variation of the above whereby executive judgments are reconsidered and refined by the executives over two or more resubmissions of the information
- *The salesforce composite*—a technique whereby you ask your salespeople for estimates of the amounts each individual will produce, and then tally these estimates to produce an overall forecast
- *The survey of customer intentions*—which is precisely what it sounds like

Of course, you'll need to narrow down and reconcile discrepancies in the data you collect.

Quantitative approaches make use of historical information and statistics. In addition to such quantitative techniques as trend extension and time series extrapolation, there are the correlation methods. The latter seek to tie company sales to specific variables in the economy, such as the level of consumer spending, the prime rate, and the Gross National Product. Thus we have *leading, coincident,* and *lagging* indicators, depending on whether they seem to rise or fall before, during, or after fluctuations in sales.

Prepare your production budget just as carefully as you prepare every other component of the master budget. Consider your budgets for labor, for materials, for manufacturing overhead, for maintenance, and so on.

Plot your production with great care every step of the way. Set up a foolproof production reporting system. Involve your senior people in planning, preparing work orders, routing, scheduling, expediting, and other activities.

Set specific objectives: Your quickest route to process improvement is *production-by-objectives.* Indeed, fuller utilization of all production resources leads to a higher return on investment.

Work on moving away from intermittent production and toward longer, uninterrupted machine runs. Gang orders where possible during slack periods. If your products are branded, investigate the benefits of running private-label merchandise. Build up your finished goods inventories in advance of selling seasons.

If inventory levels exceed sales or if you can foresee the need for more cash in the near future, offer "early-bird" discounts that will induce your customers to place orders earlier than usual.

*For more information, see: Robert S. Sobek, "A Manager's Primer on Forecasting," *Harvard Business Review* 51 (May-June 1973), 6–28; Earl H. Anderson, "Probabilistic Forecasting for the Small Business," *Journal of Small Business Management* 17 (June 1979), 8–13; John G. Wacker and Jane S. Cromartie, "Adapting Forecasting Methods to the Small Firm," *Journal of Small Business Management* 17 (July 1979), 1–7.

In the production process, two or more pieces of equipment are often used in sequence. The machines usually operate at different speeds; this raises the strong possibility that bottlenecks will form. Bottlenecks can be avoided by balancing the flow lines; use flow process charts and flow diagrams to work out the ideal flow of materials. Additional machinery, proper scheduling, and the application of queuing theory can all be of assistance in this problem area.

Apply cost-accounting techniques to all manufacturing operations; watch variances from all standards; take action whenever indicated; and use ratio analysis to improve efficiency.

Layout

Many small manufacturing establishments use the *process* type of layout whereby the machinery and equipment needed for each distinct type of production processing (cutting, stamping, grinding, polishing, and the like) are grouped together. This enables plants to manufacture different products on the same equipment, thus ensuring flexibility. However, there are some drawbacks: excessive materials handling costs, inefficient utilization of both machinery and labor, unnecessary delays, and so forth. By combining or anticipating orders (and by writing more business!) you may be able to introduce some line production, or *product layout,* into your manufacturing. In this kind of layout, both machinery and equipment are set up to follow a specific sequence of operations that culminate in the production of one kind of product. This will give you the best of both types of processes—namely, lower-cost production-line output and the flexibility you need to handle job lots.

Plan all layout changes yourself with the aid of a qualified consultant. Always consider your future requirements (three to five years hence); think in terms of additional facilities, offices, new electrical wiring, plumbing, waste lines, and the like. Use drawings, plans, and renderings. Machinery can be represented by templates of cardboard or other materials, and dimensions indicated on these. Scale models are also useful.

Many smaller plants have a U-shaped layout where both the shipping and receiving departments are at the same end of the factory. This way, the same loading area and single bay can be used for both purposes. These setups are often supervised by one person.

Machinery and Equipment

Survey all machinery: Check performance records, purchase dates, and warrantees. Replace antiquated equipment or machines of below-par performance with newer models of higher capacity. Remember that used equipment is often costlier in the long term.

When considering new machinery, strive for trouble-free operation, good-quality work and materials, reliable performance, and a good service contract with the manufacturer. Where possible, deal directly with the manufacturer and not with the distributor.

If not already in existence, a strict preventive maintenance program should be instituted. This should include regular inspections, prompt repairs, and spare parts on hand for important equipment. Work out procedures and even backup equipment for floods, power failures, fires, and other major events that could affect production.

Leasing arrangements are at times (when cash is "tight" or interest charges are low) more beneficial than outright purchases of equipment, especially those that provide options to buy.

All maintenance supplies and tools should be controlled with a careful recordkeeping system. Maintenance personnel should represent a range of skills and should include electricians, carpenters, machinists, and mechanics (depending upon the particular needs of your plant).

Materials Handling

Where possible, contract for six months' or a year's supply of materials that you use in large quantities. Make sure that the price you pay is guaranteed for the life of the contract and that quantity discounts apply. Have deliveries made to your plant as they are needed.

Materials are forever being moved about within a factory. All types of power equipment and conveyors are available for this purpose. Suppliers will submit various proposals to you over the year; evaluate all of them with an eye to economizing on movement and thereby increasing plant efficiency.

Follow two principles commonly used by experienced warehouse people: The *straight-line principle* teaches you to minimize the distances materials must travel within a plant (not adhering slavishly to straight lines but avoiding sideways or backwards movements). The *unit load principle* holds that the greater the quantity of merchandise moved at the same time, the less it costs to move each individual item in the load (usually palletized).

Many kinds of materials used in manufacturing require special care: handling precautions, proper storage containers, temperature-controlled and/or moisture-free atmosphere, ventilation (or lack of it), specially built tanks or drums, and so forth. Proper attention to these needs prevents deterioration, spoilage, and other "wastage" of materials.

In this connection, plastic and fiber containers can frequently be used to replace more expensive and heavier items such as steel drums.

Personnel

Productivity improvement in a manufacturing plant should begin with your employees. Having the right people, with the right skills and the proper training, in the right positions within your organization, lays a strong foundation for eventual improvement.

If your company does not already have them on hand, written and detailed job specifications should be prepared for all positions. New hires should be matched against those specifications. If at all possible, try to hire people who are proficient in two or more skill areas. This way, you can build valuable flexibility into the personnel component.

Set up an operations manual as a guide for your people. Seek a professional personnel specialist to help you produce this guide.

At all times, train your employees in good work habits. Then, insist on careful adherence to rules and instructions. Don't tolerate sloppy performance.

Strive for good management-worker relations, and safe and comfortable working conditions. Encourage worker input and suggestions.

If yours is a one-shift operation that runs for five days each week, this means that your machines are lying idle for sixteen hours a day on weekdays and twenty-four hours per day over the weekend. Aim at building up business to the point at which two shifts are needed (perhaps 8 A.M. to 4 P.M. and 4 P.M. to 12 midnight). This will bring your per-item overhead costs down sharply.

Quality Control

The quality-control function in manufacturing is an essential one. Ordinarily, its foremost application is to the product or products being made. It's used to detect inferior or defective work early enough so that adjustments can be made quickly in production. Indeed, quality control should embrace all purchased raw, semifinished, or finished materials used in the plant, and equipment, machinery, and supplies as well.

In a small plant, there's often no quality-control department per se, simply one or several technicians who perform necessary tests and report the results to the production head.

It's not unusual for a small manufacturer to request that suppliers conduct quality-control tests on their materials before shipping them. This is a helpful type of arrangement that will save you time and money. (It's wise to verify the results from time to time yourself.)

IMPROVING YOUR SALES EFFORTS

In the beginning, the new manufacturer may rely on his or her own efforts (or those of partners) to obtain the company's first regular customers. Later on, the firm will most likely select one or more manufacturer's representatives to take charge of the selling end of the business, thus leaving the owner(s) more time to concentrate on production.

Eventually, a sales force may be initiated. While the salient details of managing a sales force have already been treated (see chapter 14), the following description of the selling process itself may provide small plant managers with insights leading to improved results in the direct selling area.

Good selling is often tied to the well-known *AIDA Principle.* In this case, the name of an opera is employed as a mnemonic to help you remember the following key words:

*A*ttention—Your first task is to secure the attention of your prospect.

*I*nterest—Next, you must arouse his or her interest in knowing more about what you're selling.

Desire—You then begin to build desire on the prospect's part to have what you're selling.

Action—Finally, you get action by securing the order.

To a large extent, good selling is also based on the so-called *needs-satisfaction approach.* Simply put, this means that you (1) ascertain the customer's wants and needs, (2) match the proper selection of merchandise to meet those needs, (3) show the prospect what those products can do for him or her, and (4) convince the person to buy.

The Selling Process

The job of personal or direct selling can be more easily understood if it is broken down into a series of steps. Then, by applying both analytical and creative thinking to each of these steps in succession, a new salesperson can develop a professionalism and skill that will improve his or her sales results:

Prospecting. The salesperson knows how to look for potential customers and knows where to hunt for them.

Qualifying. (Also called the *preapproach*). During this step the salesperson tries to find out as much as he or she can about the prospect, so that the presentation can be tailored to the prospect's needs.

The Approach. This is the first contact with the prospect, normally conceived of as the first minute or so after meeting the prospect. Among the better-known approaches (and rather easy to comprehend, just from the titles) are the introductory, referral, and product approaches.

The Presentation. This is the main exposition regarding the product or service being sold. The salesperson shows the prospect what the product or service can do for him or her, brings out all of its selling points, involves the prospect in the presentation (touching and feeling the materials, trying out the item, and so on), and tries to answer all the questions raised during the sales interview.

Meeting Objections. Almost always, the prospective buyer will raise several objections during the presentation. A crucial factor in the selling process is the proper handling of such objections: How you handle them can make or break the sale. The majority of objections fall into one or another of the following classifications: objections to price, objections to the quality or workmanship of the product, objections about the firm the salesperson represents, and, perhaps, objections to the salesperson him- or herself. A large percentage of intermediate or advanced training time is devoted to teaching sales personnel how to counter the more common objections.

The Close. This is the culmination of the presentation, the point at which the order is written. There are any number of "closes" to use in different situations; any good book on selling will familarize you with at least half a dozen.

The Follow-Up. Writing up the order doesn't end the selling process. Before departing, the experienced salesperson thanks the customer for the order and promises to call the customer shortly after the order has been delivered to check that everything is satisfactory. In the final analysis, the key to sales success is *repeat business* over the long term.

You can be sure that the right training will contribute substantially toward improving your employees' selling skills. Bear in mind, too, that you can take some rather specific steps to increase your firm's sales volume. For one thing, you can devise a type of compensation plan that accents and rewards productivity. For another, although you need to get rid of unproductive salespeople quickly, you should use everything at your command to ensure that your top producers remain with you.* You might also improve revenues by reviewing the production records of individual salespeople and by reassigning territories.**

Managing the Sales Office

An essential element in the marketing of goods by the manufacturing (or, for that matter, the wholesaling) organization is the company's inside sales office. This is where orders from field sales representatives arrive each day. They may come by mail, be called in over the telephone, or be brought in by salespeople or messengers. Typically, the orders are "logged," or registered, and then routed through the firm's customary order-handling procedure—perhaps being forwarded first to the credit section for approval, then to the shipping department to be filled, and thereafter to bookkeeping where packing slips and invoices are made out.

To ensure a healthy operation, the sales office must be run efficiently. Incoming orders should be processed quickly and accurately. The office staff needs to keep current with just about every phase of operations: orders, prices, terms, special promotions in effect and those planned for the future, the salespeople in the field, and so forth. These inside people need to keep in close touch with customers as well; they must be able to respond intelligently to questions and to make suggestions, when necessary.

As is the case with offices of any type, of course, improvements can be effected in the sales office, too. Little more is required than a detailed study of the existing situation, reference to one or two good books on office management

---

*Charles M. Futrell and A. Parasuraman, "The Relationship of Satisfaction and Performance to Salesforce Turnover," *Journal of Marketing* 48 (Fall 1984), 33–40.

**Raymond W. La Forge, David W. Cravens, and Clifford E. Young, "Improving Salesforce Productivity," *Business Horizons* 28 (September-October 1985), 50–59.

(or the hiring of a consultant on a temporary basis), and the development of a list of worthwhile suggestions for upgrading office productivity.

You may find the recommendations below of some value when you get ready to undertake this task:

1. Start by keeping close track of your own work activities for a week or ten days. Record everything you do, hour by hour and day by day.

2. Next, pore over the detailed schedule you have kept. At this point, your main objective should be to begin working toward a sensible reorganization of your workload. You also need to think in terms of prioritizing the many tasks you need to perform. Even though this may prove difficult for you to do, you should learn to make order of these tasks—from most essential to least essential.

3. Bear in mind that your time—like everyone else's time—is limited. You must learn how to manage your time ably, how to make maximum use of it.

4. In this context, delegation can be a tremendous asset to you. It's also a vital tool in helping to reduce your workload.

   If you do not already know how to do so, learn how to give work out—at least most of the work that others can perform and that need not (and ought not) be performed by you.

5. Learn how to make decisions. Don't procrastinate; never put off till tomorrow any decision you can arrive at today.

6. Be sure to teach your managers how to make their own decisions and how to delegate in turn to their assistants.

7. Finally, review your office equipment and furnishings, your internal systems, the stationery and office forms you use, and so forth with an inquisitive eye toward raising productivity.

MANUFACTURING AND EDP

Much has been written about the value of installing electronic data processing (EDP) equipment in the manufacturing company. Indeed, you'll probably be visited by zealous systems salespeople who'll try to convince you that their equipment will work wonders for your firm. Refuse to allow yourself to be convinced easily; wait until your new enterprise is firmly established and shows steady growth.

Of course, we do recognize that any number of activities can be efficiently managed by EDP equipment: payroll, bookkeeping, purchasing, inventory management, sales forecasting, and so forth. EDP is generally much faster and more accurate than clerical processing. But there are several choices here for the small business: using a service bureau, time-sharing, or purchasing a computer (mini- or micro-).*

Service Bureaus

The service bureau has both trained computer operators and programmers on its staff. For a small business, records such as journals, check registers, accounts receivable, accounts payable, and major financial statements can be computerized. Even reports such as inventory and payroll can be put out. Two types of charges are made by the bureau: one for designing a program that suits your needs, the other for processing the data. (You'll be required to deliver the source documents to the bureau regularly; these include journal entries, receipts, sales slips, checks, and the like.) The programming charge is usually a one-time fee, which runs from a few hundred dollars to as high as one thousand dollars or more. The bureau might offer you a standard programming package, in which case you'll have to adapt your recordkeeping system to the required format. The typical processing charge for a small company runs to several hundred dollars a month.

Time Sharing

In time sharing, a terminal is installed on your premises and connected to a computer over telephone wires. Operating this terminal doesn't require the assistance of a computer specialist. Costs are moderate; they depend upon the amount of computer time used and include a relatively low rental charge. Your accountant, banker, or trade association can put you in touch with either a service bureau or a time-sharing arrangement.

Microcomputers

Tremendous strides have been made in EDP equipment over the past several decades. Once room-sized and even larger, computers have evolved dramatically to mini- and micro-models—including desktop and even lap-held types. An entire spectrum of these useful machines is now available; costs can range from more than $1 million (for a giant installation) down to as little as a few hundred dollars. Yes, the smaller machines have come down in price to the point at which even a small business might be able to afford one. Nowadays, for well under three thousand dollars, you can purchase a good PC (personal computer) that can handle just about all the tasks that need to be managed in

---

*The following articles offer some useful insights into the question of computerization for the small business owner: Leo L. Pipino and Charles R. Necco, "A Systematic Approach to the Small Organization's Computer Decision," *Journal of Small Business Management* 19 (July 1981), 8–16; James A. Senn and Virginia R. Gibson, "Risks of Investment in Microcomputers for Small Business Management," *Journal of Small Business Management* 19 (July 1981), 24–34.

your business. For this price you can acquire the necessary hardware, software, and even some of the supplies you will need.

The term *hardware* designates the computer itself—the cabinet and its contents: circuits, chips, and so on, including the central processing unit (CPU) that executes programs and processes information, the keyboard (input device), and a printer (output device).

As to the *software,* many hundreds of helpful programs, easy to understand and simple to run, are available for preparing your basic accounting statements (P&Ls, balance sheets); for keeping records of your firm's accounts payable and receivable; for writing correspondence or addressing envelopes for mailings; for filing; and so forth.

Moreover, little training or skill is needed to run these microcomputers. More and more, PCs are being profitably used by doctors, dentists, accountants, attorneys, and other professionals. Owners of home-based businesses also find them of value. Indeed, the cost is so low that many small business managers have one PC at their place of business and a second at home.

FOR FURTHER INFORMATION

Books

Ballou, Ronald H. *Business Logistics Management: Planning and Control,* 2d ed. Englewood Cliffs, N.J.: Prentice-Hall, 1985.

Corey, E. *Industrial Marketing: Cases and Concepts,* 3d ed. Englewood Cliffs, N.J.: Prentice-Hall, 1983.

Hayes, Rick S., and Gregory B. Elmore. *Marketing for Your Growing Small Business.* New York: Wiley, 1985.

Johnson, H. Webster, and Anthony J. Faria. *Creative Selling,* 4th ed. Cincinnati: South-Western, 1987.

Johnson, James C., and Donald F. Wood. *Contemporary Physical Distribution and Logistics,* 3d ed. New York: Macmillan, 1986.

Kordahl, Eugene. *Telemarketing for Business.* Englewood Cliffs, N.J.: Prentice-Hall, 1984.

Laufer, A. C. *Production and Operations Management,* 3d ed. Cincinnati: South-Western, 1984.

Lee, Lamar, Jr., and David N. Burt. *Purchasing and Materials Management: Text and Cases,* 4th ed. New York: McGraw-Hill, 1984.

McClain, John, and L. Joseph Thomas. *Operations Management: Production of Goods and Services,* 2d ed. Englewood Cliffs, N.J.: Prentice-Hall, 1985.

Mali, Paul. *Improving Total Productivity.* New York: Wiley, 1978.

Reynolds, Helen, and Mary E. Tramel. *Executive Time Management: Getting 12 Hours' Work Out of an 8-Hour Day.* Englewood Cliffs, N.J.: Prentice-Hall, 1979.

Rohrs, W., and R. Colton. *Industrial Purchasing and Effective Materials Management.* Englewood Cliffs, N.J.: Prentice-Hall, 1985.

Rosenbloom, Bert. *Marketing Channels: A Management View,* 3d ed. New York: Dryden, 1987.

Rothschild, Michael. *Advertising: From Fundamentals to Strategies.* Lexington, Mass.: D. C. Heath, 1987.

Shonberger, Richard J. *Operations Management: Productivity and Quality,* 2d ed. Plano, Tex.: Business Publications, 1985.

Stanley, Richard E. *Promotion: Advertising, Publicity, Personal Selling, Sales Promotion,* 2d ed. Englewood Cliffs, N.J.: Prentice-Hall, 1982.

Storholm, G., and L. Kaufman. *Principles of Selling.* Englewood Cliffs, N.J.: Prentice-Hall, 1985.

Stroh, Thomas F. *Managing the Sales Function.* New York: McGraw-Hill, 1978.

Pamphlets Available from the Small Business Administration

MANAGEMENT AIDS

MA 1.017—"Keeping Records in Small Business"
MA 2.011—"Fixing Production Mistakes"
MA 2.014—"Should You Lease or Buy Equipment?"
MA 3.010—"Techniques for Problem Solving"
MA 4.002—"Creative Selling: The Competitive Edge"
MA 4.005—"Is the Independent Sales Agent for You?"
MA 5.009—"Techniques for Productivity Improvement"
MA 7.003—"Market Overseas with U.S. Government Help"

Booklets Available from the Superintendent of Documents

S/N 045-000-00133-4—*Training Salesmen to Serve Industrial Markets*—$2.50.

S/N 045-000-00151-2—*Management Audit for Small Manufacturers*—$4.25.

S/N 045-000-00167-9—*Purchasing Management and Inventory Control for Small Business*—$4.50.

S/N 045-000-00176-8—*Managing Fixed Assets*—$4.75.

S/N 045-000-00181-4—*Purchasing for Manufacturing Firms*—$4.75.

S/N 045-000-00182-2—*Inventory Management—Manufacturing, Service*—$4.75.

S/N 045-000-00183-1—*Inventory and Scheduling Techniques*—$4.75.

S/N 045-000-00187-3—*Cost Control*—$4.75.

S/N 045-000-00188-1—*Marketing Strategy*—$4.75.

S/N 045-000-00195-4—*Understanding Costs*—$3.25.

23

Improving Results in Your Wholesale Business

As you will recall from the discussion of marketing channels in chapter 15, a large majority of wholesaling establishments in the country are classified as *merchant wholesalers.* The remainder include manufacturers' sales branches and offices, petroleum bulk terminals, agents and brokers, and assemblers. Since these latter types make up fewer than one-third of all wholesale distributors, the improvements suggested in this chapter are oriented toward the more prevalent type—the merchant wholesaler. Nevertheless, much of the information presented here can be of value to the other kinds of wholesalers as well.

Let's begin with a typical organizational chart for a small merchant wholesaler operation. Exhibit 23–1 is fairly representative of this type of distributor in the grocery, automotive equipment, hardware, or electrical supplies business. By studying this chart, we can arrive at a simple conclusion: To improve the firm's operating results, we should seek improvement within all four major areas of activity, namely, purchasing, warehouse operations, sales, and office management.

In order to end up with a better operating statement, you'll need to

- Buy better.
- Sell better.
- Improve internal operations.

Since both purchasing and sales were dealt with extensively in earlier chapters (10, 14, 22), little more will be added here on those two subjects. (However, you should reread the appropriate sections of those chapters on techniques for improving the purchasing and sales aspects of your business.) The concentration here is on improving internal operations, for this is the one area where able management, better procedures and systems, and improved controls can really work wonders.

EXHIBIT 23-1. SMALL MERCHANT WHOLESALER ORGANIZATION CHART

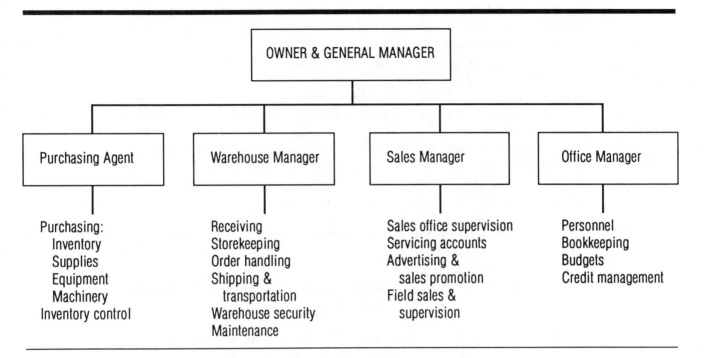

INTERNAL OPERATIONS
REVOLVE AROUND ORDERS

To maximize productivity and minimize costs, most internal operations should be designed for the sole purpose of facilitating the delivery of goods to the wholesaler's accounts. There are, then, two primary components to be coordinated: (1) the entire order flow system and (2) those auxiliary structures—such as departments and the warehouse itself—that enable the order flow system to operate.

THE ORDER FLOW SYSTEM

Except for assemblers of farm products, most wholesale companies buy goods in large quantities and then break down their inventory into smaller lots for resale to other enterprises. Since these latter types (retailers, service businesses, and so forth) require frequent, repeat deliveries, the typical wholesale distributor can count on receiving hundreds of orders every month—if not every week—of the year.

This is all the more reason why the successful merchant wholesaler gives prompt attention and quick, dependable service to incoming orders. Ideally, every incoming order should be filled and the merchandise sent on its way to its destination within forty-eight hours. However, delays and bottlenecks are characteristically encountered. This is especially true when orders come into the house in heavy quantities, as happens before a holiday season or specific holidays, or when there isn't enough labor available to fill them, or when the customary transportation facilities are overburdened.

Another fairly common problem among wholesaling firms is occasionally losing track of orders as they are processed through the internal system. When customers phone in to inquire about the current status of their orders or to add or subtract merchandise, the result is confusion and upsetting delay for both customer and supplier.

These and other problems can be avoided 95 percent of the time if you give the situation some time, diligent study, and careful thought. To help you streamline your order flow system, consider the following breakdown of its various stages and apply some thought to each one:

1. *The Order Form.* A lot of time can be saved and careless omissions or errors avoided when the order form itself is carefully tailored to the needs of your organization. Preferably, it should be prepared (or revised) with the assistance of a specialist in business forms. Preprinted snap-out carbon sets will effect substantial savings for you.

2. *Order Writing.* All sales representatives must be thoroughly trained to complete the order form properly. This applies not only to the field sales force but also to any inside salespeople. Terms, discounts, names and addresses, delivery information, and all special instructions must be written legibly. Poorly written-out order forms, or forms with mistakes, should be acted on immediately. Salespeople should be called in such instances and reproved. You must constantly keep on top of this kind of carelessness if you want to stop it.

3. *Forwarding Orders.* It's essential that orders gathered by the field sales force are transmitted as quickly as possible to the home office. A delay of even a day or two can result in customer dissatisfaction. If the sales representative's territory is within an hour's drive of the office, a good procedure is to have that salesperson deliver the day's orders in person, either immediately after completing rounds or early the next morning before starting out again.

   Of course, if the sales force operates at substantial distances from the home office, this cannot be done. Indeed, many organizations prefer to keep their salespeople constantly in the field to maximize selling time. With this method, orders must be mailed in each evening. An even better procedure is to assign specific "call-in times" to individual salespeople during the evening hours; they can then telephone their orders to a night clerk or, preferably, a recording machine. The actual order forms are then mailed in the next morning.

4. *Receiving Orders.* Regardless of the method employed in getting the orders to the office (in-person, mail, or telephone), there should be a central clerk to receive all orders. It is this person's responsibility to check all

orders for accuracy, clarity, conformance with company policy, and so forth. Those that contain mistakes or omissions should be put aside for rechecking later. This clerk must be instructed to record every order on a *daily order sheet* (which can be mimeographed or printed). Each day's sheets should have columns for writing in the order number, the time received, the customer's name, and perhaps the salesperson's initials. Additional columns should be used to indicate the routing of the order (including the time sent) to its next stop along the system.

5. *Processing Orders.* If additional copies of the order are needed (other than the set forwarded by the sales representative), avoid transcribing the information. A good office copier will speed up your operation; this fact, plus the convenience of the machine for copying other documents, more than offsets the purchase cost. Usually, all copies go first to the internal sales department where prices are checked, then to the credit desk for an okay. After approval, they're sent on to the warehouse for filling.

6. *Filling Orders.* On receiving the order, the warehouse supervisor should register it in a log book and then check over its details. At this point, priorities and routing considerations tend to be taken into account. With respect to routing, transportation "runs" to different areas are usually scheduled for different days of the week or month. Orders destined for those areas can accumulate in different boxes or trays.

Orders are distributed as the order pickers become available. These pickers then select the merchandise called for in the order. Various types of handling equipment—dollies, carts of different kinds, conveyors, even moving belts—can facilitate movement of the merchandise from the warehouse proper to the staging area. (Therefore, good warehouse layout and proper utilization of space can be of value in increasing the pickers' speed in filling orders.)

Work tables, corrugated cartons, tape, and other materials must be conveniently available when special packing arrangements are called for.

All outgoing orders, of course, should be carefully double-checked before loading.

ENABLING ACTIVITIES

Chapter 10 described such facets of operations as receiving, stockkeeping, shipping, and maintenance (albeit in connection with the manufacturing plant), while chapter 19 offered useful information about how to protect company premises. Here are just a few additional pointers on transportation and warehouse security.

Transportation

It's well worth your while to conduct a review of the entire area of transportation with the assistance of a physical distribution specialist. Investigate the pros and cons of using your own trucks versus common carriers or leased equipment. Are transportation costs adequately reflected in your current prices? Are your terms F.O.B. (Free on Board) warehouse or destination? You may consider geographical zoning in setting up your prices or arrange a flat charge per shipment (based either on total weight or a percentage of the total invoice cost).

Warehouse Security

You can always brush up on security arrangements for your premises, especially with regard to doors, locks, and key control, lighting, and the like. Review the information in chapter 19 on techniques for maintaining tight security.

Unhappily, employee stealing (*pilferage* is much too weak a term in this case!) is all too common in wholesale operations. Often, this type of theft involves collusion on the part of two or more persons. Sometimes one of them is a supervisor. Tight controls must be instituted in order to contain this type of problem. No merchandise should be moved—from the warehouse proper to the ready stocks area to the shipping department—without attendant paperwork. Moreover, those records should be carefully scrutinized on a daily basis by office personnel. If stealing is suspected, you might consider planting an undercover detective in the warehouse to work alongside the others, perhaps as an order picker.

Instruct all warehouse employees to enter and leave the premises through the same doorway. Station a security guard at that location at all times; this will help curtail the amount of merchandise that "walks out" with the help. Needless to say, security checks should be run on all workers before they are hired; this, too, will help hold down your rate of shrinkage.

Other preventive measures include fencing off the receiving and shipping areas, keeping unauthorized people out of those departments, making certain that truck bays are well illuminated both inside and outside of the building, and spot-checking incoming shipments and outgoing deliveries at different times (both day and night) and on different days of the week.

INVENTORY CONTROL

The order flow system can be adequately fueled and kept in continuous motion only if inventory levels are skillfully controlled. This means you must at all times maintain as complete an inventory as is needed to meet your customers' requirements. As you know, this is no simple feat.

Especially in the wholesale trades, inventory represents a major financial commitment. An overloaded inventory poses a serious threat to your cash position; hence, the continued need to buy merchandise at the most economical prices and under the most favorable terms. Yet, it isn't only the actual purchase costs that tie up your capital but also expenses like insurance, storage, handling, damage or spoilage, and taxes, as well as the very cost of maintaining good inventory records. For these reasons, you should decide right now to weed out and liquidate all slow-selling items so that you will end up about six months from now with a lean yet sturdy stock of fast-moving merchandise.

This kind of product-line review ought to be conducted every year; the end result will surely be appreciably faster turnover and more profit. It's true that a wholesaler is often reluctant to drop certain items from the line which it has supplied for years only out of courtesy, for fear of losing some customers' business altogether. While this attitude is understandable, it doesn't stand up very well in the face of logical business acumen.

Referring back to the now-familiar eighty-twenty principle (chapter 12), if you carry as many as 2,000 different items in your warehouse, it's likely that fewer than 400 of them account for as much as 80 percent of your yearly sales. Logically extended, this means that you now maintain an inventory of around 1,600 products just to produce one-fifth of your current sales.

Seems wasteful, doesn't it?

Your inventory control system should be organized to provide you with all the information you need to make sensible decisions about your product line.

ABC Analysis

One way to accomplish this might be to classify your products by merchandise type (for example: staple goods, seasonal items, perishable merchandise) as well as by dollar value. Then, you can examine your turnover records for the past year and divide each of these three categories into three groups, according to sales movement: fast, moderate, and slow movers. You'll want to keep close tabs on the first group of items (fast movers) in each classification by maintaining a perpetual inventory of them. There's little practical value in doing the same for the second group, and none whatsoever for the slow-selling merchandise. Indeed, these last two are best handled by occasional inventory checks.

In this regard, a government publication that deals with inventory control in wholesaling provides a method for classification.* It suggests you initiate a card file and prepare a classification card for every item you carry. In addition to the item number and description at the top, the card should contain three columns for filling in (1) the annual quantity used of that item, (2) the cost per unit, and (3) the *dollar usage-value* (the unit cost multiplied by the annual quantity used).

The leaflet explains the technique further:

> After you have cards for all items, put them in a file box according to dollar usage. Put those with the highest dollar usage-value in front as though you were counting from 100 down to 1.
>
> Now, you are ready to divide your inventory according to dollar usage. Start from the high usage-value end of the stack and measure off 15 percent of the length of the stack. Pull up a card for an indicator. From that indicator measure off another 20 percent of the length of the stack. The remainder of the stack is, of course, 65 percent.
>
> The first segment (15 percent) of the cards represents items which account for the bulk of your annual sales volume. The next segment (20 percent) is your medium usage-value items. The remainder of the stock (65 percent) represents items which add little to your sales volume but a lot to your inventory costs.

*"Controlling Inventory in Small Wholesale Firms," *Small Marketers Aid No. 122* (Washington, D.C.: U. S. Small Business Administration, 1966).

Other valuable details are contained in this publication, including data on perpetual inventory records, bin reserve, and when (and how much) to order.*

SALES ANALYSES AND EXPENSE CONTROL

Regular, frequent sales analyses ought to be part of your modus operandi. These are vital for effective stock planning and control, for generating recommendations for increasing sales volume, and for holding down expenses.

In the area of merchandising, we have already touched on the merits of analyzing inventory movement item by item, both by unit and by total dollar contribution to sales. The sales area is the place where a perceptive and aggressive management can make the most headway.

A number of different tactics can be taken here. Sales and expenses may be investigated from a variety of vantage points: Those of the customer, the salespeople, company finances, and geography are among the most common.

Typically, the customer list may be broken down by type of firm, size (in assets value), annual volume of purchases placed with the wholesaler, location, and other characteristics. The results of such analyses are useful in the decision-making process, in establishing objectives, and in setting plans for business growth. (This also holds true for other types of sales analyses.) You can take steps to measure the relative performances of all salespeople (individually as well as collectively) in the number of accounts opened each month, average size of orders taken, total contribution to gross profit or sales, expenses incurred, dollar value of orders returned, and the like. Or you can analyze the *territorial yield,* that is, obtain the same data indicated above but examine the results from the various sales territories instead of from the individual salespeople.

PUSHING UP SALES

In chapter 14 we explored in considerable depth the three vital ingredients of the promotion mix: advertising, personal (direct) selling, and sales promotion. More specifics on direct selling appeared in chapter 22; and more details are yet to come, in the next chapter. Despite this rather extensive treatment of the entire promotion area, there are still additional steps to be taken that are singularly appropriate for the wholesaling company.

At the very core of these approaches lies the raison d'être of your operation: *to render services to your customers.* Indeed, you ought to adopt this simple concept as your motto. Internalize the thought; make it part and parcel of every action you take; accept it as your prime directive. If you can convince your customers—and new prospects as well—that you can be of more value to them than your competitors, you'll have little difficulty boosting that sales curve of yours!

*For more information about ABC analysis, refer to: William L. Fuerst, "Small Businesses Get a New Look at ABC Analysis for Inventory Control," *Journal of Small Business Management* 19 (July 1981), 39–44.

This is within your grasp *if* you broaden the list of services you now offer, either by adding to that list or by improving on the quality of those services. You should preferably aim at doing both.

As an illustration, here's a representative list of services that may be offered by the merchant wholesaler. Match them against your current offerings, one by one:

- Introduce your customers to modern methods of stock control.
- Provide them with instructional materials on all aspects of managing their operations.
- Once or twice each year, run problem-solving clinics where your customers can talk over mutual business problems.
- If you make use of EDP equipment, offer assistance in stockplanning and inventory counts.
- Furnish stands, display racks, signs, and other point-of-purchase materials at nominal cost or (if possible) free of charge.
- Keep your customers abreast of newer methods and techniques that they can apply in their own businesses, through your salespeople and perhaps through a monthly newsletter.
- Offer more favorable payment terms and (without going overboard) higher credit limits than your competitors.
- As a service, offer free newspaper mats (or templates) of professionally prepared advertisements, making sure to leave space for the individual retailer's name and address. (The same treatment, incidentally, can be accorded to brochures, flyers, and catalogs.)
- Give extended terms and small loans to financially troubled businesses; this kind of service can help cement long-term relationships.
- Organize occasional contest promotions; they can create both retailer and consumer excitement and boost sales. "Demonstrators" (people sent to stores to demonstrate one or more products to shoppers) and "PMs" ("Push Money," a promotional technique whereby retail salespeople earn small sums of money for "pushing" a particular product) are also helpful.
- Customers outside your territorial coverage can be serviced by mail through your wholesale catalog and order form. It's sometimes worthwhile to open a "cash-and-carry" branch in a distant city where there is sufficient demand for your products to warrant such an outlet.

As a final thought, don't overlook the public relations value of maintaining close contact with your customers. You can build rapport with them via newsletter, but it's far better to get out of your office as often as you can to visit them in person.

BETTER OFFICE MANAGEMENT

As concerned citizens, we chafe against the sluggishness of bureaucracy. We rant about the red tape that ties its operations into knots. We applaud ongoing efforts to extricate government agencies from the mountainous paper blitz that practically immobilizes their activity, wishing ever so strongly that those agencies could be run more like private enterprise.

Sometimes it seems that the merchant wholesaler is the private sector's counterpart to a government agency. For there are mounds of paperwork in a wholesale operation. Some of it is necessary; other paperwork can and should be discarded. Not only are there customary accounts to keep track of (like payables, and the larger number of receivables) but the whole, intricate affair of controlling both merchandise and order flow is also in and of itself a tremendous task. In addition, the operation requires bounteous correspondence and collection letters ad infinitum for delinquent accounts.

Other than the obvious techniques of good human resources administration, the answers to better office management lie in the study, systematization, and elimination of paperwork, and the introduction of specialized office equipment to save time and labor. (Review the section on electronic data processing in the preceding chapter.)

Paperwork

Errors in paperwork can be costly. Here we are referring not only to typographical errors but also to errors in manual writing, beginning with the initial order written by the salesperson, through the transcription and processing of the order, to all the internal forms used for conducting business. Delays, too, can be costly. So can an office with too many typists, stenographers, and other clerical help for the quantity of work present. You need a capable office manager well versed in organizational methods to set objectives (together, of course, with the employees), to uphold performance standards, and to monitor output. If necessary, an outside consultant might be brought in to help in the process.

The following factors, among others, can affect the output of your office staff:

The working environment: poor ventilation, heating, or lighting; uncomfortable chairs, desks; poor sanitary conditions; too much noise or activity; and so on.

The management itself: unclear company goals, little or no supervision, faulty management attitudes and poor personnel relations, incapable management, poor personnel recruitment and selection policies, and the like.

The employees themselves: lack of experience, poor training, ineptitude at mathematics or poor writing skills, personal and emotional problems, and the like.

The system: improperly worked-out methods, badly designed forms, poorly functioning office equipment, a predominance of "rush jobs," and so on.

FOR FURTHER INFORMATION

Books

Ballou, Ronald H. *Business Logistics Management: Planning and Control,* 2d ed. Englewood Cliffs, N.J.: Prentice-Hall, 1985.

Barkas, J. L. *Creative Time Management.* Englewood Cliffs, N.J.: Prentice-Hall, 1984.

Corey, E. *Industrial Marketing: Cases and Concepts,* 3d ed. Englewood Cliffs, N.J.: Prentice-Hall, 1983.

Danenburg, William P., Russell L. Moncrief, and William E. Taylor. *Introduction to Wholesale Distribution.* Englewood Cliffs, N.J.: Prentice-Hall, 1978.

Heinritz, Stuart F., et al. *Purchasing: Principles and Applications,* 7th ed. Englewood Cliffs, N.J.: Prentice-Hall, 1986.

Johnson, H. Webster, and Anthony J. Faria. *Creative Selling,* 4th ed. Cincinnati: South-Western, 1987.

Johnson, James C., and Donald F. Wood. *Contemporary Physical Distribution and Logistics,* 3d ed. New York: Macmillan, 1986.

Kallaus, Norman F., and B. Lewis Keeling. *Administrative Office Management,* 9th ed. Cincinnati: South-Western, 1987.

Rosenbloom, Bert. *Marketing Channels: A Management View,* 3d ed. New York: Dryden, 1987.

Stanley, Richard E. *Promotion: Advertising, Publicity, Personal Selling, Sales Promotion,* 2d ed. Englewood Cliffs, N.J.: Prentice-Hall, 1982.

Welch, Joe L., and Charles Lapp. *Sales Force Management.* Cincinnati: South-Western, 1983.

Pamphlets Available from the Small Business Administration

MANAGEMENT AIDS

MA 1.011—"Analyze Your Records to Reduce Costs"
MA 1.017—"Keeping Records in Small Business"
MA 2.014—"Should You Lease or Buy Equipment?"
MA 3.010—"Techniques for Problem Solving"
MA 4.002—"Creative Selling: The Competitive Edge"
MA 5.009—"Techniques for Productivity Improvement"

Booklets Available from the Superintendent of Documents

S/N 045-000-00133-4—*Training Salesmen to Serve Industrial Markets*—$2.50.
S/N 045-000-00167-9—*Purchasing Management and Inventory Control for Small Business*—$4.50.
S/N 045-000-00187-3—*Cost Control*—$4.75.
S/N 045-000-00190-3—*Inventory Management, Wholesale/Retail*—$4.50.
S/N 045-000-00196-2—*Employee Relations and Personnel Policies*—$4.50.

24

Improving Results in Your Retail Store

The average small store is shaped much like a shoe box with a top, bottom, and sides. At one end are the entrance and show window; at the other, a partition and back room. Its inner surfaces are lined with ceiling, flooring, and wall coverings. The store also contains fixtures, merchandise, displays, store personnel, and, hopefully, shoppers.

This description is accurate wherever the store is located: on a busy thoroughfare in downtown Los Angeles or midtown Manhattan, on a neighborhood shopping street, in a strip or regional shopping center, or in an off-street location.

In brief, your store and all its sundry parts combine to form a selling system. As with any other system (or machine), if you improve one or more of its parts, chances are excellent that the system's entire output will increase. To help you maintain a clear, conceptual overview of your business, study the chart in exhibit 24–1.

If you're serious about improving your retail operation—and netting more profit by the end of the year—then a good approach is to tackle each of the seven major areas indicated in the chart, preferably one at a time. There are two "prime directives" that you'll need to bear in mind at all times: (1) increase your sales and (2) lower your costs. Only from these two directions can any real improvement come. A combination of the two produces the best results. As you know, however, the second direction is by far the less important of the two. Certain expenses, such as rent, cannot be reduced; among the "reducible" ones, you'll only be able to go so far and no further. Of course, you should always try to hold down your controllable expenses.

Reducing costs will indeed increase net profit, assuming your sales volume remains intact. Yet, what about next year—and the year after that? If you want your business to grow, then you obviously must increase your sales over time.

When it comes down to reality, there are only two ways to take in more

EXHIBIT 24-1. Retail store management

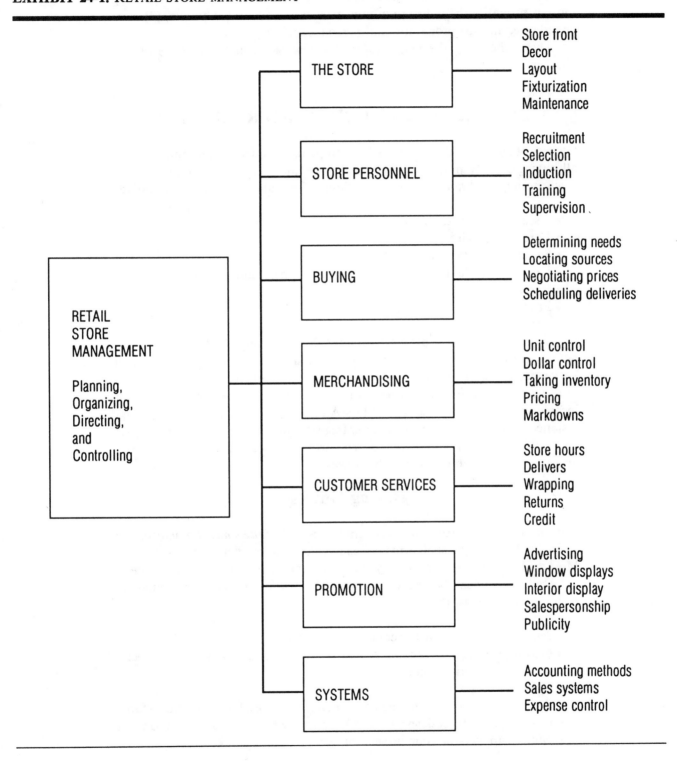

sales dollars. Either you sell to more customers than you now have or you sell more to your present customers. (For the sake of simplicity, let's set aside the strategic use of pricing as a device for increasing sales volume.)

Although all aspects of store operations touch on this business of boosting sales, three areas are more critical than the others in this connection. Selling more is primarily the outcome of improvements made in (1) buying, (2) merchandising, and (3) promotion and personal selling.

These, then, are the major topics for discussion in the balance of this chapter.

BETTER BUYING FOR HIGHER PROFITS

Owners of small retail enterprises have to plan, organize, direct, and evaluate all buying activity properly. They need to decide *what* to buy, *when* to buy, *where* to buy, and *how much* to buy. Some of the attendant activities include

- Ascertaining customer needs
- Forecasting sales
- Selecting merchandise
- Deciding on the breadth and depth of the merchandise variety
- Receiving and marking
- Pricing

Usually it is you, the owner, who must do the buying, for the business has not yet grown to the point at which you can afford a specialist. Yet you're a busy person. You're probably tied to your store and find you cannot spare much time away from it in search of new sources of supply. Moreover, if you're not located in New York, Chicago, or Los Angeles, you can't afford many long-distance trips to visit showrooms there. Instead, you must rely for the most part on wholesalers' sales representatives who drop in to see you, or, in some cases, on catalogs from wholesale supply houses.

Buying Offices

One alternative that exists in many retail lines is the *independent buying office*. There are hundreds of such firms in business to assist retailers, large and small. Most are located in New York City and a few other major metropolitan centers.

The independent buying office operates as your market representative. Among other things, this firm will

- Send their buyers out to scout the marketplace
- Provide a steady stream of advice on new items, new sources, special promotions, and the like
- Place orders for you
- Keep you abreast of changing consumer preferences, fashions, and so forth
- Provide you with desk space and a telephone when you do come into town
- Notify suppliers of your impending arrival

The customary charge for their services runs about ½ of 1 percent of your store's annual sales, most often payable in monthly installments. However, if your sales are too low, they may request a minimum fee and payment each month. Usually, they'll require a signed agreement for the term of one year, cancelable by either party.

A second type of buying service that may be available to you is the *merchandise broker.* These firms are far fewer in number than the independent offices. They'll place orders on your behalf and, to that end, keep you informed of the latest market information. There's no charge whatsoever to the retailer. The merchandise broker earns commissions from the manufacturers who receive the orders. (Commissions run generally from 2 to 5 percent.)

Some retailers are attracted to the merchandise broker because the services are free. This might be a shortsighted view for two reasons: (1) the services provided are far fewer than those offered by independent buying offices, and (2) the broker's primary responsibility is to sell goods for the companies that he or she represents.

After all, wouldn't it be worth ½ of 1 percent of your sales to have competent, experienced buyers—and a whole supporting staff behind them—working on your behalf?

To locate a buying office suited to your needs, check with your trade association, local Small Business Administration office, or the National Retail Merchants Association in Manhattan. You might also consult the yellow pages in telephone directories of such major metropolitan areas as New York City, Chicago, Dallas, and San Francisco.

The Art of Negotiating

While you may not be able to do too much about the prices of merchandise offered to you for resale (simply because yours is a small operation and you buy in limited quantities), there are ways to lower your cost of goods. Other than the price itself, you can frequently do better in areas such as discounts, special allowances, terms, job lots, and so forth.

Buy directly from the manufacturer, if this is at all possible. This will save you money. More likely than not, however, most of your purchases will come from wholesalers. Bear in mind that the wholesaler has a vital stake in keeping your business alive, hale, and hearty, in order to retain you as a good customer. Some distributors offer valuable services and terms that others do not. Among the many possibilities are advanced dating of invoices, special allowances, providing information about market conditions, special point-of-purchase materials, preticketing of merchandise, and free delivery.

Rating Your Suppliers. One worthwhile approach in your buying endeavors is to work up a simplified supplier rating plan. You can use this to compare sources of similar merchandise not only on the quality of goods offered but also on the variety carried, dependability of service, prices, production capacity, special services offered, and so forth. Use simple ratings, such as:

1 = Poor
2 = Fair
3 = Good
4 = Very good
5 = Excellent

Of course, you may wish to "weight" some of the criteria you employ more heavily than others.

During Negotiations. Before you even begin the bargaining process, you should have a clear idea as to the overall average markup you need to cover all store expenses and to provide at least a modest profit by the year's end. If you have done your planning and kept good inventory turnover records, you'll know whether or not you have been maintaining the necessary markup. If you need to "pull it up" somewhat, then you should look for a higher-than-usual gross margin on your new purchases.

In considering merchandise offered to you, you must first decide whether or not it's merchandise that you can comfortably integrate with your present stock, that your customers would want to buy, and that is within the price range your customers are willing to pay. Only if you can answer these questions affirmatively should you begin weighing the markup needed against the price asked by the supplier. If there's a considerable discrepancy between the price asked and the price you can pay, the need for bargaining becomes apparent. In the bargaining process itself, be open and honest with the sales representative. Say the price is too high and that you can't sell the particular item to your customers because you won't be earning enough gross margin dollars.

The salesperson may attempt to convince you that your judgment is faulty and assure you that you'll be able to sell the merchandise readily at prices higher than you believe you can get. Be careful. Don't be swayed by clever, persuasive sales talk. You might even suggest that the rep's company let you try out the merchandise on a small scale—placing it in your store on consignment. Sometimes this works.

After you've settled on the price, you then have an opportunity to garner available extras. These will help you not only to reduce your overall costs but also to increase your store's sales. Explore with the salesperson the terms you'll obtain. Will the goods be shipped directly to your store at supplier's cost or will you have to pay for transportation, F.O.B. warehouse? How much time will you have before you must pay the bill—thirty days from invoice date, forty-five days, sixty days? If you pay your bill early, how many points can you count on earning as a cash discount? What about repeat orders—will the same prices and terms still be valid? What about quantity discounts, either noncumulative or cumulative; that is, if you buy a certain quantity within a six-month period, can you get a discount in the form of a rebate?

Also find out whether the supplier offers any advertising aids, such as mats for reproducing newspaper ads, copy for radio commercials, signs or posters you can display in your store, special contests or promotions you can tie into, cooperative advertising moneys, and so on.

Job Lots and the Like

From time to time, you'll receive offers of *closeout* or *job lot* merchandise. Generally, this represents stock that the vendors have been unable to sell or that has been left over toward the end of a season. The articles are offered at attractively reduced prices; consequently, the temptation is great to seize this opportunity to increase your store's average gross margin.

Exercise caution. Often, this kind of merchandise doesn't reflect the proper balance you need in selection appeal. There may be too many of the less common sizes and not enough of the popular ones. The mixture of colors may not be in proportion to your customers' needs. The styles may be currently in vogue or in a downtrend. This doesn't mean that you should ignore these offers. In considering the purchase of such goods, try to separate them into three groups: (1) merchandise you'll have no trouble selling in your regular price lines, (2) articles you might be able to sell at higher prices, and (3) items you know will have to be sold off at marked-down prices. If you then tally up the total amount of sales you believe you can easily derive from the entire lot, you'll be in a good position to know whether or not you should "make the buy."

The best time for you to buy such merchandise is probably right after the peak of each season. However, you need to be careful in your judgment of anticipated sales; obviously, you won't want to carry any goods over for a full year.

Occasionally you'll come across merchandise that is not entirely perfect; these goods are referred to as *irregulars* or *seconds*. (Never bother with "thirds"!) Some retailers prefer to avoid such products at all costs, believing that to carry seconds would cheapen their store image. Other merchants do put them on display and find they enjoy brisk sales on these items. The latter approach certainly wouldn't damage store image at all if (1) such merchandise is clearly identified as seconds or irregulars; (2) the total supply of these items represents only a small percentage of the store's inventory; and (3) these goods are offered only occasionally during the year.

MERCHANDISE MANAGEMENT

Initial success and steady growth in your retail enterprise are contingent on having the right merchandise at the right time in the right quantities at the right prices. The control of the ebb and flow of the goods you offer for sale isn't a simple matter. Indeed, improper merchandise management practices are commonplace in small-scale retailing.

Many small independent retailers keep track of store inventory by means of the "eyeball control" method. For the most part, they depend on a practiced eye to ascertain whether or not they have enough on hand of any particular item, if more should be ordered, or if they are overstocked. Over time, this elementary form of stock supervision usually leads to an inventory much heavier than what's needed and the carryover of outmoded, shopworn, or otherwise unsalable merchandise.

Furthermore, unless you maintain a sensible inventory control system and good stock-movement records, you'll have little factual knowledge of the sales enjoyed by each classification of goods relative to your overall sales volume.

Data processing, whether through a service bureau or your own home or desktop microcomputer, can be of considerable value in controlling your inventory.

The Importance of Taking Inventory Regularly

One essential ingredient of good stock control is the taking of physical inventory, preferably on a regular monthly basis. To accomplish this properly, you need to prepare an inventory sheet on which you list all items carried in your store, grouped according to merchandise classifications. For example, a menswear shop might find it convenient to use such categories as shirts, sweaters, slacks, underwear, neckties, and the like. A grocery might use classifications such as cereals, dairy products, canned fruits and vegetables, cookies, salad dressings, and so forth.

Descriptions (including names, brands, sizes, and other variants) and prices of the individual items should be spelled out in detail underneath each of the major headings. Ample space must be provided for writing in the various amounts of each product found in the bins, on the shelves, in the back room, and so on. A column for totals should be provided, and another for indicating how many (if any) should be ordered.

By reviewing your monthly inventory sheets and your delivery records, after a while you'll be able to determine approximately how much you sold of every item in stock and its average rate of movement per week, month, or season.

Your Basic Stock List

In managing your inventory, it's helpful to think in terms of a *basic stock list*—a list of goods to be carried at all times. Break it down into kinds, types, and quantities. In most retail lines, the majority of items handled by the typical store unit are considered *staple goods.* These are products which consumers ask for repeatedly; demand for such products is typically of a continuous nature. Examples in the grocery field include sugar, salt, flour, eggs, butter, bacon, ham, baby foods, and canned vegetables.

Even within these common categories there are some products not properly classified as staple goods but rather as *selection types* or *nonstaple* merchandise. In the grocery business, for instance, items such as a new kind of breakfast cereal, an imported French cheese, a new brand of pancake syrup, and the like are nonstaples. In the apparel and related fields, selection-type items are referred to as *fashion goods.* The demand for such merchandise is not continuous; indeed, it is often characterized by wide fluctuations due to any number of reasons.

Automatic Reordering

You can easily control items for which there is regular, repeat business by setting up a basic stock list and establishing a simple *automatic replenishment system.* A retailer who takes inventory monthly can accumulate enough information within a few months to figure out the average weekly rate of sale for all such items. Regular reorders are tied to the inventory (except, perhaps, for fast-moving merchandise, for which a telephone order may have to be placed with the supplier).

To maintain an in-stock position, you can use the following formula:

$$O = (a + b)R - I$$

Where:

O = the quantity of the item to be ordered
a = the amount of time between inventory counts (expressed in weeks)
b = the amount of time that will elapse between order placement and the actual delivery of the merchandise into the selling stock (also expressed in weeks)
R = the item's average weekly rate of sale
I = how many are in stock (and are expected in) at inventory time

To illustrate, let's assume you take inventory on a monthly basis (every four weeks or so), and you've determined the following facts:

You have eighteen pieces of Item X on hand.
Another dozen are due to arrive within a day or two.
Delivery from the particular supplier usually takes two weeks.
You sell about thirty-six pieces each week.

Now, we apply the formula:

(Step 1)	$O = (a + b)R - I$
(Step 2)	$= (4 + 2)36 - 30$
(Step 3)	$= (6 \times 36) - 30$
(Step 4)	$= 216 - 30$
(Step 5)	$= 186$

Obviously, you'll need to order 186 pieces of Item X to make sure you'll have enough. Just as obviously, you won't need to have all 186 pieces on hand at one time, since these will be sold over a period of four weeks. If you lay in one month's stock for every item you carry, this could unnecessarily tie up a sizable chunk of your operating capital. It's more prudent to phase in your deliveries, preferably over a number of weeks, if this can be done.

Perhaps a simpler approach (once you have the hang of things) might be to determine both a minimum and a maximum stock figure for every staple item in your line, and order only when the inventoried amounts approach minimum levels.

Adding "Safety Stock." After some months of experience with the automatic replenishment system, you can take care of chance fluctuations in demand by building a reserve factor into the formula.

As an example, consider this dilemma faced by the proprietor of a menswear store:

Ordinarily, the proprietor maintains in stock at all times six pieces of each commonly-asked-for size of a particular brand and style shirt, in each of four basic colors: white, blue, tan, and gray. He has found that these quantities are usually sufficient to take care of consumer demand for at least one month. One afternoon, a shopper drops by, likes the particular shirt, and decides to purchase six, all of the same dimensions (16″ neck, 33″ sleeves). He selects three blue and three white, thereby depleting the store's month's supply of the two colors by 50 percent.

Chances are good that, unless the merchant can arrange for speedy replacement delivery of the inventory, the store will be out of stock on the two varieties long before the end of the month.

To reduce drastically the number of "stockouts" in your store, you'll need to make a slight adjustment in the basic formula, as indicated below:

$$O = (a + b)R - I + r$$

The small r that has been added represents the amount of *reserve,* or *safety stock,* needed. The additional merchandise should take care of about 99 percent of all extraordinary fluctuations in demand due to chance factors.

To calculate $r,$ use the following formula:

$$r = 2.3 \sqrt{(a + b)\,R}$$

In the earlier example involving Item X, r is worked out in this manner:

(Step 1)	$r = 2.3 \sqrt{(a + b)R}$
(Step 2)	$= 2.3 \sqrt{(4 + 2)36}$
(Step 3)	$= 2.3 \sqrt{216}$
(Step 4)	$= (2.3)(14.7)$
(Step 5)	$= 33.8$

To build in the reserve factor, the proprietor should add 34 pieces to the order, which would then total 220 pieces of Item X.

Controlling Nonstaples

The regular, automatic fill-in approach used for staple goods is not applicable to the control of nonstaple or fashion merchandise. Here it's better to think in terms of setting up seasonal *model stocks.* They may be set up on a twice-yearly basis (spring-summer; fall-winter) or, ideally, on a quarterly basis. You plan your stock in advance, using merchandise classifications and breaking down each class according to selection factors (brand, style, color, size, material, and so on).

For the sake of illustration, assume that one component of your model stock is the *sweaters* classification. Before preparing your projections for the coming fall-winter season, you should (a) study the records of last year's performance in this category and (b) take into account any trends you may have perceived (in your store, in the trade literature, and from knowledgeable suppliers). Of course, you initially need to make an estimate of the total dollar volume you expect to reach in this classification during the season, then break this down into two more manageable three-month periods.

Dollars are then easily translated into units by dividing the total dollars for each basic sweater style by the price points you've set. Total dollars for those

TABLE 24–1. Determining units needed within a classification

Type of Sweater	Percent of Total	Number Needed
V-necks	30%	90
Cardigans	25%	75
Turtlenecks	10%	30
Pullovers	35%	105
Totals	100%	300

Source: Compiled by the author.

styles are derived by approximating how much of the total sweater business is enjoyed by each style (percentage-wise).

Now, let's assume you've worked through your dollar projections for the three-month period September through November, and you estimate that you'll need about 300 sweaters of all types for that period. You stock four basic styles: V-necks, cardigans, turtlenecks, and pullovers. (For simplicity's sake, we're not at this point concerned with either brands or materials.) Your planning indicates that the four different styles will enjoy the percentages of total sweater sales shown in table 24–1 along with those percentages translated into units. Of course, you haven't finished with your homework as yet. The *number needed* for each of the four types of sweaters must be analyzed further: by sizes (small, medium, large, extra-large), and by colors. When it's finally worked out, your resulting plan for the *sweaters* classification might look something like the chart in exhibit 24–2.

HOW TO IMPROVE RETAIL SELLING

You *Can* Compete with the Larger Stores!

Having a capable, well-trained sales staff is one decided advantage the small store can enjoy over today's chain, discount, and even department stores. Over the past few decades, a high proportion of the larger retail companies have curtailed personal selling activity in favor of self-service and self-selection approaches. This long-term trend reflects the retailers' efforts to control operating expenses where the single biggest cost factor, other than the cost of goods itself, has been (and still is) the payroll expense.

As a rule, the larger stores rely more often on stacked shelves, massed displays, and an overall "impersonal" approach to sales. Thus, the singular potential of the small retail firm lies in the caliber of its personal selling efforts.

Types of Shoppers

An interesting tidbit from a classic study may prove illuminating in this context.* In his investigation, the researcher queried women shoppers on their

*Gregory P. Stone, "City Shoppers and Urban Identification: Observations on the Social Psychology of City Life," *American Journal of Sociology* 60 (July, 1954), 36–45.

EXHIBIT 24-2. SAMPLE STOCK-PLANNING CHART

Period __Sept.-Nov., 1986__ CLASSIFICATION __Sweaters__ Total Needed __300__

Types Carried	SIZES			COLORS			
	Size	%	No.	Blue 25%	Gray 25%	Tan 20%	White 30%
1. V-Necks % 30% No. 90	S	10%	9	2	2	2	3
	M	30%	27	7	7	5	8
	L	40%	36	9	9	7	11
	XL	20%	18	4	5	4	5
TOTALS:		100%	90	22	25	18	27
2. Cardigans % 25% No. 75	S	10%	7	2	2	1	2
	M	30%	23	5	6	5	7
	L	40%	30	8	7	6	9
	XL	20%	15	3	4	3	5
TOTALS:		100%	75	18	19	15	23
3. Turtlenecks % 10% No. 30	S	10%	3	1	1	0	1
	M	30%	9	2	2	2	3
	L	40%	12	3	3	3	3
	XL	20%	6	2	1	1	2
TOTALS:		100%	30	8	7	6	9
4. Pullovers % 35% No. 105	S	10%	10	2	3	2	3
	M	30%	32	8	8	6	10
	L	40%	42	11	10	8	13
	XL	20%	21	5	5	5	6
TOTALS:		100%	105	26	26	21	32

Adapted with permission of Prentice Hall, Inc. from *Mathematics of Merchandising*, 3d ed., by A. P. Kneider. Copyright 1986 by Prentice Hall, Inc.

attitudes toward store shopping. An analysis of their responses enabled him to group the women into four major categories: economic shoppers (33 percent of the total), personalizing shoppers (28 percent), ethical shoppers (18 percent), and apathetic shoppers (17 percent). (There were about 4 percent who couldn't be assigned to any of the four listed categories.)

The key features of the four groups follow:

Economic shoppers are more interested in prices, values, merchandise quality, and other "economic" considerations than in other store aspects (including sales personnel).

Personalizing shoppers seem to enjoy personal relationships with salespeople. They prefer to shop where they are recognized and feel welcome.

Ethical shoppers avoid large stores and the chains because they feel that such firms are cold and impersonal. They prefer doing business with independent retailers since they believe that these merchants also need to earn a living.

Apathetic shoppers dislike shopping and only shop because they must. For them, the most important store attribute is convenience of location.

Here's food for thought. Set aside for the moment the one-third of "economic shoppers" who may be attracted elsewhere by better prices/quality/values than you offer. (We'll return to these consumers later on.)

Wouldn't you agree that those 18 percent known as "ethical shoppers" would almost automatically favor your store, given the right degree of "warmth" emanating from your salespeople? Moreover, with good treatment, prompt and courteous attention, and excellent interpersonal relations, there should be no doubt that the 28 percent in the "personalizing" category would respond quite well, too!

So, you can already count on nearly one-half of all the shoppers in your area as potential customers. You should have little difficulty "stealing" them away from your competition.

You can even expect to acquire some of the "apathetic shoppers" in your neighborhood. After all, your location must be more convenient to some percentage of them than the location of your next nearest competitor!

As a final point, let's return to that one-third that we discounted at the very beginning of this discussion—the "economic shoppers." It's completely up to you to garner some of those people by monitoring your prices, quality of goods, and assortment mix. No reason why you can't do some competitive merchandising!

Are you convinced by now that you ought to take a good hard look at your current sales staff and your selling approaches?

Retail Selling

No matter how fortunate you've been in selecting and training your salespeople, and no matter how good a job you've done in this area, your people probably haven't yet reached their peak efficiency. (No one ever does!) Consequently, there's still room for improvement.

The basic way to improve your staff's selling performance is through a planned, continuous program. The keys to mastery here are

- Training
- Training
- Training
- More training

An integral portion of your success in training employees resides in your attitude toward them. Salespeople are not simply "bodies" or "hands and feet" to help you make sales. So many retailers wrongly think of their selling personnel only in terms of "store coverage"—that is, how many salespeople ought to be on the floor at which hours of the day or night to take proper care of the shopper traffic. These are people and not robots that process orders for you. They can make or break your business.

Among the more desirable personal attributes your salespeople should possess are

- A good appearance (including good posture and cleanliness)
- A pleasant personality
- Courtesy and tact
- An enjoyment of selling
- An understanding of psychology (practical, not theoretical)

Typically, small business owners are quick to teach their salespeople about all of the following topics:

- The merchandise carried in the store
- Where to find the merchandise
- The prices of the goods
- How to ring the register and make change
- Store policies
- Bagging and wrapping merchandise
- How to keep things neat

Rarely does the typical independent retailer spend much time teaching employees *how* to sell (other than, of course, advising the new salesperson to greet the incoming shopper with a prompt "May I help you?" and to thank the customer after ringing up the sale).

Small-scale retailers are not alone in this respect. An analysis of (among other things) the initial formal training programs of department stores in New York and California revealed that the median time allotted to the training of sales personnel in a classroom setting came to only 12.5 hours. The topics covered broke down as follows:

Company knowledge	1 hour
Product knowledge	1.5 hours

Store knowledge	2 hours
Customer knowledge	1 hour
"Art of selling"	1 hour
Register/policies/systems	6 hours*

Note that only *one hour* was devoted to the "art of selling."

The Selling Process Analyzed

Selling in the retail store follows much the same lines as the personal selling process described in chapter 14, except that the retail salesperson doesn't need to do any prospecting. Show windows, interior displays, advertising, and sales promotion take care of this. Happily, prospects are drawn to and into the store.

It might be advantageous to take apart this personal selling process, step by step, with an eye to study and improvement. If you, the owner, spend some time mulling over each step, you'll doubtless come up with at least two or three usable ideas in each case. Only a few comments are made below; they are designed to set you thinking:

The Approach. Salespeople often confuse this first step with the salutation or greeting; for example, "Good morning, sir!" or "Can I help you?" All the greeting does is initiate a conversation; this has little or nothing to do with selling. Actually, the approach ought to be the beginning of the sales presentation, for what goes on in that first minute or so of contact should facilitate the presentation.

Give customers time to "get into" the store. Neither lurch at nor pounce on them. If they know what they want, they'll most likely walk directly to you (or a salesperson). If they're not sure what they want, they might enter hesitatingly, look around at the displays, or glance perplexedly toward the salesperson. The salesperson who is approached directly should smile, greet the shopper cordially (preferably by name), and ask, "How may I help you?" This, of course, implies that you have trained your employees to recall customers' names; this technique could be especially valuable if yours is a specialty goods store. (A "guest register" in which your customers can record their names and addresses would be helpful here. It can also come in handy when you run occasional special promotions for "favored customers.")

When shoppers seem to be "just looking" or appear otherwise not ready for service, the salesclerk should at least comment on the fact that he or she is available if the customer needs assistance (after greeting the customer, naturally).

When a shopper is evidently interested in an item on display, your employee should approach the person and point out some interesting feature of the product or, better still, some benefit that the item can bring to the customer.

When there are several shoppers (and not enough sales help), the experienced salesperson will assure those who are waiting that they will be served shortly.

*Irving Burstiner, "Current Personnel Practices in Department Stores," *Journal of Retailing* 50 (Winter 1975), 3–14, 86.

The Presentation. Having learned of the shopper's needs during the approach, perhaps with several well-chosen questions, the salesperson then makes a smooth transition into the presentation itself. Here, the object is to arouse the interest of the prospect, build desire on the consumer's part to purchase the item, and then "close" the sale. In reality, people buy benefits, not products per se. Therefore, concentrate on what the merchandise can or will do for the consumer. Try to involve the prospect in touching the material, holding the item, putting it on if it's a garment, and so on.

To make an effective presentation, the salesperson must

- Know the selling points of the merchandise
- Be familiar with its qualities and characteristics
- Know how to care for it, and if it's a mechanical item, how it is operated

The effective salesperson is also familiar with your competitors' merchandise and with how your products compare.

Meeting Objections. As in any type of personal selling, shoppers may raise all sorts of issues during the presentation. Objections are to be expected. These obstacles to making the sale challenge the imagination of the good salesperson. Some comments may be no more than excuses that people present so that they don't seem like easy targets for sales pitches. Others are real objections: to price; to style, quality, or other features; to the store's service policies; and so forth. Sometimes, objections are not spoken aloud. In such cases, it's up to the salesperson to determine why the shopper is reluctant, perhaps by asking a few probing (though tactful) questions, perhaps by observation alone.

A variety of techniques can be used effectively in meeting shopper objections. Sometimes, these can be "turned around" so that what has been proposed as a negative by the consumer can be made into a positive selling point. Another method, called the "Yes, but . . . " technique, enables the salesperson to appear to agree gracefully with what the consumer has been saying while, at the same time, giving him or her the opportunity to point out one or more additional, positive facts that may help to clear up the problem.

There are other methods, too. The bibliography at the end of this chapter, as well as those in chapters 14 and 22, can assist you in your selling efforts.

The Close. The *close* or *closing* represents the culmination of the sales effort. At this point, the salesperson takes down the customer's order (if you use the sales-slip method), rings up the register (if you don't), and delivers the merchandise to the customer (or arranges for its delivery). However, knowing *when* and *how* to close a sale is perhaps a more difficult feat for the sales employee. Again, a good book on retail selling methods should help tremendously.

Suggestive Selling. While suggestive selling may be used during the sales presentation itself, it is most commonly used after the close. All too often, the salesperson will ask, "Will there be anything else?" before proceeding with the bagging or wrapping of the merchandise selected. How superfluous can a question be? The phrase *anything else* marks the lazy, inefficient salesperson. Unless the customer intends to buy something additional—in which case it would already have been mentioned—a negative response is certain.

On the other hand, statements such as the following may elicit a completely different sort of response:

At a confectionery shop: "Did you know that our salted cashews are on sale for this week only, at one dollar less than the regular price?"

At a gift shop: "We're now taking orders for delivery on Mother's Day. May I show you a display of unusual gifts for your mother?"

At a men's store: "I believe we have just the right necktie for the shirt you've selected. May I show it to you?"

At a hardware store: "That's a fine pair of pliers you've picked out. Would you be interested in a good hammer?"

At a bakery: "Here's a sample of our chocolate chip cookies. I'd like you to taste one to see how delicious it is."

Concrete suggestions do pay off. When you suggest an additional item, you plant an idea in the customer's mind, thus confronting the shopper with the necessity of making a decision. While the response may still be "No, thank you" in many cases, there's a good chance of an occasional affirmative answer. Remember that old adage, "Nothing ventured, nothing gained."

Closing suggestions are aided by a display of the suggested item near the register so that the salesperson can point to the merchandise while talking about it. These kinds of suggestions are particularly effective with inexpensive items of the "pick-up" variety or with products that are timely, on sale, or related to the merchandise the customer has already selected.

Many experienced salespeople claim they can sell additional merchandise to at least three out of every ten customers.

USING PROMOTIONAL CREATIVITY

You'll recall that there are essentially three facets to the promotion mix: personal selling, advertising, and sales promotion. We have just discussed the first area in this chapter; the remaining two facets were treated in some depth in chapter 14. It's true that the typical small retail firm does little media advertising throughout the year. When it does advertise, it generally does so in the busy season or around holiday times. In view of this fact, little more need be said on this subject other than:

• Refer back to the material presented in chapter 16.
• Strive for more creativity in your ads.
• Try to make your advertising dollars go further.

In this connection, some additional "hints" are given in exhibit 24–3.

EXHIBIT 24–3. SOME HELPFUL SUGGESTIONS ABOUT YOUR ADVERTISING

1. Doubling the size of your ad will not double the number of people who read it.
2. Do not overwrite. Layout and copy should be simple, clear, and understandable.
3. Use active, not passive, words and phrases.
4. Feature the right merchandise in your advertising.
5. Stress the benefits—the major selling points. Build in the right appeals.
6. A photo or illustration is much more compelling than copy alone.
7. Your store name, address, and telephone number should be readily discernible.
8. A series of advertisements will have a more powerful effect on your targeted public than an occasional, one-shot ad. (Continuity!)
9. Exercise care in your media selection.
10. An advertiser can often obtain free publicity from a local or area newspaper, radio station, or television station.

Source: Compiled by the author.

FOR FURTHER INFORMATION

Books

Brannen, William H. *Practical Marketing for Your Small Retail Business.* Englewood Cliffs, N.J.: Prentice-Hall, 1982.

Burstiner, Irving. *Basic Retailing.* Homewood, Ill.: Irwin, 1986.

———. *Run Your Own Store.* Englewood Cliffs, N.J.: Prentice-Hall, 1981.

Edwards, Charles M., Jr., and Carl F. R. Lebowitz. *Retail Advertising and Sales Promotion,* 4th ed. Englewood Cliffs, N.J.: Prentice-Hall, 1981.

Gillespie, Karen R., Joseph C. Hecht, and Carl F. Lebowitz. *Retail Business Management,* 3d ed. New York: McGraw-Hill, 1983.

James, Don L., Bruce J. Walker, and Michael J. Etzel. *Retailing Today,* 2d ed. San Diego, Cal.: Harcourt Brace Jovanovich, 1981.

Kneider, A. P. *Mathematics of Merchandising,* 2d ed. Englewood Cliffs, N.J.: Prentice-Hall, 1981.

Mason, J. Barry, and Morris L. Mayer. *Modern Retailing: Theory and Practice,* 3d ed. Plano, Tex.: Business Publications, 1984.

Mills, Kenneth H., and Judith E. Paul. *Applied Visual Merchandising.* Englewood Cliffs, N.J.: Prentice-Hall, 1982.

Mueller, Carol S., and Helena De Paola. *Marketing Today's Fashion,* 2d ed. Englewood Cliffs, N.J.: Prentice-Hall, 1986.

Phillips, Pamela M., Ellye Bloom, and Dr. John D. Mattingly. *Fashion Sales Promotion: The Selling Behind the Selling.* New York: John Wiley & Sons, 1985.

Reid, Allan L. *Modern Applied Selling,* 3d ed. Santa Monica, Cal.: Goodyear, 1981.

Spitzer, Harry, and F. Richard Schwartz. *Inside Retail Sales Promotion and Advertising.* New York: Harper & Row, 1982.

Storholm, Gordon, and Louis C. Kaufman. *Principles of Selling.* Englewood Cliffs, N.J.: Prentice-Hall, 1985.

Troxell, Mary, and Elaine Stone. *Fashion Merchandising,* 3d ed. New York: McGraw-Hill, 1981.

Wingate, John W., and Joseph S. Friedlander. *The Management of Retail Buying,* 2d ed. Englewood Cliffs, N.J.: Prentice-Hall, 1978.

Pamphlets Available from the Small Business Administration

MANAGEMENT AIDS

MA 1.011—"Analyze Your Records to Reduce Costs"

MA 1.016—"Sound Cash Management and Borrowing"

MA 1.019—"Simple Breakeven Analysis for Small Stores"

MA 3.005—"Stock Control for Small Stores"

MA 3.010—"Techniques for Problem Solving"

MA 4.012—"Marketing Checklist for Small Retailers"

MA 4.018—"Planning Your Advertising Budget"

Booklets Available from the Superintendent of Documents

S/N 045-000-00152-1—*Small Store Planning for Growth*—$5.50.

S/N 045-000-00177-6—*Retail Buying Function*—$4.50.

S/N 045-000-00178-4—*Retail Merchandise Management*—$4.75.

S/N 045-000-00180-6—*Credit and Collections: Policies and Procedures*—$4.75.

S/N 045-000-00189-0—*Managing Retail Salespeople*—$4.75.

S/N 045-000-00190-3—*Inventory Management—Wholesale/Retail*—$4.50.

25

Improving Results in Your Service Business

The service sector of our economy includes so many varied business types that it's difficult to generalize about improving the service operation—other than by suggesting ways to reduce expenses, increase sales and profits, or specify approaches other than the customary ones. Service firms range the entire spectrum: from tiny, one-person enterprises to large corporations such as advertising agencies, universities, and other multiemployee institutions.

Nevertheless, in addition to good overall management and plain common sense, there are other guidelines for improving results in your service business that merit your attention. Some of the more important ones are listed in exhibit 25–1. Frankly, they're just as applicable to the small service undertaking (tutoring, typing service, crafts or music school, dry-cleaning service, and so on) as to the large corporations mentioned above. They are, in fact, useful keys to successful business growth, aids that will help you build a loyal clientele.

THE MARKETING OF SERVICES

The marketing of services must, of necessity, differ substantially from product marketing. Whether the services are destined for organizational use (*industrial* services) or for use by the final consumer (*consumer* services), most reflect three characteristics that clearly distinguish them from products:*

*For some insights into the area of service marketing, see: Duane L. Davis, Joseph P. Guiltinan, and Wesley H. Jones, "Service Characteristics, Consumer Search, and the Classification of Retail Services," *Journal of Retailing* 55 (Fall 1979), 3–23; Gregory D. Upah, "Mass Marketing in Service Retailing: A Review and Synthesis of Major Methods," *Journal of Retailing* 56 (Fall 1980), 59–76; Valarie A. Zeithaml, A. Parasuraman, and Leonard L. Berry, "Problems and Strategies in Services Marketing," *Journal of Marketing* 49 (Spring 1985), 33–46.

EXHIBIT 25–1. TEN KEYS TO REPEAT SALES IN A SERVICE BUSINESS

1. *Make a fetish of honesty.* Customer confidence and loyalty are logical outcomes of fair, ethical treatment. Do not try to fool other people. Never embroider the truth. Never oversell yourself, your capabilities, or your service.

2. *Practice good human relations.* Treat others as you would want to be treated yourself. Be responsive to community problems; join in local activities. Never, never lose control of your emotions.

3. *Become the epitome of dependability.* Never make promises you cannot fulfill. Have things ready for the dates promised. Keep your word; become known by others as someone on whom they can rely.

4. *Take pride in your work.* Demonstrate a professional, proprietary attitude in whatever you do. Proficiency and technical skill should characterize your service operation.

5. *Do not stint on materials.* Always use the best-quality parts, materials, and equipment. Do not be penny wise and pound foolish; be willing to spend more on better materials than your competition does.

6. *Give freely of your time.* The service business is unique in that customers often ask endless questions (as in the tool or equipment rental service) and present a variety of complaints. Be patient. Spend time explaining and giving advice. This kind of personal attention and helpful service can only enhance your firm's reputation.

7. *Know your trade.* More than in any other type of business, the service enterprise demands mastery of the area of specialization. Learn all you can about your craft through reading, attending seminars and conventions, from your trade association, and so forth.

8. *Train your personnel well.* Customers will come to judge your business by the way they are treated at the hands of your employees. Courtesy and tact are always expected; no doubt, you have already inculcated these two traits in your employees. However, it is equally important to the service business to make certain your employees are knowledgeable, continually informed, and technically proficient. Training should be a continuous process.

9. *Offer better guarantees than your competitors.* Find out the details of your competition's guarantees/warranties. Then, set your own standards, going well beyond theirs. Where others offer a six-months' guarantee, for instance, offer yours for a full year.

10. *Improve all internal systems.* Work-in-process, materials and supplies, and schedules must all flow smoothly in your operation. Accompanying paperwork and records should be detailed and exact to assist this flow. Cut down on excess reports; simplify the forms you use; substitute office equipment for manual clerical operations.

Source: Compiled by the author.

- *They are intangible.*   Potential buyers cannot touch or handle them. This makes it difficult for people to compare and evaluate similar offerings, as they can so easily do with products (and brands) that are on the market.

   Unlike products, too, services cannot be "produced" (performed) at one place and then delivered to another. This means, of course, that to sell the service to many customers, the producing firm needs to offer it at a number of different locations. To "mass market" the service successfully, then, substantial promotional effort is indicated.

- *They are perishable.*   They cannot be stored or warehoused. As a simple example, a failure to sell all available admission tickets to a stadium for a particular football game results in the stadium's loss of some income for the day.

   Thus, a service operation occasionally may experience a "lost sales" problem, simply because it lacks a reserve "inventory" upon which to draw.

- *They cannot be separated from those who perform them or who personally contact the customer.*   Because of this fact alone, standardization of services becomes nearly impossible. Then, too, it makes it difficult for potential buyers to "shop around," since the quality of a service so greatly depends on the people involved. Thus, the need for capable and well-trained "contact personnel" is quite evident.

It would appear, then, that marketing services may be more difficult than product marketing. However, one useful tactic the service company might take in pursuit of the mass marketing ideal would be to try to expand distribution and increase its sales revenues "by routinizing operations and systems and through mechanization."*

The importance of other aspects of the operation, such as the service personnel and the physical plant itself, also cannot be underestimated. As one business writer pointed out:

Services marketing planning and execution should focus attention on seven Ps: the traditional 4 Ps plus three additional marketing mix elements that are crucial to service success—personnel, physical assets, and process management.**

Thoughts about Service Quality

As we have already noted, most service offerings resist attempts at standardization. One of the more crucial aspects of service marketing, then, is that of the *quality* of the service. To a substantial degree, of course, this is dependent on the caliber of those who deliver the service. A management intent on improving

*Irving Burstiner, *Basic Retailing* (Homewood, Ill.: Irwin, 1986), 39.

**A. J. Magrath, "When Marketing Services, 4 Ps Are Not Enough," *Business Horizons* 29 (May-June 1986), 50.

business results will work toward upgrading, over time, its people, systems, procedures, and all other facets of the enterprise.

The following quotation from an article in *Business Horizons* underscores the importance of this aspect:

> The service quality challenge is to meet—or better yet, exceed—customer expectations. For most firms, this is a complex undertaking. Most service businesses are labor intensive and the service is subject to variability. Customers are frequently present when the service is performed, in effect witnessing its production. Even if customer contact personnel have the talent, training, and motivation to deliver high-quality service, they may nonetheless be dependent on "good service" from the operations part of the firm to be fully effective. . . .*

The same article summarized the findings of an exploratory study of some retail services (banking, securities brokerage, product repair, and so on). The researchers interviewed business executives and made use of consumer focus groups as well. They stressed the following "ten determinants of service quality":

1. Reliability ("consistency of performance," "dependability")
2. Responsiveness ("willingness," "readiness")
3. Competence ("knowledge," "skill")
4. Access ("approachability," "ease of contact")
5. Courtesy
6. Communication ("keeping customers informed," "listening to customers")
7. Credibility ("believability," "honesty")
8. Security ("physical safety," "financial security")
9. Understanding the customer
10. Tangibles ("physical evidence of the service")**

MAKE THE MOST OF YOUR FACILITIES

Your premises may be just right for your current needs. On the other hand, they might be inadequate, or even more than adequate. If you're like most owners of service enterprises, you feel that your premises are too "tight" and that if you had larger quarters you would be able to enjoy more business. Yet you may feel a sense of helplessness about all of this because you are tied into your present location with a lease that still has a few years to go.

What to do?

The answer may lie in making a thorough appraisal of your present layout. Hire a consulting firm with experience in your line of business. Often by

---

*Leonard L. Berry, Valarie A. Zeithaml, and A. Parasuraman, "Quality Counts in Services, Too," *Business Horizons* 28 (May-June 1985), 52.

**Adapted from Ibid., 45–46.

rearranging your stock and work areas, and by updating your equipment, you can gain extra space. Reserve inventory, for example, can be relegated to a basement, office, the second floor of a taxpayer (a small building, usually two stories, with a retail store on the street level), or other nearby site.

The ideal layout depends on the kind of business you're in. Some types require a great deal of space for *customer contact* (beauty salons, dance studios, and the like come readily to mind). In other kinds of businesses, *working space* is at a premium—for example, pet-care establishments, auto repair shops, upholsterers, laundries, and so forth.

In all these firms, some space is needed for meeting and serving the customer. Whatever your business, the surroundings for "customer contact space" should be attractive. They don't have to be in high-fashion design; neither should the furnishings or decor be cheap or shabby. It's not always necessary or desirable to convey too expensive-looking an image. New, attractive wall covering or even a good paint job can work wonders for your place of business. The interior can easily be enhanced by better lighting or a new floor or ceiling. These relatively minor changes can have a positive effect on upgrading the public's image of your firm.

You should also check both entrances and exits to make certain they're clear and inviting, so that traffic won't be impeded in any way. Make sure doors are easy to open and close and that company identification (signs, lettering) is completely legible.

Incidentally, the terms of your present lease should not preclude you from planning seriously for an eventual move to larger quarters. Such preparation should be started well beforehand so that you can, together with experienced advisors, project not only your long-term space requirements but also the optimum layout and even the exact equipment you'll need.

REFINE OPERATIONS

Just as with any other type of business, a service enterprise can benefit by your probing into various fundamental aspects of its operation. With some thought and application, you can refine your approaches and techniques to all of the following areas:

- The purchasing of materials, supplies, and equipment
- Inventory methods and inventory control
- Advertising, sales promotion, publicity, and public relations
- Personal selling methods
- Budgets and other financial controls
- Personnel administration
- The internal work flow and other systems

All of these have been amply discussed in earlier chapters; you can locate detailed information on these areas by checking the index at the back of this book. However, the general promotion area that embraces advertising, sales promotion, publicity, and public relations merits more extended treatment here, in the following section.

INCREASING YOUR SALES VOLUME THROUGH PROMOTION

Word-of-mouth advertising is the cheapest of all forms of promotion. It costs nothing, yet it is the most effective. The keys to repeat sales mentioned earlier in this chapter, if followed, will generate plenty of this kind of advertising. You can precipitate even more of it by being more active: visit offices, retail stores, and factories in the vicinity to introduce yourself, to talk about your business, and to outline the services you offer. Carry along business cards and leave one with everyone you speak to. Better still, distribute 4-by-6 index cards printed with necessary details. The cost of a thousand such cards is minimal.

Many supermarkets make bulletin boards available for local notices; put up an eye-catching flier in your neighborhood market. A special offer on the flier will bring results and so will delivering the same flier to all residents in the area. (The benefits of using this technique for one service firm are mentioned in the section on "Advertising" in chapter 14.)

If you have a service shop of any type, the U.S. Small Business Administration advises you to "let people know" about it:

> Customer confidence is of little value if people don't know that your shop is there and ready to serve them. Keep reminding people. A small ad in the classified section of the telephone directory won't do the job if your competitors are constantly reminding people about the advantages of their offerings.
>
> Some repair shops let people know what they offer by using direct mail advertising. Such flyers, designed by a local print shop, can also be delivered door-to-door.
>
> Other repair shops promote themselves by mailing out a small item which can be used in the home. A list of emergency telephone numbers—such as the fire station and police station and your own number, of course—makes a good item. Customers can attach it to their telephones. . . .
>
> Sometimes a shop's location can be used for promotion. The owner-manager offers his basement or other space as a community meeting room. He announces its availability with a sign in the window. As people use the meeting room, the shop becomes an unofficial community center instead of just another small service shop.
>
> Special contests are another promotional tool. One radio repair shop holds an annual contest for the best "homemade" radio built by teenagers. Besides the goodwill, the contest helps the sale of radio parts, and it may help you to spot individuals who would make good part-time employees. An auto repair, hardware, hi-fi or appliance shop may be able to do the same thing. Sometimes, the owner-manager can interest newspapers and radio and television stations in doing a feature story about the contest.*

---

*"Building Customer Confidence in Your Service Shop," *Small Marketers Aid No. 122* (Washington, D.C.: U.S. Small Business Administration).

The SBA also suggests that you prominently display a framed copy of your industry's code of ethics in your shop.

A listing in the yellow pages of the telephone directory is essential for a service firm. Paying for a bold-type listing and a small advertisement would be even better. The costs for these are quite reasonable.

Ask your customers to register in the "Guest Register" book when they come in. The book should have columns for names, addresses, and telephone numbers. This will help you build and maintain an up-to-date customer file, a valuable list that you can periodically "milk."

Keep your clientele posted on upcoming specials either by mail or by telephone. In fact, there are a number of ways you can profitably use the telephone: to call people when their repaired items are ready, to discuss with them any problems that come up, to give them advice, and so forth. Be sure to ask your customers for recommendations, too; work out an inexpensive giveaway promotion to encourage them.

If you have a storefront and some selling space, do a little merchandise retailing to help pay the rent. Put in a display of fast-selling items that will appeal to your customers. (Beauty salons have long profited from this technique.)

Look over your list of services. Are you able to make deliveries in the neighborhood free of charge or for a nominal amount? How about credit? Can you make a "promotion tool" out of extending credit by publicizing it? Can you furnish an appropriate substitute for your customers' use while their appliances, tools, and the like are in the shop for repairs? Can you afford to finance large purchases?

Finally, apply some of the creative thinking approaches described in chapter 12 to the problem of how you can successfully differentiate your service business from those of your competitors.

FOR FURTHER INFORMATION

Books

Collier, David A. *Service Management: The Automation of Services.* Reston, Va.: Reston, 1985.

Connor, Richard A., Jr., and Jeffrey P. Davidson. *Marketing Your Consulting and Professional Services.* New York: Wiley, 1985.

Gray, Ernest A. *Profitable Methods for Small Business Advertising.* New York: Wiley, 1984.

Kotler, Philip, and Paul N. Bloom. *Marketing Professional Services.* Englewood Cliffs, N.J.: Prentice-Hall, 1984.

Lovelock, Christopher H. *Services Marketing: Text, Cases, and Readings.* Englewood Cliffs, N.J.: Prentice-Hall, 1983.

Morton, Tom J., and Dean Stout. *Real Estate Marketing.* Reston, Va.: Reston, 1985.

Norris, James S. *Public Relations.* Englewood Cliffs, N.J.: Prentice-Hall, 1984.

Pederson, Carlton A., and Milburn D. Wright. *Selling: Principles and Methods,* 8th ed. Homewood, Ill.: Irwin, 1984.

Reynolds, Helen, and Mary E. Tramel. *Executive Time Management: Getting 12 Hours' Work Out of an 8-Hour Day.* Englewood Cliffs, N.J.: Prentice-Hall, 1979.

Stanley, Richard E. *Promotion: Advertising, Publicity, Personal Selling, Sales Promotion,* 2d ed. Englewood Cliffs, N.J.: Prentice-Hall, 1982.

Storholm, Gordon, and Louis C. Kaufman. *Principles of Selling.* Englewood Cliffs, N.J.: Prentice-Hall, 1985.

Wheatley, Edward W. *Marketing Professional Services.* Englewood Cliffs, N.J.: Prentice-Hall, 1983.

Pamphlets Available from the Small Business Administration

MANAGEMENT AIDS

MA 1.010—"Accounting Services for Small Service Firms"

MA 1.017—"Keeping Records in Small Business"

MA 4.015—"Advertising Guidelines for Small Retail Firms"

Booklets Available from the Superintendent of Documents

S/N 045-000-00165-2—*Managing the Small Service Firm for Growth and Profit*—$4.25.

S/N 045-000-00180-6—*Credit and Collections: Policies and Procedures*—$4.75.

S/N 045-000-00189-0—*Managing Retail Salespeople*—$4.75.

S/N 045-000-00190-3—*Inventory Management—Wholesale/Retail*—$4.50.

S/N 045-000-00203-9—*Management Audit for Small Service Firms*—$4.50.

IX

THE FUTURE OF YOUR BUSINESS

26

Growth and Continuity

Do you recall, back in chapter 12, the discussion of the *product life cycle* concept? Businesses—like products and people—evidence several different stages during their life spans.

THE BUSINESS LIFE CYCLE

The newly launched small business, if successful, begins to grow. It passes through a perhaps turbulent adolescence, attains maturity, and then, eventually, fades away. Like the life cycle of the innovative product that meets with customer acceptance, the new enterprise will most likely pass through four phases: the *introductory, growth, maturity,* and *decline* stages.

Introductory Stage

It's during the initial stage of the business life cycle that the entrepreneur starts up operations, hoping to carve out the beginnings of a niche in a particular industry. This introductory stage is the most perilous of the four; success or failure lies in the offing. If the enterprise is viable, well-managed, and if the owner is lucky, the end-of-year bottom-line figure will be registered in black ink instead of in red. At this point, the entrepreneur directly controls all the major business functions. Sales thereafter will continue to grow, albeit perhaps slowly. If tight reins are held on spending, the business will continue to prosper.

Several employees (part-time or full-time) may be added and profits repeatedly ploughed back into the business. This, however, is more of a holding operation or a clinging to survival than real business growth. This type of situation may prevail for a year or two, sometimes longer. Indeed, some businesses may never fully attain the next phase.

Growth Stage

This next phase is characterized by more accelerated progress, the consolidation and strengthening of the enterprise's position relative to its industry, an ascending sales curve, and a growing number of employees. The entrepreneur may purchase more capital equipment, thus increasing the total value of company assets. More capital may be brought in, perhaps through the original owner's taking on one or more partners, borrowing substantial sums from a financial institution, or selling some of the corporation's stock. Supervision is gradually given over to employees; several layers of management soon evolve between owner and rank and file. During this stage, profits are excellent. Expansion begins. Indeed, some firms at this stage begin to consider such moves as acquisitions and mergers in addition to internal growth and relocation.

Maturity Stage

Eventually, the company appears to reach its limits in size and performance. No one knows, of course, how many years it will take for any particular firm to enter the maturity stage. By now the firm may enjoy a sizable market share. Perhaps it can no longer be called a "small" business. When growth slows down to a mere crawl, the future cannot look promising.

Decline Stage

Any no-growth situation will inevitably lead to decay, to that fourth and last stage of the business life cycle—the decline stage. At the end of this final phase, one can only expect the demise of the company.

For any one enterprise, each stage in the life cycle may be lengthened or shortened. In the final analysis, it's management's vision (or lack of it) that is responsible for the pacing.

Growth is essential to the well-being of your business; so is continuity in management. Both of these ideas are developed further in the balance of this chapter. Before we continue, however, it might prove illuminating to read through the brief synopses of small business growth in exhibit 26–1.

CONTROLLED VERSUS EXPLOSIVE BUSINESS GROWTH

Growth means expansion. It creates additional revenues—and additional profit. It must be planned for, organized for, and then guided and nurtured. To realize company growth, top management must be highly motivated along these lines and must possess the ability to grow.

A distinction needs to be made between deliberate, planned growth, and unchecked, even explosive growth. The first is cautious and carefully charted—carried along through regular planning sessions, periodic progress reviews, and program modifications. The second embraces a substantial element of peril that may actually destroy the potential of the budding company. Unprecedented

EXHIBIT 26–1. Typical Examples of Initial Small Business Growth

Greeting-card stores. In a metropolitan area on the West Coast, two competitive greeting-card shops were located within three blocks of each other. Both had started in business seven or eight years earlier. The owner of one store decided to expand his operation by renting the stores on either side of his location, breaking through the walls, and thus quadrupling the size of his original establishment. He added several new merchandise lines (records, stereo equipment, high-quality chocolates) and departmentalized the premises.

The owner of the other shop took in two partners, along with their additional investment capital. They found desirable locations in several neighboring towns and built a small chain over the next several years. By then, only three of their six stores were profitable; leases for the others were not renewed.

Hardware Distributor. A hardware wholesaler expanded her operation into a contiguous state. She advertised for, interviewed, and trained three additional sales representatives for the new territory. Subsequently, a new compensation plan was prepared for the entire miniature sales force, and both a sales manager and a "trainer" were employed. Within two years, the new territory had been built up substantially and the company went on to "attack" two neighboring states.

Gift Shop. A middle-aged couple, successful operators for twenty-three years of a gift and souvenir shop in a New England resort area, sought a warm climate in which to spend their winters and their eventual retirement. They opened another outlet in southern Florida, an almost exact copy of their northern store down to layout, fixturization, and merchandise carried in stock. Unhappily, the newer store does less than half of the sales volume that the older store enjoys. They do not seem to be able to reach their breakeven point. Nevertheless, the couple decides to use the profits of the first store to carry along the second one, hoping to build it up over time.

Land Developer. A small land developer placed a down payment on some wooded acreage in the mountains of Pennsylvania, bulldozed roads through the property, and then subdivided the land into homesites. The property was offered in its semideveloped state, one lot at a time, for vacation or retirement homes. Within two years after start-up, more than $10 million worth of land had been sold through television, direct mail, and telephone solicitation. Meanwhile, the company expanded to the point at which several hundred salaried employees and commission salespeople were on the books.

Soft-drink Stand. After registering an instant, sound success with their first soft-drink-and-frankfurter stand, three partners managed to open up two additional outlets within the next six months. This way, they reasoned, each stand could be operated and tightly controlled by a partner. All three units enjoyed brisk sales. Soon thereafter, the owners decided to go the franchise route. They hired a franchise director on a commission basis, worked out all details of the franchise "package" with the director's assistance, and succeeded in blanketing the state with fourteen additional stores.

EXHIBIT 26-1. (*Continued*)

Manufacturer of Kitchen Furniture. An Arizona firm that manufactured kitchen dinette sets perceived the profitability of installing a similar plant in the Midwest close to several of its major, though long-distance customers. This way, not only are they better able to service these accounts and add new customers to their books but they will save considerably on transportation costs.

Source: Compiled by the author.

initial success often leads to serious complications. In those firms that experience runaway growth patterns, we see many of the following symptoms:

- An excessive number of employees
- The proliferation of departments
- Confused lines of authority
- Runaway costs
- A lack of coordination and thus a loss of control
- Improperly trained department heads and supervisors
- A climbing employee turnover rate
- General dissatisfaction and even dissension.

PLANNING FOR GROWTH

Planned growth is by far the more sensible approach. This planning, incidentally, may be even more vital to the small firm than to the large company simply because the former cannot afford to make many errors. It does not have the financial reserves to make amends for mistakes.

How to Develop Your Company Growth Plan

Once top management has made the commitment to pursue a growth pattern, the very next step ought to be the preparation of a "master plan" for growth. This document should embrace all of the required elements:

- The specific targets set (including objectives such as desired return on investment, the number of additional units to be opened, new plants or warehouses to be set up, the sales levels to be attained, and the like)
- The schedule for organizing and putting into operation the successive stages of the plan
- Methods of gathering and allocating company resources (labor, management, methods, materials, goods, and so forth)
- The arranging for needed financing; the setting up of checks and balances to ensure that all activities are on track; and so on

At the very least, a plan coordinator (or even better, a two- or three-person committee) should be charged with overseeing the necessary coordination for developing the plan. Responsibility must be assigned since day-to-day activities need to continue uninterruptedly throughout.

WAYS TO GO

Planned growth may be either an internal or an external affair, or perhaps a combination of the two. By ploughing back each year's profits, acquiring one or two new partners, selling stock to friends and relatives (if a corporation), or securing a large loan, the small company can generate sufficient capital to finance an appreciable degree of internal growth. Such growth is usually accomplished through new product development, the purchase of additional machinery, innovation, product line expansion, automation, different methods of distribution, promotional creativity, and a variety of other approaches.

However, external growth can be made to proceed at a more rapid pace; this is sometimes more expedient for the healthy young firm. Management's attention may be directed toward going public, becoming franchisors, acquiring another company, or merging with another firm—all of which generally takes more capital than can be generated by reinvestment of profits or borrowing.

MERGERS AND ACQUISITIONS

In the typical merger, two companies of roughly equal market strength and asset value decide to combine. This "marriage" usually results in a new and stronger entity, with all of the resources of the original two at its command. In the acquisition situation, the two firms are unequal in net worth, sales volume, and so forth. The larger one buys out the smaller—lock, stock, and barrel. Payment may be made entirely in cash or in some combination of cash plus common stock, bonds, and so on.

The majority of combinations are of the so-called *horizontal* type, in which companies conducting similar business operations combine, such as two supermarket chains, two hotels, two appliance manufacturers, and the like. Other types include the *vertical combination* (in which companies integrate backwards or forwards along the marketing channels—as when a large wholesaler acquires a manufacturing plant or a manufacturer opens retail outlets for its own products; and the *conglomerate,* whereby a company will buy up other firms in entirely different industries in order to diversify its holdings.*

For the interested firm, the names of prospective candidates for acquisition may be obtained from banks, management consultants, investment bankers, CPAs, business brokers, law firms, and other sources.

---

*For some background reading about this area of mergers and acquisitions—along with suggestions that may facilitate such moves—see: George Hamilton, "Start Your Acquisition Program Ten Minutes from Now," *Business Horizons* 28 (September-October 1985), 12–16; David B. Jemison and Sim B. Sitkin, "Acquisitions: The Process Can Be a Problem," *Harvard Business Review* 64 (March-April 1986), 107–116; Robert W. Swaim, "Mergers—The Personnel Squeeze," *Personnel Journal* 64 (April 1985), 34–40.

Many of the potential advantages offered by mergers and acquisitions are outlined in the paragraphs below:

Marketing: increased turnover; more intensive use of existing markets, adding new markets, perhaps expanding from local or regional markets to national markets; access to new market-research information; adding new products or services to the product line to help existing customers and/or add new customers with associated needs; offsetting any seasonal or cyclical fluctuations related to the existing product line; acquiring brand names and any special market reputation.

Production: new products and/or markets making greater use of existing plant and machinery, thus leading to increased economies of scale; acquiring patent rights, licenses, etc., and additional R. and D. facilities; augmenting or complementing productive capacity, additional factory buildings, plant and equipment; new manufacturing processes; vertical integration, acquiring sources of raw materials and/or customer outlets.

Finance: better utilization of joint resources, employing idle capital or gaining additional funds (as, for example, a progressive company acquiring a dormant company having little ambition, but ample cash or marketable securities); taking advantage of a tax loss situation; spreading the business risk; minimizing stockheld balances; increasing the market value of shares; exploiting large-scale opportunities; enhanced profits and reserves.

Management and Personnel: outlet for excess managerial capacity; acquiring additional management skills, key workers, trained staff, etc.; access to training facilities, management development plans, etc.*

MANAGEMENT SUCCESSION

Along with growth and expansion, there is mounting pressure on top management to devise a strong talent acquisition program. Additional specialists are needed to fill the new supervisory and executive slots as they are created in the developing organization and to replace those managers who leave or are weeded out due to incompetence. Managerial talent is difficult to locate; in this country there has been a serious shortage of executives for years.

Usually, management that is sophisticated enough to embark on an expansion program rises to the challenge by initiating needs assessment for five or more years into the future. Simultaneously, a personnel talent inventory is prepared. Promising employees, those deemed to have the potential for growth and promotion, are identified; a comprehensive training and development program is begun; and the management skills of the selected candidates are nurtured through a variety of methods, including university courses, job rotation, committee work, and project assignments.

Strangely, though, while most entrepreneurs provide for this continuity of management talent long into the future, they rarely apply this concept to themselves. In the entrepreneurial personality, an owner is not only regarded

---

*W. F. Coventry and Irving Burstiner, *Management: A Basic Handbook* (Englewood Cliffs, N.J.: Prentice-Hall, 1977), 399.

as indefatigable but as indestructible. Soul-searching questions such as "What will happen to my business if I become ill and am unable to carry on my duties?" and "Who will take over the reins later on?" are shunted off into the distant future. Yet, as the key in the entire business, the owner should realize that more than anyone, he or she needs a backup for eventual replacement. Certainly, the firm would suffer most if his or her services were to be lost.

The Family-Owned Business

Often, one or two family members are active in the business. This leads the founder(s) to look forward to the time when sons or daughters—or perhaps sisters or brothers—will take over at the helm. Several friction-generating possibilities accrue to this type of situation:

- No one else in the family may possess the vision, requisite skills, desire, or self-direction to manage the business someday.
- Personality clashes between owner(s) and relatives—or among the latter alone—will probably occur from time to time.
- Jealousy and rivalry among family members can ruin their relationships, if not the business itself.

Frequently, it's wiser to think of hiring a capable administrator, perhaps someone with an excellent track record as president or executive vice-president of another company. This is preferable to designating one of the family as your eventual successor.

In any event, that new executive should be brought into your business as early in the game as possible, despite the fact that it's an expensive move. More likely than not, several years of thorough training and hands-on application will go by before this manager will acquire mastery of your operations. You'll also want to maintain close supervision over this person and make frequent evaluations before deciding that you have sufficient confidence in his or her capabilities to turn over the major portion of your own responsibilities when it becomes necessary.

FOR FURTHER INFORMATION

Books

Cooke, Terence E. *Mergers and Acquisitions.* New York: Basil Blackwell, 1986.

Crawford, Edward K. *A Management Guide to Leveraged Buyouts.* New York: Wiley, 1987.

O'Flaherty, Joseph S. *Going Public: The Entrepreneur's Guide.* New York: Wiley, 1984.

Marren, Joseph H. *Mergers and Acquisitions: Will You Overpay?* Homewood, Ill.: Dow Jones-Irwin, 1985.

Rock, Milton L., ed. *The Managers and Acquisitions Handbook.* New York: McGraw-Hill, 1987.

Scharf, Charles A., et al. *Acquisitions, Mergers, Sales, Buyouts, Takeovers: A Handbook with Forms,* 3d ed. Englewood Cliffs, N.J.: Prentice-Hall, 1985.
Siegel, William L. *Franchising.* New York: Wiley, 1983.

Pamphlets Available from the Small Business Administration

MANAGEMENT AIDS

MA 2.004—"Problems in Managing a Family-Owned Business"
MA 3.002—"Management Checklist for a Family Business"
MA 7.003—"Market Overseas with U.S. Government Help"
MA 7.007—"Evaluating Franchise Opportunities"

Index